Praise for *Enduring Courage*

"[Rickenbacker's] life has been recounted in his own autobiographies and by many other authors, yet arguably none get the telling more right than John F. Ross in his exhaustively researched and exquisitely written biography, *Enduring Courage*." —*Air & Space/Smithsonian Magazine*

"A brisk and informing read . . . [Ross's] engaging new book, surveying the risky realms of racing and air wars, reminds the reader how fast the world changes—and how much remains the same. . . . Rickenbacker's life provides ample grist for thrilling narrative (and gruesome detail). Yet serving the good purposes of history, Mr. Ross artfully strikes resonances between eras. . . . Portraying the ultimate daredevil in an age of daredevilry, Mr. Ross wrings out as much excitement as the material holds in describing Rickenbacker's violent worlds." —*Washington Times*

"[A] lively and engaging portrait of Rickenbacker . . . Ross has a real gift for sitting the reader beside "Fast Eddie" as he thunders down the straightaway of a 1913 racetrack or leans forward in the cockpit of a Nieuport 28 climbing toward a flight of Fokkers. . . . an admiring biography . . . *Enduring Courage* offers a compelling portrait of an American hero."
—Tom Crouch, *Washington Independent Review of Books*

"Energetic . . . Exciting . . . Ross sweeps readers along in Rickenbacker's thrilling tale." —*Kirkus Reviews*

"Entertaining . . . Ross peppers the text with quotes that place readers right alongside the ace through nearly every moment of his life. Obviously this is exciting material to work with—after all, Rickenbacker was a man who drove in the first Indy 500 and dueled with the Red Baron's flying circus— but Ross is never fawning in this thoroughly enjoyable and downright rollicking read." —*Booklist* (starred review)

"Ross has a knack for exciting, visual narrative, and the life-defining moments of race and dogfight.... A highly entertaining portrait, which reveres its subject as a hero defined by his high-speed feats."

—*Publishers Weekly*

"John Ross is that rare soul who writes narrative history with the verve and timing of an accomplished novelist. *Enduring Courage*—a heroic portrait of the aviator ace Eddie Rickenbacker of Ohio—is a bona fide page-turner. The Indianapolis race car scenes and World War I dogfights ripple with excitement. I couldn't put it down."

—Douglas Brinkley, bestselling author, professor of history at Rice University, and historian for CBS News

"Daring, beautiful, and masterfully told, *Enduring Courage* puts you shoulder-to-shoulder with one of the great American spirits of all time, Eddie Rickenbacker, who does in each chapter what the rest of us dream to do with our lives."

—Robert Kurson, *New York Times* bestselling author of *Shadow Divers*

"Before Charles Lindbergh, before Chuck Yeager, before Neil Armstrong, there was Eddie Rickenbacker, American aviation's first mega-celebrity. In *Enduring Courage*, John F. Ross gives readers a brilliant and compelling biography of a man who led a remarkable life, illuminating as well a more innocent and hopeful period in American history, when the common man could make for himself a very uncommon future. This is an unforgettable treasure of a book."

—Dr. Richard P. Hallion, former United States Air Force historian and author

"The dawn of the twentieth century saw the advent of two world-changing technologies: automobiles and airplanes. With these came new breeds of risk takers and heroes—the race car driver and the fighter pilot. Eddie Rickenbacker was both.... Rickenbacker clearly had the 'right stuff' for this brave new world. But what was the right stuff circa 1918? Biographer John

F. Ross grapples with this and other questions in his new book.... Many books have been written about Rickenbacker.... Ross writes about many of the exploits described in those works, but he also mines primary sources, including thousands of pages of transcribed interviews with Rickenbacker, to get beneath what he calls 'the veneer of untouchable hero.'"

—National Geographic.com

"In 1941, [Rickenbacker] suffered serious injuries and narrowly escaped death in a devastating aircraft crash near Atlanta.... Following his recovery, Rickenbacker was selected by Secretary of War Henry Stimson to transport and personally deliver a reprimand to General Douglas MacArthur, then supreme commander of the Southwest Pacific Area, headquartered in New Guinea.... The B-17D Flying Fortress ferrying Rickenbacker got lost in the Pacific and was forced to ditch at sea. Together with the rest of the crew, Rickenbacker spent twenty-four harrowing days adrift on a life raft without food or water. The story of his survival and rescue is the most gripping part of *Enduring Courage*. Nowadays, of course ... we don't have national heroes remotely like Eddie Rickenbacker."

—*The Weekly Standard*

"Every World War I aviation enthusiast knows the story of 'Captain Eddie' Rickenbacker.... So, why yet another book about Rickenbacker? The answer is simple: John F. Ross has told Eddie's story in a way no other author has. *Enduring Courage* is set apart from other books by taking the Rickenbacker story beyond simply the biography of the man. Writing for a universal audience, Ross ushers readers behind the scenes to tell, rather eloquently, the story of early-twentieth-century culture and the development of auto manufacturing and racing, as well as aircraft and aerial combat as they evolved in 1914–1918. In recording these events—factually and in adequate, but not overbearing, detail—Ross masterfully explains Rickenbacker's significance in terms of the world in which he lived, where his "enduring courage" in the new age of speed destined him for greatness."

—*Over the Front*

ALSO BY JOHN F. ROSS

*War on the Run: The Epic Story of Robert Rogers and
the Conquest of America's First Frontier*

Living Dangerously: Navigating the Risks of Everyday Life

ENDURING COURAGE

ACE PILOT EDDIE RICKENBACKER

AND THE DAWN OF THE AGE OF SPEED

JOHN F. ROSS

ST. MARTIN'S GRIFFIN 🌊 NEW YORK

For Grace and Forrister

www.stmartins.com

Designed by Steven Seighman

Maps © 2014 by Jeffrey L. Ward

All section-opener photographs courtesy of Auburn University, Special Collections and Archives

The Library of Congress has cataloged the hardcover edition as follows:

Ross, John F.
    Enduring courage : ace pilot Eddie Rickenbacker and the dawn of the age of speed / John F. Ross.—First edition.
        p.   cm.
    Includes bibliographical references and index.
    ISBN 978-1-250-03377-2 (hardcover)
    ISBN 978-1-250-03378-9 (e-book)
  1 Rickenbacker, Eddie, 1890–1973.   2. Air pilots—United States—Biography.
3. Fighter pilots—United States—Biography.   4. Automobile racing drivers—
United States—Biography.   5. World War, 1914–1918—Aerial operations,
American.   6. World War, 1939–1945—Aerial operations, American.
I. Title.   II. Title: Ace pilot Eddie Rickenbacker and the dawn of the age of speed.
    TL540.R54R67 2014
    940.4'4973092—dc23
    [B]

                                                                    2014008039

ISBN 978-1-250-03384-0 (trade paperback)

St. Martin's Griffin books may be purchased for educational, business, or promotional use. For information on bulk purchases, please contact the Macmillan Corporate and Premium Sales Department at 1-800-221-7945, extension 5442, or write to special markets@macmillan.com.

First St. Martin's Griffin Edition: May 2015

10   9   8   7   6   5   4   3   2   1

CONTENTS

ACKNOWLEDGMENTS

This book began three decades ago when I first opened a copy of *Fighting the Flying Circus* as a boy. Eddie Rickenbacker's exhilarating tale of biplanes dueling in the skies of World War I kindled not only a strong love of history but a desire one day to tell these stories myself. I have room here to thank only a small fraction of those who have helped me on this long journey from dream to finished manuscript.

One of the great benefits of writing is that it enables me to meet people that might not otherwise cross my path. I spent a recent afternoon, for instance, with Carlton Pate III, who cheerfully sat me in the seat of his meticulously restored Ford Model C and calmly instructed me as I careened around the back streets of suburban Connecticut. Or Ted Hamady, an independent aviation historian, who patiently answered all my questions about the Nieuport 27 and SPAD XIII, on occasion pulling out pieces of them to illustrate a point about design and construction. And I spent a pleasant day with the members of the mid-Atlantic chapter of Over the Front, the League of World War I historians, who generously opened me up to new worlds about not only early airplanes but how innovation and necessity so often work hand in hand.

No book of this nature would be possible without the assistance of many archivists, researchers, and librarians. My deep appreciation goes to the archivists and researchers at Auburn University Libraries, which houses the single largest collection of Rickenbacker materials: Dwayne Cox, in charge of the Special Collections and Archives; John Varner, Tommy Brown, and Midge Coates, digital projects librarian. Many thanks to the staff at the Library of Congress, particularly manuscript reference librarian Bruce Kirby. At the National Archives and Records Administration in College Park, Maryland, archivist Eric van Slander and archives specialist Theresa Roy proved particularly helpful. I'd like to thank museum specialist Brian Nicklas at the Smithsonian's National Air and Space Museum. Also my gratitude goes out to Paul Barron at the George C. Marshall Foundation; Mary Marshall Clark, Columbia Center for Oral History, Columbia University; Karim Hussain, Modern Domestic Records, the National Archives, UK; special collections archivist Becki Plunkett, the State Historical Society of Iowa; archives technician Sylvester Jackson Jr., Air Force Historical Research Agency, Maxwell Air Force Base; assistant curator Rebecca Jewett, Rare Books and Manuscripts Library, the Ohio State University Libraries; John Pulford, head of collections and interpretation, Brooklands Museum, UK; manuscript curator Bert Stolle, the National Museum of the United States Air Force; Sarah Swan, U.S. Air Force Museum at Wright-Patterson Air Force Base.

For reading the manuscript at various stages and offering critical insight, I'd like to thank William Casey, Joe Meany, Alexis Doster III, Larry O'Reilly, Dick Hallion, Duke Johns, and Tom Crouch. Cindy Scudder gave indispensable help with picture research and design, not to mention her good counsel about publishing. Thanks to Cathi and Phil Smith, not only for assembling tiny biplane models and finding a recipe for French 75s, but for their enthusiastic support and friendship. And thanks also to the often brilliant essayists of the Literary Society of Washington, upon which I tried out many new ideas. I'm particularly indebted to—and honored to count as a friend—Tim Dickinson, whose guidance and long, rich conversations about all things Rickenbacker both sustained and stretched my thinking in many new directions.

My editor at St. Martin's Press, Marc Resnick, believed in this project enthusiastically from the beginning, and navigated the project's many curves with a sharp editorial eye, good judgment, and a great sense of humor. His backup, Kate Canfield, always proved up to the task at hand. I'd also particularly like to thank SMP's indomitable director of publicity, John Murphy, and ever-competent and energetic senior publicist Christy D'Agostini. My warm thanks also go out to Jeff Dodes, Dori Weintraub, Laura Clark, Michael Hoak, and Kathryn Hough. My thanks also to copyeditor India Cooper, cartographer Jeffrey L. Ward, and indexer Peter Rooney.

I couldn't have a better agent in Stuart Krichevsky. Without his wisdom, clarity, enthusiasm, excellent judgment, and market savvy this book would not have happened. I'm also deeply grateful to Stuart's colleagues Shana Cohen and Ross Harris.

To my parents, Jane and Phil, and my brother, Jim, who have always, always been there. And to my children, Grace and Forrister, to whom this book is dedicated. The joy they give me is a constant source of my inspiration. And to my wife, Diana. It is impossible to imagine a writing life without her warm support, presence, and sagacity. I truly won the lottery when I met her.

THE WESTERN FRONT

CHÂTEAU-THIERRY SECTOR

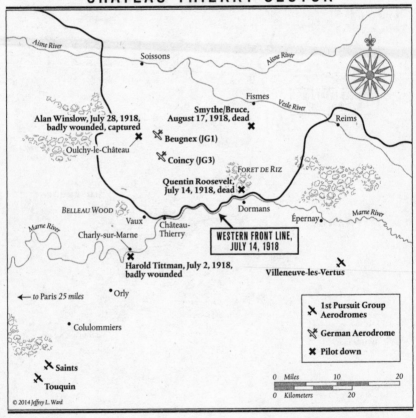

Aisne River

Soissons

Aisne River

Fismes

Vesle River

Reims

Alan Winslow, July 28, 1918, badly wounded, captured

Smythe/Bruce, August 17, 1918, dead

Oulchy-le-Château

Beugnex (JG1)

Coincy (JG3)

FORET DE RIZ

Quentin Roosevelt, July 14, 1918, dead

BELLEAU WOOD

Vaux

Dormans

Épernay

Marne River

Marne River

Charly-sur-Marne

Château-Thierry

WESTERN FRONT LINE, JULY 14, 1918

Harold Tittman, July 2, 1918, badly wounded

Villeneuve-les-Vertus

← to Paris 25 miles

Orly

Colulommiers

Saints

Touquin

© 2014 Jeffrey L. Ward

1st Pursuit Group Aerodromes

German Aerodrome

Pilot down

0   Miles   10   20

0   Kilometers   20

SAINT-MIHIEL SALIENT

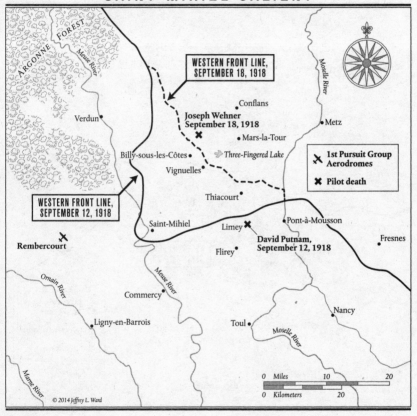

ARGONNE FOREST

Meuse River

WESTERN FRONT LINE,
SEPTEMBER 18, 1918

• Conflans

Verdun •

Joseph Wehner
September 18, 1918

Moselle River

• Metz

• Mars-la-Tour

Billy-sous-les-Côtes •

Three-Fingered Lake

Vignuelles •

Thiacourt •

WESTERN FRONT LINE,
SEPTEMBER 12, 1918

Saint-Mihiel •

Limey

• Pont-à-Mousson

Rembercourt

Flirey •

David Putnam,
September 12, 1918

Fresnes •

Ornain River

Meuse River

Commercy •

Nancy •

Ligny-en-Barrois •

Toul •

Moselle River

Marne River

| 1st Pursuit Group Aerodromes |
| Pilot death |

0   Miles   10   20

0   Kilometers   20

© 2014 Jeffrey L. Ward

MEUSE-ARGONNE SECTOR

Cunel
Heights

Murvaux

✖ Frank Luke, September 29, 1918

Walter Avery, October 3, 1918

✖ Wilbert White, Jr., October 10, 1918

Hamilton Coolidge,
October 27, 1918

Dun-sur-Meuse

Damvillers

Grandpré

Aisne River

Epionville

A R G O N N E   F O R E S T

Mountfaucon

Meuse River

Orne River

•Varennes

•Verdun

•Brabant

•Clermont

Aisne River

Aire River

WESTERN FRONT LINE,
SEPTEMBER 26, 1918

•Souilly

Meuse River

	1st Pursuit Group **Aerodrome**
	German balloons
✖	**Pilot death**

0   Miles   10   20

0   Kilometers   20

✖Rembercourt

Saint-Mihiel

© 2014 Jeffrey L. Ward

INTRODUCTION

WHEN A MAN FACES DEATH

One bright spring afternoon in May 1918, a column of German infantry halted on a muddy road in northeastern France, craning their necks skyward as four biplanes locked in mortal combat. More like butterflies than human creations, their double wings bobbed and dipped capriciously. For long moments, the men forgot their blistered feet and aching shoulders to marvel at the seeming effortlessness of these airborne gladiators.

In his cockpit high above, the twenty-seven-year-old Eddie Rickenbacker fought for his life in a machine that battered his body at every turn, delivering a disorienting cocktail of dizziness, vertigo, nausea, pounding noise, extreme cold, and, always, fear. Only fifteen years downwind from Kitty Hawk, these aircraft were little more than controllable box kites with engines, flimsy contraptions of wood, fabric, and baling wire so insubstantial as to appear dangerous just sitting on the ground.

Half an hour earlier he had left his aerodrome on patrol, taking some twenty minutes to reach 17,000 feet, the air thinning to where he struggled to breathe. His head grew light, his vision tunneled. (Oxygen deprivation so fogs judgment that the Federal Aviation Administration today prohibits flights above 10,000 feet without pressurized oxygen.) As he climbed, his Nieuport's rotary engine spattered him with castor oil, which he could not help but inhale, churning his stomach and loosening the bowels. Nausea stalked him relentlessly, often drenching his cockpit in vomit. His fur-lined teddy-bear suit afforded little protection against temperatures that dropped well below zero in the unheated, open cockpit. Pilots would often find themselves peeling their stiffened, numbed right-hand fingers off the joystick one by one.

Perhaps most unsettling was the pilot's knowledge that he might need to make a terrible decision at any moment. Rickenbacker sat within a highly combustible deathtrap, its heavily doped fabric stretched tight across wooden frames prone to catching fire from a single hostile bullet or sparks from his own engine. Once fire took hold, the wind would whip it into an inferno. Although effective parachutes existed, he did not carry one: Headquarters had deemed them defeatist. In such ever-possible catastrophes, he must choose between jumping or staying with his machine and risk burning up long before the charred plane struck ground. That bitter range of choices, unprecedented in the history of warfare, sat heavily on Rickenbacker's shoulders—as it did for every flyer on the front—and this was only what he knew. What he didn't know was at least as bad.

New to the war, the Americans had lacked the time to build a fleet of their own design, so instead they bought French aircraft. The French dished up the Nieuport 28, an aircraft they had already rejected for their own service, given that it was outclassed by German machines. Furthermore, it contained a design flaw likely to assert itself with sudden finality at the height of combat.

As Rickenbacker guided his machine over enemy-occupied territory beyond the medieval city of Nancy, he spied three German Albatros aircraft far below him, whose pilots had clearly not seen him. His senses possibly skewed from high-altitude oxygen starvation, he threw the Nieuport into a precipitous dive—the so-called zoom—and screamed down upon the tail of an adversary, getting close enough to see his enemy's head bobbing in frantic astonishment. One squeeze of the trigger of his Lewis machine gun loosed fifty rounds into the Albatros's fuselage, sending it catapulting into a death spin.

Exhilaration lasted only a second as the other two enemy planes swooped from the height advantage that his attack had conceded and broke into a "dogfight," a newly minted term, which, like much military slang, captured the savage immediacy and concentrated violence of the action.

Seeing a dramatic reversal, Rickenbacker jerked back hard on his stick, "bouncing" his nose upward in a gut-wrenching change of direction. With a loud crack, the fabric over the leading edge of his upper starboard wing peeled back from the spar and began to snap like a flag in a stiff wind. The French technology had failed, as it would do repeatedly until the Americans could change planes.

Deprived of half its lift, the Nieuport slid into an uncontrolled tailspin, the Germans blazing long ropes of bullets at it. With the detachment of the fatally wounded, it struck Rickenbacker as odd that they should waste good bullets on a goner. Surely his lower wings would go next . . . but somehow they held. With every revolution he felt "a regular jar as the shock of the air cushion came against the left wing after passing through the skeleton of the right one." His engine cut out.

Then, galvanized, he kicked into activity, wrenching the stick from side to side, stomping on the rudder, even banging his body with all his force against the cockpit, but still he could not "modify, even in the slightest, the gyrations of the Nieuport." Everything suddenly slowed, "My whole life seemed to go through my mind like a moving picture" as the plane plummeted two miles downward. "I wondered whether the airplane would disintegrate around me and let me fall free, whistling through the wind. Would I strike the ground and splatter all over? Maybe I would be lucky and land in the trees with only a few broken bones."

He saw the soldiers watching his Icarus-like fall, imagining how they would pick over his body and carry off pieces of the shattered machine for souvenirs. He envisioned his mother opening the door of their little house in Columbus to receive the cablegram announcing his death. A "spasm of longing" rose up within him.

Only a few seconds remained. No emergency procedures came automatically to mind—none had yet been devised. For Rickenbacker there remained only the crippling reality of a wildly disorienting, stomach-screwing spin into the earth.

Then his panic suddenly shifted into steely resolve. Just a couple of hundred feet from the ground, he threw all his "weight to the left hand side over the cockpit and jammed the controls, crossed them and jammed the engine wide open." An explosion lit the cowling with blue flame, but "the whole thing suddenly sputtered and vibrated violently, and finally went off on one wing headed for France." Ordinary reasoning would suggest that engaging the engine should only have sent him more quickly to his death, but instead the speed so gained imparted just enough lift to free him from the spin. In those frightening moments, he had manifested a creative, rational response that somehow tempered the nearly overpowering storm of fear and confusion, enabling him to innovate a nearly instantaneous solution. His long-trained preparation for the worst had produced a mastery honed over years of managing just this depth of extremity.

Flying almost horizontally, he jerked on his stick with all he had and reversed the rudder to counter the dominant gyroscopic momentum of the rotary engine. At last the Nieuport was moving forward faster than it was losing altitude, but only just barely. He pitched around in search of his two enemies, bracing at every moment against the smash of bullets into his back, but the two Albatros pilots had unsurprisingly left him for dead. He nursed, cajoled, and fiddled his crippled bird home—and, after landing, promptly threw up behind the barracks.

The following day he climbed aboard a different Nieuport, this time with a little more knowledge about its flawed design. In a matter of months, he would become America's ace of aces, with more enemy aircraft shot down than any other U.S. pilot in that war.

Rickenbacker lived at a time when the latest machines of the industrial revolutions were ripping apart the ages-old rhythms of plow and steam. When he was seven, the first car race reported average times of a little over 7 miles an hour; by his teenaged years, he would routinely clock speeds of 100 mph in competitions. When he was twelve, no one had flown in a heavier-than-air, powered machine or was expected to anytime soon; by his twenties, he was dogfighting at Mount Olympus heights. The motorcar and airplane each enabled its operator to experience dimensions of speed and time that no human being had ever encountered before. Again and again, Americans would watch as Eddie Rickenbacker climbed into these machines and pushed them faster and harder, escaping death by a heart-beat, only to flash a broad aw-shucks grin and go out and do it again.

Rickenbacker and the handful of fellow pioneers who straddled the early automotive and aviation worlds, often tempering the ingenious machines of Ford and Wright with their blood, exhibited the first truly modern "right stuff," working without manuals or more than rudimentary instruction and pushing themselves and their machines to places where they didn't know what would happen next. The pure creativity and imagination deployed by these young men who flew by the seat of their pants, innovated on the fly, and cheated death at technology's outer edges were breathtaking.

No mere thrill seeker or arrogant fatalist—men fitting those descriptions died in droves around him—Rickenbacker mastered new frontiers, at the very edge of spine-tingling speed, with the steady nerves of a professional risk taker. As amateurs turned professionals overnight, he and his colleagues had to forge a new, cool-headed approach to risk, staking out the early approaches to risk analysis. No longer did the old icons of American courage and manhood—cavalry officer, cowboy, lumberjack—suffice in the modern industrial world. The generations-old exhortations of "Don't shoot until you see the whites of their eyes" or "Damn the torpedoes!" needed reinterpretation. In his exploits and temperament, Rickenbacker would help frame new personifications of the American hero as race-car star and fighter ace. With his exceptionally businesslike approach to risk, Rickenbacker inspired confidence in others who were struggling to adapt to the challenges of a fast-accelerating world. He was always reinventing, forever working, wielding an immense imagination upon a world he was recasting as he swept through it. Americans would come to know his face as well as that of the current president's: It was far more memorable than handsome, yet in a group photograph, it is his face that demands a closer look, to search its overly long, chiseled features and bushy eyebrows for some clue as to the nature of courage. Like few others, he seemed to embody the very word.

A generation after his World War I exploits, a catastrophic airline crash left him hanging to life by a thread. The nation held its breath, daily braced for word that he was gone, then was recharged by how he had willed himself back from an almost certain death. Little more than a year later, the fifty-two-year-old endured one of the most grueling ordeals ever recorded while adrift for three weeks in the South Pacific. Those with him on the lifeboats later admitted that it was Rickenbacker—and he alone—who had kept them alive. When newspapers published photographs of the rescue, readers saw that while Rickenbacker's body lay emaciated and battered, his defiant spirit remained intact and shone just as brightly as ever. Americans seemed collectively to sigh in relief. They had been with him through so many adventures that they couldn't believe that anything, even the vast plane-swallowing Pacific, could ever dim that indomitable will.

Paradoxically, Rickenbacker's very hero status—what the nation so needed him to be—has obscured the man behind that perpetual boyish grin. His life's exploits dazzle with such blinding light that most biographers haven't pushed beyond them, or can't. Even though he is long dead, his presence remains so strong that one feels as if he has reached out beyond the grave to rap knuckles and chide us for somehow not being tough enough and willing to stand up to challenge. A man completely and naturally in control, he never asked to be liked—and certainly many did not like him—but everyone certainly watched and listened to him. He was not emotionally accessible, preferring to let his actions speak, and it's clear that only a few really got to know him. That was fine with him.

When faced with such an inscrutably heroic risk taker, one struggles to explain his success, too often settling for the easy answers that his survival was attributable to luck, fate, or access to heightened animal instincts deriving more from his brainstem than the cerebral cortex. However, pushing beyond the flames and awful crackups, the flourishes of his ghostwriters, and his own formidable will in dictating the narrative of his life, one finds a true rarity—a thoughtful man of action who conceived of the next task before him much as a mathematician sees an equation. His successes came not only from hands and nerves but from head and heart, and his choices were often ingenious as well as unorthodox.

Examining his life offers us an extraordinarily rich salient into the intersection of fate, luck, courage, will, and intention—as well as the early-twentieth-century American spirit that launched a self-absorbed nation into becoming a world power. Ultimately, Rickenbacker's story boils down to courage. Not the kind of raw courage that comes in a blinding rush to push a car off a child or charge a machine-gun nest, but one that is trained to purpose and gets stronger, wiser, and more effective with experience. This courage—enduring courage—doesn't just happen but must be worked for and earned. George Washington had it; so did Ulysses S. Grant and Teddy Roosevelt. No other single trait has so forcefully shaped the American nation.

When Eddie Rickenbacker's brand of courage intersected with the new frontiers of speed brought by car and airplane, extraordinary things started to happen. Hold on to your seats.

BOOK I

RACING

I to my perils
Of cheat and charmer
Came clad in armour . . .

The thoughts of others
Were light and fleeting,
Of lovers' meeting
Or luck or fame.
Mine were of trouble,
And mine were steady;
So I was ready
When trouble came.

—A. E. Housman, *More Poems*

1.

LOVE AT FIRST SIGHT

One warm day in 1905, a scrawny, towheaded fourteen-year-old raced down the sidewalk toward a crowd gathering at High and Broad streets in Columbus, Ohio, easily overtaking several horse-drawn wagons plodding along the brick-lined pavement, bells jingling on their reins. He dodged around customers exiting wide-awninged stores as a trolley hummed down the middle of High beneath a series of iron arches hung with still-novel electric lights.

Eddie Rickenbacher wriggled through the crowd to reach a glittering object that he would soon learn was a brand-new 10-horsepower Ford Model C, first of its kind in this midwestern city. He had never seen anything so beautiful. Its brass steering column hovered over an elegant black leather, horsehair-stuffed bench seat; its chassis rested upon large grayish wheels with yellow spokes, accented with mudguards resembling startled eyebrows. Often enough the boy had watched the earth-shaking steam behemoths of the Second Industrial Revolution rumbling through Columbus's vast yards, but locomotives were dirty, rail-bound monsters. Here was a creation clean, sleek, and streamlined, not constrained to rails and, most important, designed to human scale and individuality.

Only after a minute or two did the boy register the salesman's voice extolling his chariot's miraculous new features. The pitchman's vaudeville-inspired flourishes left the crowd dubious. The claim that everyone would soon own one seemed the wildest snake-oil hyperbole. To sit atop a box barely able to contain a series of violent, noisy explosions was surely dangerous, if not downright suicidal. Trusting something that exuded not natural horsey sweat but oil and smoke—and made an unholy clamor as well—must be folly indeed. "It is a far step from the innate intelligence of the horse and the companionship of the dog to the blind power and mere possession of the machine," wrote one journalist ominously in 1900. Furthermore, its inner workings were inscrutably hidden, the stuff of sorcery. The crowd had heard about these "crazy firewagons" ripping at dangerous, unpredictable speeds through the measured, long-established, and reassuring rhythms of horse-drawn traffic, past the commerce of steam and canal. These juggernauts were visibly quixotic, unreliable, and uncontrollable. All of this was true enough. Yet this vehicle of the future nonetheless declared itself with mesmerizing boldness.

Searching the faces of the crowd, the salesman locked onto Eddie's dark brown eyes. Little distinguished this immigrants' son from the thousands of other urchins roaming the streets of every American city. On his thin frame hung clean but threadbare clothes. Between two winglike ears sat a nose bent where a punch had broken it. One scar grooved his chin, another his cheek. Yet perhaps the salesman saw early what others would soon recognize: a deep, burning fire in the eyes, made the more vivid by contrast with their soot-dark brows, which bespoke not desperation and brute endurance but a deep and abiding curiosity.

Maybe the salesman could sway his tough audience by giving this boy a ride. After all, what could be so dangerous if a kid could take a spin? The hawker needed to score a deal soon; Mr. Ford drove his salesmen hard.

"Want to go for a ride?" he asked. "Yes," gasped Eddie. The man reached to the steering column and elevated a lever just beneath the wheel to retard the spark plug. (By doing so he prevented the engine from firing prematurely while he cranked the car to start, inflicting a kickback powerful enough to break a hand or wrist.)

Reaching under the floor, he flicked a dowellike pin under the kickboard beneath the seat to turn on the ignition. He grabbed the foot-long crank handle and fitted its clawlike end into a brass-rimmed hole just above the running board on the driver's side, jerking the handle's wooden grip from its downward orientation into the twelve o'clock position. The two-cylinder engine shuddered and rat-tat-tatted into noisy animation. The crowd tittered in anticipation. A wisp of smoke escaped from the exhaust. The spoked wheels rattled with promise. To Eddie and the others assembled, the loud clicking hum was entirely foreign, what John Dos Passos would call "the new noise of the automobile."

Having depressed the steering-column handle, the salesman walked around to pull himself aboard with a fluid tug on the wheel. Eddie hopped onto the running board and slid in beside him. His host drew on a rope to swing free the wooden chock locking his rear right tire and shoved back the brass lever by his right elbow. The machine slid forward. Shouting that he'd be back for others, the salesman shifted the lever again, the car slowly picking up momentum as he pulled out onto the street. In moments, they had reached an impressive 13 miles per hour. The boy had hit higher speeds on a bicycle, but this ride's sheer exhilarating freedom was different. Instead of being pushed forward like a bicycle or pulled on a horse cart, he felt lifted up and along—and carried away. Aproned shop owners, tired teamsters atop their wagons, and annoyed gentlemen on horseback gazed at this portent with little short of wonder. Sitting in that marvel, Eddie was no longer the poor immigrant's son but something altogether more glorious and potent: the personification of speed, modernity, and movement at will.

Perched higher than in a modern-day SUV, yet without the protection of a windshield or even a dash, the driver and his passenger experienced the dizzying, electrifying raw rush of motion that jangled the senses and watered the eyes while the scenery blurred and the wind plucked at their clothes. The seat swayed pleasantly, like a ship at sea. The salesman leaned forward, his hands clenching the wheel. The Model C's steering was not geared, and so even the slightest jerk from a pothole or bump could careen this king of the road into a nearby carriage or ditch. Nor, furthermore, had Henry Ford and his engineers yet come up with an effective means of stopping. Braking was a carefully choreographed dance of shifting to low gear and madly pumping the footbrake. The driver devoted his attention to anticipating possible hazards and steering well clear of large obstacles.

To Eddie and the salesman, such difficulties weren't limitations; the car was all possibility, a taste of sensations never before so satisfactorily encountered, which delivered an exhilarating sense of rumbling headlong into the future. In those electric moments, as the car described a circuit around Ohio's white-marbled, Greek Revival Statehouse, a dream took shape for that wide-eyed boy: a point where instinct, joy, and rational thought fused together. He would build and drive these new creations—a determination that he would ride into becoming one of the most famous Americans of his generation. In a few short years, everyone in Columbus would know his name; a decade later, every American would recognize the wide, confident grin that broke the craggy angles of his face. As for the salesman, his crazy claims would prove right far more quickly than most anyone had dreamed. By the next decade a significant part of a car-crazy nation would own cars.

At the turn of the twentieth century, the everyday world of America, still framed around technologies from the age of Andrew Jackson, was being upended by a prodigious sequence of breakthroughs. Americans were putting industrial machinery to unprecedented large-scale use, inventing petroleum fuel, the telephone, pasteurized milk, and the cinema. At the World's Columbian Exposition just a few years earlier, visitors had gawked at typewriters, refrigerators, and flexible artificial limbs. Flush toilets and Edison's bright incandescent bulbs created a particular stir, one breathless writer announcing in *Scientific American* that this effervescence of discovery was like "a gigantic tidal wave of human ingenuity and resource, so profound in its thought, so fruitful in its wealth, so beneficial in its results, that the mind is strained and embarrassed in its effort to expand to a full appreciation of it." In scope and magnitude, the Yankee ingenuity of America's independent inventors—Thomas Alva Edison, Orville and Wilbur Wright, Henry Ford, Alexander Graham Bell—rivaled if not surpassed the inventive power of Periclean dramatists, Renaissance artists, late-nineteenth-century Berlin physicists, and Weimar architects in the 1920s.

The year that Eddie climbed onto that glistening Ford, an obscure German-born scientist named Albert Einstein had advanced his special theory of relativity, which would burst out its profound practical consequences before midcentury. The ripples of this and other discoveries tore the fabric of society—and knocked down many traditional modes of living and working. Wassily Kandinsky executed his first abstract painting, *Picture with a Circle,* in 1911, and that same year Cubism emerged. Virginia Woolf claimed that "human character changed" in 1910, as modernity itself was born and novels shook off their Victorian crinolines and experimented wildly in form. Syncopated jazz and ragtime rhythms introduced new tempos. Early Hollywood films, shot at sixteen frames a second but shown in theaters at twenty-four frames a second, showed their actors racing along in hyperfast apparent motion, frantic to get to wherever they were going at superhuman speeds. Pocket watches, once owned only by train conductors and the rich, became suddenly cheap and generally available. For the first time, people began systematically to mark time in increments of five and ten minutes.

Yet there is a powerful case to be made that no invention would propel the twentieth century forward with greater force than the newly configured internal combustion engine, which would power its first practical car in 1895 and make sustained, heavier-than-air flight possible only eight years later. These new technologies captivated the nation's imagination as they burst cometlike into American life. Within a few short years of Ford's introduction of the Model T in 1908, the chance to control, exercise, and enjoy speed passed into the eager hands of hundreds of thousands of ordinary Americans. Seated behind his wheel, a driver effortlessly multiplied choice as well as speed. For the first time in history, multitudes without specialized skills could operate a machine regularly capable of outdistancing the fastest stallion. Nor did the driver have to interact with a creature with its own mind, which might decide to pull up midstride or even pitch its rider. Speed was now tamable to a whole host of new purposes.

Drivers related breathlessly how the countryside dissolved into an Impressionist blur as they rattled down even terrible roads; this would prove just the first taste of the new perspectives that individual high-speed mobility would bring America. It wasn't only the thrill of high velocity but the feeling of being lifted by the rush of acceleration itself, as well as the mild g-forces that pressed the body at turns, even the mystery of swift deceleration. While the experience of flying itself would remain out of most people's reach for decades, the increasingly more common sight of men soaring among and above the birds dissolved whole categories of the impossible.

"The world loves speed," wrote a journalist in 1902. "All mankind would in some form indulge in it, if it but could. He who cannot, finds zest in watching him who can and does indulge ... The love of speed is inherent and increasing in intensity. The automobile is spreading and will continue to spread the desire for swift and exhilarating flight through space." Tasting the excitement of speed regularly—being able to divert it, revel in it, and put it to astonishing use—Americans would break open new horizons. The frontier lay not beyond the forest or across the river but at the end of a clutch. Nothing had ever quite so intoxicated the nation.

When Eddie climbed into that nearly prototypical Ford, there was no Indy 500 or NASCAR; there were no hot-rodding clubs or drag-racing cliques. Not one single person had water-skied, let alone gone out on a Jet Ski. The notion of doing everything much faster began to pervade all aspects of American life. It was happening in surgery and radio, and very soon on the edge of war. Zipping into the American lexicon would be new words that would communicate previously unimagined realities: zoom, rpm, mph, revving, and redline. Beyond that stretched new reaches of car-possibilities: car camping, drive-in movies, road trips, cruising the strip, Route 66 and the interstates, rest stops, suburban commuting, tailgating, and soccer moms.

One late night in 1881, an attractive young woman with a shock of tied-back red hair and dark circles under her blue eyes stepped off a train at

Columbus's Union Station. The shadowy figures of workmen in the yard made her nervous, so she hurried into the grand brick and stone terminal, which sprouted two tall mansard-roofed towers along with arched portals and windows with elaborately carved stone lintels. Still unsteady from her recent Atlantic crossing, she walked into the immense waiting room. Certainly she had visualized this moment, her imagination providing far more sustenance across the Atlantic than the small wheel of cheese she had hidden in the folds of her long dress. The only powerful relic of her former life was a black leather-bound family Bible.

That she was alone and spoke no English did not slow her determined stride across the platform to find the stationmaster. He did not understand the words that tumbled out of her mouth, which only grew more insistent under his blank stare. Her eyes welled up. She pulled out a letter and held it out to him. Recognizing that it was written in German, he sent an employee running off into the dark. Her brother's letter made it plain that she must leave the stubborn, infertile mountain slopes of the Swiss canton of Basel-Landschaft. He offered brief words of encouragement, but the enclosed money for her passage—earned so quickly in America!—spoke more than anything else to this new land's possibilities.

A German-speaking man, who she learned was the sheriff, came to the station and took her to the farm where her brother worked. When they finally met, she cried so hard that they thought she wanted to go home. No, she explained, *no*. So she set to farm chores, eventually finding her way to a factory job.

The United States was indeed a world apart from the farmhouse into which two Swiss families had been crammed. The sixth of ten children born to a poor ribbon maker, Lizzie had inherited a fiery disposition that often brought her trouble. As one of the youngest girls, she had to wind thread onto the little bobbins that her older sisters used on the loom. Bored to distraction, she tied knots in the thread. Her angry father shut her for hours in a cramped storage closet.

When her best friend—a similarly redheaded sprite named Louisa—died at age thirteen, Louisa's father came to ask Elizabeth's whether she might come to live with them; it was not uncommon to farm a daughter out. Eavesdropping from behind a door, she heard her father say, "She is no good around here, she may go."

Lizzie could not—or pretended not to—understand her mother's tears nor her father's stern looks when he delivered the news. "I only saw adventure ahead," she later remembered, with the positive spin on past events that decades later would shape her son's own recollections. She had spent four years in her new home when her brother's letter arrived.

Lizzie joined hundreds of thousands of Germanic immigrants who had come to the United States in the wake of several mid-nineteenth-century revolutions. Railroad lines and canals provided cheap transport for those seeking a new start in the American heartland. Most of the newest and poorest German-speaking immigrants to Columbus settled in the German Village, which arose south of a deep, spring-fed ravine that cut the neighborhood off from the more established parts of town. Cheap land and access to water had already attracted the noxious tanneries, which supplied leather products to the booming buggy-making industry. The most successful immigrants raised one-and-a-half-story brick houses, like those in Europe, on solid limestone foundations with gables facing the street, their faces decorated with stone lintels and tall windows. The poorer arrivals crowded into tenements that sprouted like weeds between hulking factories that crowded the Scioto's filthy banks. By 1890, Columbus boasted, in iron processing alone, thirteen foundries, two ironworks, a steel-rail mill, a rolling mill, and twelve galvanized-iron works.

Lizzie fell in love with another recent Swiss immigrant, William Rickenbacher, a man with capable hands and a strong back, whose dark, bushy eyebrows seemed to emphasize his fiery spirit. He was stern, in keeping with the Teutonic traditions of men from the cantons of the old country. She thought that he would make a good father for her children. He worked in one of the numerous breweries west of the German Village, which had emerged to slake the thirsts of a hard-toiling immigrant population by fermenting large quantities of cheap, dark ale. The couple married and moved into a cramped space at the back of one such brewery, the reek of hops soon penetrating their few possessions.

The same forces that had opened up Columbus to economic boom brought correspondingly hard times when a chain of recessions struck in the late nineteenth century. Still, the city's population grew by 70 percent from 1890 to 1900, and another 70 percent between 1900 and 1910. The pioneering Congregationalist preacher Washington Gladden decried the social decay he saw all around him: drunken public officials, prostitutes so thick on High Street in the evening that "decent women" needed an escort. In 1886, four years before the Rickenbachers' third child and second son, Edward, was born, Samuel Gompers had founded the American Federation of Labor in downtown Columbus to narrow the deep divides between the "masters and men" of the Gilded Age.

Just as his family grew, William was laid off from his brewery job, got another but was laid off again, and had to settle into day labor on the city's growing infrastructure of bridges and sidewalks. The couple had bought two cheap lots in southern Columbus, several blocks west of the last electric trolley stop, but William's sporadic employment threatened their dream of someday building a house. They sold one lot to survive.

Without consulting her husband, Lizzie took advantage of her father's visit to America to borrow his return fare, which she promptly turned into a down payment on another lot and the funds to build a small house with a bedroom and sitting room on the first floor. The children would crowd into an unheated loft to sleep. When she told William that the house was almost complete, he balked, his pride deeply wounded. She told him she was moving there with or without him. Lizzie managed to repay her father by taking on endless loads of laundry. In 1893, when Eddie was three, the young family took up their new residence, which had no gas, let alone electricity, running water, or heat beyond a fireplace, and light only from a single kerosene lamp. Eddie grew up watching his fiercely self-reliant mother doing whatever it took to survive.

His passion for risk taking declared itself early. Human beings exhibit wide ranges of tolerances for danger, from those who recoil from its slightest manifestation through the great majority who live with it uncomfortably and the very few who vigorously seek it. This last response first showed in Eddie as an accident-prone child, starting at four when a streetcar hit him. Over the next several years, he fell into a well and knocked himself out, slipped from a walnut tree, scarring his chin, and had to be rescued by his older brother after getting his foot caught in a railroad track with a train bearing down.

As he grew older, he more actively courted risk. Among his fellow urchins he formed the Horsehead Gang, which took its moniker from the wooden sign of the Columbus Driving Park, a horse-racing track only three blocks away. One Saturday afternoon, the gang commandeered a small square rail truck inside a gravel pit, dragging it up the steep hundred-foot incline to the mine's stony lip. The boys placed wooden chocks under the wheels, then piled aboard for a number of runs. On the last, Eddie was trying to kick the chock out with one foot when he fell in front of the cart and a wheel cut his shin to the bone.

Growing wilder, the gang spent an evening breaking the gaslamp globes on every block from Livingston to Main and Miller streets. So brazen was Eddie that he stole the catcher's mitt of an African American player in the midst of a Sunday game against a white team. Racing away from the field, he stuffed his prize under a bridge and went home, only to meet members of both teams and an angry father, who forced him to confess and then beat him badly.

Years later, Eddie would recall one fight after another, not always brought on by his pugnacity but often by his poverty and heavy Swiss-German accent. Among his classmates at East Main Street Public School, he stood out as one of the poorest—no small feat in that town jammed with struggling recent immigrants. In the depths of winter, Eddie and his siblings couldn't go to school for lack of winter clothing. During one particularly bad time, his father sent him there wearing mismatched shoes, one brown, the other light tan, the right pointed, the left blunt-nosed. His fellow students cruelly ribbed "Dutchy" about that and practically everything else, which often ended in another fistfight. One punch broke his nose, but anything was better than passively enduring the sharp sting of shame. The thin, gangly youth didn't sit back but seemed regularly to push things just a little bit too far. His rebelliousness never seemed fueled by malice or mean-spiritedness— rather by a fierce will to survive, and to do so by standing out and never letting others define who he was.

At school Eddie drank in the new, strong, and rising nationalism sweeping the United States. Earlier immigrant generations had brought great waves of patriotism, but this was different: America was repitching its identity in the classroom as a nation defined by its technological prowess, innovation, and limitless possibility. The Pledge of Allegiance was written in 1892, "America the Beautiful" in 1895, and Memorial Day celebrations had become common. Soon-to-be-president Teddy Roosevelt rode to a victor's glory over the Spaniards in Cuba in 1898 when Eddie was seven. Although the U.S. annexation of the Philippines from defeated Spain would set off a bloody insurrection that might have put Americans on notice of the dangers of imperialism, the country stood confidently braced for its manifest destiny. Emerging, too, were marching orders for America's young sons, new codes of conduct articulated in such books as the humorous "Peck's Bad Boy" series about a lovable troublemaker by journalist-politician George Wilbur Peck. In the preface to one volume, he wrote an ode to the typical American boy, who "does not cry when he gets hurt, and goes into all the dangerous games there are going, and goes in to win . . . who takes the hard knocks of work and play until he becomes hardened to anything that may come to him in after life."

While Peck could imagine how the school of hard knocks would build character in middle-class children, he knew little of the extreme poverty of immigrant families in the new American cities. When Eddie and his older brother prowled the Toledo & Ohio Central (T&OC) railroad tracks with a wheelbarrow and sack, they understood that failure to return home with pieces of coal that had fallen from passing locomotives would mean a cold kitchen; even these slim pickings would leave the scrawny young brothers clutching each other at night for warmth, made the more difficult by empty bellies. Eddie worked not long after he could stand up, delivering newspapers at five years old. He kept goats to sell the thick milk to neighbors, sold rags, cadged cigarettes for himself, and hustled anything he could.

William's inability to adapt to the New World didn't help matters. The mounting series of reverses to his father's pride heaped ever higher, and he took it out on his children, Eddie in particular. The big, heavy laborer hit his boy hard; Eddie later recalled him as always trying to "lick the old nick out of me with switches." At one point, a mutt named Trixie that Eddie had adopted went furiously for William's ankle, so aroused was she by William's brutality toward her master. A moment that could have turned ugly suddenly broke up in laughter. Perhaps it was Lizzie who set off the giggling. She often provided the only safe port after her husband's frequent storms ripped the household. Lizzie could remember all too well the anger of her own father against her own small defiant acts. Eddie, it seems, had inherited her proud, scrappy toughness: Like many mothers' favorite sons, he would become the "conquistador" that Freud describes. The battered but enduring boy learned how to take his father's bone-rattling punches without crying, to stand up to a formidable presence.

These increasingly difficult encounters with his father ended in a minute one July day in 1904. That summer noon, William and five or six other laborers were resting under a tree after a hot morning laying a cement sidewalk at Linwood and Mound streets. An African American drifter named W. A. Gaines, who had been putting in sod at a nearby yard, walked over to ask, "None of you fellows want to share your dinners with a fellow, do you?" Something about this innocuous request deeply angered William, who responded that "if I had any dinner to share with any person I would share it with my children." Profanity then flowed. What lit Rickenbacher into a blue rage that day remains unclear, perhaps that he felt keenly the ever more vise-tight grip of poverty and his inability to succeed in this land of plenty. Gaines hustled away, but Rickenbacher went after him. Gaines, who later claimed that Rickenbacher had brandished a knife, swung a steel spirit level, a tool used to even the sidewalk, breaking William's left forearm below the elbow. William kept coming. A second blow struck the back of William's head, knocking him out. A sheriff later found the frightened Gaines, blackjacked him, and then charged him with assault to kill.

William slipped into a coma at nearby St. Francis Hospital but tenaciously clung to life. The community threw benefit picnics for the distraught Lizzie and her children, one a "lawn fete and dance" at the Driving Park, to which the Columbus Light Company provided free transportation. Only after five weeks, and after a brief awakening in which he recognized his wife and children, did William slip away. Lizzie went into debt to buy her sons dark suits for his funeral. As the family started out for church, she gathered the children together. "I want you all to promise me that, no matter what happens, you will always help one another," Eddie remembered her saying. "Don't you worry," he replied. "I'll take care of everything—don't worry." Yet he absorbed the important lesson that not even he could survive without the help of all his family pulling together. The failure of any of them could bring failure on all.

Three weeks after Eddie's fourteenth birthday that October, a jury took more than an hour to convict Gaines of manslaughter. He drew ten years in jail, slight punishment indeed at a time when a black man often faced death itself for killing a white man, regardless of guilt or intention. The judge's leniency articulated what most in the courtroom already knew: The hotheaded, often profane, elder Rickenbacher had brought this upon himself. The shame that front-page newspaper gossip brought on the family was intense, especially for a boy just reaching adolescence, who harbored extremely mixed feelings about his father's readiness to deliver punishment. He would never forget what could happen to those who lost their tempers.

Eddie could never bring himself to tell the truth publicly about how his father died, claiming in his bestselling autobiography that his father had been no plain laborer but rather a manager on an important bridge-building project. He related how a swinging timber had struck his father fatally in the head one evening as he was operating a pile driver. His mother's credo of doing what it took to survive had taken deep, firm hold; he buried humiliation and guilt by brushing the facts away. He would survive with dignity, even if that meant falsifying the record. He would also correspondingly downplay the grinding poverty, shame, cold, and fear of his early days, inventing a hard but somehow ennobling childhood.

Unable to sleep the evening of the funeral, Eddie walked downstairs and found his mother head in hands at the kitchen table. Standing beside her, the undersized thirteen-year-old solemnly promised never to make her cry again. Lizzie reached out and patted his head. A profound change had come over the boy. He drew up the chair to take his father's place at the head of the table; from then on, he would assume the man's role in her house, despite the presence of older siblings.

The following morning Eddie left with the other children, but instead of going to school he walked over to the Federal Glass Factory, where his brother Bill had once worked. After inflating his age to fourteen and lying that he had finished eighth grade—a requirement of Ohio's otherwise rudimentary child-labor laws—he was hired to start that evening, a twelve-hour night shift carrying freshly blown tumblers to the ovens on heavy steel platters. He walked two miles home and quickly overcame his mother's objections. Weeks later, when a truant officer visited the house, Lizzie walked the man upstairs, where they peered in on the boy collapsed fast asleep on his bed, still wearing his grimy work clothes. Aware of the family's difficulties, the officer finessed his report. Years later, an interviewer asked Eddie whether his elder brother had felt any resistance toward his taking the lead as the family's breadwinner. Bill was industrious, conceded Eddie dispassionately, but he just didn't have the same "push."

Years before mandatory high school institutionalized adolescence, it was far from unusual for children to enter the workplace. Neither the Wright brothers nor Thomas Edison graduated from high school. The word "adolescence" itself had only recently entered the lexicon, and the cult of the teenager, hastened by the mobility conferred first by the bicycle, then by the automobile, would not blossom for some time. Even so, there was something eerily foretelling about a boy who could will himself from childhood to adulthood overnight, from rambunctious troublemaking to full-blown responsibility. Never again did he feel the pull of his friends in the Horsehead

Gang, which quickly dissolved without his leadership. It was as if he just skipped adolescence entirely—and missed that often difficult period when young people become so painfully aware of what others think of them. He grew a thick skin. He learned to survive by taking command, focusing on the task at hand. In this new role, Eddie had no time for the anger that had become his father's Achilles' heel, nor for emotion of any sort. Much later a close friend would characterize him as "completely undemonstrative," while Eddie's wife recalled his "emotional shyness." He never said nice things to her—"the words would choke in his throat"—although he did say flattering things about her to others when she wasn't around. It's not that he didn't have feelings, but he buried them, because they were vulnerabilities that could compromise the imperative to survive. He would become a man whom people automatically called by his first name the minute they met him but whom few, if any, really got to know.

The sudden death of a parent rarely energizes a child; it is taboo for him or her to express even the most justified feelings of liberation in the wake of so profound a tragedy. Eddie, however, seemed only to relish his new freedom. Over the next two years, he would prove far more adept in the workplace than his father ever had—at the glass factory, then as a molder for the Buckeye Steel Castings Company, a bottle capper in a brewery, and a cobbler. At Goodman's Shoe Company on West Broad Street, he stamped out heel-shaped pieces of leather, then laboriously nailed one piece to another, and another, to build a heel. Tired of this sleepwalking routine, Eddie fashioned a wooden heel template to save time by stacking three or four pieces, then nailing them together. The supervisor noticed and congratulated him.

He came to feel a strong confidence in his abilities, which, tempered by a precocious ability not to take offense or indulge in self-pity, ripened into an earnest industriousness that employers came rapidly to value. Carving marble at a monument works yielded praise from his boss and the skills to craft his father's tombstone. His mother still ruled the house, though, and pulled him off the job after he developed an itchy throat and slight cough from the dust. It was an index of his growing manual talents and overall competence that the shop's owner offered to double his salary on the spot, but his mother refused to let him compromise his health. Still, money was somehow coming in; with the help of his siblings, the family not only paid off the mortgage but fixed up the little house and yard.

On Sundays his mother would give him a quarter, and he would take the electric trolley north to Olentangy Park on the outskirts of town, where he gobbled down Cracker Jacks and rode a wooden roller coaster. He particularly enjoyed fourteen-year-old Cromwell Dixon's crazy contraption, the Sky-Cycle, which often floated high above the park, its creator precariously astride a horizontal pole hung beneath a 32-foot-long football-shaped hydrogen balloon. Squinting into the bright summer sky, Eddie watched him pedaling furiously to turn a propeller, imagining himself at the controls, free for long minutes from the earth.

When a light breeze blew the Sky-Cycle beyond Olentangy's confines, Eddie would chase it through the neighborhoods. The whole world—not just the fitful zephyrs brushing over Olentangy Park—was crackling with change and possibility. Newspaper reports had recently appeared about a couple of bicycle mechanics from Dayton, only 70 miles away, who had roused their engine-powered machines above the dunes off North Carolina's Albemarle Sound. Across America, independent inventors were heroes, the imaginations of most every boy fired by stories of Edison's electric light, Marconi's radio, Eastman's camera, and Bell's telephone. In 1910, dime-novel entrepreneur Edward Stratemeyer packaged this spirit of youthful inventiveness into one of fiction's most enduring characters: Tom Swift, the peppy, hyperoptimistic boy supergadgeteer, whose backyard tinkering swept him into a wonderland of dirigibles, submarines, and electric cars. In spirit, Tom—"Swift by name and swift by nature"—stood for Eddie or any one of millions of their American brethren. Invention and tinkering had simply hijacked the country's imagination. As Peck squarely put it at the turn of the century, the typical American boy "will investigate everything in the way of machinery, even if he gets his fingers pinched, and learns how to make the machine that pinched him."

Such motivations sent Eddie into his own backyard to construct a perpetual motion machine. Under the light of a coal lamp at night he wound springs and fooled with bits of machinery. "My idea was a series of springs—as one unwound, the other would wind up and so forth, carrying the power with it and the balance." He would have to engage the problem with his hands before he finally understood why it could never work. That didn't stop him from trying to fly off a roof on a bike under a large, tightly gripped carriage umbrella. Fortunately the mound of sand that he and a friend had carefully heaped up beforehand broke his precipitous drop when the umbrella immediately turned inside out.

Ordinary Americans did not just thrill to Jules Verne's fantastic world, in which Captain Nemo cruised the world's oceans in a palatial submarine, but believed that they themselves were drawing upon a multitude of world-changing inventions—in essence, becoming their own Nemos. Eddie carried around with him a pocket tool set—an adjustable wrench, a screwdriver, and pliers—all wrapped in a piece of leather; sufficient, if you commanded his natural skills, to most any task. At no time, perhaps, since the generation that fought the American Revolution had U.S. citizens felt so empowered to create a world to their own designs.

After his marble-carving gig, Eddie took a job cleaning cars with the Pennsylvania Railroad, which morphed into a spot in the machine shop, where he learned how to turn ungainly pieces of rough steel into beautifully symmetric forms. The men liked to tease the youngster, sending him around the shop in search of half-round squares or left-handed monkey wrenches. In return for the laughs and raspberries, this resilient, good-natured kid, who took their ribbing with a wide grin, received valuable lessons at the lathe, and help with making canes and baseball bats during lunch break. His appreciation of the beauty of fine-precision parts and well-designed machines grew into a lifetime love. He might well have stayed there but for a misadventure he did nothing to precipitate when a wheel popped off a cart stacked high with lumber as it passed his workstation. The whole load toppled onto him and pinned him to his lathe. They urgently pulled off the boards to find the youngster's shin badly lacerated but Eddie otherwise okay.

The accident sent Eddie to the Livingston loft bed for some days. His mother nursed him, her energetic care fueled by guilt over her son's early entrance into a man's workplace. Had the lumber slid into him at a slightly different angle, it could easily have snapped his leg bones, crippling him for life. In that hard world where little care was taken for worker safety, accidents were a man's problem, not the company's.

Eddie dwelt little on much beyond the most recent past. His ride in the Model C almost possessed him. In his waking dreams, the thrill of speed, freedom, and powerful motion claimed his imagination as nothing had before—and sent him down the road over and over again.

His short career had made him passably handy at lathing, stonecutting, cobbling, and glassmaking, all practical skills employed toward tangible, traditional uses, which nevertheless offered little chance for imaginative reinterpretation. In this boy's prescient eyes, the Model C was a mere charcoal sketch of what was to come. On first impression, few people recognize an object's transcendent possibilities—to most, for instance, the automobile was simply a horseless carriage. Eddie looked beyond its shiny exterior and saw the promise of a new frontier, one that could be continually recast and made ever more formidably useful. Reflecting in old age on a life of unceasing initiative and enterprise, Eddie would muse justly that "I was a dynamic part of progress and life."

By the turn of the century, the American geographical frontier was no more. Intrepid explorers would soon reach both poles; others had long since rounded both capes by sail and pushed overland into the jungles of Africa and the deserts of Australia and across the ranges of South America. Deep in its genetic makeup, the restless nature of Americans yearned for new challenges, new horizons, which they would find in the obsession with going ever faster and higher. If speed was America's new religion, then the car was its mobile temple. Eddie would soon become one of its most powerful prophets.

2.

A MOST DANGEROUS JOB

The streets of Columbus that young Eddie knew so well churned, ground, and pulsed with the unbridled promise of a world remaking itself. The gods of the industrial age were its machines, which legions of hardworking men and women worshipped in long, wearing factory shifts, so irretrievably were these inanimate contraptions connected to the promises of the American Dream. Dominating the eastern bank of the Scioto, the multiacre, multistory Columbus Buggy Company employed eight hundred people, enough to spit out one carriage every eight minutes around the clock. Day and night, the river cast back the glare of its furnaces and lights; the fume forever issuing from its smokestacks gave an eerie impression of the Scioto's being ablaze. The vast Triumph Artificial Limb Company and Columbus Ice and Cold Storage Company pushed out life-strengthening products. Giant cauldrons stood like obedient soldiers in the manifold breweries to the city's south, permeating the air with the fragrance of hops. New York Central trains thickened the air with their smoke as they pounded through neighborhood after neighborhood into the city's heart, shaking windows, shattering conversations.

The marked resemblances of some parts of the city to the upper reaches of Dante's hell—the stacks pumping out thick dark smoke, the sewers belching industrial waste into the river, the nose-hair-curling reek of the foundries and tanneries—were not yet seen as harbingers of environmental degradation, but rather as the embodiments of innovation, wealth, and prosperity. Beneath the stacks rumbled the engines that were delivering monumental changes to upend the sleepy rural rhythms of the field and plow, replacing them with the modern, the urban, the speedy—progress itself. Great iron arches spanned more than a half mile of the main street, each festooned with a multitude of electric lights that blurred the distinction between night and day. In the evenings, light pushed into the far corners of alleyways and streets, erasing the flickering, danger-making shadows flung by the gaslights of old. No longer did the sun alone dictate the rhythms of commerce and life itself; now human ingenuity was playing an ever greater role. The giant Lazarus department store blazed like a great urban lighthouse pointing to a future full of material wizardry and comforts. A splendid new facility had recently replaced the Union Station that Lizzie had entered years ago, this one an immense gleaming marble monument, grand and seemingly imperturbable by time and fashion. Trains now no longer routinely killed pedestrians crossing busy downtown streets but instead entered the station beneath traffic-choked bridges. Indeed, miracles were manifesting around each corner. Everything was up to date, and not just in Kansas City.

Of course, such full-speed growth came with costs. Pockets of squalid, stubborn poverty stuck and grew like mold in the interstices between factory and warehouse, a sign that the American Dream had not blessed everyone with prosperity. Human changes inflicted on the landscape, too, bore not so sweet fruit. By clearing the oak-maple forests whose roots had shored the banks and environs of the Scioto, industrious pioneers had unwittingly opened the city to flooding. In March of Eddie's eighth year, the river again overflowed its banks and ripped through ineffective levees, putting west Columbus under several feet of water. Eddie and his friends happily splashed through the submerged streets. Perhaps except in the pulpit, there were no discussions of how or why: The flood moved simply and ruinously in, a capricious act by a darkly whimsical god. Citizens dealt with it as humans always have with natural catastrophe, focusing on the small moments of light when heroism and humanity exhibit themselves. In Columbus that early spring, they celebrated a dog named Joe, who had saved a young family from the rising waters.

Such warnings went largely overlooked, in large part due to the hubris nurtured by that mounting sense of power that comes from (more or less) taming nature, defying fate, and enjoying its returns in comfort and luxury—for a while. There was but one speed, and that was full steam ahead.

In turn-of-the-century America, opportunity—at least for those graced with a head start and ambition—seemed plentiful enough. The burgeoning automobile market set off a gold rush of innovators and tinkerers, hucksters and opportunists in the Midwest. Columbus itself saw the birth of more than forty automobile makers between 1895 and 1923. The vast promise of the Wild West world of automobiles drew brilliant, quirky, and resourceful men who brought all manner of industrial experience to the task of building cars. David Dunbar Buick had started out manufacturing plumbing fixtures; Walter P. Chrysler repaired and built locomotives; Henry Leland, who brought Cadillac into existence, made firearms. George N. Pierce, who eventually created the legendary Pierce-Arrow, made birdcages, valuable experience that led him into manufacturing bicycle spokes and thence into automobiles. Fortunes were to be made, all right, but no one knew exactly how the business would play out.

Stir-crazy from lying bedridden with his injured shin, Eddie snuck out one afternoon, limping over to 140 East Chestnut Street, to peer through the windows of the Evans Garage, which serviced bicycles and had recently branched out into automobiles, offering one of the few places for pioneer enthusiasts to park their cars under cover. There amid broken bicycles sat several horseless carriages—the name still assigned to most motor vehicles—which looked as if someone had cut their traces and shooed the horses away, their engines sitting underneath the seat, facing small dashboards or none at all. Eddie made out the frame of a Waverly Electric from the Pope Motor Car Company of Indianapolis, a tiller-steered two-seater mounting an enormous hooded headlight. Priced at $850, more than the yearly income of an average American family, it remained far beyond the reach of most. Next to it sat an outlandish Locomobile steam buggy, which combined bicycle-type spoked wheels and suspension with a horse-carriage chassis, seating its driver above the boiler.

Then Eddie's eyes fell eagerly on an automobile powered by an internal combustion engine. This Packard boasted three speeds and reverse but only one cylinder. Like most American boys, Eddie knew all about the epic 1903 journey of Horatio Jackson, Sewall Crocker, and their adorable pit bull, Bud: how the three (Bud was picked up on the way, eventually being fitted with his own goggles because the alkali-flat dust inflamed his eyes) triumphantly underwent the sixty-three-day ordeal of reaching New York City from San Francisco in a used two-cylinder Winton. Their northern route, although chosen to avoid the steepest Rockies, had still been disrupted for days of hourly resorts to block and tackle on nearly impassable pitches. The exhausted trio became heroes, the first of what would become a stream of automobile adventurers.

The three vehicles before Eddie's eyes neatly encapsulated the three different technologies competing in the automobile arena. Two of them would soon wither. No technical problem ever has a single solution, and the quest for a self-powered mechanical vehicle not guided by rails proved no exception. Between 1895 and 1903, there had arisen a furious race for dominance, each of the three technologies taking turns to lead the pack. At first the quiet-running, battery-driven electric car took primacy in sales and popularity, in large part because it was the easiest to operate. A simple lever started the car and controlled acceleration. Pope's Columbia electric became the first offered as a stock car rather than a custom model. However, electrics would be doomed to little more than running errands around town because of the endless need to recharge their batteries—which themselves weighed a great deal, generally amounting to 40 percent of the vehicle's weight. (A fully charged battery today provides 10 watt-hours per pound, while a gasoline engine delivers 6,000.) Nor did electrics do well on hills or rough roads.

In 1900 the steamer surpassed electrics in sales. That year 1,681 steamers, 1,575 electric, and 936 gasoline vehicles were sold in the United States.

To many the steam car seemed the obvious answer; after all, that technology had carried the continental-nation-making railroads from coast to coast, while steamboats plied the Mississippi, Ohio, and Hudson, and the USS *Monitor* had transformed naval warfare. Decades of innovation had reduced the size of the unwieldy early water tanks to small, efficient tubular boilers. While steam locomotives could carry great quantities of coal for their boilers, a small wheeled vehicle could not. The Locomobile relied on kerosene to make steam in a so-called flash boiler, doing away with the constant need to stoke a firebox and remove ashes; now a driver could raise a head of steam and get started in about twenty minutes. During the Second Boer War of 1899–1902, the British pressed the Locomobile into service as a tractor to drag supplies, particularly relishing its secondary capacity to boil water for tea. The Stanley Steamer would become the most famous steam car—and one would break the land-speed record by reaching 127 mph on a South Florida beach in 1906.

Like all steam-driven cars, the Stanley was limited by the very small boilers that it could carry, compelling the operator to assiduously monitor the steam-generating process to maintain proper pressure. As a result, the Stanley Steamer displayed a dizzying array of gauges: boiler-water level, steam pressure, main tank fuel pressure, pilot tank fuel pressure, oil sight glass, and tank water level. To start a Stanley, the driver had to adjust thirteen different valves, levers, handles, and pumps. The kerosene often started fires. The boilers had to be refreshed with filtered, clear water after only 20 to 40 miles—highly impractical while touring. As the water steamed away, the car's speed dropped considerably. Water simply proved too heavy to carry in quantities necessary to travel long distances without refilling.

Compared to these still substantial achievements, the internal combustion engine seemed an afterthought, a promising technology only in its infancy—and one confronted by possibly insurmountable difficulties. Unlike those powered by steam and electricity, the petroleum engine could only work efficiently within a narrow range of rotational speeds, thus requiring a transmission system of clutch and gearbox. Whereas steam engines featured easy sliding-lever throttles, the gearshifts of gasoline-powered engines scraped, grabbed, and ground, making every shift a chore. One critic noted in 1900 that the internal combustion engine was "noxious, noisy, unreliable, and elephantine. It vibrates so violently as to loosen one's dentures. The automobile industry will surely burgeon in America, but this motor will not be a factor." Internal combustion devices not only stalled frequently but were frightfully loud, hard to start, and required endless adjustment. They still offered, however, one huge advantage over steam and electric cars: When they worked, they could negotiate America's atrocious unpaved road system. (In 1900 there were so few paved roads outside major cities that it wasn't possible to drive on pavement continuously between New York and Boston.) By 1903 the gas-engined car surpassed the other technologies when the Olds Motor Vehicle Company sold four thousand Oldsmobiles.

As Eddie continued to stare through the window at the Evans Garage, the flame ignited within him by the Model C boiled into a raging fire of near-desperate adolescent longing. These cars crouched in the darkness beckoned him as if animate, promising him a world not only exciting but new and even dangerous. Amid these inchoate visions of speed and freedom lurked the intoxicating knowledge that these machines were ultimately knowable and explainable. There was clarity in that dusty shop, each car the composite of hundreds of parts working in union, unsullied by the fickle uncertainties of emotion or chance. For Eddie, there was no looking back: He would need to work here. He strode right up to William Evans, who was running the garage by himself. Admitting that he needed help, Evans offered the teenager seventy-five cents an hour, a third of the wage at the railroad. "You have yourself a boy, mister," answered Eddie, delighted to be working at last with the next great thing. Over the next eight to ten months, he studied the different machines, eventually starting their engines up when Evans left the shop. On one occasion, he drove the Packard inside the garage, and the engine seized. Opening the crankcase and finding a bone-dry piston stuck to the cylinder wall, he jammed a crowbar beneath the rod connecting the piston to the crankshaft and heaved. It yielded. Eddie poured oil inside, cranked the engine once to lubricate it, and then restarted it. To his relief, the engine came to life, although he had done it permanent damage. Evans returned to find him quietly patching a tire.

During another of his boss's absences, he picked up his mother and some friends for a spin in the Waverly. After they had eaten dinner and he had dropped them off, he started back to the garage. The car slowed to a halt, its batteries drained. With darkness setting in, he still had a mile and a half to go—and couldn't afford a tow. Remembering how Evans had commented that a battery frequently regained a little current if left idle, Eddie waited an hour, his Ingersoll dollar watch "in and out of my pocket a dozen times." Finally he got the Waverly up and running, at least for several blocks, until it ran down. He repeated the process again, then again, at last reaching the garage about 3:00 A.M. He hooked up the battery charger and took the streetcar home.

Evans must have had a sense of Eddie's growing boredom. With his ear-to-ear grin and likeable earnestness, the boy disarmed any of his boss's concerns. In the meantime, at the recommendation of a teacher with whom he remained in contact, the sixteen-year-old signed up for an "international" correspondence-school course in automotive engineering. At first baffled by the reams of technical drawings, he soon found them starting to make sense. In the inner workings of machines he found a world of order and purpose. For a boy brought up in a household often upended by the unpredictable outbursts of an angry father and the silent disappointments of a loving mother, it was a haven. His growing familiarity with engines only increased his yearning to build the cars themselves.

Several blocks from Evans's garage, the Oscar Lear Automobile Company was jammed into a shabby little three-story building on a 50-by-100-foot lot, which housed a hive of mechanics and engineers assembling cars from scratch. Eddie took to visiting the shop in his free time, pushing inside to watch the men bent over engines or machine parts. However small their facilities, the owners turned out one quality car a week, crafting every single component, except the rubber tires. The namesake principal owner, previously a typewriter and bicycle merchant, had turned to solving a key problem of the early automobile internal combustion engine: how to disperse the heat generated by thrashing pistons before it melted the engine parts or boiled the lubricants dry. Water-cooled engines often boiled over or spouted whalelike geysers of scalding coolant. Lear experimented with a system in which air played the main reductive function. In relatively short order, he and two partners were building large air-cooled engines, the first of their kind in America, enclosing each cylinder in an aluminum shell, which left a space between the inner jacket and the outer cylinder surface, through which a large fan drove air that exited out the jacket's open top.

Then it came time to put this notion to the test. Few considered that early gas automobiles could run for long periods; Lear decided to prove that conceit wrong. Lee Frayer, one of his partners, entered a stripped-down Frayer-Miller in the world's first twenty-four-hour race, held at the race-track near Eddie's home in the summer of 1905. Their entry looked more like a gigantic go-kart than an automobile, its massive spoked wheels supporting a frame upon which sat an exposed, cylinder-displaying engine and a small wicker basket for a seat. Three cars roared off on the afternoon of July 3, each nearly shaking its driver senseless. Repeated sprinkling with water did little to keep the track dust down. Within the first hour the Peerless, operated by a Columbus brewer, popped a tire, ran through a fence, and struck a water barrel, shearing off the car's starting crank and caving in the radiator. Frantic engineers soon got it back into the race. In the next hour, the Pope-Toledo blew out a tire and chewed up 100 feet of wooden fence before flipping into a ditch. The *Columbus Evening Dispatch* simply recorded that "the frame was straightened, a new radiator was installed and a new set of wheels put on and everything adjusted for more record-breaking time in sixty short minutes." As darkness fell, fifty giant arc lamps around the track's periphery bathed the track.

At 9:20 P.M., after Frayer had set a then-blistering record pace of just over 60 miles per hour, a flying rock broke the teeth of his main gear and bent the camshaft. Before 4:00 A.M. he was back in the race, making up 150 of the 250 miles thus lost. He had completed 728 miles to the Pope-Toledo's 828 when the latter zoomed over the finish line on July 4 in front of 15,000 screaming fans. Without the long repair, Frayer would have clearly taken first. He became something of a hometown hero, a pioneer of new worlds in a city hungering for the latest, fastest, and most enduring skills.

In spring 1906, Eddie started hanging around the Oscar Lear shop on weekends, evenings, and holidays. Finally Frayer asked the gangly teen what he wanted. There was work needed to be done, answered Eddie, so he would come back the following day. Arriving at 7:00 A.M., he scrubbed the garage floor and work surfaces, sweeping away great piles of metal and wood shavings, carefully leaving one section untouched to make the contrast apparent. When Frayer walked in and saw the grinning boy and his handiwork, he offered him a job on the spot. In this taciturn, hard-bitten engineer, Eddie found a father figure who never lost his temper, never drank to excess.

Henry Ford had yet to revolutionize car manufacturing with the assembly line, so workers still painstakingly handcrafted each part. Frayer placed Eddie with a German toolmaker assembling blower fans for the main engines; the boy's job was drilling small holes through the steel rim attaching fan to engine. Although a mere apprentice, he crafted a little jig of hardwood that let him drill four or five holes, not just one, at each pass. Learning how to make his own tools, Eddie worked on steering gears and carburetors, the latter being the devices that blend air and gas into the mixture that fuels internal combustion.

During lunch, Eddie went over his correspondence course, eating his sandwich while poring over the crude drawings of engine parts: hard work, especially for a seventh-grade dropout with no one to help him understand the details. Frayer startled him one day by asking about the course and inspecting the materials, soon giving him a raise and the chance to learn from skilled craftsmen about operating drill presses, lathes, shapers, and grinders, as well as how to make, axles, transmissions, and ignition systems. He learned, as do many engineers, with his hands: making, shaping, tweaking. Frayer discovered a preternatural quickness in the boy, a desire to learn and master.

He proved such a quick learner that Frayer offered him a place in the engineering department alongside the men crafting, or rather designing, Frayer-Millers—for this kind of skilled work remained so brilliantly idiosyncratic that each car was a slowly developing work of craft, not the offspring of an established blueprint. His team was hard at work building three cars for the 1906 Vanderbilt Cup on Long Island, a road race organized by "Willie K." Vanderbilt, the great-grandson of the Commodore, in still-rural Nassau County out of concern that the American car industry was falling far behind Europe's. "I wanted to bring foreign drivers and their cars over here in the hope that Americans would wake up."

On the day before the team set out, Frayer handed Eddie a leather helmet and a pair of Zeiss racing goggles and asked him to race with him, adding, "You've got a good head on your shoulders." Dizzy with delight, Eddie replied that he'd need only an hour to get ready. Sprinting home, he jammed clothes into a duffel that had belonged to his father and raced back. The train ride to New York City was a blur; a touring car ferried them out to Long Island. It was Eddie's first time outside Columbus.

Early race drivers competed in cars that were little more than engines, tires, and two steel bucket seats mounted on a chassis, lacking windshields, seat belts, or harnesses. Nor did drivers use helmets or fireproof suits. Suspension systems were rudimentary at best; racers manhandled the steering as bone-jarring ruts threatened to rip the wheel from their gloved hands. Brakes frequently burned out long before the race ended.

Drivers raced with riding mechanics, known as "mechanicians," crowded next to them, responsible primarily for adjusting gasoline and oil pressure. While gravity-fed fuel systems and splash boilers might work for touring cars, they were woefully inadequate at racing speeds. The mechanicians manipulated bicycle-tire pumps to pressurize the gas tank and pressed plungers to lubricate the searingly hot engines. Should a gas line break, the mechanician might fish out a roll of adhesive tape from his pocket and try to fix it temporarily. In one race, a mechanician hung across the vibrating hood of a Marmon for 50 miles to adjust a faulty carburetor by hand.

"The next thing you've got to watch for is the tires," Frayer told Eddie. "Keep your eye on them, especially the rear tires, and let me know when the rubber begins to wear off. You can tell it easy, the fabric's a different color."

Besides these tasks, the mechanician must watch for overtaking competitors. "I'll be looking straight ahead, of course, so if another car is coming up to pass me, I won't see it," explained Frayer. (It would occur to no one to install rearview mirrors until 1910.) Eddie was to "keep a lookout to the rear, and let me know if anyone wants to pass." Because wind and engine noise drowned out even the loudest shouting, mechanicians and drivers worked out physical signals. "Tap my knee once if somebody is coming up to pass me. Two taps mean a tire is going bad." Perhaps the most important if unspoken element of the mechanician's code was to watch out for the driver, who, hammered by the monstrous conditions, lost a little bit more edge on each lap. "Many's the time my mechanic beside me has to kick me to keep me waked up," Eddie himself later told a reporter.

It's hard to imagine a more dangerous job. Unlike the drivers, who could brace against the wheel and anticipate corners, mechanicians had little more than a handle on the side of their seats and one behind the driver to hold on to, not infrequently being pitched out at a corner taken too fast or when the car hit a particularly bad bump. They died at a rate three times that of drivers. "He is the Damon of the gasoline circuit, a Damon to the race driver's Pythias," wrote Eddie and, perhaps obviously, a coauthor, in a purple ode to the mechanician in a 1915 issue of *Motor Age*. After risking his life for his driver, "he drags himself wearily to his garage. His legs are weak, his hands are cut, his back is bruised and swollen."

The 1906 Vanderbilt Cup offered a $10,000 prize. Europeans had roared off with victories in the first two years, but now Frayer was only one American of many set on challenging their supremacy. France, Germany, England, and Italy were well represented. A motley assortment of cars began the time trials; only five cars from each country would compete in the actual cup race. There was a chain-driven Locomobile, a mammoth Pope-Toledo, an Oldsmobile, a Panhard and Darracq from France, an Italian Fiat, and a German Mercedes.

On the first day of the qualifying heats, Frayer and Eddie careened around the course, Eddie delighting in the wind on his face, avidly checking the dials, and bracing with Frayer against the bucket seats as they took curves.

With no windshield the wind grew extremely loud; one writer in the mechanician's seat reported that "I thought sure my ear drums would be crushed beneath the pressure." The engine turned over at a maximum of 800 to 1,000 revolutions a minute, providing a ride that was not smooth, Eddie reported, "but a series of lunges." The journalist complained that "the oil and sand spattered my face. The incessant hum of the motor and roar of the exhaust, thundering like the regular fire of cannon, terrified me."

On the second day, Frayer drove even faster. On a stretch of the Jericho Turnpike, Eddie turned to look at him with alarm as they approached a sharp curve far too fast. Frayer's face went white as he jammed the failing brake to the floorboard.

"Hold on!" yelled Frayer; the road curved, but the car continued flat-out into a ditch, blasting out the other side and, however frantically Frayer yanked at the wheel, slammed into a dune. The sand brought the car abruptly to a stop, sending it flipping over and launching its occupants. Remarkably, neither suffered more than cuts and bruises. Mechanics fixed the dents and scratches overnight. They were still in contention.

The following daybreak, they made a practice run. This time the brakes held; Frayer hit the same turn carefully, gunning the engine as he came out of it at about 70 mph. At that very moment, a flock of partridgelike guinea fowl burst across their path. To lighten the car, Frayer had removed the screen over the large circulation blower in front. One unfortunate creature was sucked in. "It killed him, feathered him, carved him and broiled [him] right then and there," recalled Eddie. The blower tore apart in a cloud of black and white feathers, quickly overheating the cylinders. Frayer nursed the damaged car back to the starting line, far preceded by a reek of unintentional roast fowl. The mechanics scraped and cleaned the engine.

On September 22, the day that would determine the five American entrants, the pair roared off to an excellent start, Frayer driving hard. Maybe he pushed too hard, because their rear tire blew on a curve, their back end swerving to the right, then fishtailing at 60 mph, while Frayer struggled to regain control and avoid a copse. Finally he pulled over. Both jumped out to untie the wheel attached to the side of their hood and replace the blown tire, a procedure they had practiced.

Not long after, the temperature gauge shot up into the red and the oil pressure dropped, which Eddie could not reverse no matter how hard he worked the pump. The wind fell away; they heard a faint knocking grow louder. The big Locomobile approached from behind, and Eddie dutifully tapped Frayer on the knee. Frayer nodded and gave way; although aware that the piston would freeze in the engine block at any moment, he couldn't bear to quit. Even so, in the end he took his foot off the accelerator, pushed in the clutch, and turned off the ignition, and they rolled to a stop by the side of the road. There they sat. Frayer sighed and looked at Eddie.

"We're through," he murmured. Eddie marveled at Frayer's equanimity, particularly after "a year of seven-day weeks [and] an outlay of $50,000 or more," which had not even qualified them to compete. "You've got to learn how to smile and take it," Eddie would later write. If he got licked, "why I'd forget it, close the chapter and go on and smile"—a homespun philosophy, but one that carried him through a life of perilous extremes.

The early crowds at these road meets blithely disregarded their considerable dangers, often spilling right onto the track despite the sixteen policemen per mile whom Vanderbilt had deployed. Rarely if ever had the public seen something terrestrial go that fast. Onlookers would part a hundred feet before an oncoming car, closing up immediately afterward, with sometimes lethal consequences. One man, struck by a Hotchkiss, landed dead at the feet of two horrified women. "Many Marvelous Escapes," announced the *New York Herald* of spectators who just couldn't get close enough, as if they were running with the bulls in Pamplona. "Again the scrambling, screaming, swearing!" wrote a *Collier's* reporter of one vehicle fishtailing into a crowd. While bruises and scratches were many, fatalities were relatively few, at least this time. The police tried to move the crowds back with hoses, but not even that seemed to work. Wild with excitement, the spectators of this blood sport just couldn't get enough of the ungainly machines with overlarge wheels and daredevil drivers. "A good God looked down, I think, was sorry for the fools, and let them live," the reporter continued. The Connecticut-built gas Locomobile clocked the fastest lap, giving the Americans hope, but eleven consecutive tire failures forced it out of the race. A Frayer-Miller did win a spot in the elimination round, running well until it pulled over with a broken crankshaft in the seventh lap. A Frenchman won, averaging 61.43 mph in his Darracq. As for the young man from Columbus who watched the race from the sidelines, he was hooked, the taste of speed and excitement lingering at the edge of his consciousness for a long, long time.

No other Frayer cars would ever race again, although many of their creator's innovations would survive: the left-handed drive, wire wheels, and low-slung chassis. Back home after this heroic if disastrous showing, Frayer took a job as head engineer at the Columbus Buggy Company, which for decades had produced some of the nation's finest horse-drawn vehicles. It, too, was adapting its technology to the automobile, building a high-wheeled carriage not unlike its original product with a small, two-cylinder engine beneath the seat, a small gearshift on the side, and a steering bar instead of a steering wheel. The company called upon Frayer to build a large, air-cooled, internal-combustion-engine-powered model. He brought along his seventeen-year-old protégé as chief of design to oversee a dozen far more experienced and much older men.

Learning to ride in the passenger seat at high speed seemed nothing compared to getting through the mechanics' initial wall of resentment there in those dirty, lathe-filled garages. Eddie deployed an arsenal of crude jokes that he delivered with an appealing veneer of confidence—which, mixed with an authentic modesty in practical matters and a remarkable ability to listen and learn, soon overcame the entrenched hostility. He thus honed leadership skills that would never have come his way so early had he stayed in school. A group photograph of the shop shows men in dirty overalls standing supportively around Eddie, almost as if he were not their boss but their mascot. He is the only one wearing a tie. He had also become the company's chief test driver.

One morning Frayer told Eddie to go help the business's owner, Clinton

Firestone, whose car had stalled on the way to work while crossing a storage dam on the Scioto. Eddie jumped into one of the stripped-down high-wheel buggies, which he had taken to calling a "mosquito, because it looked just so, bereft of fenders or a body, just an engine, four wheels, and a little makeshift seat." Pulling up behind Firestone, he hopped out in his overalls and cap, his frame still scrawny and anemic. The sight struck Firestone dumb. He finally sputtered in his high, reedy voice, "Hell, I asked for man, not a boy."

"Maybe I can help you," said Eddie. Turning the engine over with the crank on the side of the car, he could immediately tell that one of the cylinders was not emitting the appropriate *swoosh*—a sign of no compression. He knew that cars' bouncing motions sometimes shook free the springs that held the intake valves, which admitted the gas mixture into the cylinder. Without them the valves could not close. In a moment, Eddie walked around to the engine in the back of the car, pulled out the valve cage, and knocked back several small locks meant to hold the spring in place, reinserting the valve into the cylinder. He turned on the spark and cranked the car, which roared to life. It had taken all of five minutes.

"It's okay, Mr. Firestone," said Eddie. Truly astonished, his big boss drove away without a word, but he would later tell Frayer that Eddie was the "seventh wonder of the world." Somewhere along the line, Eddie had developed a rare diagnostic skill, difficult to learn—certainly there were no texts on it—and mystifying to most people. "Put simply, engines have always talked to me," he would write years later. "I would simply listen to [the engine] for several seconds and pinpoint the trouble." He had developed almost a musician's ear for such warbling, interpreting an engine's pops, grinds, and pings as chords that directed him to the carburetor, transmission, or gearbox, almost as if he were communicating with a sentient being. "I could understand it and it would respond to my mental desires," he told his ghostwriter.

From then on, Firestone himself dispatched the prodigy to troubleshoot problems for salesmen out demonstrating his company's cars. In one case, the high-wheel motor buggy was frustrating buyers in Atlantic City who wanted to drive on the beach. The sand caused the clutch to slip, stranding prospective buyers until a harness team towed them off to annoying calls of "Get a horse!" Experimenting for several days and nights, Eddie bought an old brake band from a junkshop, which he adapted to the clutch mechanism—a modification so successful that the Buggy Company made a point of delivering it to its customers for emergency use. It also earned him his first picture in a newspaper. Sent to Texas and Tucson to deal with overheating engines, he again handcrafted a solution, this time a forced-cooling circulation system.

His money now easily covered his mother's mortgage and family expenses, still leaving him a little extra in his pocket. Feeling master of the universe as only a seventeen-year-old can, he bought a diamond ring for the lovely young Blanche Calhoun, whom he had fallen for in Sunday school years ago. He proudly presented it to her on a trip home with no idea what it represented. Blanche glowed, and news spread rapidly that they were engaged, but, sputtered Eddie to his family, it was only supposed to be a gift, nothing more. Supremely embarrassed, the young mechanical virtuoso took his tone-deafness in matters of the heart quietly out of town on Buggy Company business. From then on, for well more than the next decade, he would enjoy the company of beautiful women but never let them distract him from his immediate goals.

Firestone eventually put him in charge of the company's five-state north-central sales district—Iowa, Nebraska, the Dakotas, and Wisconsin. Instead of fixing cars, he would sell them. It didn't take Eddie long to realize that the smartest way to do this was to "race on Sunday, sell on Monday." Rich from a booming market in wheat and red meat, midwestern farmers' sons were eager to turn cash into speed.

In 1909, the company stopped building the high-wheeler and instead started manufacturing more conventional Frayer-inspired four-cylinder cars. In June of that year, Eddie entered a stripped-down Firestone-Columbus at a race in Red Oak, Iowa, walking the dirt oval the day before to gauge how fast he could take the corners, and wondering why none of the other drivers were doing the same. At Red Oak, as at all the earliest racing venues, speculators had taken over a horse track with flat ovals, not the banked corners of future, purely automotive arenas. On these soft curves, the wheels would dig in as the car turned, often sending it sliding sideways.

Only in the midst of the race—and far too late—did it dawn on Eddie that race dynamics had been radically changed, because the heavy cars cut deeply into the surface. Hitting the first corner far too fast for the wheel-torn curve, he blew out his right rear tire and lost control. The car crashed through a fence, leapt a ditch, and rolled, tossing his riding mechanic, Glen Spies, into the air. A local newspaper reported that Eddie was "seriously bruised and cut up about the face, but Spies had several ribs broken and for a while it was thought sustained internal injuries, but [this] proved to be a mistake." Such adversity only seemed to strengthen Eddie's steely resolve.

Soon he started winning, first in Iowa, then in Nebraska, where Teddy Roosevelt was among the spectators cheering him on. He seemed to possess that right combination of an unflinching need to win and an abundance of moxie. The intensity of high speed didn't faze him as it would most, but instead seemed to focus and calm him. Then he got the break he was looking for. Frayer entered them into a 100-mile competition at the Columbus Driving Park featuring America's most famous racer, Barney Oldfield.

Oldfield had begun his remarkable career in 1902, when as a twenty-four-year-old bicycle racer he climbed behind the wheel of the 999 race car at the invitation of the designer, a little-known Detroit carmaker named Henry Ford, who did not have the nerve to race the mammoth, stripped-down vehicle, with its wooden clutch and 230-pound flywheel. Oldfield loved the power and speed, winning his first race by spinning unbraked around corners. "The rear wheels slid sideways for a distance of 50 feet, throwing up a huge cloud of dirt," reported The Automobile. "Men were white-faced and breathless, while women covered their eyes and sank back, overcome by the recklessness of it all." Whether at the wheel of a Peerless Green Dragon, Stutz, Blitzen Benz, or Miller Golden Submarine, Oldfield would go on to break most records, including the sound barrier of its day, the mile in a minute on a 1-mile oval track, as he did on June 20, 1903. The following year he hit 84 miles per hour on the hard-packed sands of Ormond Beach, Florida. Given his consummate showmanship, it was not long before most

American boys were familiar with his round goggles, square, fleshy face, and the 6-inch Perfecto cigar clamped between his teeth to cushion them against the violent shaking on the course. Not bad for a poor kid from an Ohio farm, who had once operated an elevator at Toledo's Monticello Hotel.

Oldfield's PR team pumped the legend up to heady heights, weaving a mystique around the physical qualities it took to master tracks as dangerous as the machines that defied them. "Average lungs can't overcome the outward force and the result is like strangulation. Blood rushes to the head; temporary but complete paralysis of mind over body occurs." Indeed, there was something truly formidable and somehow heroic in itself about climbing into a machine that was all power and no safety features, with iffy brakes and wretched steering. The public loved the burly, brawling Oldfield, who cut a Babe Ruth–like figure before that legend ever hit the majors. "I did more fighting in saloons getting old Barney out of scrapes than I ever did in the ring," said his friend the heavyweight champion Jim Jeffries. Oldfield simply seemed larger than life, even appearing on Broadway as himself, grimacing in pretend determination as he gunned his car on a huge treadmill. For Eddie, the chance to race against him was a crazy dream, the fantasy that a sandlot hotshot might entertain about being called up to pitch against Ty Cobb.

Oldfield had sealed his reputation by driving formidably large, overpowered cars. An earlier Winton Bullet had been subject to the shaking violence of cylinders as wide as coffee cans. His six-cylinder Knox would simply blow Frayer and Rickenbacher off the course—unless, figured Frayer, they could win by guile. The pair determined that the Knox's tires, too thin and unreliable for the weight they bore, could prove Oldfield's undoing. Neither Eddie's four-cylinder car nor Frayer's Red Wing could outrun Oldfield in the flats, but both could recover lost ground on the corners, which Eddie could engage furiously, goading Oldfield into taking them faster than he sensibly should. In this scenario, the larger Knox would simply wear its tires out faster and send Oldfield into the pits while Frayer triumphantly followed up to take the prize.

Whatever the strategy, lining up against Oldfield must have been both electrifying and intimidating for Eddie, who as a boy had sold soda pop at the track while avidly following Oldfield's career. He sprang out to a fast start, then cornered at near—but not quite—reckless speed, having tested the surface at sunrise when no one else was watching. Facing a run that lacked both a solid surface and banked corners, he had pushed his stripped-down roadster to determine at just what speed he could master these difficulties without skidding out of control. No two tracks were the same, Eddie would write later, and "you have to practice to feel it." Nor were any two sets of tires identical. Other unpredictables included the weather, engine balance, engine power, acceleration, and the car's balance. Already the young contender was learning to integrate a supremely complex series of factors— much less instrumentally quantifiable than today—into deciding how, when, and where he would push his machine. "It's a very fine dividing line, and it's often just as dangerous to be below it as to be above it, because things can happen below the danger line; everything changes so far as the feel of that car went, as far as the balance of it went." Hitting a 60 mph corner at 55 would get a driver in trouble. "You would be off balance at that particular point."

Eddie was finding his "groove," as racers call the point at which a driver discovers the perfect line where speed, course conditions, and assimilation of skill to vehicle come into focus. "That's where the tuning comes in, the language that you learn to understand." It takes as much mental effort as physical to hew consistently to that line over a long race, and that tuning would be refined during the race as conditions changed, tires wore thin, the track crumbled, and drivers tired.

Irritated that the young upstart was besting him, Oldfield snapped at the bait and pushed his Knox too hard, blew out two tires, and had to pit. Eventually Rickenbacher's own light model also broke down, but the time Oldfield had lost enabled Frayer to win by almost a lap. Unequivocally beat, the sporting Oldfield hailed Eddie as a "clean, square racing man," who "took his share of track and no more. The sole of his right shoe is heavy as lead, and it keeps the accelerator pressed into the floorboard." It wasn't lost on Eddie, as he rubbed shoulders with this great performer, that race-car driving was, like boxing, one of the few ways that a poor kid could hammer his way to stardom. No one could take away from Oldfield, however much the press vilified him as a boozer and brawler, that he had been the first to reach a mile a minute on a track in a gasoline-powered car. For Eddie, the possibility of gaining something that no one could challenge gleamed more brightly than Oldfield's sparkling four-carat diamond pinky ring. A won race was incontrovertible and unassailable.

Seeing Oldfield up close also underscored for Eddie the importance of showmanship. He needed to invent an image that cast him as "reckless" and "crazy," even though he was already assessing risk as the experienced pro he was so rapidly becoming.

In Omaha, he went back to peddling, but with mounting boredom as he came to realize that selling worked best by showing farm boys a good time rather than by invoking a car's high-performance qualities. His office lay on the Omaha Viaduct, near the Union Pacific terminal. One day, while he was watching a train from his second-floor window, a burning cinder flew into his right eye. A doctor dug it out without anesthesia, leaving him with a permanently dancing black spot.

He told no one. With such an injury, most men would have come to doubt just how well they could do in the highly physical theaters of the racetrack and later the sky. Lowering the threshold of risk had never been an option for Eddie. As risk rose, so must he discover how to improve his response, quickly and intensely.

3.

DEATH ON THE TRACK

On October 1, 1910, auto racing reached a new peak in the running of the Vanderbilt Cup on Long Island in New York. Enthusiasts rose at 3:00 A.M. to find a spot at Krug's Corner or the snaky S-twist at Old Westbury on the Nassau County road course. Those coming in cars parked under the route's broad shade trees, their passengers spilling out to picnic in some of the first examples of tailgating. Drinking began immediately and kept up all day. When a course marshal finally yelled, "Car coming!" the crowd erupted into a frenzy of pulsing and pushing, oblivious to police, fences, and dangers, to the road's very edge. "A black spot in the distance grew larger as the roar deepened, suddenly took shape," wrote one observer. "The glaring radiator numerals smashed you in the eye; blue flames spurted from exhaust vents in the bonnet; gay streamers, whipped horizontal by the wind, flared backwards from the helmeted heads of driver and mechanic. Here was speed that you could feel as well as see, speed that burned your cheeks, filled your eyes with oil clods and your nostrils with the stench of gas."

Spectators would pay the price for their enthusiasm: Four died, and twenty-two sustained serious injuries. Late in the race, Joe Dawson pulled his yellow Marmon from the lead into the pit and sat stock-still, tears channeling his dust-blackened cheeks, convinced that he had just killed a spectator. Minutes passed under the pit crew's horrified eyes before his manager was able to report that the man he had struck was still alive, and Dawson pulled back into the race, missing victory by twenty-two seconds.

Such carnage proved too much for the governor of New York, who banned road racing from the state. Meanwhile, a brazen group of entrepreneurs, led by a half-blind showman named Carl Fisher, had dedicated the first purpose-built auto track at Indianapolis, a harbinger of future racing venues. Like Eddie, the Hoosier-born Fisher had quit school early, fending for his divorced mother with a series of odd jobs. Severe astigmatism hadn't slowed him down: Members of the Zig-Zag bicycle club nicknamed him "Crip" after his penchant for spectacular crashes. Nonetheless, he kept racing bicycles, became good friends with Barney Oldfield, and soon graduated to cars. Somehow this poorly sighted daredevil even established a world record on Chicago's Harlem dirt track in 1904 by clocking 2 miles in just two seconds over two minutes.

Fisher's greatest talent lay in his salesmanship, which often verged into Barnumesque hucksterism. After opening an Indianapolis car dealership with Oldfield, he floated across town in one of his Stoddard-Dayton cars, buoyed well off the ground by an immense red balloon. After landing it outside town, he purported to drive back, although the car he started out in had been stripped of its engine for lightness's sake and quietly switched for an intact model. With one of his former bicycle-club brethren, he founded the Prest-O-Lite company, which built car headlights fueled with compressed acetylene gas. Driving at night was extremely hazardous, not only because of the dearth of road lights but because the metal filaments of Edison's lightbulbs (as well as the drip acetylene torches) could not withstand bumps and jolts; nor could early engines generate sufficient power to run them—one more factor in the age's bloodcurdling roster of accidents. Eddie experienced several nighttime mishaps himself, including one in rural Texas in which he smacked into the back of a surrey carriage drawn by two horses. His car nosed under the buggy, ripped off the horses' harness, and pitched a young couple headlong into a cornfield. Fortunately they were unhurt.

Delivering high-pressure gas to the headlamps, the Prest-O-Lite canister provided reliable illumination on America's atrocious roads. Fisher couldn't help but generate headlines, even inadvertently, as his acetylene-filled factories kept blowing up, including, most famously, the flagship India-napolis plant in 1907—a blast that also took out a nearby sauerkraut-processing facility and covered the sidewalks with cabbage. Despite such interruptions, Union Carbide bought the company for $9 million in 1911.

Fisher still loved racing. Having visited Brooklands, the world's first ded-icated car-racing venue (soon to become one of Britain's first major airfields under the stress of war), on a trip to London, he fixated on building a similar track for his hometown. Doing so, he believed, could help Indianapolis ease past Detroit into the forefront of the automobile industry. With partners from his early cycling days, he scraped together enough for a 2.5-mile oval course with banked corners, lined by 3 miles of whitewashed fence. The grounds contained a landing field, 41 buildings, 4 miles of gas pipe to inflate balloons, 3,000 hitching-post spaces for horses and buggies, and several grandstands, each capable of holding 7,500 people.

These pioneer speculators were among the first to realize that auto-mobile racing could be big business—not as an amateur effort but as a savvy business enterprise showcasing professional racers. They opened their track in 1909 but made the huge mistake of economizing on the sur-face, selecting crushed limestone and gravel over a harder, more durable material. On the first day, the cars kicked up such a murderous stone-laced fog that two drivers died. In a 300-mile event on the third day, one driver lost a tire and plowed into the crowd, killing his mechanician and two spec-tators and critically injuring others. Yet another driver, blinded by the track shrapnel, flew off course, missing a large crowd only by a matter of yards. Only then did Fisher stop the race. "More brutal than bull fighting, gladiatorial combats or prize fighting," declared the *Detroit News*.

Nevertheless, this persuasive, not to say obsessive, operator somehow convinced his investors to double down on their commitment and resur-face the course with 3.2 million paving bricks at thirteen cents apiece, thus giving birth to "the Brickyard." Yet the races of 1910 failed to draw a crowd, even when admission included an exhibition by the Wright brothers them-selves. Fisher needed something big, splashy, and bold. At a single pivotal meeting, the partnership reached the make-or-break decision to sponsor a

single long race—but not so long that the entire 500-mile event couldn't fit
into the Memorial Day holiday. Admission prices would reflect the epic
quality of the enterprise: A prodigious purse of $25,000 would attract the
nation's top drivers. This proved one of the most brilliant decisions in
sports history. The high-spring holiday released vast crowds—and the ordeal would test men and their cars as nothing had before. On display would
be several of the values Americans so cherish: audacity, courage, toughness,
and the unrelenting will to win. The coming competition was loudly proclaimed to be the canonical annual event of racing, the Brickyard a mecca
for what one modern journalist has called "that secular deity, the internal
combustion engine," consecrating speed in its purest raw form.

Indy was on the tip of every race-car enthusiast's tongue, and by now
these were legion, so Eddie jumped at the chance to serve as Frayer's relief
driver. On May 30, 1911, 80,000 people poured onto the grounds, a large
number crowding the infield. A special grandstand had been built for two
British engineering societies that had crossed the Atlantic just for the race.
A company of militiamen augmented hundreds of special policemen hired
for the event.

The track could accommodate only forty-four entrants. The best drivers
in America showed up: Ray Harroun in a single-seater Marmon, Ralph
Mulford in a Lozier, Spencer Wishart in a Mercedes, Bob Burman in a Benz,
Arthur Chevrolet in a Buick. Frayer let the twenty-year-old Eddie take the
start. Every participant knew that driving more than six hours, even if some
alternated the wheel with others on their team, would be more punishing
than any race they had entered before. One journalist who took a spin in
the mechanician's seat wrote, "One second my insides were up against my
back teeth and the next they were flattened against the seat of that speed
engine. There was always a vacancy in between. The only connection was
my backbone and that came near snapping several times." This had only
been over a few laps. "My kidneys would scare me," wrote Eddie, who took
the precaution of wrapping a 20-foot-long, 8-to-10-inch-wide strip of burlap from his hips to his armpits. One of the pit crew pulled the makeshift

corset tight, but by the end of the race, it would bunch loosely about his waist.

At the start line, Eddie revved up his four-cylinder scarlet and gray Firestone-Columbus. The barking of the machines chorused at the dangerous outset, each exhaust belching smoke and flame. The tightly packed drivers, especially those at the back, experienced a curious sensation as the flat-out departure created a partial vacuum. Curiously, throttling down did not reduce speed. At no other time has driving been so physically difficult: Not only did drivers have to endure bone-jarring vibrations, they also had to muscle these powerful but barely maneuverable power plants around a banked oval designed to induce maximum speed. Absent windshields, the wind battered them mercilessly. "You've no idea how the breeze forces a fellow's cheeks back and distorts his face when he's going good and fast," reported Eddie. Drivers had to squeeze their steering wheels to keep their cars from leaping suddenly off course when they encountered a bad bump. "Take this track out here," Eddie told a reporter. "It's as smooth as a boulevard when you're going at 60 miles an hour, but when you get up to 105 it feels like a rough road beneath you." The tremendous vibration made a car feel as though it were "built of magnified corrugated iron," wrote another reporter. Tight springs on the clutch and accelerator exhausted the calf muscles and numbed the feet to an almost crippling degree. Even so, the cacophony and physical pressures, underscored by the high danger, concentrated the minds of these consummate risk takers. Eddie found elation in the sheer absolute power and control, as everything but the race dissolved away. Drivers talked about how the peripheries of one's vision contracted to mere streaks of color while the front maintained an adrenaline-heightened crystal clarity. "When things are right, you can feel the tires in your nerve ends," asserted the future longtime Indy veteran Johnny Parsons.

On the thirtieth mile in the backstretch, a front tire flew off Art Greiner's car before Eddie's horrified eyes, twisting and hopping about the track before the shrieking crowd. Greiner and his mechanician flew into a fence 20 feet away. Eddie whizzed by as the infield crowd mobbed the unconscious

Greiner, who miraculously had only broken his arm—and pushed so close to the fatally mangled mechanician that the militia had to use their gun butts to clear a path for the ambulance.

Not long after, another car's steering mechanism broke. In a bad split-second decision, the mechanician jumped out to direct the driver into the pit, only to slip on the oil-covered surface. Another driver, Harry Knight, bore down at 88 miles per hour, managing to swerve at the last possible moment before crashing into a pitted car, which plunged like a bumper car into a neighboring pit, four mechanics diving away just in time. Knight and his mechanician went airborne, while their car hit yet another car in one more pit. No one died, though Knight fractured his skull. It was all over in seconds. The race hammered on, battering the cars, and especially their tires, whose frequent blowouts flipped them across the track and over the rail. One woman fainted dead away, while most of the crowd stood cheering themselves hoarse—a roar that drowned out the screaming clamor of the engines as Harroun's bright yellow Marmon Wasp tore past the checkered flag.

It had taken 6 hours 42 minutes and 8 seconds, an average of 74.59 mph. Harroun had chosen—in direct challenge to the rules—to ride by himself, relying on that newfangled contraption, the rearview mirror. No small device, it looked like a huge alien spider had jumped on his hood, four long metal rods holding the mirror right in front of his face. However uncomfortable, the mirror enabled him to drive solo, thus making it possible to streamline his car to huge advantage. All this took a toll. At race's end he sat dazed in the Wasp, behind a mask of grease and dirt. "This is my last race," he said. "It is too dangerous."

The rules committee grumbled about Harroun's innovation but finally allowed it, although ruling that the two-man teams would be required for years to come. In this effervescence of new technologies, it seems remarkable in retrospect that certain developments—such as the rearview mirror, windscreen, seat belt, and hard helmet—were conceived so relatively late. (Eddie and his mechanician Pete Henderson would pioneer the use of steel hard hats instead of leather or cloth aviator-style helmets in the 1916 Indy.)

In the lurching, trial-and-error world of innovation, whole swathes of the implications of any new technology's impacts frequently go unexamined, most often because the context has not been mapped nor the language of engagement been created to consider them. In the unthinking rush to throw cars faster and faster around a track, for example, the idea of minimizing risk for the driver and mechanician didn't much occur to anybody. Certainly, course operators lined their tracks with straw bales and placed spectators behind walls, but it was taken for granted that the business was inherently risky and that participants alone must shoulder the unusual dangers. It wasn't that drivers didn't want to improve their chances of staying alive—but just that no one considered it the industry's job to devise and then impose safety standards and equipment on the drivers. In the same way that Eddie's accident in the lathe factory was his misfortune to bear alone, race-car drivers took on the entire unconceptualized dangers of their risky craft. Only when the sport itself took responsibility for avoiding some of the terrible toll did the opportunity open up to systematize risk-mitigating factors; once that came into play, precaution became a matter of common sense.

Frayer finished a respectable thirteenth in that all-star field, leaving Eddie smitten anew with the thunder of engines, the roar of the crowds, and the hurtling competitiveness of it all. Despite the extraordinary hazards of the world's most dangerous sport, he could no longer imagine a future without racing. Going back to jollying midwestern farmers' sons through boozy late nights held little interest for him now. Racing appealed on a level far more deeply satisfying than fame and money; besides the pure adrenaline rush, it gave him an outlet for taking control and conquering life's uncertainties. Observers have long noted that many race-car drivers have endured difficult childhoods; racing gives them a chance not only to impose order on something dangerous but to cast aside feelings of inadequacy. Such drivers tend to believe they alone have the power to tame a frightening, often unpredictable machine. For Eddie, winning became not just a means of commanding adulation but the ultimate, rock-solid proof of an ongoing power to survive.

Eddie's irritation with the Buggy Company's owners grew as they remained bound by the conception that automobiles were simply replacements for buggies, nothing more than carriages without horses. Indy had confirmed what his first glimpse of the Model C had suggested: that automobiles represented a new order of mobility, speed, mastery, and power. As the once lucrative firm slipped toward insolvency, its proprietors seemed able to recall only an antiquated—decades past—golden age, often with tears in their eyes. Wanting none of that, Eddie quit. Despite his good showings and possession of an American Automobile Association (AAA) license, he lacked both sponsors and money of his own, and so had to launch himself on what pro racers derisively termed the "Cornstalk Circuit"—a tour of county fairs, mostly in Iowa. He spent the summer of 1912 racing in small midwestern towns, some with little more than 2,000 inhabitants. Cars came by rail, then sat for a few days in dealerships for the locals to ogle. Eddie probably did odd jobs as well as coordinating publicity and other details. Catering to an audience that emphatically put speed over safety, such operations ran afoul of an AAA Contest Board justly appalled after several racers had plowed into crowds. Although not involved in any such horror, Eddie had participated in unsanctioned events, and so his license was suspended from late October 1912 to July 1913. Prevented from racing for the larger purses, he traveled to Des Moines and looked up two brothers who had established a promising reputation for building fast two-cylinder cars. He felt an instant affinity with Fred, the brilliant elder Duesenberg, who held a certificate from the same correspondence course Eddie had taken. Fred and his brother August ("Augie") had immigrated to the Midwest from Germany to set up house with an older brother, much as had Eddie's mother. Years later, the Duesenberg name would become synonymous with excellence, even giving birth to the acclamation "That's a Duesy," conferred on something particularly desirable. Duesenbergs would take the Indy 500 in 1924, 1925, and 1927—phenomenal success, but coming all too slow for these undercapitalized pioneers struggling to survive the years right before World War I.

Eddie hired on at only three dollars per week. It was a big cut from his buggy-works salary, but he had found another fatherly mentor as he worked alongside Fred sixteen hours a day in the back of a Des Moines Dodge dealership, fine-tuning his skills as an automotive engineer, at most briefly pausing to gulp a chocolate-milkshake lunch fortified with two eggs. The Duesenbergs developed a four-cylinder car with an innovative engine powered by horizontal valves and vertical rocker arms, developments that would eventually be widely adopted, every piece a model of careful handcrafting. "We used to take a connecting rod, hammer it out and forge it by hand and then cut the highest spots off with a planer, a shaper," recalled Eddie, "and then you got down to the old elbow grease, a file, and you had a pair of scales there to keep from going too far, and then you'd balance them out and file them into shape, the shape that they should have been, weigh one against the other so that they won't be out of balance." One of Fred's mechanics observed that "we worked for him like football rookies trying to please a great coach." A broad-faced figure with big ears, tangled thick hair, and fingers so arthritic that they could hold a pencil only with difficulty, Duesenberg would finally concede late each evening, "Well, why don't we all knock off and get a good night's sleep?" The men well knew that they were due back at 8:00 A.M., but Eddie didn't mind. A half-century later, Enzo Ferrari gave words to Eddie's feeling. "When a man has taken something, some material and, with his own two hands, transformed it into something else, he has made not a machine out of it, but a soul, a living, breathing soul." Eddie fell under that same spell.

The team barely finished three cars in time for the 1913 Indy 500, painting the cars on the train to Indianapolis. Still banned from driving, Eddie watched from the pit as one came in ninth in a field of twenty-seven. By the Fourth of July 1913, the reinstated Eddie was racing a Duesenberg in his hometown, teamed up with the deeply religious "Smiling" Ralph Mulford, a driver who had won the Vanderbilt Cup and placed second in the 1911 Indy. (He was so nationally famous that an imposter traveled the country persuading young women that he wanted to marry them.) In front of his mother, relatives, and friends, Eddie went out dangerously fast, panicking other drivers until Mulford could come triumphantly up from behind.

Eddie began driving regularly for the Duesenbergs at Cincinnati and in the Elgin Road Race near Chicago. In a 300-mile race at Galveston, Texas, later in July, one of his tires blew at 90 mph, leaving a strip clinging to the rim that lashed him violently and repeatedly across the arm and chest. Fearing that his arm would break, Eddie looked to pull over, but then felt his mechanician Eddie O'Donnell's arms over his shoulders. The slapping ceased as now O'Donnell took the blows—and had to be lifted out of the car after it crossed the line. Eddie suffered a severely lacerated arm and chest, O'Donnell a separated shoulder.

In one race in San Antonio, Eddie knew that his primary opponent had a faster car—and could force him to take corners quicker than he'd like—so he riveted half a buggy-wheel rim to the cowling to form a rudimentary roll bar. When his left tire stuck on a patch of mud and flipped the car three times, he ducked under the cowling and suffered only a dislocated collarbone.

Mounting victories brought Eddie the Duesenberg managership. In the gritty young twenty-three-year-old, the brothers saw the compelling underdog front man that their team needed, a pit-bull driver with the raw power to put necessary intensity into ever-more-telling skill and effort. They desperately needed a winner. Building cars was even then an expensive business, and the Duesenbergs were teetering on the edge of ruin. They focused on the 1914 Indy, which offered the richest purse to date. Eddie was their man.

As the date approached, Eddie walked into the garage one day to discover a small blue-black alley cat trapped between the wire spokes of a jacked-up wheel. The kitten clung to the hub, balancing it. "Well," he thought, "you like this car so well . . . I'll take you for a ride when we get to Indianapolis." He built a little box for "Lady Luck" behind the seat of his red-white-and-blue-painted Duesenberg. "The cat loved it, and it sat out there right behind my shoulder, taking the air at 110 and 115 mph."

Driving the Indy proved a little less enjoyable for Eddie—and every other competitor. "The direct effect of the jar upon the driver's hands," wrote a journalist, "is the raising of great blisters, and when these break the surface the palm is left absolutely raw." Such pounding also busted rods, camshafts, rocker arms, and frames; only thirteen out of the thirty entrants finished. French drivers in their Delages and Peugeots dominated the race. Oldfield came in fifth in his Stutz, Eddie a respectable tenth.

The Duesenberg seemed capable of withstanding the extreme punishment of the longest race—but that would become immaterial should the company dissolve beforehand. Cash had always been tight, and they now faced the wrecker's yard if they didn't pull in some purse money. The upcoming 300-mile Sioux City race on the Fourth of July offered an impressive total purse of $25,000, $10,000 of this to the winner. It had also attracted the best drivers in America, including the cigar-chomping Barney Oldfield and Spencer Wishart, the "Millionaire Speed King." Ralph Mulford and "Wild Bob" Burman arrived with their Peugeot team, the latter announcing that "this track is very fast." The local paper noted that Eddie "has a savage style of driving, and is one of the hardest chaps in the world to overhaul." Even with his reputation for a heavy foot and as an up-and-coming talented driver, he still hadn't broken into the sport's top ranks. He would have to beat the best to do so.

Sioux City sits in the prairie-grass plains of northwestern Iowa, just about the geographical center of the continental United States; a decent, modest city far from large bodies of water, it grows hot and extremely humid during summer. Word that the race would field the best drivers in any event west of the Mississippi, the second-largest purse ever offered, and the boasting rights for the dirt speedway championship flew across the Midwest like a prairie fire under hot south-blowing winds. Days before the event, "speed bugs" poured into town on every conceivable conveyance, only to find hotels and boardinghouses packed, restaurants jammed. Fifty rich Chicagoans camped in private railroad cars.

Night after night, townsfolk strolled the streets to marvel at the tent city that had materialized overnight, public parks full of recumbent forms, and car tonneaus crowded with sleeping bodies. They pushed to the grandstand fence to stare at a track carved from a cornfield. Under the bleachers sat three Duesenbergs, encircled by cots for two drivers and four of the pit crew. Lady Luck wandered around nearby. Carpenters serenaded them all

night as they sawed planks to extend the grandstand seating for the unanticipated hordes. License plates from New York, New Hampshire, Georgia,
and Nevada were spotted. No tent revival or vaudeville show had ever attracted so strong a crowd, estimated at 30,000. The municipality deputized
an extra three hundred men to help keep the peace. Evangelists set up a tent
on the outskirts of town to preach against free love, card playing, and tango
teas. When drunken young men tried to break up a service, the minister
chased them away at pistol point.

The Duesenberg team had arrived by night train several days before.
Only six silver dollars were left in Eddie's pocket after paying the railroad
charges—certainly not enough for garage fees or putting up the crew, but
rent was free under the grandstand. Needing time to think and prepare, Eddie himself found lodging at a farmhouse for $2.50. The raceway's ham-
burger shack gave the team food on credit.

Workers had poured thousands of gallons of hot oil over the 2-mile dirt
track, whose surface now seemed in fine shape; with 10-ton steam rollers
"practically petrifying the top soil," reported one magazine, until it was as
"hard as macadam." Qualifying heats saw speeds of 90 miles per hour on
the curves and nearly 100 on the straightaways. Sooner or later, though, this
surface would begin deteriorating and letting fly the dreaded "gumbo," the
drivers' term for clods of packed dirt and gravel kicked up by the tires. Eddie
knew he was in for it: As usual at the wheel of a smaller, less powerful, but
more nimble car than most of the competition, he would again need to
make up speed on the curves, which would leave him often in the wake of the
larger, gumbo-spitting machines. In anticipation, he fashioned a protective
mesh screen for his dash.

When Lady Luck ran away the day before the event, Eddie nearly pan-
icked but reassured himself that she had left to have kittens. His backup
plan, one he and his mother had hatched over the kitchen table during a
recent visit, centered on a grisly central European practice, probably origi-
nating among the Tyrolean gypsies. A bat's heart preserved in a silk handkerchief or red ribbon brought good fortune at cards. Even better for a dealer

was to tie the organ to his hand with a silk string. A bat heart twined to his finger certainly couldn't hurt his chances.

Eddie promised his last silver dollar to the son of the farmer with whom he was staying for a live bat, which was delivered at 10:00 P.M. the evening before the race. Placing it in a little box, he poked out a breathing hole and then drove the eight miles into town in search of red silk. Most of Sioux City had already pulled its blinds, but he found a spool in a side-street shop. Arising at 4:00 A.M. next morning, he beheaded his tiny captive, carved up the limp body, and bound the minute organ tightly to his right middle finger.

Big betting went on right up to the traditional starting detonation. The local pool had anointed the dashing, slight-framed millionaire's son Spencer Wishart as the favorite; his custom-built yellow Mercer had set the lap record during the trials. A Chicago paper noted his consistently excellent record—he had placed second at the 1913 Indy—and his "confidence in his own ability to win." He was popular among the other drivers, although some believed him reckless. "He's out to prove something, and that's no way to drive a race," commented Ralph De Palma, the Italian American who would win the 1915 Indy.

The dark-haired, charismatic Wishart could have been scripted for a part in a silent film. Married less than two months earlier to an Indianapolis debutante, the handsome twenty-four-year-old was racing for glory, not money. Everything about him bespoke wealth and privilege; rumors abounded that his publishing-company-magnate father had poured $100,000 into his cars. Everybody's idea of a hero, he seemed the consummate risk-driven prince. His sister was even married to a German baron. The contrasts with Eddie could not have been more dramatic. While Wishart patronized the finest restaurants, his angular-featured adversary, who bore a foreign name and the hint of an accent, chased around Sioux City looking for a black cat and bits of silk, his fingernails dirty from working alongside his mechanics. Oddsmakers gave Wishart 4:1; Bob Burman, Ralph Mulford, and Billy Knipper ran at 6:1. Also racing would be Harry Grant in his English Sunbeam, who had twice won the Vanderbilt Cup and taken seventh at the recent

Indy, and Billy Carlson, who had come in two places behind Grant in a kerosene-fueled Maxwell. Oldfield boasted to journalists that his considerable experience in the dirt arena ensured him victory. The papers dutifully noted Eddie as a contender, but little more.

Seventeen cars lined up in ranks of three for the ten o'clock start. The temperature had hit 91 degrees in the stands, but it was far hotter amid those great revving engines on the track. Eddie probably wore his favorite headgear, a woman's sock, which was light and did not pull on his head, and may well have once more wrapped his lower body in burlap; the already withered bat heart was sticky on his right hand. Eddie O'Donnell sat wedged up against him. Although no more than 2 feet separated their heads, they would not be able to hear one another over the unmuffled clamor of the pistons however loud they shouted. Eddie gripped a wooden wheel broader than a big pizza, fiddling with his goggles to make sure the suction was good. Without a good seal, gas fumes would severely—and dangerously— irritate the eyes.

The drivers blasted off at 9:58, kicking up such a thick cloud of dust from the outset that it obscured the crowd's view, but the whine, growl, and roar of the engines left no doubt that the unseen racers were now going flat-out. Thirty thousand spectators screamed in delight, awaiting, as one reporter wrote, "the thrill of blood." Ambulances from the South Dakota National Guard Medical Corps waited to cart the casualties away. The race began officially as the cars crossed the tape on the second lap, the drivers now jockeying furiously for position. Wishart established a blistering pace of nearly 80 mph, going far higher on the straights, slowing a bit to handle the 10-foot-banked turns. Dust—actually more a hail of pebbles than a shower of tiny particles—begin to batter faces and goggles. Many drivers wore an extra set around their neck for when their original pair grew opaque from scratches and thick layers of dirt, or simply broke outright. The wind of motion at least cooled their sweat-sodden driving gear. Although they were not outfitted in insulated suits as racers would be generations later, the heat was oppressive from the start. Many did not drink liquids before the race, fearing this would force a premature pit stop. "It can be very painful if you get caught," wrote Eddie, "and it will impair your efficiency and end up in a disaster"—but this in turn entailed battling dehydration that dizzied vision and severely compromised the power to concentrate. Drivers routinely sweated off 10 to 15 pounds over the course of a long race.

As each driver and mechanician settled in, the mad vibrations pounded their backsides. Suspension systems remained rudimentary at best—basically feeble batteries of leaf springs and primitive arrays of shock absorbers. The state-of-the-art Hartford system resembled a pair of scissors whose two arms could be tightened at the joint to impose more stiffness and resistance through increased friction. Unlike modern hydraulic absorbers, which grow stiffer the harder they are compressed, these started out at their stiffest, chopping and jerking on small bumps, sometimes wholly ineffective against serious jolts.

However banked the turns, cars skidded wildly as they cornered, their spray of gumbo not unlike a skier's taking a sharp turn in powder. Clearly fading behind the larger, more powerful machines in the straightaways, Eddie angled to find the fastest line on the corners and hit the best possible moment to tap the brakes—that one sweet spot where he could push as fast as his tires could take the curve without spinning out of control. His chance to win lay in keeping as close to the limit on as many corners as possible. He settled into a rhythm of running into the curve, touching the brakes, sliding, then hitting the gas, but appropriate speed would steadily change as sixty-eight screaming tires chewed up the course. Eddie maneuvered the corners, slowing down not just by using the brakes but by throwing his rear wheels around in a sideways slide, a technique that a later driver would call "drifting." In a four-wheel skid, more gas would deepen the angle of the slide, until a delicate touch on the brakes straightened the car out.

All worries and doubts, all chilling memories of past accidents, vanished before the ferocious concentration necessary to retain control of that shuddering, skidding, and growling machine. Paradoxically, it brought Eddie great equanimity and peace; he felt at one with the car, even as he bent it to metal-straining velocities it had not known. O'Donnell and he leaned away at the turns in anticipation of the g-forces that would force their bodies into numbing changes of direction.

In the fortieth mile, Wishart's big Mercer swept into the lead after Bob Burman's Peugeot had to pit after blowing a tire. A Sunbeam trailed him; Eddie kept third. The leaders set a blistering average pace of 77 mph. Oldfield fell out with a leaking radiator. Eddie continued to hit the corners hard and fast, finding the best line through, then straining to keep up in the straights. He reacted nervously as the track broke up, ruts growing on corners and soft spots forming where piles of rock and dirt gathered, as mounting unevenness clawed at the steering wheels.

At the 80-mile mark, Eddie was only ten seconds behind Wishart, who had kept up the pace of the first 40 miles, and 2 miles later took the lead, only to lose it to the Sunbeam in the next lap. Wishart pulled the fastest lap of the race to recover the lead at 86 miles.

The on-track bombardment was worse than anything Eddie had ever experienced. Following Wishart into turns, Eddie found himself lashed by amalgam. "It would hit us like a stream of water, but it was gumbo." His mesh screen did little to deflect the torrent, which hammered his forehead and bloodied his elbow where it stuck out of the car. Drivers started dropping out. A rock shattered the goggles of the Sunbeam's driver, but he nevertheless kept stoically in contention, blood running down his cheeks. The other Duesenberg heated up so badly that it caught fire. Its driver, Tom Alley, was taken to the hospital, burned on head and chest; Ralph Mulford, with astounding grit, let the car cool down, then climbed behind the wheel to resume the race. "As the race wore on," reported one newspaper, "the strain began to tell on drivers and machines, and all precautions for safety were forgotten by the hooded, begoggled men who crouched behind the steering wheels of their cars urging them to the limit of their capacity." The ruts finally broke Burman's steering mechanism, so he, too, was out.

Nothing else mattered to Eddie now but catching up with the shuddering, maddeningly close yellow backside of Wishart's Mercer, each corner a painful repetition of the last. He repeatedly faced the same difficult choice:

take a curve too fast and quite likely die, or take it too slow and lose. He kept up his focus, still hitting the corners hard to stay in contention, right on Wishart's bumper. Sweat ran down his back, his lower body growing bruised and numb under the vibration. He sensed that now he could make his move—but suddenly his oil pressure plummeted.

Reflexively he dug his elbow angrily into his mechanician's ribs. Why was O'Donnell not doing his job? The pressure continued to drop. Eddie wrested his eyes away from the disintegrating track to find O'Donnell knocked out cold by a piece of gumbo, blood spattering his face. Eddie ignored the strong urge to pull over—he hadn't put up with so much to quit now and hand the race to Wishart. Although his arms shook like jelly from the pounding, and his outside elbow was numbed by repeated blows, he leaned over to grab the pressure pump from O'Donnell's inanimate grasp and worked the plunger with one hand, his other bringing superhuman strength to bear on the steering wheel. He bent his head low so as to avoid as much gumbo as possible. Finally the oil pressure began to rise. After nearly fifteen minutes, O'Donnell revived and grabbed the pump. Now Eddie redoubled the effort to overtake Wishart and did so at mile 260, never again relinquishing the lead. The Sunbeam pulled over to fix its gumbo-pierced radiator.

After 300 grueling miles—3 hours 49 minutes later—Eddie roared by the checkered flag nearly two minutes ahead of Wishart. Remarkably, he had almost kept the same pace that he had established in the first 40 miles over a clean, hard track, keeping his speed even as the surface had deteriorated badly. SPEED DEMONS ANNIHILATE SPACE, announced the Los Angeles Times breathlessly. "The drivers were unanimous in declaring this the hardest race of their experience," wrote the Chicago Daily Tribune's Reed Parker. "The heat was terrific, the track slippery and badly rutted on the turns. The speed was terrific, and the cars which had a chance of victory plentiful."

Only moments into Eddie's "assurance" lap, a tire blew. Had that occurred just seconds earlier, it would have cost him the race. The sister Duesenberg, which had caught fire, miraculously rolled in third, bringing the team solid winnings. In celebration, Eddie took his crew out to the finest hotel in town, where they took hot baths, enjoyed a fine meal, and retired to feather beds.

The race, however, was not over. As the team dined in high spirits, word came that Wishart had challenged the finish order. Claiming to have lapped Eddie when he pitted, he asserted that he had been ahead overall across the line. The techniques for judging and timing races remained an imperfect discipline in 1914. Such protests were frequently raised but did not often go to review. In this case, the human counters holding stopwatches had recorded Eddie's victory, while the wires over which each car drove (discharging an electric impulse on each lap) had given the race to Wishart, whose protests grew so exceedingly strong and angry that the head referee reluctantly ordered a recount. Wishart could not let go of the exhausting, bitter competition that he had so fiercely waged. He was enraged by the idea that a rough-around-the-edges upstart from nowhere had deprived him of rightful triumph.

That afternoon's gathering of timers wrangled on to 2:30 A.M. and resumed at 10:00 A.M. the following morning, finally finishing only after eighteen hours' discussion. The referees determined that the electric monitoring system had malfunctioned. Eddie had won the race fair and square. However, something had apparently gone wrong with the accounting for the second Duesenberg. Realizing that it had spent too long in the pits to have earned the third spot, Eddie, as head of the Duesenberg team, headed off another challenge. "Seeing an endless controversy in sight, [Eddie] consented to move his second car, driven by Ralph C. Mulford, from third to sixth place," reported the *Los Angeles Times*. He had not merely kept the Duesenberg enterprise alive but, more important, had shown that he had what it took to race and win against the finest drivers while still making rational choices. He had earned a place among the best.

Six weeks later, Eddie and the still-angry Wishart met again at the August 22 Elgin road race, on whose twisty 8.5-mile course Wishart had established records the year before. Some 60 miles into its 300 miles, Eddie had to pull over with mechanical problems. Although he was no longer physically on the track, his long shadow chased Wishart, who pushed harder than ever, determined to let nothing deny him a dominating victory. Holding the lead 7 miles after Eddie's exit, he lapped his teammate Otto Henning in a narrow turn at Coombs Farm but took the corner a little too fast, his front wheels losing just enough traction to make him swerve and brush Henning's rear wheel. The brief contact threw his own front wheels 20 feet into the air and somersaulted the Mercer through 100 feet of wooden fence, shattering palings and splinters into a crowd of spectators. The car slammed into a tree, and Wishart and his mechanician, Joe Jenter, went flying with savage impact. The unconscious Wishart lay near the car, Jenter a full 50 feet beyond. The Mercer's gas tank stood like a tombstone near Jenter's crumpled form. If not for the tree, many of the almost twenty spectators standing nearby would have died.

Someone ripped a paling from the wrecked fence to splint Wishart's leg. Borne off on a barn door, he briefly regained consciousness that afternoon, gasped "Ruth" to his new wife, and died. Jenter soon followed.

Eddie reentered the race at twenty-two laps, probably unaware how bad Wishart's crash had been, intending to set a course record. Then a misleading hand signal from another car's riding mechanician sent the Duesenberg hurtling off course. Avoiding a telephone pole, Eddie slammed into a ditch whose contours happily slowed down driver and mechanician rather than slamming them to a total halt, saving them from potentially major injuries. The Duesenberg suffered a bent axle and broken drive shaft.

That Spencer Wishart should perish so brutally chilled the racing world. Eddie and the others had spent so much time right up against the wall of destruction, seeking to push the limit without going over it, that all had gained a "nodding acquaintance with death," as a journalist would later describe the champion Stirling Moss's experiences. So while death was no stranger, the sudden extinction of so bright a light among their small fraternity struck every driver personally. Had it just been bad luck? Or a momentary lapse of attention? Every one of them had to ponder his own relationship to these inescapably perilous flirtations with mortality. "I tried to dominate death with mental willpower and self-discipline and a desire to stay alive," Eddie would later write. There was nothing poetic in his attitude toward racing. He responded to the frantic risks that the sport exacted by going full bore. Even so, something seemed to separate his brand of racing from that of the glory-seeking Wishart. He romanticized the dangers far less, kept his eyes more clearly cool. Not for the last time was he going to see friends and competitors die violently. Eddie walked over to the crash site to pay his respects, later claiming to have seen the imprint of Wishart's head on the tree.

Among the horrified onlookers had been twenty-two-year-old Lowell Thomas, soon the most famous broadcaster of his generation, renowned for bringing Lawrence of Arabia into world mythology. Impressed that Eddie had stood up so well against much older and more experienced drivers, he described how this young interloper had "already thrown himself into the maelstrom of life, dreaming big dreams, unafraid to test himself against the roughest and toughest." The two men, who would define so many of their generation's standards and dreams with their different adventurings, would become lifelong friends. Both would face—and embrace—truly extraordinary times opening up ahead.

4.

AEROPLANE VS. AUTOMOBILE

On the windy gray midafternoon of Friday, August 28, 1914, all 20,000 people in the grandstands of the Iowa State Fair in Des Moines sat hushed, work-callused hands turning nervously in their laps, eyes glued on a frail aircraft bumping along the muddy track below them. Lincoln Beachey, as always impeccably turned out in woolen suit and tie, his checkered-cloth golfing hat jauntily reversed, masterfully gripped the controls as a stiff crosswind dangerously wobbled his *Little Looper* biplane. Like the early Wright aircraft, the clipped-wing Curtiss-style *Looper* was a "pusher" aircraft, its air-cooled Gnome rotary engine and propeller operating behind the pilot like a ship's screw. No plane ever appeared more Icarus-like, or its pilot more nakedly vulnerable as he sat upright as though ready to pound out a piece on a piano, bracing his feet against the front-tire axle, held in only by a slim belt around his waist. Beachey seemed to have sprouted a mythic pair of wings along with the machinery to realize the ageless da Vincian dream.

Finally *Little Looper* picked up enough momentum to lift just barely away from the thick Iowa topsoil, then whizzed around the track at a mile a minute. Swaying less than 20 feet above the track, Beachey waved both hands at the slack-jawed crowd as he roared past the grandstand. They could see the stripes on his suit, the wind whipping his pants leg, and heard him laughing as he zoomed, dipped, and twisted terrifyingly close to the ground, lapping the track again and again. Then, as if with some divine capriciousness, this human dragonfly creature broke entirely loose of earth, climbing up and up until he vanished into a cloud. Forty thousand eyes swept the sky in search of that tiny figure. A few seconds later, *Little Looper* burst back into view in an awkward twist, which turned into a full-fledged, uncontrolled tumble. The crowd sucked in its collective breath; this could only be the end. The vivid white letters BEACHEY on the upper wing unequivocally declared that its namesake was falling upside down.

A few hundred feet above ground, Beachey wrestled his tumbling craft out of what had appeared to be a total submission to gravity, swooping down smartly in front of the grandstand. The spectators roared themselves hoarse, knowing that they had just witnessed Beachey's famous dive of death. Two hours later, he was up again, this time climbing 2,000 feet, then diving until the bracing guy-wires whined in protest; then he jerked up the airplane's nose, forcing it upside down and all the way over in a perfect loop. He looped again, then circled the track and looped once more, landing to wild applause, although some felt nauseated and a few even fainted. Beachey curtly acknowledged the crowd, then turned unhurriedly to chat with one of his assistants.

That day Eddie Rickenbacher sat among the awed corn and wheat farmers, small businessmen, housewives, and well-scrubbed children in denim who had just fallen beneath the spell of America's most famous daredevil. Few had not heard about Beachey's stunts. The first to fly upside down, first to loop the loop in America, he had crash-landed on parked cars and frozen rivers, raced trains, shot ducks from his cockpit, and pirouetted amid the thunderous downpours of Niagara Falls until his wings dripped and his carburetor coughed water. He had donned a flaxen wig and fluttering skirts to impersonate a famous aviatrix. With one simple miscalculation, he had killed innocent bystanders. The year before, he had taken off inside the Machinery Palace on the Exposition grounds of the San Francisco World's Fair, reaching 60 miles an hour without leaving the building. That year alone, his promoters claimed that 17 million Americans had watched his acrobatics in 126 cities—a remarkable feat in a nation of 100 million inhabitants. Orville Wright called Beachey's acrobatics "a thing of beauty to watch."

No one had seen his like before; no one had ever so routinely defied fate with such seeming recklessness and charm. He was short, boyish, arrogant, and irresistible. When asked what it felt like to fly with such daring, he rakishly proclaimed, "You know when a man's in love? A feeling something like that." Watching automobiles speed past in blurs of dust and engine whine was one thing, but the airplane imparted new, unexplored meanings to daring the devil. Every time he took to the sky, he drove back the line separating human and machine that bit further. "I can do things the birds cannot do," he boasted. "I can loop the loop and fly upside-down." Where should a man's humility lie, or need it know no bounds? The crowds fixating upon him waited for a crash, not so much out of morbid anticipation but because he was so clearly assailing the natural order of things. That didn't bother him. "If I did tumble from the air, I did not want my final bump to stamp me as a piker. I wanted to drop from thousands of feet. I wanted the grand stands and the grounds to be packed with a huge, cheering mob, and the band must be crashing out the latest rag. And when the ambulance, or worse, hauled me away, I wanted them all to say as they filed out the gates, 'Well, Beachey was certainly flying some.'"

Tempt fate he did. Over the Iowa fair's first few days, the winds mounted, but still he threw the biplane into awful contortions aloft. His contract dictated that he would be compensated only for the days that he performed both his signature loop-the-loop and dive of death. The fair paid him to perform, so perform he would. Not that Beachey ever shied away from flying in bad weather. His promoter advertised BEACHEY FLIES 3 P.M. RAIN, SHINE OR CYCLONE. He relished the challenges of gusty skies. On Monday, only an hour or two after he touched down, a gale-force wind crashed through the fair—a "real tent-leveler," wrote one journalist—knocking out the grandstand lights and leaving most spectators shivering there for hours. A giant tent serving as temporary stables partially collapsed, setting off a furious effort to rescue terrified horses in the dark. Flying timbers and broken glass injured spectators and workers alike. Fair organizers halted the actors warming up for the fair's signature presentation: Pain's "Opening the Panama Canal and Uncle Sam's Reception to the World," a firework extravaganza set on a 300-foot stage with hundreds of actors and dancers.

The British act celebrated the United States' inauguration of the ocean-shrinking 48-mile canal dividing the Americas earlier that month. Now ships could pass from the Atlantic to the Pacific without making the lengthy, gale-thrashed passage "round the Horn." America had succeeded where the French had bitterly failed, in one of history's greatest engineering feats. Yet only two months before the fair, the assassination of Archduke Franz Ferdinand of Austria by a Bosnian Serb student at Sarajevo would stain the century by setting off the first true world war, far overshadowing the engineering marvel of the canal. Long-simmering antagonisms boiled over as ineffectual national leaders muddled through a tangle of alliance obligations, threats, and dithering. While few actively worked for war, no one could see a way out of their particular path into it. Nor was anyone quite sure why everything had come to a boil so terribly fast: Only thirty-seven days after the assassin's bullets felled the archduke and his wife, the majority of the world's strongest powers were at each other's throats.

Few dreamed that such a bloody conflict would grind on so long—and so savagely. The German Schlieffen Plan had called for a strike that in early August 1914 would take its army to Paris within a month. Overly optimistic, although nearly successful, the offensive broke down in the teeth of a determined French and British stand just 40 miles from the French capital. Struggling for advantage, each side attempted to outflank the other, leading to the misnamed "Race to the Sea," which ended in frustrating deadlock on the Belgian coast. In its wake lay a thin series of battlements stretching hundreds of muddy miles to the Swiss frontier. No options existed but to construct vast trench systems, ultimately known as the Western Front—a businesslike term, but a nightmare stalemate in reality. Pinned down in these trenches, the armies beat themselves bloody, raiding and lobbing shells into each other's lines. The fatal combination of the machine gun with barbed wire made frontal assaults mass executions. Poison gas found its first large-scale use. The new technologies of the Second Industrial Revolution showed their darker powers of creative destruction in incendiary shells, mines, and land torpedoes, which showed repeatedly and tragically how human life could be crushed by industrial-strength weaponry. "Our world has passed away," observed British writer and poet Rudyard Kipling, "In wantonness o'erthrown. / There is nothing left to-day / But steel and fire and stone."

Americans would watch these events unfold with some alarm. Few believed that the nation should plunge into age-old European quarrels, which were surely none of their business. Strong voices, including the pacifically minded President Woodrow Wilson, lined up against intervention. Most still thought of Britain, on whose sprawling empire "the sun never set," as the world's preeminent power. Before the Great War, America remained at most a formidable but provincial presence, no more than an admittedly opulent suburb of the European power system; by the Armistice, no one argued that America did not muster world power. Not only America's brawn but its distance would eventually make the difference in world conflict.

At that Iowa State Fair in 1914, the concerns of embattled Europe seemed far off indeed. Once the natural storm subsided, green recruits from nearby Fort Dodge paraded past the grandstand; that aside, little of the overseas catastrophe seemed to ripple through these midwesterners' lives, or those of most Americans. When a reporter asked Beachey how airplanes might figure in the new war, he replied confidently that dropping bombs showed promise—but, he stressed, more important would be the power to scout over enemy lines. While he wowed the crowd with the miracle of flying, many Europeans were learning that aircraft could also bring about death and destruction.

Eddie hadn't been at the fair for fun but rather on Duesenberg business. On the fair's final day, Beachey squared off against him—airplane versus automobile, a vaudeville-inspired performance not far removed from the medieval matching of bull and bear in a fight to the death. How would these two new kinds of machine fare against one another? Workers spread shovelfuls of calcium chloride on the track to keep down the dust, but even so Eddie kicked up a dark cloud in his wake. Beachey, who spotted Eddie a lap, careened dangerously and seemingly out of control as Eddie raced a mere 10 feet beneath him. *Little Looper*'s swaying wings passed a little too close to the grandstands as Beachey struggled to keep the plane within the track's tight confines. Perched over his wheel, Eddie took the straights wide and hit the corners tight, the handicap affording him the margin of victory. The audience left well satisfied, certain that they had seen the best that aircraft and automobile had to offer. Eddie, however, couldn't help admiring the moxie of his ice-blooded showboating rival, so brashly confident in the skills he was creating as the world watched.

Certainly nonmilitary thrill seekers had defied extreme risks before— conquering ice-clad peaks, going over Niagara Falls in barrels, diving off bridges and cliffs, swinging and tumbling from trapezes under the big tent—but Beachey, Eddie, and a handful of other daredevils were exploding into the American consciousness in ways entirely different. While the sober sons of a bishop might have assembled the first powered heavier-than-air craft capable of sustained flight, a new breed of adventurer was bringing off feats that were simply not to be entertained only a half-dozen years earlier, riding contraptions that took the human body ever farther and faster. Those begoggled car-racing "Mercurian monarchs" and their even wilder brethren, the magnificent men in their flying machines, pioneered new frontiers as unknown then as space was when the astronauts first challenged it in the 1960s. In the early twentieth century, Americans hungered for new breeds of heroes who could step into the dangerous steel machines that the previous generation had created and not only master but transform them, as one historian has put it, into "resplendent art and myth." These ironnerved, sometimes foolhardy souls complied.

They died in alarming numbers. On March 14, 1915, came Beachey's turn. At the Panama-Pacific International Exposition in San Francisco, 50,000 spectators—including Eddie—saw the bird man perform his heart-stopping loops in his new monoplane high above Alcatraz Island. Rounding one out, he dove from 1,000 feet and jerked the stick back at 500, but the spectators heard loud cracks as first the left and then the right wings flapped uselessly backward. Beachey smashed into 40 feet of water; it took just under an hour to fish him out. The coroner solemnly announced that he had suffered a broken leg and some superficial scratches but had actually died by drowning. At least he had attained his dark wish that were he to die, it should come during a blood-chilling maneuver before a mighty crowd. The cold fact was that he had not figured out his new machine's wing tolerances.

In 1910 alone, thirty-seven prominent fliers died, a horrific rate for the small number actually getting aloft. They were of the first generation to step into machines so new, untested, and unrealized that simply to operate them entailed embracing extreme risk. The speeds now attainable exponentially increased the dangers—which this new breed of risk seeker either fatalistically ignored or began working out new modes of overcoming.

"Chance-taking is not a business with me," Beachey had claimed. "It is a delightful diversion, and no music lover ever is more charmed by listening to the inspiring strains of his favorite opera, superbly sung by a great artist, than I am charmed by the hum of my motor when I am sailing in or out of a loop and upside-down flight." Although perhaps intended to pull in larger audiences, these words suggested to Eddie a formula for killing oneself, illustrating the poet Thomas Gray's caution that "the paths of glory lead but to the grave." Reckless bravado had killed Spencer Wishart and now Lincoln Beachey. Being dashing wouldn't brush aside the Reaper, but approaching risk in a businesslike spirit just might. Eddie and a handful of other early risk takers therefore pioneered colder-eyed, less romantic methods; before ever undertaking supreme feats of derring-do, they sought radically new techniques of managing risk, inventing and perfecting tactical and strategic responses to extreme danger that clearly shape those of their rational successors today.

"It wasn't always recklessness," Eddie wrote of his early driving. "It was a pre-determined chance or hazard and you tried to think ahead to what would happen to you if. And in doing so, you usually kept away from that breaking point." He insisted that he wasn't the maniac everybody thought him, "but I had to keep the reputation of being a carefree daredevil."

Now he entered the most dangerous time of his most dangerous calling. Whatever the demands of practical common sense, he must continue to win. That would push him into some ill-considered decisions as he sought every possible advantage, an approach now becoming particularly hazardous because he was no longer new to driving. It isn't the first few times that someone climbs onto a motorcycle that prove the most dangerous—unfamiliarity imposes caution. Real danger begins to close in when the rider has mastered the basics of shifting and feels confident to reach for the edge, yet has not yet amassed experience enough to adequately judge road conditions, traffic, cornering, and stopping—or, as Wilbur Wright wrote to his father, "carelessness and overconfidence are usually more dangerous than deliberately accepted risks." Eddie, said the *Chicago Daily Tribune,* had developed "an inclination to bust up his mounts," pushing his cars so hard that they fell apart in midrace. Even so, 1915 would still prove a good year for him.

Despite the war's ongoing havoc, the 1915 American racing season was the best to date, offering twenty-three road and speedway races, their average winning pace nearly 20 miles per hour faster than only two years before. On the tracks alone, the top recorded speeds jumped from 82 mph in 1914 to 105 mph the following year. Americans' interest in their own cars had risen dramatically as well: By June 1, the number in private hands reached 2 million (and this did not include more than 200,000 motor trucks). To feed this insatiable hunger, the Packard Motor Car Company's payroll swelled to 8,200, its Detroit plant being enlarged to 48 acres. New racing venues were steadily popping up—Speedway Park in Chicago, for instance, needed 14 million board feet of lumber to cover its 2-mile oval track and structure, along with 100 carloads of sewer and drain tile, 15,000 concrete piers, 50,000 cubic yards of cement, 500 tons of nails and spikes, 1,000 tons of steel, 2,000 carloads of cinders, and 6 miles of road to afford access.

Competition was the fiercest yet. Twenty years of furious improvement of engines, tires, and gearing had finally created high-compression, steadier machines, more reliable and nearly as fast as drivers could handle on the present surfaces. Eddie's record enabled him to jump from the still-struggling Duesenberg team to Peugeot, which boasted some of the fastest cars on the circuit. (Duesenberg would replace Eddie with his mechanician, Eddie O'Donnell.)

A family manufacturing firm since the eighteenth century, Peugeot had entered the automotive business by way of making steel rods for women's crinoline dresses, which soon morphed into creating umbrella frames, saw blades, and eventually bicycle spokes. Eddie's experience with it lasted for only two disappointing races, mechanical problems dogging him all the way. For one he built paired helmets and masks for driver and mechanician, connected by rubber speaking tubes, "his mouth to my ear and my mouth to his ear." They wore white sweaters and white leather head guards and masks, which along with their white-painted machine gave them the appearance of deep-sea divers; the press flocked to take pictures. The alien-looking apparatus worked fine, but Eddie scrapped it because it proved too hot and uncomfortable. He sold his Peugeot to a talented car designer named Harry A. Miller, who promptly began modifying it to get it back racing.

Eddie couldn't have chosen a worse time to leave Peugeot, later acknowledging this to have been one of his poorest decisions. Years later, he fondly recalled driving their cars, "From the minute you touched the pedal, you could feel the thing squat. It really squatted like a cat with the four paws and claws. Try to pull a cat off something that she doesn't want to get away from." A European racer would grab the wheel Eddie had relinquished, becoming the circuit's best driver and his greatest adversary. In February 1915 Louis Coatalen, the design and mechanical genius behind British Sunbeam cars, had brought to the United States a hotshot driver: Dario Resta, with a long record of victories at Brooklands behind him. The war had transformed Brooklands into a flying school and aircraft-manufacturing center, leaving British racing all but dead. Coatalen announced that both he and Resta would drive Sunbeams at Indy, but when Eddie's Peugeot became available, Resta immediately signed up for the competition.

Resta had emigrated with his family from Italy to Britain when he was two, and his father had become a successful studio photographer. The short, dapper man had dark eyes and a crop of dark, wavy hair, and he spoke impeccably precise English. He had become the British amateur figure-skating champion before the lure of racing cars cast its spell. His auto-sales company had sent him to America on several occasions in 1909, during which he sold a Mercedes to one Mr. Wishart, who gave it to his racing-inclined twenty-year-old son, Spencer. The handsome Resta may have met Spence's then fourteen-year-old sister Mary, who would later figure prominently in his life.

With barely enough time to get to know his new machine, Resta entered the season's third big event, the 400-mile Grand Prize road race at the Panama-Pacific International Exposition in San Francisco, the venue at which Beachey had died the year before. On February 27, he appeared in his hastily prepared Peugeot, still bearing Eddie's signature white paint job. Oddsmakers gave this unknown odds of 50:1. Rain battered the course into a mire, moving officials to layer the track fronting the main grandstand with boards and then with cross-planking. So jury-rigged a construction offered a dangerously slippery surface, and water shot up several feet from the board cracks when cars flew over them. Eddie showed up in his Maxwell, holding a large beach umbrella over his head, much to the amusement of the crowd.

"I am glad to be back at the wheel of an American car," Eddie rationalized his switch to reporters. The Maxwell Motor Company's 1915 product, the 25, would take off after a marketing campaign boasted that its owners didn't have to put it away for the winter. In early December 1914, the company's charismatic, mustachioed driver, Billy Carlson, had torn up the narrow curves of the nearly 6,000-foot Mount Wilson outside Los Angeles, negotiating wet snow that frequently sent him sliding to within inches of precipitous drops ("Almost any place along the course the car would have been wrecked and the driver probably killed had he blown a tire," reported the *Los Angeles Times*) and still shaved thirteen minutes off the record, completing the ascent in twenty-nine minutes. The popular Carlson, son of San Diego's youngest elected mayor, had cemented his reputation—and that of the company he represented.

The 25 offered more prosaic advantages, including the first adjustable front seat, with a range of 3 inches. Rumors from Detroit ran hot that Maxwell's chief engineer, Roy Harroun, who had won the 1911 Indy 500 without a mechanician, was building a race car whose aluminum alloy parts and counterbalanced crankshaft promised to minimize engine vibration significantly—innovations that could make a car hard to beat. Although it would not be ready for the 1915 Indy until Memorial Day itself, Eddie joined the team, which mustered not only Billy Carlson but also Barney Oldfield. Eddie was to play his familiar role as the "rabbit," racing out to a fast, commanding lead and tempting others to push too hard, whereupon Oldfield and Carlson would come up from behind.

Irresistible fodder to the papers, this stellar threesome found a crowd of young women trailing them wherever they raced. Early in 1916, the team parked at the Venice, California, fire department, which was besieged by admirers desperate for a glimpse of Oldfield. Maxwell's chief mechanic, Harry Goetz, and Eddie's slight mechanician, Eric Shrader, stood guard. When one young woman reached over a metal chain to touch Oldfield's car, Shrader touched a switch, mildly electrifying the chain and reeling her backward with "squeals and shrieks," reported a newspaperman. "Good thing, that electric adviser," said Goetz. "It's a shame to pick on the ladies, but we have to protect Barney and Carlson. We don't care about Rickenbacher, he's not married."

For reasons of economy, the Maxwells had been designed to run on kerosene. This clean petroleum distillate would power aircraft jet engines generations later, but it did not vaporize as efficiently as gasoline, often fouling the carburetor. On the rain-soaked Grand Prize course, this slowed Eddie down considerably, while Resta was able to maintain a fast pace in the Peugeot. The rain continued apace, sending cars sliding terrifyingly long distances and sometimes spinning them on the corners like tops. More than a third of the drivers simply gave up. Accepting that he had no chance of victory, Eddie concocted a ridiculous plan: If he could get the judges to call the race for being too dangerous, then he might have his carburetor cleaned and start again. Every time he passed in front of the grandstand, he threw his Maxwell into a skid, deliberately swinging from side to side, apparently on the edge of crashing. "Everybody was watching, standing up, thrilled to death," he remembered. The judges considered calling the race until someone pointed out that only one contestant was having such trouble, and so it continued while Eddie was pulled in. Resta hung on through the toughest conditions, thrilling the crowd with mind-numbing command over the greasy course for seven hours. A moment's lapse in that marathon might easily have killed him, but he won conclusively—although one magazine reported that he had taken a "terrible beating of the rain in his eyes and face." He had proved his toughness. Never again would the oddsmakers call him a long shot. A week later he won the Vanderbilt Cup in San Francisco.

The Maxwells switched over to gas after Oldfield, Carlson, and Eddie threatened to quit—and their team began to win. Oldfield set a world record at the Tucson road race in March without once shifting or pitting. Eddie won a 25-mile race at his hometown Driving Park with his mother in the audience. During the same event's 100-mile race, he lost his way for a moment in a thick cloud of dust, swinging too far to the outside and taking out 200 yards of wooden fencing. A 12-by-1-inch paling shot like an arrow through the radiator, knocking the magnetos off the side of the engine, and crashed through the dashboard, nearly piercing Eric Schrader's crotch. "Another inch," wrote Eddie, "and he would have been cut in two. We had to lift him out, in fact, pull him out. He was so tightly pinched into the seat." Eddie ran up into the grandstand to reassure his mother, but she had already left to cook dinner.

No other sport requires such sustained, intense concentration as a long-distance car race, and in no other sport is death so close for so long. In this frightening new arena, Eddie was discovering not just that he could stare down death and risk—but that he was really good at it.

5.

NEW ORDER OF TERRORS

Four days of near-constant rain compelled Carl Fisher to postpone the fifth Indy 500 from Saturday to Monday, May 31, 1915. The event had already cemented its reputation as America's premier race. Neither thick mud on the local roads nor the overall sloppy conditions deterred thousands of spectators from their appointment with howling machines throwing themselves at high speeds around the Brickyard. Hotels overflowed. Talk centered on how the rain-chilled bricks would yield record speeds.

Eddie was eager to test his skills against the field of fifteen other American and nine foreign cars, the world's best drivers pushing the world's fastest makes. His new Maxwell Special was something to behold. Painted in Eddie's signature milk white, the race car featured Ray Harroun's latest brainchild, a powerful gas-driven engine drawing on a double-overhead camshaft and four valves per cylinder. At the same time, Eddie felt deep trepidation, knowing what the Peugeot's high-torque engines could do. Even though the war had arrested European car design and production, the Peugeots still led the field with a series of innovations dating back to 1912, which included four-cylinder engines with twin overhead camshafts, hemispherical combustion chambers, and two sets of valves per cylinder—improvements so far ahead of the others as to set the standard for most race cars.

At the wheel of the very car Eddie had abandoned not that long ago, Dario Resta appeared unbeatable. For this race, as he had in Sioux City, Eddie drew again on his bloody superstitions, keeping a bat supplied by his brother Albert. When he opened the cigar box, though, the tiny mammal soared off, sending Eddie into a dark mood. Feeling the underdog, he plotted how to game the system—and if that meant pushing the rules, then so be it.

Experience had taught him that the first 100 miles of a race over the dry, abrasive bricks wrought havoc on tires; after that, however, wear abated significantly from the film of ground rubber and oil drippings that the cars deposited on the track. Eddie hatched a plan to reduce friction by lubricating his outside tires for the first part of the race—not illegal per se, though only because the AAA Contest Board had not yet envisioned somebody's doing it. Drivers often cooled their tires with buckets of water, but oil was a different matter. Knowing that he was sailing a little too close to the wind, Eddie carried out the preparations secretly. Under his instruction, his team hid a pressurized 1.5-gallon tank beneath the Maxwell's seat, then lined a copper tube out to the steering knuckle, the connection point between tie rod and wheel. Thence, a light, special arm of his own design would extend an oil-squirting tube in place over each tire. The record remains mute on whether or not his team built the special contraption during the rain delay, but it does smack of an idea born of haste and desperation.

On race day, so as not to call attention to the device, the pit crew brought the car out to the track at the last possible moment and casually draped overalls over the right front and right rear tires. The official starter seemed, Eddie recalled, "to smell a mouse, but he couldn't imagine what I was getting away with, for it was the last thing in the world anyone would have thought of."

The conspirators had neglected to attach the oil pump to the crankshaft, and so halfway through the race, a bearing burned out and he pitted. An official who noticed oil dripping immediately discovered the device. One biographer claims that Eddie grinned "sheepishly," then confessed. Officials disqualified his car; Eddie narrowly avoided suspension because the system was not technically illegal. When asked about the incident years later, he showed no remorse or embarrassment, merely conceding it a setback only because he had been caught. "The plan was perfect, but the bearings weren't."

Here was the sign of the emerging pro, the craftsman who in his bid to win did not cheat exactly but certainly pushed the system and played for every advantage. Such amateurs as Beachey and Wishart lived from one glamorous high moment to another in search of applause above everything. Not Eddie. For him it was all business, the business of survival. While he watched from the sidelines, Resta and Ralph De Palma repeatedly exchanged the lead in one of the most exciting of all Indys. Resta's dark blue Peugeot beat De Palma's cream-colored Mercedes in the straights but lost on the corners. Still, only a late blown tire cost Resta the contest. One observer later called him "not only a masterful driver but also a mechanical tactician. [He] won [elsewhere] because his machine was mechanically fit. He knew exactly how long his tires would 'stand up.' And he knew how many times he would be forced into the pits." Eddie had never raced someone of this finesse. As another observer put it, "Resta appeared to drive with his eyes on the stopwatch, Rickenbacher with his eyes on the car ahead of him." Right now, Resta was clearly the better driver—and Eddie would learn all he could from him.

Little immediate notice would be taken in America of a landmark event in Europe that evening when a German zeppelin bombed London, killing and wounding a number of civilians. The kaiser had expressly forbidden targeting major civilian centers, but a navigator's error had sent one ship unwittingly over a London suburb. It marked a momentous change in a war of unprecedented scale that had dragged on for nearly a year. A line had been crossed, and both sides would soon consider it fair game to target the civilians living in cities.

Eddie's next tactic proved more sensible: He hired Harry Van Hoven, an Iowan whom he had met in San Francisco, to run his pit crew. Van Hoven came from a sharp-witted family—his vaudeville-performing brother's gag-rich routine had earned him the sobriquet "the Man Who Made Ice Famous." The pit crew loved his wisecracks and passion for chocolate malts. Staggeringly obese, which made it hard to serve as a riding mechanic, Van possessed not only an outgoing personality but a quick mind, which he quickly put to economizing the time his car spent in the pit. Just four years earlier, the time and motion pioneer Frederick Winslow Taylor had published his breakthrough *Principles of Scientific Management,* which targeted the mass inefficiencies of American industry. There were, he wrote, "perhaps forty, fifty, or a hundred ways of doing each act in each trade," but only one method or tool was better than all the rest. Taylor articulated to the business community that maximum efficiency lay not in finding the mythical best worker but in installing the most efficient system—a radical departure from ancient traditions of craftsmanship. Van brought these ideas into the pit for the first time, carefully choreographing tire and oil changes before race day and directing the whole frantic undertaking through a megaphone during the event—startling new efficiencies that shaved many valuable seconds off Eddie's pit time. Efficient motion was no insignificant skill when the crew had to wrestle 70-pound racing wheels. Eddie's team could now change four tires, in thirty-three seconds, testimony to scientific management in this unexpected context. They could change the tires, fill the radiator, and check the oil in under fifty seconds. Later in the season, Eddie would acknowledge that at least one race had been won "in the pits." Other teams would soon follow the Maxwell lead. "I have come to the conclusion," noted a prominent Chicago journalist, "that these star drivers are good executives and that to succeed in racing one must have something more than the mere nerve to drive fast."

The new pit system promptly began yielding dividends. The pressure to beat Resta mounted. Half the season had flown by without a major win for Eddie when the Sioux City race came up on July 3. The papers anointed Resta the favorite. Eddie would also be competing against his former riding mechanic, Eddie O'Donnell. It was on this track a year earlier that Eddie had dueled with Spencer Wishart.

For the six days prior to Saturday's race, 6 inches of rain had fallen on Sioux City, leaving the track spongy and fissured. "The speedway is a fearsome sight," reported the *Chicago Daily Tribune,* "with its surface a mess of ruts, any one deep enough to wreck a car should a side skid of sufficient force throw the wheels from one to another." Resta called it "a second bog of Kildare" and sensibly deemed the course dangerous. Nevertheless, the race would go on.

Eddie pushed hard and got out to a fast start. While he had always shone on the routine ovals of the speedway, he had particularly excelled on the more unconventional layouts of road races: "I liked road racing better because you had right angle turns and you had curves of different types ... You've got to be careful that you don't follow someone else into the hay stack on the corner." In contrast, a high-speed track was like swinging a ball attached to a string round and round one's head, "There aren't any ups and downs, twists and God knows what all." Eddie raced the track for money, roads for the thrill. The press would dub him "the King of the Dirt-Track Racers" when he went on to be the only driver to win three open speedway events in 1915.

After only 12 miles, Resta dropped out with a broken oil lead and center-bearing bolt. Very soon afterward, it turned into a race between Eddie and O'Donnell. After 70 miles, Eddie, dangerously cutting in and out of traffic, came up to lap a slower Ogren Special driven by thirty-year-old Charles C. Cox of Cincinnati. Cox swung out of the way but then swerved back behind Eddie as his mechanician signaled that someone else was right on his tail. Cox's right front tire glanced off Eddie's back left, sending Cox flying through the outer fence and down a steep embankment, to die a few hours later; his mechanician survived. Eddie himself had to fight against crashing into the fence. His claim that he was concentrating so hard that he didn't know what had happened to Cox until after the race seems suspect, especially since he had to pit to replace the wheel whose spokes had been jarred loose by the collision. Had he pushed a less experienced driver just a little too much? Certainly Cox had underestimated Eddie's speed.

O'Donnell used that break to swing out into the lead, but Eddie caught up after 2 miles when O'Donnell pitted with a punctured tire. At 148 miles, the lead referee flagged Eddie in for a warning. The ruts had sent slower drivers scattering in search of the smoothest surface, which lay at the outside of the track, making it hard for faster cars—most conspicuously Eddie's—to pass on the right and compelling them to pass on the left, contrary to the rules. It looked as if O'Donnell would regain the lead while Eddie was pitting, but again he had to pit himself. The warning did little to slow Eddie, his focus now unbreakable; indeed, he beat his former mechanician by a little more than three minutes.

Two days later in a 300-mile board-track event in Omaha, he beat O'Donnell again, never losing the lead, but reporters saw him sobbing as he crossed the line. He had just learned from his pit crew that Billy Carlson, his good friend and racing associate, had died that morning from injuries sustained in a terrible crash the day before at the Tacoma Speedway. One of Carlson's tires had blown out as he hit a high-banked turn in a headlong lead. His young riding mechanician, a medical student turned racing fanatic, died also. Van had withheld the news until Eddie finally came in. "Billy was a most lovable chap," wrote Oldfield, a feeling shared by the whole circuit. Three and a half months earlier, his movie-star wife of almost seven months, Margaret, had told the *Los Angeles Times* that he had made her sign a prenuptial contract stating that she was "absolutely to 'not worry.'"

At Omaha, Eddie had averaged a stunning 91.07 mph. Only twenty years earlier, the winners of America's first road race, in Evanston, Illinois, had averaged 7.5 mph. "Gasoline has robbed the milestones, which formerly marked weary leagues of travel for men and beast, of their terrors and has carried man through space at a speed none but a superman should dare attempt," opined a 1915 editorial in *Motor Age*. Eddie had all too closely seen the new order of terrors that such speed had created. By the following summer, five of his eight teammates since the Vanderbilt Cup would have perished on the track.

After Omaha, the demoralized Maxwell team disbanded and sent their cars back to the Detroit factory. Maxwell had already decided before Carlson died that racing was too expensive, and the catastrophe sealed the decision. Van tried to cheer the boys by telling a reporter that "I have heard—on good authority, too—that the Maxwell people are afraid that, the way Rickenbacher drives their car, the back wheels won't be able to keep up with the front wheels, and they will have to build it in two sections, one known as Ricken and the other as Bacher." Little could lighten the gloom hanging over the team.

Eddie had jumped from Duesenberg to Peugeot to Maxwell in just a matter of months, but just as he had settled the Maxwell's problems and logged victories, the team was shut down—bad luck indeed. He immediately went to Indianapolis to meet with Carl Fisher and James A. Allison, whom he convinced to create the Prest-O-Lite Racing team, buy Maxwell's four cars and refurbish them, and tap Eddie to become its manager. Fisher felt the frustration of a great many Americans who had seen Europeans sweeping up U.S. titles with apparent ease. When Oldfield dismissed Resta's successes with "I'll teach that spaghetti eater he can't come in here and take over," he was speaking, however crudely, for much of a nation that felt American predominance in racing should be an enduring right—a major reason for Eddie's leaving the French-built Peugeot to drive the American-made Maxwell. With European racing and car manufacturing mired by the demands of war, and many of Europe's best drivers taking quite other risks at the front, Fisher saw a chance. He also agreed to sponsor the experienced Indianapolis driver Johnny Aitken, who had approached him with an idea similar to Eddie's. Aitken's lackluster driving career had sidelined him of late into working as pit manager for Peugeot. The new Indianapolis Speedway Racing Team under Aitken would field two aging Peugeots—and quickly become a thorn in Eddie's side. The canny Fisher had carefully hedged his bets by backing two serious contenders.

No longer a hired hand, Eddie was now a racing entrepreneur with new opportunities opening up before him. His signature on the contract with Fisher and his associates on September 14, 1915, reflected a new man with a strong sense of himself as a change master, grasping opportunities unavailable even months earlier: *Edward V. Rickenbacker*, replacing the *h* with a *k*, thus Americanizing his Teutonic name. Eddie's parents had given him no middle name, so the New World star of conspicuously Old World stock decided that the patrician Anglo-Norman "Vernon" sounded just right.

The contract dictated that Fisher would buy the cars and pay for replacement parts, repairs, and rebuilding. Eddie in turn would give Fisher and Allison 25 percent of his winnings and cover operating and travel expenses, salaries, and maintenance. It also stipulated that every driver he hired would be single, thus focused exclusively on racing; that was just fine with Eddie. As the *Chicago Tribune* waxed, "Famous as a speed mad, matrimony insulated bachelor, [Eddie] has but one love, and that the thoroughbred of steel with which he pursues prize money."

Before the 1915 season was over, he pulled out one more trick from his growing kit bag at the Narragansett Park in Cranston, Rhode Island, whose gently banked, asphalt-surfaced track awakened an idea for Prest-O-Lite's first outing. Tire wear remained a key factor in each race. If he switched his fast but vulnerable thin tires for wider ones, he could conceivably avoid pitting at all over the race's 100 miles. Everybody else would be running on skinny tires because less friction delivered higher speeds, but avoiding the pit altogether would buy Eddie valuable minutes that might more than make up for the time lost on the track. He arranged for a truck to pull up just minutes before the race started, and his competition watched in amazement as Van's crew jacked up the chassis, popped off the conventional tires, and switched them out for fat new ones—all in sixty-three seconds. Fouled plugs forced Eddie to pit anyway, but he came back to win against De Palma and Burman. He ended the 1915 season as the only driver to have won three open major speedway races, rising from seventh to fifth on the AAA circuit. A key to his growing success lay in his ability to devise unorthodox solutions to problems, especially when up against faster cars or better drivers, "You've got to have an imagination so that you can anticipate things happening and what would you do if they did happen and be prepared for it." Behind the rough exterior and hard eyes lay a mind never ceasing to turn over difficulties that seemed at first to have only one solution—and coming up with completely novel answers.

Over that winter of 1915–16, Eddie overhauled the Maxwells in a 12,000-square-foot facility that Fred Allison had carved out of Prest-O-Lite's Indianapolis plant. Money was little object as the team worked to create a car that could finally trounce the Europeans. Eddie threw himself into the task with an energy that would have made Fred Duesenberg proud, hiring three mechanics and one mechanician for each car, along with three other drivers. He bought a Victrola and a stack of records for each of the four teams, which proved particularly motivating as they worked late into the evening. Marches and "I Love You, California," which they had heard at the San Francisco exhibition that year (and would later become the California state song), lightened the hard hours. "It was like turning night into daylight when we would start playing it," remembered Eddie. He engineered an incentive program to reward high-level performance among his team and elevated a young Canadian mechanic, Peter Henderson, to mechanician, to show that he was open to internal promotion.

Out of those long days emerged the Maxwell Special, boasting more efficient intake manifolds, a system to keep oil cooler, strengthened connecting rods, and a new set of valves. The team had streamlined the body, adding a conical tail similar to that used by Peugeots, which contained the main fuel tank. An auxiliary tank was also added, accessible through a lever on the steering column. A larger inlet enabled gas to flow faster from tanks into the engine.

Eddie broke up his team into two-car units, figuring that travel time and overlapping races dictated that he dispatch teams to different venues simultaneously. In the upcoming summer his teams would cross the country four times and race in sixteen different major events. In the pit, Van wielded a stopwatch and scrawled times on a chalkboard. Should he judge that Eddie had established a commanding lead, he could signal to slow down and conserve tires and engine. Some twenty-five symbols could be combined to communicate a hundred or more instructions and observations. A squiggle, for instance, indicated that something was dragging under the car.

Over those winter evenings, Eddie started drafting a loose-leaf notebook that conversationally prescribed "every move, human, mental, physical, mechanical," instructing mechanics in the pit, for example, on the use of a copper-headed hammer to loosen the single large wing nut, appropriately called the "knock-off," that attached each tire. It also recommended that drivers and pit crew relieve themselves before a race commenced.

Fine-tuning the engine and preventive maintenance to minimize the car's liklihood of "turning to cheese," as Van liked to say, were handled very specifically. The book admonished team members not to lose their tempers or to brag. They were to get to bed early the night before. Toward the front of the typewritten copy appeared, "Above all, I want my men to keep cool during any pit work, regardless of trouble, and there must be harmony in the pits during a race, regardless of personal feelings." Anyone injured was to be taken to the finest hospital to receive the best care. Anyone unable to abide by these rules was welcome—and indeed encouraged—to leave. Not one did. This was Eddie's family. As his mother had said after her husband was killed, survival meant that all brothers and sisters must look after each other. Everybody had to pull his or her weight.

When rumors surfaced of an affair between him and silent-screen film star Irene Tams, Eddie sent her a telegram that included the lines "I much prefer to travel with Herr and spell it with a double 'R' / For a woman's only a woman / My soul mate's a racing car"—doggerel that received wide press. "I was entirely too busy trying to be a successful racing driver which automatically eliminated my youthful love life," he later conceded. His fellow racers, many of whom fell for rich debutantes or beautiful actresses—Dario Resta wed Spencer Wishart's sister—could little understand Eddie's extraordinary preoccupation. For him, however, his entire being pushed at the highest pitch toward winning and the resulting success that would buffer him from his hard past. He simply would not make room for anything else. Winning meant survival, and his businesslike approach to risk did not permit anything that would throw it off track.

Even so, the wife of a fellow driver would crack this tough veneer. The former vaudeville singer Adelaide Frost was married to Cliff Durant, playboy son of William Crapo Durant, founder of General Motors. Eddie met Adelaide at a party thrown by the junior Durant at his Los Angeles mansion. Something about her smile and voice stole into his heart. Adelaide was Durant's second wife, and his legendary womanizing (he had been married four times when he died at forty-six) and drinking had already taken its toll on her. Word around the circuit was that he knocked her about. The spark of attraction would catch fire when Eddie and Adelaide met again after the war.

Racing year 1916 started out with yet another shocking accident. Longtime ace "Wild Bob" Burman lost control of his Peugeot when a tire blew during an April road race in Corona, California, that didn't even count in the standings. The car overturned into a crowd, injuring a number of spectators and killing Burman and his mechanician, Eric Shrader. Eddie had fought many a hard race with the slight Shrader right next to him.

In the first official race of the season, a 300-mile speedway event at Sheepshead Bay, Long Island, on May 13, Eddie ran against Resta and Ralph Mulford. The thirty-two-year-old former long-distance runner Carl Limberg, who had not won a major event, pushed his orange-painted Delage hard into an early lead. Lap after lap, Eddie tightly bunched with him, Resta, and De Palma—to the point that, said Eddie, "you could almost cover us with a blanket." Observers have noted repeatedly how narrow the track becomes at speed, how little room there seems.

"None would be first to obey the cry of caution to release to some slight degree the pressure of the foot on the accelerator pedal," wrote a breathless reporter for *The Automobile*. "Never did the gladiators of Rome battle better." In the north turn of the saucer, Limberg had just passed two cars, Eddie 50 to 75 feet behind him, when his right back tire blew like a gunshot. High up on the steep wooden banking, Limberg's Delage jerked and smashed into the guardrail. In the stands, Mrs. Limberg screamed as her husband and the mechanician flew out of sight beyond the embankment.

The Delage's chassis, engine, and rear axle slid down the curve in front of Eddie, the front axle and steering apparatus crashing behind him. He missed the wreck by a whisper as the body and engine burst into towering 25-foot-high flames that charred a hole in the track amid great dark billows of smoke. He knew conditions would be worse when he came back through again. Moments after he had passed, a physician scrambled up the incline on his hands and knees, unmindful of two cars that nearly clipped him, reached the rail, and slipped down the other side to find Limberg dying, impaled on an upright piece of timber. The mechanician had been killed on impact.

Although officials frantically waved warning flags and all the others slowed down in the smoke, Eddie, knowing that the wreckage had slid downslope to the track edge, took it high at full speed even though his vision was badly obscured. Even so, Resta still held the lead "in the teeth of the worrying pack of steel hounds." The Englishman's Peugeot settled the contest when it broke a valve in mile 114, Eddie cruising on to win handily. On the track that day, his actions had run right up to the line separating cunning opportunism from recklessness, but his nearly instant assessments had proven right. His confidence was growing in his ability to handle with nerve and clear calculation those insanely chaotic moments at the edge of speed and fear.

The Automobile's reporter tried to rationalize the horrors of the track by considering that "each broken car should prove a foundation for greater reliability . . . on the family stock car." A *New York World* editorial took less satisfaction. "The test of the car of utility . . . is in its daily, practical work. It needs no try-out at forced, death-inviting speeds. The interests of its makers would be helped, not hurt, by dissociation from a murderous sport."

By mid-1916, the contest for the national championship had settled into a three-way battle between Eddie, Resta, and a savvy older pro, the tall, thin driver universally known from his spontaneous crooked grin as "Happy" Johnny Aitken. The Indianapolis native had seen it all since he took the lead on the first lap of the first Indy 500. A skilled mechanic, he had quit the business in late 1910 after two of his racing partners had died on the track. After serving as a pallbearer for one of them, he said, "I will never drive again. The tragedy of the racing game has gotten on my nerves." Yet he would be back at it soon enough. As the high-wire artist Karl Wallenda famously said after climbing back up to perform after two of his troupe had fallen to their deaths, "To be on the wire is life; the rest is waiting." Overall

Aitken would win fifteen races at Indianapolis, more than anyone else in history. Like Eddie, he was a student of the sport, working on the development of the annual National models for years, traveling to Europe to study race-car construction and design, and serving as a pit manager and strategist for Peugeot.

The contest between Aitken and Eddie hit fever pitch at the September 9 Harvest Classic sponsored by Fisher and Allison at the Brickyard. The third and final contest, over 100 miles, counted in the AAA standings; both needed a win to keep up with Resta. No race in Eddie's career would prove more exhilarating for driver or spectator.

The day dawned bright and breezy, good conditions for a record-setting pace. It became immediately apparent to everyone, as Aitken's blue Peugeot and Eddie's white Maxwell easily distanced the pack, that this would be a battle of titans. For 90 miles, the pair pushed each other to faster times than the track had ever seen, frequently exchanging the lead as Eddie played his familiar strategy of losing the straights but winning the dangerous turns. An hour later, as they hit mile 90, the right front steering arm of Aitken's Peugeot snapped, considerably slowing him down, but he didn't pit or stop. Control of his car now depended on one slim rod, less than an inch thick, which could break at any moment from the stress and send him flying into the wall. The broken arm dragged on the track.

Eddie raced up triumphantly from behind to grasp victory, but at mile 95, comfortably ahead of the determinedly limping Aitken, he felt his right rear wheel start to wobble. Van and his crew madly signaled for him to pit, but he kept up his speed, knowing that such a delay could cost the race. About a half mile from the checkered flag, he heard the rifle shots of wooden spokes beginning to break on his left back tire. As both rear wheels began wobbling dangerously, the officials tried to flag him in. Eddie ground on, but now with painful slowness.

Others on the circuit whom the two champions had long since lapped began to tear by both crippled cars, which their drivers kept pushing to the edge in what was now a special, private duel. Coming out of the west turn into the homestretch, Eddie heard a "helluva bang" as his left rear tire let go, sending him into "a Devil's spin," as one journalist noted. The Maxwell careened right, then left, then back again, the rear axle crashing to the track, as Eddie frantically sought to control the wildly buffeting machine. Then the right tire dished and detached. Parts of the Maxwell flew across the track as it began sliding down into the path of four speeding rivals. His front tires blew. Somehow he manhandled what remained of the Maxwell to give the others right of way "just in the nick of time," then narrowly missed a retaining wall and came to a stop.

"How Aitken got through [the car parts] I'll never know but he was only going about 25 or 30 mph," Eddie would later recall, "but I was out and the race was over." Aitken crawled the last few miles "with only one front wheel attached to his steering apparatus" but still managed to win.

"Much credit is due Rickenbacher for his masterly control of the Maxwell under these conditions," observed *The Automobile*. Miraculously unhurt, Eddie and his mechanician climbed out of the wreck to thunderous applause and walked to the finish line.

Eddie earned even more kudos than Aitken for his calmness in extremity. "It came to me," he wrote later, "that I could control that machine with my mind, that I could hold it together with my mind, and that if it finally collapsed, I could run it with my mind. It was a feeling of mastery, of supreme confidence." Nonetheless, it was Aitken's victory, much narrowing Eddie's chances for first place.

A third place in mid-October at the Chicago Speedway virtually ended any chances of beating Resta or Aitken. Bitterly disappointed, Eddie abruptly disbanded the Maxwell team, paying off salaries and all expenses, but able to keep about $40,000, the most he had yet earned. Still, the big one had eluded him—and that burned more than all the praise and lesser triumphs could offset. With ample resources he had done everything possible to transform the Maxwell into a winner, but time and again Resta's and Aitken's older Peugeots had beaten him.

Then a tempting offer came over the transom. Louis Coatalen, the brilliant chief engineer of the British Sunbeam company and a fierce rival of Peugeot, asked whether Eddie would like to come over to England to check out the new race car they were building. It had been Coatalen who had brought Resta to America, before the young champion had jumped over to Peugeot to drive the car Eddie had left behind. The Sunbeam could be just the machine to put Eddie into first place in 1917, so he accepted. First, though, he would finish out the year's last three championship races in a Duesenberg provided by an eccentric Philadelphia millionaire.

Because the Vanderbilt, Grand Prize, and Ascot races all were set in California in November, Eddie took a train west. One free afternoon, he drove out to Riverside, California, and found an aircraft parked on a grassy runway. He pulled over to take a look at something still startlingly rare. The Martin TT exemplified the second generation of aircraft after the original Wright models. Pilots no longer perched nakedly and precariously in front of a "pusher" engine but sat somewhat protected by a boxy fuselage. More powerful engines had begotten larger aircraft, moving the propeller and engine forward.

Outside he met Glenn Martin, already a somewhat legendary pioneer flier and designer, destined to attain yet greater fame and real fortune after founding the major aircraft company that would eventually turn into Lockheed Martin. His flying career had begun modestly in 1912 when he converted an old Methodist church in Los Angeles into an airplane factory, financing it mostly by stunt flying at fairs but sometimes in more original ways—for instance, with $100 for a record-breaking 68-mile flight from Newport Bay, California, to Catalina Island and back, carrying mail and newspapers. Three years later he responded to a filmmaker's ad seeking a pilot with a plane to swoop the Hollywood darling Mary Pickford around in *A Girl of Yesterday*. Less than a year before meeting Eddie, he had patented the packed parachute.

Eddie had always been acrophobic, even growing dizzy at moderate heights, but his race with Lincoln Beachey had sufficiently intrigued him to push fear aside. He readily accepted Martin's offer of a quick run, taking the trainer's tandem seat. For thirty minutes, Martin flew him around the area, bellowing comments on the sights below over the roar of the engine. Rickenbacker yelled questions, unable to contain his exhilaration at experiencing this new kind of speed. Martin let him take the controls—surely a telling gesture of confidence in an absolute greenhorn—and Eddie pulled the TT into a smooth bank. Free from any racetrack friction, the aircraft easily responded to his careful manipulations. Only after they touched down did a wave of nausea and fear wash over Eddie. Why, he asked Martin, had he felt perfectly fine until he landed?

"Because there's nothing to judge height by," explained the expert. "There's no edge to look over."

After Martin showed him the engine and some of the controls, Rickenbacker knew for the first time—confidently and totally—that he could, and would, fly. He could feel it through his fingers as he ran his hands over the controls and the smooth contours of the laminated wooden propeller: not the rush of realization that he had felt as a boy passenger in that Ford two-seater, but a riper, more confident awakening.

Not long after this first venture, again out driving in California, Eddie spotted a single-seat military biplane in a cow pasture. Engine troubles had forced down Major Townsend F. Dodd, in charge of aeronautics for the Army Signal Corps. Recently Dodd had accompanied General John J. Pershing down to Mexico as pilot during the punitive expedition against Mexican revolutionary Pancho Villa. Dodd's engine ran but did not generate enough power to keep the aircraft aloft. Eddie offered to help, fiddled around, noticed that a coupling had slipped off the magneto, and fixed it in a couple of minutes. He took out a spark plug, got the piston up on dead center, locked the coupling, and replaced the plug. "Try it now," he told Dodd, then swung the propeller and was rewarded with a roar as the craft came back to life. Yelling his thanks, Townsend rolled down the pasture and took off. They would meet again aboard a ship on the way to war.

After a stripped gear forced Eddie out early in the Vanderbilt, Resta clinched the national championship. In the Grand Prize race, Eddie pitted after twenty-six laps with a broken drive shaft. Having nailed the first and second spots in the rankings, Resta and Aitken declined to race in the Thanksgiving Day running of the 150-mile Championship Award Sweepstakes at the Ascot Speedway. This time Eddie's Duesenberg held together and he finished first, a victory only mildly rewarding in that tough year. Between them just four drivers had won all of the fifteen major championship races: Resta (five), Aitken (five), Eddie (three), and De Palma (two).

On the train home to prepare for his trip to England, reflecting about his luck and the superstitions that had driven him to bind a bat's heart to his finger and drive with a black cat, he suddenly felt extremely foolish. Walking to the bathroom, he pulled out an assortment of "lucky elephants and four-leaf clovers; Billikens and tail buttons of rattlesnakes; rabbits' feet and other charms in dozens," pitched them into the toilet, and watched them scatter over the tracks. Something had changed within him, a power-conferring recognition that fate was his to master, not the other way around.

He could have had no idea that the race he had just completed at Ascot Park, Los Angeles, would be his last—and that his life, as well as that of the nation and the world, was about to be transformed.

BOOK II

FLYING

The third excellence is courage, the perfect will, which no terrors can shake, which is attracted by frowns or threats or hostile armies, nay, needs these to awake and fan its reserved energies into a pure flame, and is never quite itself until the hazard is extreme; then it is serene and fertile, and all its powers play well.

—Ralph Waldo Emerson, "Courage," *Society and Solitude* (1870)

6.

STORM CLOUDS OVERHEAD

In late December 1916, Eddie excitedly strode up the gangplank at West Twentieth Street in Manhattan to board a ship bound for Europe. The idea of crossing the Atlantic was heady enough, but the chance to work with Sunbeam and finally put Peugeot behind him was yet more thrilling. The year had ended disappointingly, but he had money in his pocket, a top ranking, and solid national name recognition. His mother need never again want for anything.

The ship sounded a long blast to claim the channel, threading a shoal of coastal schooners swarming in and out of New York, then passed by the still-charred ruins of Black Tom Island, the most visible witness to date of America's inexorable slide into war. Eddie gazed upon the remains of an island laid waste by the largest human-caused explosion the nation had ever seen.

Four and a half months earlier, one eyewitness recalled the concussive shock that had literally knocked him out of bed a little after 2:00 A.M. one Sunday morning. Father Anthony Grogan, who ran a mission for homeless Irish girls in lower Manhattan, plunged down the brick steps onto State Street and stared in disbelief out across New York Harbor. The glass from thousands of shattered windows crunched under foot.

"It seemed as if Ellis Island were on fire," he would recall. "Sparks were falling on the water in myriads in all directions like a fiery rain. It seemed as if they came from the big red balls which shot up into the air and then burst with a muffled report, which added to the tenseness of the scene." Dozens of his charges and swarms of tenement dwellers poured onto the street, struck dumb by the light show and explosions that just kept rolling along, as though the Western Front had opened up without warning onto New York State—as, in a grimly prophetic way, it had. "A great pillar of flame . . . lit up the sky with a red glare," reported *The New York Times*. Others awoke convinced that the very world was coming to an end.

The massive munitions depot on Black Tom Island in New York Harbor, which up till then had stocked some 2,132,000 pounds of artillery shells, nitrocellulose, high explosives, fuses, and TNT in railcars, barges, and warehouses, had gone up with a force equivalent to an earthquake measuring 5.5 on the Richter scale. Nothing like it had ever thus rocked a major American city, and nothing would do so again until terrorists crashed airliners into the Twin Towers a long lifetime later. Shrapnel stopped the clock on the *Jersey Journal* tower, more than a mile distant, and savaged the plinth of the Statue of Liberty. Ellis Island resembled a war zone, harboring 353 now terrified refugees from the European conflict. A photograph shows a nurse cradling a large shell that had sailed unexploded into the island's hospital. "Where on Saturday stood huge brick warehouses there remain only giant mounds of blazing and smoking ruin, while all about them are the wreckages of barges and railway rolling stock and other debris," reported the *Times*. Fires that took nearly a week to extinguish consumed mountains of sugar destined for Europe.

The revelations that emerged over the following days would prove even more momentous than the blast itself, which German saboteurs had set off to destroy munitions bound for Britain and France. Until that midsummer's evening, Americans might have lulled themselves into the assumption that the unprecedented bloodletting and industrial-strength destruction of "the Great War" would not cross their shores. Any doubts that German agents were operating in the United States—and there had been other evidence— vanished in the munitions' red glare. Theodore Roosevelt railed at "hyphenated Americans," and citizens of German descent became suddenly suspect. President Wilson spoke solemnly to Congress of betrayal by "citizens of the United States born under other flags but welcomed here under our generous naturalization laws to the full freedom and opportunity of America, who have poured the poison of disloyalty into the very arteries of our national life." A generation later, when the Japanese struck Pearl Harbor, this memory had remained so raw that it was conscripted into the next Roosevelt administration's case for interning Japanese American citizens. "We don't want any more Black Toms," FDR instructed the assistant secretary of war in charge of implementing the program.

Suspicions about the loyalty of German Americans had bubbled long before the blast. Ever since war had broken out in Europe, Eddie had been hassled in the United States for his Teutonic origins. The *Chicago Tribune* had commented seven months earlier that "Rickenbacher's ancestors hailed from the land of the Alps, although his name sounds more like a German pot roast than a Swiss cheese sandwich." The sportswriter J. C. Burton, with whom he had coauthored a story on riding mechanicians, had penned a few lines in *Motor Age* when the German racing star Christian Lautenschlager won the French Grand Prix in July 1914, ending:

> Great Kaiser Bill has had his fill
> > Of Pilsener and lager;
> He loudly boasts and drinks deep toasts
> > In praise of Lautenschlager:
> Across the sea a victory
> > Has led this peace-plan knocker
> To plan to knight in his delight
> > That Deutscher, Rickenbacher.

This doggerel appeared next to a drawing of a boyishly beaming Emperor Wilhelm II juggling two toy race cars. The most damaging account of Eddie's heritage was fabricated by another sports journalist, Al Waddell, in a bid to drum up interest in an early Vanderbilt Cup race. Deciding that the poor boy from Columbus needed a public relations boost, the *Los Angeles Times* newspaperman concocted an elaborately absurd story that Eddie was none other than the "Baron von Rickenbacher," a young Prussian nobleman who had bested the famous Lautenschlager in an informal road race and for this had been kicked out of his military academy. Thus disinherited—so went the story—the young patrician worked his way to the United States on a cattle boat to race cars. "I decided the baron touch would give Ricken-backer a play he otherwise would not have had because he was just beginning his career and was just another driver in the talented company," Waddell later recalled. He had fun playing with Eddie's imagined noble past, at one point asking him to pose in top hat, tails, and monocle. "I'm no baron," Eddie reputedly responded, "and no German. I'm an American citizen, born in Columbus, O., and I'm going to stay that way." Still, however toughly independent, he could smell rising ethnic bigotry and took precautions, one of them being to Americanize his name to Rickenbacker and add the sober middle name of Vernon.

There was little else he could do. In 1914, it had been anyone's guess whether the United States might ever be shaken loose from its staunch neutrality. Events soon warmed up America's relations with Britain and soured them with the Second Reich. Britain's declaration of war mobilized the Royal Navy, the most powerful in the world, and drove the kaiser's formidable but still not quite equal forces into port—not just his battle fleet but also the magnificent German merchant marine, more than ninety ships in American harbors alone. This stranglehold prevented Germany and Austria-Hungary from importing foodstuffs or war materials; Britain, France, and Russia could buy whatever they could afford from Americans eager to sell. President Wilson steadfastly held to America's neutral right to do business with whomsoever it chose. The extraordinary volume of commerce now beginning to flow would for the first time transform the United States from a debtor to a creditor nation and sweep it onto the world stage with new, as yet unimagined, powers.

Germany's complaints at such one-sidedness made little impact, so the kaiser fought back, ordering his submarine fleet to sink any ship, hostile or neutral, that as of February 4, 1915, plied a zone encircling Great Britain. Three months later, the inevitable befell: U-20 torpedoed a British liner bearing U.S. citizens. RMS *Lusitania* sank in only 18 minutes, just 11 miles off the southern tip of Ireland, drowning 1,198 people, 128 of them Americans. That it had been clandestinely carrying 4.2 million rifle cartridges and 1,250 cases of shrapnel shells, which made it a legitimate target, took a long time to emerge and made little difference anyway. Theodore Roosevelt called for an immediate declaration of war. Only with considerable difficulty did President Wilson overcome the clamor and maintain neutrality. By the time that the German high command rescinded unrestricted submarine warfare under the force of American fury, the damage had been done.

German intelligence assigned Captain Franz von Rintelen to New York to implement an aggressive sabotage offensive. That well-funded naval officer, fluent in English, who carried a Swiss passport and passed himself off as a businessman, immediately took command of the German crews aboard the blockaded ships, making his headquarters the engine room of the *Friedrich der Grosse* in the North River. There he planned dock strikes to disrupt munitions shipments to Europe. His team also built explosive devices that they secreted in the holds of Europe-bound merchant vessels. The United States lacked both a national counterintelligence service and laws forbidding peacetime espionage and passport fraud, so efforts to track down the saboteurs were difficult. After the *Lusitania*, Wilson ordered the Secret Service—usually detailed to protect the president and pursue counterfeiters—to keep an eye on German diplomats, but they had little luck. Then came Black Tom.

Anti-German sentiment rose to a fever pitch; soon vigilantism would rip the country, neighbors denouncing immigrant neighbors. Some 2.5 million German immigrants were living in the United States in 1915; another 4 million Americans had been born to parents who grew up in Germany. Once the most respected of all immigrant groups, which had included such notables as industrialist John D. Rockefeller, U.S. Senator Carl Schurz, and the brewer Adolphus Busch, now found itself subject to what one historian has called "a violent, hysterical, concerted movement to eradicate everything German from American civilization." Eddie's Columbus neighborhood, the German Village, would feel its pinch and soon have all the Teutonic flavor wrung out of it.

When some warned that his Germanic surname might bring him

trouble overseas, Eddie had simply shrugged. Already an American hero, what did he have to fear, even if his parents had come from German-speaking Switzerland? Even so, he did not anticipate—though perhaps he should have—the hostility of the reception he would soon receive.

On board ship, Eddie struck up a conversation with two men who introduced themselves as Goodyear and Immerman, Chicago wheat traders. He thought their accents a bit odd but chalked it up to their being Canadian, and he was soon enjoying their jovial company, joking with Immerman about the difficulty in those days of traveling with German-sounding names. On docking at Liverpool, Eddie casually noted the absence of his two friends in line.

"Rickenbacker?" barked a long-nosed English sergeant. When the racing star stepped forward, the man further snapped, "What's your name?" Strange, Eddie later remembered thinking, because the sergeant held his passport.

"What is your purpose in England?" his inquisitor went on in harsh Cockney. Eddie began to explain his visit to Sunbeam, only to be interrupted.

"Don't you know that there's a war on?" Eddie realized that something was up. Who didn't?

"Do you know there's an embargo on everything pertaining to steel, including automobiles, from leaving the British Isles for the duration of the war?" continued his inquisitor, who then paused, eyes boring into Eddie's. "Or don't you know that racing cars would come under that category?"

The sergeant moved Eddie down the hall and into a cabin where Goodyear and Immerman were waiting, "colder than the coldest, damnedest icicles that I've ever seen in my life." Introducing themselves briskly as agents of the Metropolitan Police, they produced a thick dossier, which laid out his supposed birth and upbringing in Germany—a rehash, realized Eddie with mounting alarm, of the newspaper fantasies outlining his past as a speed-drunk Prussian blueblood—after which they accused him flat-out of being a German spy. In retrospect, Eddie thanked God for his sense of humor; he understood immediately that only charm would get him through. "The whole thing was so ludicrous that, instead of getting mad, I treated it as a joke."

His amusement was distinctly tempered when the three men strip-searched him, rubbed lemon juice on his skin to bring out any messages in invisible ink, pried off the heels of his shoes, and rifled his suitcase. He was told that he must stay aboard and return to the United States. Nor might he place a call to his British sponsor.

Eddie finally convinced the agents to allow him to spend Christmas Eve ashore under their direct supervision. If the tangle with Scotland Yard had not yet opened Eddie's eyes to the strains of wartime on a homefront population, then his walk from the Albert Dock did. Millions of troops would pass through this vast pierage and complex of naval installations along the River Mersey, giving the area the tone of a permanent armed camp. The war effort had claimed so many men that details of dark-clad women wearing lettered armbands had been deputized as police. Many of the sailors aboard the *Lusitania* had called Liverpool home, so the sinking had hit the city particularly hard. Rioting had targeted many British people of German descent, often long-established, prosperous cobblers and butchers, who saw their homes and businesses destroyed. Authorities whisked most away to internment camps.

Under the blackout imposed that November after zeppelin raids on industrial centers farther south, Liverpool was dark except for "little blue shafts" of light at intersections. The agents brought Eddie to the newly rebuilt Adelphi Hotel, whose rooms Jules Verne's Professor Pierre Aronnax had compared to the sumptuous interiors of Captain Nemo's supersubmarine in *Twenty Thousand Leagues Under the Sea*. Goodyear and Immerman took rooms on either side of Eddie's. Eddie kept his equanimity in the face of the outrageous accusations. Since childhood he had expected things to go wrong, and he was usually ready when trouble came.

He bought his companions a few beers, and they loosened up, finally permitting him to phone Coatalen on Christmas morning. His sponsor quickly arranged for his release. On Boxing Day, after his passport had been stamped by the Alien Office in Liverpool, he boarded a London-bound train, which arrived at Waterloo Station after dark. A Jack the Ripper fog, one of the "London particulars" of damp and coal smoke, had already blanketed the city. Unable to get a cab, Eddie got altogether lost trying to find the Savoy Hotel. He was impressed by how Londoners made their way through the darkness by walking along the gutters, occasionally kicking the curbstones to stay oriented. Finally one seasoned Londoner told him to grab his coattails and guided him to the entrance, but the front desk wouldn't permit him to check in without his having registered at the appropriate police station. Only after Eddie had threatened to lie down right there on the floor and sleep because he was so tired did the manager assign him a porter as his guide to getting fingerprinted. He finally climbed into bed at 3:00 A.M. The next day Coatalen came over, promising to take him to the Sunbeam motor works in Wolverhampton once he was cleared for travel. Eddie spent the next ten days in London. "All of England's young men are in khaki and I must admit I feel strange when walking down the street—rather out of place," he cabled home. He observed no new car designs.

His window at the Savoy overlooked the Thames; he could see Big Ben towering above the Palace of Westminister and thrilled at the sight of four or five Handley Page trainers and de Havilland DH-2s winding along the river at 75 mph. They weren't particularly elegant, merely engines tacked to crude biplanes, but their powerful presence in loose formation impressed him deeply. He learned that they came from Brooklands, the great British car-racing venue (Carl Fisher's visit to which had inspired the Indianapolis Speedway), now an aerodrome 20 miles southwest of London.

What he saw on a visit to Brooklands astounded him. The 3-mile concrete-banked oval enclosed a large grassy infield containing dozens of aircraft and a long strip from which they took off southward. The 100-foot-wide track itself now served as a road over which 5-ton Royal Flying Corps trucks delivered supplies to a "flying village" of wooden hangars, offices, and barracks ringing the outside perimeter. Brooklands's civilian owner, who had named the track for a favorite racehorse, had turned over the entire facility to the government when Britain went to war in early August 1914. The café was now an officers' mess. Before the hostilities, the management had encouraged early fliers to put on demonstrations between the races—thus, above land once belonging to Henry VIII, a British pilot had pulled off his country's first loop-the-loop. Soon shacks popped up, each barely large enough to accommodate a biplane, a cot and stove, some extra yards of fabric, and repair equipment. Vickers Ltd. and Thomas Sopwith had started flying schools here in 1912, and both would erect facilities for building military aircraft during the war. With Blériot and Martinsyde also setting up shop, Brooklands would become Britain's largest single center of aircraft production. By the end of that first August, aircraft from Brooklands were engaging German planes over France and Belgium. The aggressive British approach to combat flying served up many if not most of these craft—and their pilots—as fodder for German aviators flying better planes with more effective armament.

At the outbreak of war, the Royal Flying Corps had consisted of only five squadrons, totaling 125 planes and 1,100 men. Prewar attempts by civilian manufacturers to get Whitehall to buy more airplanes was met with word from the secretary of state for war's office, "Gentlemen, much as we would like to help you by placing orders, we regret we cannot do this as we are trustees of the public purse and we do not consider that aeroplanes will be of any possible use for war purposes." The guns of August blasted the RFC into overdrive. By 1918, Britain was producing 3,500 planes a month.

The hard, determined faces of the young combat pilots Eddie met revealed that even after two years they were still getting pounded out of the sky. The current backdrop of war was particularly grim: The year 1916 had proved one of the bloodiest in history; advances in artillery and the use of water-cooled machine guns had shredded life on the Western Front with industrial precision. On July 1 alone, the first day of the Battle of the Somme, the British incurred 57,420 casualties, 19,240 of these deaths—and most of those within the first hour. Such was the bloodletting that every British soldier Eddie met had most likely known people who had died, or at least their families. One of F. Scott Fitzgerald's characters in *Tender Is the Night* describes the Western Front as "a whole empire walking very slowly, dying in front and pushing forward behind. And another empire walked very slowly backward a few inches a day, leaving the dead like a million bloody rugs."

As "the winter of the world" bore down, millions of shell-shocked infantrymen and stunned civilians longed for some glimmer of humanity amid the unimaginable bloodletting. They found brief respite in the increasing number of duels—which they could envision as tournaments—visible overhead, in which frail fabric-and-wood steeds reared up against one another, their pilots a new order of knighthood locked in heaven-high fights halfway between fairy tale and science fiction. Mired in gore and mud below, the worn-out infantry had only to gaze upward to be briefly transported out of their world of filth, lice, and suffering, refreshed by the sight of these colorful crates of baling wire and fabric soaring across the sky. Victory in these encounters came not through launching volcanic barrages onto the heads of terrified soldiers huddled in trenches but from the skill and cunning of individual young men locking into deadly three-dimensional chess. There seemed something altogether glorious, honorable, and heroically artistic about this new breed, who took these box kites into the thinning air in search of yet deeper dangers. Across bars and kitchen tables from San Francisco to Vladivostok, the myth of the winged knight errant thrived. The hollow-eyed pilots at Brooklands could tell a different story; their average survival rate dropped precipitously as the sheer demands of aerial combat came close to outreaching even the most ferociously talented. Yet even they played up to the myth, so desperate were they and the nations they served to offset the horrors on the battlefield.

Eddie paid rapt attention to the tales of intricate gladiatorial contests in the air, strangely resembling the gritty, bloody car races of which he was a master. News of these still-unprecedented combats had filtered piecemeal to the United States. In June 1916, *The New York Times* reported the death of Victor Chapman, an American volunteer in French service and descendant of the first chief justice, at the hands of twenty-five-year-old Lieutenant Oswald Boelcke, flying in a small, fast, black-painted fighting scout. In December, after the forty-kills ace himself went down, *The Washington Post* published brief tantalizing details of the strange new world of aerial combat from Boelcke's reports, one of which described coming upon an enemy airplane in serene flight, a dead pilot at the controls. Early in 1916, after Boelcke had disabled an enemy's rudder, the observer had climbed out onto the left wing and hung there precariously, the only way to keep the craft airborne—notes as exotic as reports from arctic explorers.

A little over a month before Eddie visited Britain, a remarkable engagement had come about, the details of which were only just emerging. The pilots at Brooklands described how the British ace Lanoe Hawker had met the rising German superace Manfred von Richthofen, the "Red Baron," with all the trappings of a prizefight. When first they joined, they spiraled, as the baron would later write, "round and round" one another "like madmen," each gauging his opponent's skills. Hawker, commander of number 24 Squadron and a holder of the Victoria Cross, at one point even waved merrily at his opponent. They went around twenty times to the left, then thirty to the right. Hawker's British DH-2 turned more tightly than Richthofen's Albatros, but the latter held the edge in flat-out speed and climbing capacity. There followed a tangle of loops and banking turns, as each sought the critical moment of advantage. At several points, Hawker's bullets passed close to Richthofen's head: But when the British ace registered that his fuel was running out he broke for home, only to find that the most desperate zigzagging could not escape Richthofen's pursuit. A bullet caught him in the head. He crashed 50 yards inside enemy lines.

This, the Baron's ninth kill, marked an early chapter in an extraordinary career that would make him the deadliest ace of the entire war. Handsome, with a finely chiseled chin and silky blond hair, the twenty-four-year-old seemed born to kill artistically. When the up-and-coming German ace Ernst Udet first saw Richthofen, he was struck by his "quiet, self-controlled face, [and] large, cold eyes, half covered by heavy lids." Richthofen enjoyed an aristocratic upbringing, learning to ride, hunt wild boar, and fish on various family estates. He served as a cavalry officer until it became apparent that the trench deadlock had rendered the "white arm" obsolete. Quite by chance, he met Oswald Boelcke; Germany's top ace at once recognized a natural-born flying genius and took him as a pupil. Richthofen would soon outshine his master. As his kills mounted, he painted his plane bloodred so that friend and foe alike might recognize him. The men of his squadron followed suit, each, however, painting one part of his aircraft in another bright tint to acknowledge their leader's primacy—a ferocious showiness that earned them the sobriquet of "the Flying Circus." While other squadrons might go up two or three times a day, Richthofen and his men would do so five times; when bad weather shut down most other squadrons, they flew under almost any conditions. German newspapers reported that a British squadron had been formed just to kill the baron; the pilot who did so would receive £5,000. Richthofen coolly joked that the prize should be his if he shot down the entire squadron, and he nearly did so in February and March 1917, adding ten more kills to his roster.

Hearing about Richthofen and the Flying Circus thrilled Eddie—but seeing the machines that the Royal Flying Corps was throwing against them was even more intoxicating. Like any other engineer learning through his eyes and hands, Eddie walked among the aircraft, examining the hell-bent tide of innovation that extremity had brought about almost overnight. Here was, for instance, the Sopwith 1½ Strutter, the first British military airplane to mount the engine in front and to fire a synchronized machine gun through its propeller. He stroked the massive wooden propellers and eyeballed the graceful cut of its wings. The engineer in him marveled at how perfectly technology had been interpreted toward deadly purpose. He was hooked, and he knew it. From that moment, he became intent on learning how to fly so he could become a combat pilot—a desire that gelled rapidly into iron-hard resolution, not unlike the moment years earlier after his father's death, when he knew he must quit school at once to support the family.

After ten days, Coatalen secured permission for him to travel to Sunbeam's plant in Wolverhampton, well to the north of London. *Motor Age* reported that Eddie had also crossed the Channel to visit Peugeot but been turned away at Bordeaux. At Wolverhampton, he closely examined engines at the factory during the week, then returned to London on the weekends. Every morning and evening he checked in with the relevant authorities, something Coatalen had warned him to take seriously. In Wolverhampton, he took a flat with Cecil Reed, a bachelor mechanic at Sunbeam. Eddie enjoyed Reed's homemade crumpets, bacon, and scrambled eggs in the morning but had to teach him how to make coffee. A quarter century later, Reed would tell him that he had been steadily funneling information to Scotland Yard. "All the time you were at the Sunbeam plant, you were under surveillance. Yes, my friend, your mail was opened, your conversations reported, your every move was scrutinized."

Eddie was particularly struck by the high compression of the English cars, acknowledging to a reporter that their speed, perhaps even up to 120 mph, would "open American eyes." The Sunbeams looked like solid racing material, but his experiences at Brooklands truly excited him. He told Coatalen that he wanted to join the Royal Flying Corps, but Coatalen managed to convince him to drive a Sunbeam in the 1917 season back home. Still, Eddie vowed to fly should the United States join the war.

That was coming soon enough. On February 1, 1917, Germany announced that it would renew an unrestricted submarine campaign, whereupon the United States broke off diplomatic relations. German strategists knew that this offensive would likely drive America into the war but figured that the U-boat fleet could sink so catastrophic a tonnage of merchant shipping as to bring Britain to its knees long before the American military could mobilize—a calculated gamble that they would lose ruinously. The Germans gave merchant ships a five-day grace period. An American offered Eddie a place in his stateroom on the SS *New York*, but only if he got there within four hours. One of Coatalen's drivers sprinted him to Liverpool over 150 miles of what then passed as highways with minutes to spare. As he came aboard, Eddie again met the overbearing sergeant.

"Ah, you're back again. You'll have to have your baggage checked, you know, and all your papers." Again Eddie was ushered into a cabin; again Goodyear and Immerman awaited him. They delayed the ship two hours with their questioning. Eddie was forced to leave his engineering drawings, notes, and books. As the *New York* steamed downriver and out to sea, he encountered Gene Buck, a songwriter and showman friend from Detroit, who passed along the rumor that a German spy was aboard. "That'd be me," joked Eddie in relief. *Motor Age* would later comment on his European adventure: "As a fitting close to the experiences of an American race driver in Europe, it must be recorded that during the first day out, a stowaway spy was hauled out of the coal bunkers; also, that the menacing eye of a submarine was sighted."

Aboard ship, Eddie hatched a scheme that he outlined to reporters after arriving in New York. "I leave for the West tomorrow," he said, to talk to racing drivers and their mechanicians about joining a flying corps. "We are experts in judging speed and in motor knowledge ... I expect to get up a body of not less than fifty of us who will volunteer if war is declared." Among some whispers of warmongering, Eddie traveled to Detroit, visited his mother in Columbus, then went on to Chicago and Los Angeles to canvass the racing fraternity. Along the way, he got the impression that a blond Englishman whom he kept running into might be shadowing him; when he checked in at Los Angeles's Alexandria Hotel, there the stranger was again. Shortly thereafter, the man approached Eddie and admitted to being a British agent. His superiors, he announced, no longer believed Eddie to be a spy. "But I do want to thank you," continued this naively engaging spook, "for the wonderful trip I've had, following you about this interesting country." Eddie never saw him again.

Even more strikingly, the air corps idea went over well with many of America's top drivers—notably Ralph De Palma, Ray Harroun, Earl Cooper, and Ralph Mulford—who all agreed to join the putative Aero Reserves of America. "Mature men of proven and swift reflexes developed at high speeds in competitive racing—what flyers they would make!" wrote Eddie.

With enough names in his pocket, he traveled back east, stopping only for a tonsillectomy in New York, figuring to wrap up business before being sent to France. Coming out of the anesthetic, he found himself bleeding profusely from the throat but was at first groggy enough to think it normal. It wouldn't stop. He called out for a nurse, who came but could do nothing. The operating surgeon had left the hospital to attend another patient. The nurse tracked down an intern, who proved equally ineffective.

"I began to feel my life flowing away with my blood," Eddie recounted later. He felt no pain or panic; indeed, everything seemed serene and peaceful. He began seeing beautiful colors and shapes; memories of his childhood flashed by. "How easy it was to lie there and, with a heavenly sensation of contentment, die."

He had always fought, though, and fought to win—reactions that kicked in to give him the strength to shout however painfully against his closing throat for the nurse and intern to fetch the head doctor quickly. Somehow he hung on until the returned surgeon diagnosed and clamped a nicked artery. The just-conscious Eddie stayed awake long enough to hear the doctor berating his subordinates for not summoning him sooner. It had been a very close call. He couldn't get over the irony that this was the closest he had come to dying, in the brief intermission between racing and what he was certain would be a second career as a combat pilot—and that during a routine procedure.

As he recuperated, relations between the United States and Germany deteriorated further. While Eddie was in England, Arthur Zimmermann of the Imperial Foreign Office had sent a coded cable to the German ambassador in Washington for transmission to the legation in Mexico City. Anticipating that the imminent renewal of unrestricted submarine warfare would push America into belligerency, the so-called Zimmermann Telegram promised Mexico financial and military support should it declare war on the United States, its reward for joining hands with the kaiser being the recovery of Texas, Arizona, and New Mexico. The British decoded the cable, then leaked it to outrage American public opinion. This time the nation's hackles rose and stayed that way until the deadly game was fully played out.

On April 2, President Wilson called upon Congress for a declaration of war and got it after four days of vigorous debate. Figuring that the timing was perfect and that he was sufficiently recovered, Eddie dashed to Washington to impart his vision of an air corps of ace car drivers to Brigadier General George O. Squier, head of the Signal Corps, who was bringing the country's nascent air service into being.

He could have saved his breath. When asked for his college degree (then a requirement for a flier's commission), Eddie cited his engineering correspondence course. The military brass laughed in his face. When he pointed out his unmatched mechanical and engineering experience, they countered that a flier who knew too much about technology wouldn't risk his life by getting airborne if he thought something was wrong with his engine. (None of the senior officers had ever flown themselves.)

"But that's the key to the whole thing!" responded Eddie, explaining how the kind of men he had in mind could coax the most out of their engines. Nothing would convince polished authority that this man of rough demeanor and imperfect utterance was anywhere close to officer material. He had come up against an ingrained class hostility through which not even a good-natured racing star could break. If the frustrations of the past several months—roughed up as an accused spy, then denied the chance to serve his country—had ever boiled over, they would have done so in those Spartan offices. Eddie didn't grow angry; he just offered courteous thanks and silently took his leave, vowing to find another way.

Meanwhile, President Wilson had ordered General Pershing to take an expeditionary force to France and come up with a plan for American military presence on the ground. Wilson suggested to his cousin John A. Wilson, who ran the AAA, that a well-known car racer be selected to drive Pershing and his staff in Europe. Eddie received the call while preparing for one of the few racing events still running that year. If he could get from Cincinnati to New York immediately, the job was his. After the briefest visit to his mother, he tore back to New York and enlisted.

On June 5, 1917, the day that Congress instituted registration under the Selective Service Act, the *Baltic* sailed for Europe, carrying Pershing, fifty-nine other officers, sixty-seven enlisted men, and thirty-three field clerks. Aboard was a tall captain named George S. Patton Jr., as well as Major T. F. Dodd, whose aircraft Eddie had fixed in a California cow pasture. As a driver, Sergeant Rickenbacker ranked as the most junior of noncommissioned officers. When he returned just eighteen months later, this lowly noncoms had become the nation's greatest hero, his name recognition exceeding even Pershing's.

7.

FLYING LESSONS

So passionate an outpouring welcomed the American Expeditionary Forces to Paris that it startled Pershing and his men. As they rode to their hotels from the Gare du Nord, Parisians lined the boulevards and crowded the squares. Conspicuously lacking were young men, virtually all of whom had gone to the front. Throngs jammed windows and rooftops for a glimpse of the procession. Gendarmes could not prevent women from climbing onto the open cars under the rain of flowers crowning the soldiers' heads. Many, openly weeping, waved small American flags to cries of "*Vive les américains!*" "There was a terribly hysterical quality in it," wrote an American journalist. "They were laughing and crying at the same time, but the crying was held in."

"Though I live a thousand years," recalled Pershing's chief of staff, "I shall never forget that crowded hour." For Patton it "was the most inspiring drive I ever took." For Eddie it was simply "a helluva hullabaloo"—a weary people cheering with one voice for the only army capable of saving the proud city from the crunch of German boots. An American friend had warned Pershing that "there is a limit to what flesh and blood and endurance can stand," and that the French "have just about reached that limit."

The great offensives of the past two and a half years—in Artois and Champagne in 1915, on the Somme in 1916, most recently along the Chemin des Dames that spring—had left 5 million casualties on both sides and only slightly altered the trench lines. Something had snapped among

French infantry during the particularly catastrophic assault on the Chemin des Dames ridge, a stretch of the front above the River Aisne northeast of Soissons. In a fruitless advance upon the well-dug-in Germans, they had been mown down in droves by machine guns, leaving almost 300,000 dead and wounded in barely a week. Widespread mutiny broke out, and as many as 30,000 men refused to advance, some actually taking over four towns.

Only General Philippe Pétain's timely crackdown averted further catastrophe. He took the energy out of the mutinies with massive arrests, executing the ringleaders while ordering improved rations and more generous leave schedules. However, these palliatives only stemmed further desertion. Pétain realized that his army could no longer mount a major offensive without the support of the United States, which was still far from fully mobilizing. At the height of the mutiny, the minister of war estimated that only two reliable French divisions lay between the Germans and Paris 70 miles away. Pershing would later write that "this adverse situation after three years of struggle was so depressing that the prospects of Allied victory probably never before looked less hopeful." The American intervention was indispensable, and "I hope . . . not too late," Pétain told Pershing.

Pershing spent the next several weeks visiting different sectors of the front with an eye toward organizing the complex of training centers and the immense supply system necessary to host the millions of doughboys soon to descend on France. Eddie did little to discourage American press coverage, which reported that the famous racing driver was chauffeuring Pershing regularly around France—although if he did so at all, it was only rarely. Yet Douglas MacArthur, then a thirty-seven-year-old infantry colonel in the 42nd Division, remembered coming late one night across a stalled Rolls-Royce bearing the commander in chief's four red stars. Walking over, MacArthur, who would go on to command U.S. Army forces in the Far East during World War II and become one of America's most formidably successful commanders, found only the driver, a sergeant, who, when asked the trouble, squinted hard and replied that it could be "a hairpin in the clutch," a not-so-subtle allusion to the widowed Pershing's notorious passion for beautiful women. The driver, MacArthur wrote, was one Eddie Rickenbacker.

Mostly, Eddie drove a Packard for Major Dodd, recently reduced to second in command of the U.S. air component under the colorful Billy Mitchell. By September, as Pershing settled into new headquarters in Chaumont, 150 miles southwest of Paris, Mitchell and Dodd continued their tour of French aerodromes in search of suitable training facilities for American pilots. The ramrod-straight, French-speaking son of a Wisconsin senator, Mitchell had bounded precociously into the army, becoming the youngest member of the general staff at thirty-two. Eddie found him an "excitable, high-strung individual" but admired him. Mitchell often expressed his frustration with the army's slowness to recognize the revolutionary possibilities of heavier-than-air flight. In August 1913, he appeared before the House Military Affairs Committee to argue for the creation of a "permanent authority" to hasten the development of military and naval aeronautics, because "we are behind all other major powers in the matter of aviation." He learned to fly; then, almost as soon as the United States had entered the war, visited General Hugh Trenchard, the father of British attack aviation, to learn all he could about the strategic use of airpower, particularly the practical corollaries of the doctrine that aviation was an offensive, not a defensive, arm.

Eddie received confirmation from a high-placed friend back home that he remained under surveillance as a possible spy by his roommate and friend, Sergeant Frederick W. Flake, who often drove for Mitchell. Eddie's suspicions had already been ignited when he found Flake rifling through his belongings with only a lame explanation. Now a little more comfortable with the game, Eddie seized upon the opening to suggest that he was about to confide some delicious indiscretion, only to switch topics. "I used to lead him out on the end of a limb and then cut it off and change the subject."

Soon after their arrival, Eddie found himself driving Dodd and following Flake, who had Mitchell aboard, to the medieval city of Nancy, not far behind the front lines, legendary as the birthplace of quiche lorraine. Roaring up in their twin-six Packards as darkness fell, they settled with their French hosts into the Café Walter overlooking the majestic stone-paved Place Stanislas. As the three American officers discussed the war with their two French colleagues, the drivers kept their own company. In spite of Flake's spying on Eddie—or even because of it—the two had become friends, even patronizing Paris cabarets together. Just as dinner ended, howling sirens heralded an air raid, sending the citizenry headlong into the city's labyrinth of wine cellars. Mitchell hastily ordered his party out of the city center. Some months earlier, determined to stick out an air raid on Châlons, he had been lucky to escape with only a bruised leg when a bomb burst across the street.

The cars raced west 7 miles to Pont-Saint-Vincent, where they ascended a hill outside the city. Spotlights danced jerkily across the sky in search of the mighty Gotha G. bombers, three-person beasts of prey boasting nearly 79-foot wingspans, so broad that almost three fighter aircraft could perch side by side on their upper wings.

That night Mitchell's party witnessed one of the world's first demonstrations of industrial-strength bombing. Antiaircraft tracers ineffectively laced the air as the great aircraft with thrumming Mercedes engines circled their targets high above an artillery range. A flash lit up the city's farther side, soon followed by a chain of appalling blasts, the death knell of a projectile factory; next the railroad station went up as a bomb found a train loaded with gas and oil. Mitchell estimated that the flames leaped 100 feet high or more as entire city blocks burned away. The two raiders droned away into silence, soon to be succeeded by wailing fire trucks and the clattering of alarms. The authorities ordered the evacuation of the entire civilian population.

With the Gothas, war turned a bloody page. The feebly powered aircraft of 1914 could haul little ordnance aloft. The earliest pilots emptied boxes of fléchettes (weighted darts), killing little except the occasional horse. Zeppelins provided more stable bombardment platforms. In January 1915 the frightening reality emerged when two slow but silent and immense airships discharged six 110-pound bombs on Yarmouth. The destruction was less than spectacular, yet concrete enough: four dead, the town square damaged, along with several small buildings. The earliest bombs remained rudimentary, merely artillery shells trimmed with strips of horse blanket to ensure that they landed nose down. Vulnerable to the wind and attack aircraft, the zeppelins enjoyed only a brief window of success, although they achieved their most important goal of terrifying British cityfolk. The Gothas proved grimly more effective, delivering 200-pound bombs while flying fast and high.

In Paris, Paul Painlevé, the French minister of war, a pioneering mathematician soon to be prime minister, lectured Pershing on the importance of aviation. Pershing's experience had been limited to watching the pathetic performance of several Jennies in the Mexican desert during his pursuit of Pancho Villa. Aviation had changed far faster than Pershing could have imagined since then. "It enables you to have eyes yourself, to put out your enemy's eyes and to deal destruction at points not otherwise reachable," Painlevé told a journalist with Pershing, partly in the hopes of convincing America to turn its industrial might to outbuilding German airpower. Painlevé had ample experience with the subject, having flown with Wilbur Wright at Auxerre in 1908, given some of the first lectures on flight dynamics, and, in 1910, called for a thousand airplanes to be built in five years. While most still considered his words fantasy, he had struck a greater chord in France than Mitchell had in America. Unable to arouse much military interest in the United States, Wilbur Wright had toured Europe in 1908, electrifying not only Painlevé but a generation of aviation enthusiasts, including Alberto Santos-Dumont, Henri Fabre, Gabriel Voisin, and Louis Blériot. The headlong French rush into aviation made their tongue for a while the language of the new science, many terms then coined still in use, including *fuselage*, *aileron*, *longeron*, and *nacelle*.

In 1909 Blériot took only thirty-six minutes to cross the English Channel in a plane nearly unrecognizable from the original pusher Wright craft. His innovative process couldn't have been more different from the brothers' careful developments, built on the back of thousands of glider experiments at Kitty Hawk. He came up with the design of the Blériot XI after a seemingly random consideration of different, unrelated ideas that he crashed through ten iterations. The eleventh worked: a monoplane, carrying its direct-drive engine in front, which flew comfortably at 45 mph. Though fog left him flying blind without a compass, he somehow located the White Cliffs and crash-landed near Dover Castle. The impressive stone fortress known as "the key to England," which had guarded England's coast for almost two thousand years, had been reached in little over half an hour by a single Frenchman in a flimsy apparatus of wire, fabric, and wood. Britain boasted the world's strongest navy, but even the most formidable battleship could not interdict invasion from the clouds. This chord of modernity rang loudly through Europe. In America, moated by vast oceans and absorbed in the giant rumbling of its own economic engines, the implications of powered flight did not yet strike with the painful clarity they registered in a continent that now saw its historic borders of channels, rivers, and mountains being easily breached.

The morning after the raid on Nancy, as the two cars wound through the hills toward Neufchâteau, Mitchell's Packard suddenly spluttered to a stop. Sergeant Flake jumped out and flung open the hood. A certain amount of unproductive time passed until Dodd suggested that his driver take a look. Eddie was happy to oblige.

"What's wrong with it?" he asked Flake.

"I can't get it revved up. It's popping on me, backfiring."

Mitchell would remember how the "tall, lithe man" dove into the engine, undid a little wing nut on a carburetor assembly "almost as big as the engine itself," located a bent needle valve, and fixed it with a few twists. Eddie quickly established that dirt and water had choked off gas flow through the strainer. Flake's inability to identify this routine problem suggests that he had been chosen to drive Mitchell for reasons other than mechanical aptitude, a signature skill of the army driver.

"Now start it up," said Eddie. The engine roared to life. This lightning work—similar to what had compelled the attention of Firestone and Dodd—impressed Mitchell, too. Within a few weeks Eddie would become his main driver. Curiosity soon got the better of Mitchell, who grilled Eddie about his racing experiences and difficulties with Scotland Yard, although he must have known about Flake's ongoing surveillance. One of Mitchell's main responsibilities lay in establishing a major U.S. aerodrome, so for the next several weeks Eddie roared him around the Western Front. "Any job that he was given," Mitchell later wrote, his hindsight no doubt given wings by Eddie's enormous achievements soon to come, "was done in the best possible manner. He was never late and was always well turned out, neat in his personal appearance, punctilious and gentlemanly."

On one excursion, as the pair barreled along a road in a Hudson Super-Six, the engine started banging "like a triphammer" as a burned-out connecting rod bearing sounded ready to fail. Unlike Pershing, a cavalryman who judged nonrail speed by the gallop, Mitchell liked to go fast, which soon exacerbated the problem. Early that afternoon, Eddie pulled into a small town, dropped Mitchell off at a hotel, and found a tiny garage whose old mechanic could come up with nothing to fit the Hudson. He did, however, find some Babbitt metal, a soft alloy used to make bearings; melting this with a blowtorch, Eddie poured it into a mold he had improvised with astounding exactness out of sand and water, and then only had to file and scrape the crude part into serviceability. By 6:00 P.M., they had roared off, Mitchell dumbfounded at Eddie's capacity to jackleg a rural garage into effective backup without specialized tools. It would not be long before Eddie could capitalize on his growing friendship with this colonel.

In mid-August, a patch of free time found Eddie strolling down the Champs-Élysées, not far from the Signal Corps headquarters at the Élysée Palace, where he ran into Captain James Miller, a New York banker whom he had known stateside and renewed acquaintance with aboard the *Baltic*. Considering how rarely luck figured in Eddie's planning, he may well have set the encounter up.

"Eddie," cried Miller, "you're just the fellow I've been looking for!" Recently tasked by Mitchell with creating an aerodrome out of the muddy fields near the town of Issoudun, about 100 miles south of Paris, Miller needed a chief engineering officer.

"I'd be glad to do the best I could to help you, Jim," replied Eddie, "but I think an engineering officer for a flying school ought to know how to fly himself"—and let that sink in for a moment. Here was his long-awaited chance.

"I'll see what I can do," said Miller. Still needing to convince Mitchell that he belonged behind an airplane stick, not a staff-car wheel, Eddie sought his boss and found him chatting with some French officers outside the palace, as ever tapping his boots with a riding crop. Waiting until the conversation broke, Eddie approached and saluted smartly to report that he had Miller's permission to speak to him. Mitchell heard out a presentation Eddie had practiced a thousand times in his head.

"I think I can do a better job there than I'm doing here," Eddie argued. "Anybody can do what I'm doing now. I'd like a chance to prove that I can learn to fly." Mitchell recognized in Rickenbacker that quality in himself that would not take no for an answer. He gave his blessing, albeit reluctantly.

While Miller had been recruiting Eddie, he had been enlisting a lot of other talents. The green young pilots available to him were junior members of the American elite, who had qualified for air service at designated universities across the United States. In such men as Hamilton Coolidge and his Harvard classmate Quentin Roosevelt, son of the former president, Eddie would encounter a more pernicious, deep-seated hostility than he had ever previously experienced. These children of privilege would have a hard time warming to a man who was, as one described it, "big, older, tough as nails." To them his "race track vernacular, his profane vocabulary" was not the language of another nation but the jargon of an inferior caste. For the moment, though, the future looked bright. Despite his national fame, Eddie knew that his chances of entering a U.S. flying school had been negligible, and that the war might have finished long before he could escape his responsibilities as an engineer or factory inspector. Now he was heading to the Second Aviation Instruction Center at Tours for primary flight training.

Only a physical exam still stood in the way, but Mitchell somehow wangled him a physician well acquainted with Eddie's racing days who without asking changed his age from twenty-seven to a barely qualifying twenty-five. Eddie neglected to mention his eye injury.

The Tours aerodrome, which the Americans took over in November 1917, was laid out similarly to several dozen advanced air bases scattered behind the length of the front. About half a mile square, bounded on one side by a road, the facility encompassed a wide, bumpy sod field. Inside the corners closest to the road stood large wooden hangars capable of holding a dozen aircraft, boxlike affairs opening their wide doors toward the fields. Armies of mechanics, three per plane, toiled to overhaul engines at night. Nearby lay the pilots' mess and sleeping quarters. Behind the hangars the support personnel—mechanics, workmen, drivers—were crowded into small wooden buildings. Four squadrons, eighty to ninety planes in all, and as many pilots, operated out of here, each squadron requiring some two hundred enlisted men to keep its planes flying, altogether almost a thousand men when headquarters, searchlight company, telephone squad, lighting plant, Red Cross, and YMCA personnel were taken into account.

When Eddie appeared for his first day of training, a crazy spectacle scattered over the uneven grass. A dozen aircraft, resembling giant prehistoric birds with stubby wings and spindly, naked tails, were zigzagging fast and violently down the field, others spinning around like dogs chasing their tails. Some poltergeist seemed to possess them all. One pivoted like a top and flipped over, its pilot climbing out with a sheepish grin, to the mocking applause of his messmates. Several of the planes stuck their tails into the air, "like church spires in a desert," wrote an amused pilot.

"This way!" shouted the men to other planes veering off toward a hangar. "Come back!" they hooted at the endless near-collisions. At last, two of the clipped-wing Penguin *rouleurs*—or "rollers"—turned dangerously toward each other, paused, then sped headlong forward, until their propellers met with a mighty splintering crash. The onlookers howled with delight, pounding one another and laughing so hard they could hardly breathe. "*Oh, là là! Il est perdu!* [There's no hope for him!]," muttered the French instructors under their breaths. Workers dragged the machines into the hangar, where stout French peasant women reattached thick linen cloth and the mechanics fixed broken spars and mounted new propellers.

Eddie and the others new to these weird contraptions, far indeed from the great soaring turns through the sky that they had anticipated, looked on as knots grew in their stomachs. Following the duplicitous advice of some practical jokers, a few trainees had turned out in full flight suits, overboots covering their regular footwear, with thick, warm teddy-bear suits to resist the extreme cold of altitude.

It took only a moment of watching the Penguins at play for the eager novices to see that the joke was on them. Their first lesson would be at the controls of vehicles incapable of flight, craft sporting impossibly stubby wings almost as wide as they were long—or, in more professional aviation parlance, of an extremely low aspect ratio. (Until the advent of powerful jet engines, flightworthiness almost always grew as a function of ever higher aspect ratios—the progressively wider relative proportion between a wing's length and breadth naturally found in most bird wings.)

When his turn came, Eddie clambered aboard, strapped on his belt, and adjusted his leather helmet, painfully aware how ungainly far he stuck out from the cockpit, his 6'2" frame a head or two higher than that of the average Frenchman for whom the plane had been designed. In front of him perched what looked like a camera tripod, sprouting wires from its apex out to the wings.

He nodded to his mechanic.

"*Coupe, plein gaz,*" said the mechanic.

"*Coupe, plein gaz,*" returned Eddie. The mechanic spun the propeller, drawing gas into the engine, which sputtered, then stopped.

"*Contact, réduisez.*"

"*Contact, réduisez,*" repeated Eddie. The mechanic again spun the propeller, this time kicking the three-cylinder engine into roaring, shuddering life. Eddie tightly gripped the *manette*, soon to become widely known as the joystick. Repeating his instructions in his mind to apply full gas and keep the tail up, he bolted down the field, pushed back against his seat, then threw his stick forward to raise the tail, which flipped up so quickly that he cut the engine. The craft spun around in a circle and stopped. Eddie let out a breath, realizing that he had forgotten the rudder at his feet but had anyway shut off the power, thus at least avoiding a humiliating flip. He would have to overcome his habit of steering with his hands alone.

Unlike the British, the French believed that the trainees should largely teach themselves how to fly, an approach akin to learning to swim by being thrown into a lake. Instructors delivered directions on the ground, rarely flying tandem with their trainees, their broken English replaced by torrents of Gallic as their exasperation grew. From first flight through to getting his wings, the tyro was usually alone in the cockpit. The instructor would hop into an unusable fuselage from which all the fabric had been stripped so that the controls were visible. "Now so to do a left-hand spin," he would bark, "you do this to the rudder and this with the stick." With the students gathered around, he would demonstrate how to move the controls for different maneuvers. Then the trainee would exchange places with him, manipulating the controls under the loud instruction. The student then went up to 5,000 feet or so and tried it himself. "It made a splendid solid foundation," wrote one airman, "with loads of self-confidence to back it up"—and also routinely killed pilots, although not in the Penguin phase. The pursuit training program, including the most dangerous advanced preparation in acrobatics, killed eleven students out of every hundred—and that before anybody started shooting at them.

Once more a mechanic flipped the propeller, and again Eddie bounded down the field, but this time pressing his feet on the rudder, correcting the machine's tendency to veer randomly off course. Slowly he got the hang of it, a process reminiscent, he said, of "the old trick of patting your head and rubbing your stomach simultaneously." In a day or two he learned to anticipate the Penguin's turns with a tap on the rudder, much like sailing a boat, when overcorrection will send the craft too far in the opposite direction. Without getting off the ground, Eddie had learned how to use the rudder to turn from side to side, use the stick to operate the elevator and keep the machine at a proper angle, and adjust the fuel to the engine or throttle. What he had believed might never come without conscious thought now came with what one aviator would call the "quickness and sureness of instinct."

Eddie and his fellow students then moved on to aircraft that would lift only a few feet off the ground, accustoming them to getting airborne, if only for yards at a time—the thrum of the engine softening, the motion suddenly smoother.

In the midst of his training, Eddie and his comrades caught sight of an airplane flying incredibly fast, outlined against the underbelly of white clouds. It shot upward, lost speed, then toppled nose down into a vrille, tumbling around and around like a wind-tossed leaf. Eddie had seen Lincoln Beachey perform breathtaking stunts, and then what the British fliers could do at Brooklands nearly a year ago, but this demonstration was wholly different, an aerial ballet at more than human speed. The pilot pulled out, nonchalantly executed some loops, then turned completely over in a *retournement*, buzzed the startled students, and landed perfectly, an impromptu demonstration that showed just how little these beginners had yet achieved.

One pilot whom Eddie would come to know, James Norman Hall, described in the third person his adventures and those of his friends in those heady early days. "They were daily enlarging their conceptions of distance and height and speed. They talked a new language and were developing a new cast of mind. They were like children who had grown up over night, whose horizons had been immeasurably broadened in the twinkling of an eye. They were still keenly conscious of the change which was upon them, for they were but fledgling aviators."

All would not be delight and wonder, however, during Eddie's first real flight. For such initiations the French had designated the Cauldron, an outdated mammoth biplane with a 43-foot wingspan and an 80-horsepower rotary engine. It featured already-faded Wright-brothers-era technology, relying on the dihedral warping of the wings to bank, a task replaced in all more modern aircraft with flaps or ailerons on the wings' trailing edges. "It was a slow moving crate," recalled Eddie, "wingspread galore, a biplane, and wires all over—that's why they called it a chicken coop." It was more like a big kite, the top wing so low that it offered a cutout even for a pilot's head as he sat in the tiny cab.

On his first time up, Eddie grew sick to his stomach with fear. He barely fit in the cockpit, and the cut of the top wing stared him straight in the face. A crosswind buffeted the cumbersome craft, wobbling him at high speed directly toward a hangar. Swinging through hollering instructors and wildly scattering pilots, he missed this by the merest feet, managed to straighten the plane out, then pulled back on the stick. That liberating sense of escaping the earth washed over him. The aircraft stabilized, its myriad wires buzzing an off-key symphony.

That first moment off the ground was notoriously dangerous, the engine often cutting out and many students dying an instant later. Instead of continuing straight on to crash-land, a muddled novice with a dead engine might bank back around to put down on the field, only to find himself lacking the necessary altitude and momentum. For all their instructors' profane exhortations, few amateurs could anticipate the strong lateral pull exacted by the Cauldron's rotary engine, which reached an invisible hand to wrestle the stick rightward. The early model engine featured a stationary crankcase around which the cylinders wheeled clockwise—in essence, spinning the entire engine like a gyroscope—to exert a torque of several hundred pounds in that direction. Turning *against* this took some effort and slowed the turn. Turning *into* the torque rapidly intensified the turn while steeply dipping the nose into an unanticipated dive, which could prove fatal when close to the ground.

Stepping on the right rudder and pushing the stick to the left, Eddie guided the Cauldron into a gentle rightward turn—much to his relief, as he still had to balance against the tricky crosswind. The Cauldron rose easily and gently into the sky. When Eddie turned back to the field, he prepared to touch down by depressing the stick and executing what he thought was a perfect landing, only to feel no reassuring bump. Craning over, he found himself still 25 feet off the ground. He made another pass and then another, shuddering as he realized how badly the hole in his right cornea cut into judgment of depth and location. Many new fliers have difficulty establishing ground level, even those with perfectly uncompromised eyesight, but with this trouble, he "couldn't project [his] vision progressively." It would take him time to adjust for his handicap. Finally managing to put down, he bolted behind the barracks to throw up.

With repeated trial and somehow nonfatal error, Eddie learned to land, single-minded determination gaining him his brevet, wings, and promotion in only seventeen days. The pilots coming in from programs back home had been put through eight to twelve weeks of ground school, then six to eight weeks of primary flight instruction. Even with days lost to fog and rain, he packed in twenty-five hours of flying time, the exigencies of war shrinking primary training to the barest minimum.

Now he was headed to Issoudun to become its chief engineer—in the table of organization, a ground job. He would have to figure out how to wangle advanced combat-level flight training once he arrived.

8.

A STEEP LEARNING CURVE

When Eddie reported as chief engineer in late September 1917, Issoudun resembled nothing so much as an immense flea market set amid one "helluva mudhole." What proposed to be the major U.S. aerodrome in France, just 100 miles southeast of Paris, was then no more than several square miles of uneven, rock-filled fields, whose miserable soil drained so poorly that the briefest showers left them badly mud-choked. At first no duckboards crossed the morass; walking anywhere meant "you lose a few feet for every one you gain," wrote one new arrival. Quentin Roosevelt quipped, "I don't see why the Frenchmen don't turn into frogs, by natural selection, after a thousand years of it."

Great piles of lumber and gasoline barrels, stacks of bathtubs and terracotta, and huge machinery crates lay scattered across fields so vast that one aviator compared them to the sea on a calm day. In the distance, a single road cut the monotony, detectable only by the rows of poplars lining it. The area's tiny villages had changed little over the centuries, their outlying farms sparse clusters of stone buildings whose tiled roofs were swathed in moss. Large rabbits seemed the only creatures to flourish here. "The weather was mean and disagreeable," remembered Eddie.

He could see French engineers, Indochinese laborers, and German prisoners building mess halls, Red Cross and YMCA buildings, barracks, a few garages, and a hospital. Propped by wooden flying buttresses, great Bessonneau hangars were emerging like bullish monsters from the bowels of the earth, squat wood-and-canvas improvisations swallowing aircraft through their gaping mouths. Ropes staked to the ground kept rigid the canvas covers stretched over raw planks. The great tents billowed and flapped even under light winds, their timber supports creaking with, to one pilot, "the quiet sound made by ships at sea." Forty-five Bessonneau hangars would soon make Issoudun the largest of the twenty-two American aerodromes in France. By November 1917, the sprawling facility encompassed nine fields, spread over some 3 miles to minimize aerial collisions: three for basic flight training; five for advanced, including acrobatics and formation flying; and one for a cemetery, which the students called Field 13, such was the human cost of America's frantic entry into this high-tech conflict. "Yesterday Philippauteaux fell and was killed. Another Tours pal finished. The day before O. H. Wilson fell at the same field and was killed. Seems like all the bunch will be gone before they reach the front," wrote Lieutenant Walter Avery of the 95th Aero Squadron in his journal. Without a beat he continued, "Kellogg borrowed my hair soap and is washing the dog. Cute darn *chien* weighs about 5 lbs."

All was "hustle, activity . . . and loads of mud," another would put it. The men soon grasped that they were part of one of the largest and fastest mobilizations in human history. "The fact that your bunk is hard and your mattress is a layer of newspapers to keep out the cold, never so much as enters your head," scribbled pilot Hamilton Coolidge blithely. The pilots and support personnel didn't even seem to mind the mountains of "corned willy," or corned beef military rations. When they could, the men crowded around stoves, three or four games of chess, one or two of checkers, always going on.

Over nineteen months, the American air service morphed from a ghost corps of 65 officers and about 1,000 enlisted men to an effective workforce of 190,000, more soldiers than fought on both sides at Gettysburg—20,000 of them officers. By war's end, the United States was fielding 45 squadrons airborne on the front, deploying 740 aircraft, nearly 800 pilots, and 500 observers. The competition for pilot spots proved ferocious: At least 50,000 young men applied, but only 1,402 graduated from advanced training schools to fly in action. Yet by the Armistice, the air service would come to boast more aces—men who had shot down five or more enemy planes—than its entire officer complement at the outbreak of war. Issoudun would become a self-sufficient city with 150 barracks, 91 hangars, its own sewers, waterworks, fire department, hospitals, streets, target ranges—even its own newspaper.

For starters, however, Eddie and the other chosen few crowded uncomfortably under damp, chilly tents. He traveled to Paris with several million dollars at his disposal to search for machine tools to overhaul engines, find other equipment for general shopwork, and locate automobiles for transportation—difficult enough in the war-strained French capital, where coal proved so precious that visitors could only expect weekly hot water for baths, and sugar was almost priceless. He operated his first machine shop out of the back of two trucks, then started a salvage department to recycle and repurpose any materials that could be scrounged. Somehow, equipment kept rolling in over the 7-mile track connecting the railroad hub in a nearby small town to the aerodrome. They improvised when the right tools or machines weren't available, inspiring one commander to dub Lieutenant Rickenbacker and other early squadron personnel "masters of difficulties." Gradually Eddie and his many men brought shape and order to Issoudun, although the immense construction project would never quite get finished.

As irritating to Eddie as the rock-studded fields that endlessly crippled aircraft was the disposition of the pilot cadre, who showed up bright with promise and breathless to be kings of the air. The cream of the U.S. ground schools, these men proudly (if not arrogantly) wore their Sam Brownes—thick leather belts with a shoulder strap reaching diagonally across the chest to the right shoulder—brass trimmings, gold and black hats, coats, leggings, and polished boots. "These were Yale and Harvard and Princeton boys, rich men's sons, all of them grand American youth," recollected Eddie with uncharacteristic deference. He was working around the clock to put the aerodrome together and hammer the planes back into shape so these aspiring white-hot fliers could go on to advanced training—and then to the front. He had little time to fly himself. Whenever he could, he'd take up a plane, but often without watchful, guiding instructors, which seemed to suit him fine. Even—perhaps especially—in the uncharted wilderness of the sky, he had been born to learn by doing.

Short of manpower, Eddie set his pilots to building roads and sidewalks, laying hangar floors, and cleaning latrines. The young war eagles felt particularly irritated when issued tin buckets and ordered to scout the fields for rocks, "some of them as big as your head," remembered one flier. They often worked shoulder to shoulder with German prisoners, disparaging this implacable taskmaster who seemed to take everything far too seriously. Few of these university men had ever encountered someone like Eddie, much less been constrained to submit to so graceless a tradesman's directions. They whispered "Heinie" under their breath in his presence, but "the more they hated me, the more I put them to work," recalled their unmoved boss.

"Lt. Rickenbacker won't give us more planes if we bust any, so we waste good flying weather cussing him out," wrote Lieutenant Jimmy Meissner, son of a U.S. Steel board member, who had dropped out of Cornell to join the air service. While Eddie no doubt derived some enjoyment from setting his charges straight, he was laboring under enormous difficulties. "I couldn't get propellers fast enough to keep the planes in shape." Each blade had to be crafted with care and perfectly balanced with the other—failure to do so rapidly killed good men. Even working around the clock in late 1917, the mechanics at Issoudun could only turn out six propellers a day, not nearly enough to meet the ongoing wastage.

Disappearing into the shop one winter day, Eddie worked with a master signal electrician to craft a mudguard that attached to aircraft landing gear, shielding the propeller from the clods of mud and rock that it kicked up. For several days, the pilots mocked the invention. The chuckling died away soon enough as the incidence of propeller fractures dropped precipitously. Rickenbacker mudguards were soon in wide use across France.

The Nieuports' rigid construction meant that they held up poorly under hard landings, especially on winter-frozen fields. A later base commander recalled a three-day period during which not a single one of his eighty-seven 23-meter Nieuports was flyable. A certain gallows humor ruled as random-seeming accidents piled up. One pilot buzzed a young boy standing near a field and killed him. An instructor shot himself in the stomach while demonstrating gun safety. Telephone wires strung up one evening would snag an early morning takeoff the next day; a discarded meal sack would catch the landing gear of an incoming aircraft and wreck it. One pilot landed on top of a cow. Roosevelt wrote home about how mud kicked up during one of his takeoffs broke his propeller before he could clear the field. Fire burst from the debris-punctured gas tank and swallowed the entire aircraft in the thirty seconds it took him to set it back down. He leaped out, his pants and sheepskin-lined boots already ablaze.

Late one afternoon, a French instructor asked the twenty-three-year-old pilot—and future ace—Reed Chambers to fly one of the Nieuports in need of an engine overhaul over to the main field, where several of the Bessonneau hangars served as repair facilities, crowded with dozens of airplanes awaiting service. Cheekily confident of his skills—"I was very hot at that point and handled the thing like a family automobile"—Chambers skipped over the landing field, "horsed" his plane around, and landed at dusk "right on a dime, right in between all these airplanes." The cocky pilot hopped out of the cockpit only to find a man on a Harley-Davidson motorcycle with sidecar—the chief engineer, realized Chambers—skidding to a halt in front of him, yelling that he was a "blankety-blankety fool."

"Don't you realize that all we do is spend our lives here trying to keep these things working," raged Eddie, "and you come in and land right among a gob of them, with a chance of cracking them all up?" Chambers wasn't the only hotshot pilot bored silly with the aerodrome routine and eager for more dangerous action. Most of them blew off steam in their planes, skimming 5 or 10 feet above country roads in pursuit of automobiles or goats, flying through flocks of crows to knock bunches of them out of the sky. When they crashed, as often they did, Eddie's mechanics had to drive out in a truck and retrieve what was left. When one came down in the woods, they'd have to cut a new road, or build a bridge if the plane had pancaked into a swamp. The mechanics eventually stocked about 29,000 different parts to keep just the Nieuports in working order.

Seeking a little fun at the expense of this hotshot whom all the pilots loathed, Chambers called Eddie to attention and excoriated him, telling him to watch his language or face charges. Chambers's overalls hid his insignia, so Eddie couldn't tell if he really outranked him. He did, but only barely, having been commissioned first lieutenant a few months earlier. Even so, he must have known the old army adage that "seniority among lieutenants is like virginity among whores."

Eddie made a quick decision. He flashed a grin, "as only Rick can grin," recalled Chambers, and laughed. "Well, all I can say is, I wish I could make that kind of landing." Did Chambers want to hop into the sidecar and come down to the mess for dinner with him? A surprised Chambers accepted.

Eddie's ability to move at flank speed across the face of adversity again served him well that evening as he and Chambers became friends. Some men never master this valuable skill; others have it taught to them. Dwight Eisenhower, one week younger than Eddie, learned this at West Point when the boxing coach told the sour, bruised, and beaten young cadet that "if you can't smile when you get up from a knockdown, you're never going to lick an opponent." The tough streets of Columbus and the chewed-up racetracks had taught Eddie to "believe and fight like a wildcat for that which I want, and I fight to the last ditch. At such times as I have been licked, it has been my experience that 99 times out of a hundred—and I have been licked often—it was just the right thing to have happen."

Chambers found Eddie "one of the most sincere fellows that I've ever seen," and patriotic, "despite his German name." Unlike most of the other pilots, Chambers had no polished education, having been kicked out of his Kansas high school after an altercation with a teacher. He had slipped back after hours and painted the school with a pint of skunk essence collected over several seasons of winter trapping. His alma mater closed for a week, and the prank earned him a "good shellacking" from his father, "which I certainly deserved." The rambunctious young man soon left home to seek his fortune—first in the harvest fields of western Kansas, then in the Tennessee National Guard. Sheer determination finagled him into flight school at the outset of the war. In Eddie he at once discerned a kindred, self-creating, rebellious spirit. Rickenbacker vented about the difficulties of keeping the planes in airworthy condition with few spare parts and even fewer mechanics who knew a screwdriver from a pair of pliers. "I thought I'd had troubles," Chambers remembered thinking.

That evening Chambers took a bus back to Field 7 and told his fellow pilots that they'd been wrong about Eddie. "He's really a swell guy, when you get to know him." His friends, many of whom had trained with him in the United States, were more than dubious, accusing Chambers of backsliding, selling out, even of being a sucker. He was perplexed. Certainly they groused when Eddie gave them grunt work, but it was all for the common purpose. There seemed to be more at stake here, an uglier antagonism rooted somewhat in his German-sounding name but more deeply in a combination of envy about the fame already conferred by his racing career and pure class disdain. Most of those young men believed that Eddie had neither earned nor deserved the right to be one of them. He was simply not one of the band of brothers. "Really, the American of the mechanic class is a pretty fine specimen, I think," wrote Roosevelt rather unpleasantly of the men he had been forced to work alongside, an attitude that chilled Chambers to the bone.

By November the school was up and running, but Eddie still had no time to take the regular course. Between tasks he ducked into lectures and on occasion snuck a plane out, picking up what he could without benefit of direct instruction. He overheard a conversation about getting into a tailspin—a good stunt to know, opined the instructor, because a spinning plane is hard to hit in combat. To go into it, simply stall the machine and kick the rudder hard. With nothing more than that to go on, Eddie decided to give the most dangerous maneuver in aviation a try.

One chilly November day, he zipped up his Eskimo suit—government-issued, fur-lined, full-body outfits—grabbed his leather helmet, goggles, and mittens, and walked over to the waiting 15-meter Nieuport 23. (The 15-meter designation applied to the square meters of wing surface.) Most striking about this aircraft was its size. "The little thing looks like a toy," wrote Coolidge, "but its motor has the roar of a battery of heavy guns." The top wing arced much like an awning over the smaller lower wing in so-called sesquiplane (one-and-a-half-wing) design, a V-shaped spar attaching one to the other. Each wing extended only 13 feet, the whole craft weighing 780 pounds unloaded, a little more than a quarter the poundage of a Volkswagen Beetle. Its small wings made it extremely maneuverable and nimble—"delightfully sensitive," judged Coolidge—but also, as Chambers more dryly noted, "a very tricky little airplane to fly." While its diminutive size and weight enabled it to circle far more tightly than any modern fixed-wing fighter jet, it also required constant attention to the controls.

Eddie scrambled up to wriggle uncomfortably into a cockpit so narrow that a modern writer has likened such entrance to fitting a cork into a cham-pagne bottle. His shoulders nearly touched the upper longerons, and his head stuck out as usual, making it difficult for him to read the gauges—not that these tended to work well anyway.

Resting his right hand on the mahogany joystick between his legs, he glided his thumb up to the button they called the "blip switch" at its tip. Much of a pilot's effectiveness—indeed, his ability to stay alive—came from how effectively he "pressed the tit," as some fliers put it. Flying a rotary-engined machine was part science, part art, and always unpredictable. The rotary flipped the usual engine arrangement inside out: Instead of moving, the crankshaft—the crank that translates the piston's up-and-down motion into circular motion to turn the propeller—remained stationary while the rest of the engine rotated rapidly around it, propeller and all. Not need-ing a radiator or flywheel, rotary engines were lighter than conventional engines, but their main advantage lay in a spinning engine's ability to cool itself more efficiently than the traditional layout.

The cockpit was quite spare, featuring a tachometer, a Zenith height gauge, an airspeed indicator, and a compass. Just five instruments con-trolled the plane: the stick and blip switch, a single rudder bar at the pilot's feet, and, by his left knee, a large lever (controlling a tapered needle valve regulating the flow of fuel into the engine) and a smaller one (operating a slide valve that admitted air into the mix). The aircraft lacked the throttle common to all later planes—an instrument like a car accelerator that revs the engine to higher rpms. Nor did the Le Rhône rotary engine contain a carburetor, the device that determines the proper mix of fuel and air. (The air mixed with the gas to create a combustible vapor that was drawn into the engine and ignited to drive the pistons.) The pilot himself served as the carburetor by regulating that critical mix, causing one pilot to comment tersely that "you flew the engine as much as you flew the airplane." However, he could only reduce the gas flow to take the engine rpms from 1,200 to 800—below that the engine simply quit. Even at the lowest end the rpms were still too high to taxi or land safely, which was where the blip switch came in. One tap broke the flow of electricity from magnetos to spark plugs and switched off the engine, immediately dropping ground- or airspeed.

Thus when the rotary engine turned over, it roared to full power, "and you were *immediately* ready to take off!" said British pilot Cecil Lewis. With the engine whining like an angry hornet and the machine pressing insistently against the chocks, the pilot began to blip the switch on and off to tame the imminent headlong surge downfield, somewhat like driving a car without brakes but with the driver's foot continuously flooring or completely releasing the accelerator. The only means of slowing or stopping was cutting off the ignition at critical junctures. Operating the blip switch created the sound so familiar in old movies: *Br-rppp, Br-rp, Br-rp! Br-rpppppp* . . . Danger lurked for the pilot who pressed it too long. While the engine might be off, fuel was still flowing into it, accumulating unburned in the cowling, the protective nose cover. Start the engine with too much unconsumed fuel lurking there and the spark would touch off a fire, never a good idea in a plane made of shellacked fabric and wood. Most fires burned out quickly but would still cut off the engine for long moments, which could prove extremely dangerous—especially at such vulnerable junctures as landing, when the pilot most needed the blip switch.

Just before shouting "Contact" to the mechanic, Eddie adjusted his goggles, cinching the strap so tightly that the rims cut into his face and made his head ache. The goggles protected his eyes not only from the wind but also from the oil spewing from the engine, yet another inconvenience of the rotary design. The engine lubricated itself from a small tank, passing the oil through the spinning system to exhaust through a topside port. The oil of choice was not a petroleum-based product like those used today but castor oil, a vegetable derivative used in large part because it would neither mix with gas nor easily degrade. The Nieuport would expel 2 gallons or more over the course of an hour—pilots nicknamed rotary engines "whirling sprays"—much of it onto the pilot, whom it often covered, cloying nostrils with the smell of burned liquid. When ingested (and it was hard not to do), the oil induced nausea and diarrhea. (Between the wars, castor oil would become a favorite tool that Italian fascists would force down political prisoners' throats.) Oil once coated Coolidge's goggles and windscreen so thickly as to effectively blind him. "I never came so near crashing before." Some pilots carried a flask of blackberry brandy aloft to ease the discomfort of what they inhaled.

Blipping the engine, Eddie jostled downwind, counterpressing the rudder when the roaring air or a bump on the field swung him one way or the other. At the end of the field, he reversed the Nieuport and released the blip switch. As the machine shuddered forward, the wind picking up in his face, Eddie kept straight with a tap on the rudder. Within 400 feet he lifted off. Rising high above Issoudun, the air grew less densely resistant, so he slightly adjusted the large lever forward to reduce gas flow, ensuring that the engine wouldn't flood and cut out. When he descended, he'd need to do the reverse. (The French curiously built the controls contrary to most norms that increased gas flow when pushed forward.) As when driving, he listened to the thrum of consumption, alert for the raspy crackle that indicated a too-lean mixture, or the muffled sluggish rumble of undue richness. He made sure that small drops of oil were clinging to the wing's leading edge and that the exhaust was bluish white, both signs of the engine's getting oil. Wiping a smear of castor oil off his goggles with the back of his mitten, he pushed the stick to keep his tail up. The tail-heavy Nieuport needed persistent forward pressure to stay level. At every moment, the pilot adjusted rudder and stick.

Eddie pushed the joystick leftward into a gentle port bank, offsetting the strong counterclockwise torque exerted by the 300 pounds of spinning engine, which made handling it akin to "trying to fly a gyroscope," as one American ace put it. This was where Eddie's superior racetrack-honed instincts took over. He almost unconsciously registered the level of vibration, too much of which could indicate a fouled spark plug. A shift of wind on his cheek would alert him to the plane's "skidding" sideways or its failure to execute a clean turn. All senses were subjected to the purpose of flying— gauging and checking, listening and feeling, registering those pressures of a turn in the seat, which gave rise to the telling expression "flying by the seat of your pants," the overall raw interaction of human flesh and machine.

No engineers had yet devoted careers to drawing lessons about pilot behavior—and error—from the chilling roster of fatal crashes, or to establishing guidelines about when a pilot might be likely to reach critical levels of impairment from hypoxia, altitude sickness, or hypothermia. No instruments had yet been redesigned to make them more useful in deadly combat or terrifying emergency: no warning lights or buzzers to indicate an upcoming hazard, no turn or bank indicators. Pilots often flew without fuel gauges, just with the knowledge that they took off with about two and a quarter hours of flying time at normal speed. Teams of scientists had yet to determine the best angle of approach and speed to land under various conditions. No pilot knew about wind shear or could sit in a seat engineered to withstand an impact. Pilots were largely on their own, picking up insights from fellow fliers and always, if they wished to live, paying attention. Aviators in the deadly French skies of the Great War mostly just reacted when things started going wrong. When the patent clasp of Coolidge's harness— which had "a way of coming undone at the crucial moment," as he mildly commented in a letter home—sprang one day as he was looping upside down, he was nearly pitched out. So he fixed special handles inside his cockpit for such emergencies. He and his brethren were writing the new rules of safety and aircraft performance with their experience—and often their high-spirited blood.

Nor did an airman taking off expect, as is common today, that his machine would work flawlessly or easily. These cantankerous, unreliable, finicky, altogether dangerous craft remained true marvels to those who handled them and miraculously took them at speed—when things went well—to heights only infrequently attained by balloonists. If they were perilous, so was life in the trenches, and there it was much less exhilarating. Lieutenant Lansing C. Holden Jr. of the 95th Aero Squadron explained that all there was to acrobatics was getting up high, making sure your belt was tight, and just "letting her go" while keeping your eyes inside the machine.

Eddie took the Nieuport twenty miles from Issoudun over a stretch of woodland where no one would see him. In the few minutes he took to get there, the frigid air so numbed his face that he could barely move his mouth. His hands began to feel a little clumsy. The constant cold, particularly bitter under flying conditions—it dropped about a degree for every 300 feet the pilot climbed—gave many pilots persistent hacking coughs, some of them actual pneumonia. "You cannot imagine how bitter it is," wrote Lieutenant William Muir Russel of the 95th. "I put on a couple of knitted masks, then Allen's leather fur-lined helmet and my goggles. Even then, the part of my face which is exposed stiffens and prevents me from moving my mouth." Joked Roosevelt in a letter home, "I don't know how angels stand it." Quipped another aviator, "And now that we have had a chance to freeze our ass in woolen pants who dares to speak of 'sunny' France? Nobody."

Reaching 10,000 feet, Eddie tried to throw his machine into a tailspin but failed—"My muscles simply would not obey my command"—and flew back without trying again, feeling "thoroughly ashamed of myself." The next day he went back up and, steeling will over completely rational fear, pulled the plane upward into the sky until it slowed, then stalled, the moment when a combination of wing angle and decrease in speed disrupts the airflow and deprives the wing of lift, leaving nothing to support the aircraft's weight. He stomped on the rudder, forcing lift on one wing, while the other lost it. The nose plummeted, and the airplane started spinning. No situation is more dangerous for the pilot of a fixed-wing aircraft.

He pulled out after only one complete turnaround, whose couple of seconds had seemed forever. Even that fleeting experience induced the most disorienting cocktail of sensations: vertigo, nausea, and panic. To imagine a spin, as one recent writer has imagined it, visualize yourself dangling several hundred feet above the streets of New York inside a car whose back bumper is attached by rope to a flagpole sticking out from the top floor of a skyscraper. An invisible hand sets the rope swinging in a wide circle, while separately spinning the car at its end. Then the rope is cut, and the car plummets toward the concrete. Such is spin—a nightmare that sets off every alarm bell in the human brain and body.

In 1949, the predecessor of the Federal Aviation Administration took spin recovery off the list of requirements for attaining a pilot's license, because too many people were getting killed as they trained for it. Even today, one is unlikely to survive a spin anywhere within 300 feet of the ground in nearly any kind of aircraft. The most terrible aspect of the experience may well be that an untrained pilot's instinctive response—which seems entirely logical once the screaming in his or her head has reached a deafening crescendo—will not undo the crazy rotation but actually hasten impact. "If the first time you go into a spin is inadvertent . . . then it's too damned bad because you're not going to do the right thing," James Patton, chief of flight operations at NASA's Langley Research Center, told a 1980 congressional hearing. It resembles an apprentice driver's natural but disastrous response to the first skid, jerking the wheel against it instead of steering into it.

Today's pilots have the benefit of much research into the physics of spin and have been taught well-developed recovery techniques; still they are advised not to practice it. In the early days, a spin at any height was a virtual death sentence, the "graveyard spiral." It was, noted one British pilot, "something mysterious and deadly, a danger from which there was no salvation, which attacked one suddenly and for no reason in mid-air." "Nobody quite knew how, nor indeed how or why aircraft spun at all," observed a prominent scientist (and brave pilot) who would undergo dozens of spins and publish the first scientific paper on the topic in March 1918. The British pilot Cecil Lewis simply noted that "spinning was the one thing the young pilot fought shy of."

Watching Lincoln Beachey, Eddie may have seen the first pilot to throw his aircraft into a spin and recover. In general, prewar pilots conducted their loops, vertical banks, and steep climbing turns all without breaking the cardinal rule that one must never slow to stall speed. As war brought increasingly deadly fire, pilots began to see the spin as a critical evasive maneuver.

After that one turn, he "skedaddled home," frightened but exhilarated. Over the next weeks, he repeatedly put himself into extreme harm's way far from the aerodrome, until he could "flutter down almost to the ground." Just as with his driving, he methodically learned the limits of his machine on curves, how much the tires could bear, inching up to the very edge but not over. The other pilots bragged about how many revolutions they made before pulling out, but Eddie kept quiet.

Two weeks after he had turned insubordinate rage into friendship with Chambers, Eddie drummed up coverage for many of his engineering responsibilities in order to devote more time to flying. He joined the top fliers assembled at Field 7 for the final series of tests in formation flying. Of that colorful formation of Coolidge, Jim Meissner, Douglas Campbell, Roosevelt, and the rest of the dozen and a half pilots, only Reed Chambers acknowledged him. Soon the others weren't speaking to Chambers either, because of his open friendship with Eddie, which this pettiness only deepened.

Yet the officers' attitudes would soon gradually shift toward this outcast whose skill somehow offset his rawness. They noticed how he got terribly airsick every time he flew and performed acrobatics. Many times, reported Chambers, Eddie would "come in with everything in the cockpit all messed up." Doug Campbell commented that a lot of people in that situation would just have quit, "but he decided he wasn't going to quit; he was going to get on with it. And he got on with it." It took him many weeks *after* he had reached the front to completely conquer the nausea. "He had tremendous willpower," Campbell noted, which soon became obvious to everybody.

In late December, Eddie found an opportunity to shock the status quo and prove himself one of the best. On Sunday afternoons at Issoudun, many of the pilots gathered for a game of football, quite a few of the brass coming from Paris and American Expeditionary Forces headquarters at Chaumont to watch. New rules instituted in 1906 (the year after nineteen college players of this violent sport, including a West Point cadet, were fatally injured) had opened up the game, and prep-school and college men flocked to new football programs. That year the forward pass became legal, and massed formations were proscribed. Some of the players wore flimsy leather helmets resembling fliers' headgear, but many did not.

In the middle of that winter game, the players' attention was pulled upward to an airplane stuttering and popping directly overhead, clearly in some sort of distress, which then seemed to lose all control, falling into a tailspin only a few hundred feet from the ground. Players and spectators scattered in every direction to escape the flitting and bobbing Nieuport.

At just 50 feet up, it miraculously pulled out of free fall and zoomed even closer, the whine of its engine bewildering the watchers, who knew that entering such a spin that low bordered on the suicidal. Only days earlier they had buried Lieutenant John Paull, whom such a fate had overtaken. There was no latitude should the engine quit, the controls fail, or the pilot make even the smallest mistake on the rudder—any of which was a likely contingency in those early days. One pilot perished every week on average at the school, many from mishandling spins. Overall, one pilot out of nine would die in training alone, not even counting the far worse mortality rates when they met the enemy. No environment kills people more readily than when new technology intersects with war. "Since coming to Issoudun a month and a half ago," wrote Avery, "of our bunch Sawhill, Llewellyn, Woodruff in hospital. Paul[l], Leach, Wright, Turner and Hopkins killed. Who will be next? Me?—Possibly yes, possibly no. I hope to get to the front. Not croak here."

In a breathtaking demonstration of skill and daring—a tribute, really, to the showmanship of Lincoln Beachey at the Iowa State Fair years earlier—the unheralded Eddie Rickenbacker had "pulled a Brody," a phrase immortalizing the foolhardy tavernkeeper who in 1885 fulfilled his boast that he could jump off the new Brooklyn Bridge and live. Captain Carl Andrew Spatz, who had replaced James Miller as base commander, grounded Eddie for thirty days, but the chief engineering officer had boldly carved out a place among the best pilots at Issoudun. Had it been too crazy? Hardly, because it required an unnerving command of the machine. Yet Eddie would later call it a "damn fool thing to do." Nevertheless, he had shown that he would not settle for just fitting in but would excel on his own terms.

In January 1918, Eddie became the first graduate of advanced flight school. Amid all the confusion of Issoudun, he and the other pilots had proven to be quick, adept learners, finding ways over a few short months to hone new skills and prepare to meet an enemy who had spent the last three years perfecting theirs. Tasked with checking out new aircraft for problems, Coolidge flew fifteen to twenty test flights a day under the supervision of a French instructor with combat experience. "He can feel the defects of a machine in a five minute flight," wrote Coolidge, "where it usually takes me ten." When the Frenchman died in one test too many, Coolidge kept on, getting better and better at diagnosing problems, developing "an eye for little details such as missing bolts, cotter pins, warped wings, etc."—the small matters that would keep him, and many others, alive.

When the list was posted for gunnery school at Cazaux, the final step before going to the front, an exasperated Eddie could not find his name.

"You're too important and valuable here," Captain "Tooey" Spatz told him.

"I have a man who is my assistant, a much older man than I am and probably much better than I am," pleaded Eddie, "and he can do what you need done here; but he can't do what I think I might be able to do by going to the front."

"Well, those are my orders," Spatz shot back.

Eddie had not come this far to get stuck at Issoudun. Reed Chambers had also received orders to teach flying at Tours, his commanding officer only relenting to assign him to Cazaux when he saw tears in Chambers's eyes. Eddie hatched a plan. The grippe, as they then called the flu, had ravaged the camp that winter, pressing hard on the pilots, who spent long periods in the cruel cold of high altitude only to come down into the perpetual chill and damp of the barracks. Eddie had a bad bug, perhaps the grippe, compounded by exhaustion, and it showed. The head surgeon, Major Ralph Goldthwaite, put him into the hospital. Eddie enlisted the doctor in his scheme, acknowledging that part of the reason for his openly getting sick was to give his assistant engineer a chance to run the shop, so that Eddie could prove that he was not indispensable and could therefore be released for combat. Likely amused at this determination, Goldthwaite agreed, and Eddie lay flat for two weeks.

When he got out, he went over to see Spatz, whom he found signing his orders for Cazaux. Why the change of heart? he asked. "I'm onto your little game, and if you feel that way about it, I don't want you around here anyway." In the captain, as in Billy Mitchell before him, Eddie had found a kindred spirit. In the last month of the war, when Spatz had received orders to return home, he begged a week off to fly combat missions on the front, and without anyone's permission stretched this threefold, shooting down three of the enemy. Spatz, also of German descent, would, like Eddie, change his name (to Spaatz) and go on to become a general in World War II and the first chief of staff of the U.S. Air Force.

Eddie was inching ever closer to his dream of getting up to the real thing.

9.

AIRCRAFT MORPH INTO DEADLY WEAPONS

In early January 1918, a truck dropped Eddie and fifteen other pilots off for gunnery school at the picturesque French beachside resort of Arcachon, some 40 miles southwest of Bordeaux on the Biscay coast. It couldn't have been more different from the boring plains of Issoudun and its endless shoe- and soul-sucking mud. Here a pleasant esplanade separated the coarse golden-sand seashore and blue Atlantic from a parade of stately Victorian villas and hotels. For the three weeks of training, they lived in the Grand Hotel, a six-story wedding-cake white palace only steps from the beach, and ate themselves full of fresh bread and *gravettes,* the deliciously briny local oysters, all washed down with bottles of Entre-Deux-Mers, a dry white Bordeaux, or the local red. "All got mildly stewed on rouge and grenadine," reported one airman with a certain satisfaction. On Sundays, their only day off, they peered into shop windows or walked south along the beach until they came to the 350-foot-high Great Dune of Pyla, Europe's largest sand eminence, from atop which unfolded mile upon mile of low, pine-studded hummocks: "a curious country," commented Roosevelt, "nothing but sand and pine trees, planted by Napoleon's orders." For the not-long-ago poor boy from Columbus, far from the crackerjack kitsch of Olentangy Park, this expensive cosmopolitan resort must have seemed something of a dream, the faded expression of a world inexplicable and almost gone, but one that he would soon be risking his life to preserve.

The isolated, unpopulated Landes timber country—Europe's largest maritime pine forest—proved an ideal location for the École de Tir Aérien (School of Aerial Marksmanship), or just Cazaux for short. No bullet would find an accidental billet here. The aerodrome itself lay several miles inland from the town, its fields carved from the forests on the northeast shore of a 14,000-acre tidal basin lake, on whose calm waters French instructors first took out Eddie and the others. Aboard motorboats, they shot .30 caliber rifles at a cigar-shaped canvas sock, 10 to 12 feet long, 8 to 10 inches tall, dragged behind another boat. This exercise taught "deflection shooting," timing shots so that the quarry moved into one's line of fire. Had Eddie ever fired a gun before, it had been at most once or twice; his aim proved atrocious, compounded in part by the black spot floating in his injured eye. Day after day he returned, spending hours bobbing up and down, getting off 800 to 1,000 rounds, his shoulder growing sore from the recoil—until he finally started hitting the target.

The difficulties he encountered afloat paled against being sent up against a softly descending parachute aboard the pitching, bucking, rolling platform of a Nieuport. The pilot aimed by aligning two rings, a fixed back sight and a front sight, the latter attached to a wind vane designed to compensate for the aircraft's speed. Merely lining up a target, much less hitting it, proved extremely difficult. On one of Eddie's first outings, his wild shots severed the 500-foot-long rope just yards behind the tow plane. The pilot and observer dove for cover as the sock floated away and "raised more hell than seven boxes of monkeys," recalled Eddie.

"It is very difficult to keep your sight steadily on the objective," wrote Coolidge. "It means moving the hand a little on the stick, a slight pressure on one toe, then the other perhaps, and so on"—a task compounded because the school's trainers were battered Nieuports, "the most awful old crocks," in Roosevelt's estimation. The French aviators warned the Americans not to try any steep dives or fancy acrobatics, an injunction hard to follow when chasing a parachute to the ground. "You get up in the air, and get excited over trying to follow up the parachute," explained Roosevelt, "and you forget all about your machine except as a means of keeping your sights on the target." Over the next several months, the wings fatally tore off one machine, while target shooting distracted two more men into a deadly midair collision.

With no other place to land besides the aerodrome, many pilots experiencing engine problems simply put down among the pines. One commander wrote somewhat tongue-in-cheek, even in a formal report, about how a "large group of pilots developed a tendency to roost in the tree-tops, and the men in charge of the motorcycle 'trouble-shooter' got used to quick dashes into the forest to assist the aviators who had suddenly developed this tree climbing instinct. They were usually found sitting quietly on some limb waiting for assistance, while the machine hung in bits about them."

Like so much else in First World War aviation, gunnery had evolved at a breathtaking speed. At the outset, no one—not Beachey, not Blériot—had ever shot at one plane from another. Enemy aviators simply waved to one another in passing, acknowledging that their membership in the tiny airborne brotherhood confronted them with deadlier common foes—air and gravity—than national enmity. Shooting at another pilot somehow seemed unsportsmanlike. Then aircraft, which most observers had believed would prove no more than a theatrical diversion, quickly revealed their tactical worth, and the stakes began to change steeply. As the British retreated from southern Belgium into France in that first August of the war, French aerial reconnaissance warned their ally that the German II Corps would soon encircle them unless they took quick action. In late August, a keen-eyed German pilot helped the German 8th Army surround and destroy the Russian 2nd Army at the crucial Battle of Tannenberg. Perhaps most critically, aerial reconnaissance helped to bring about the Paris-saving "Miracle of the Marne" in early September, when the aircraft designer and pilot Louis Breguet established that Alexander von Kluck's army was swinging east of its planned line of advance, which opened up a 30-mile gap in the German front. Pressing decisively into this opportunity, the British and French broke the Germans' debilitating month-long offensive.

As both sides settled into siege lines, field officers began to rely increasingly on intelligence gleaned by aerial "scouts," which could spot troops massing for assault and direct artillery fire. While the ground war stalled and then stagnated, the race for air superiority went into higher gear as both sides poured in men and resources, asking for the first time whether airpower could provide a decisive three-dimensional advantage. It didn't take long to realize that interfering with reconnaissance activities could effectively blind the enemy, so pilots and their observers started carrying pistols and carbines aloft—though the chances of inflicting an incapacitating wound were slim, except at virtually point-blank range.

Lieutenant Louis Strange of the Royal Flying Corps may have been the first Allied pilot to mount a machine gun on his aircraft, but it yielded miserable results. On August 22, 1914, two German machines appeared over the RFC field at Maubeuge in northeastern France. Two B.E.2s quickly took off, armed with hand grenades and bombs, their only and highly improbable hope of inflicting damage being to drop explosives into enemy cockpits. Strange took off shortly thereafter in his Henry Farman aircraft with his observer behind a Lewis machine gun. The Germans climbed to 5,000 feet, far above the Farman as it struggled to get to 3,500 under the added weight of the gun. "The enemy machine made off while we were still climbing up over our aerodrome, and I imagine its occupants must have enjoyed a good laugh at our futile efforts," reported Strange. On landing, his commanding officer ordered him to unship the gun and mount, which "I had been at some pains to devise," and told his observer to use a rifle instead.

Only three and a half years later at Cazaux, Eddie was practicing with a Lewis light machine gun, which was mounted on the upper wing to fire forward over the propeller's arc, his Nieuport engine now powerful enough to make the gun's weight virtually insignificant. The Lewis bore what resembled a flat-head shovel handle at its butt and a drum, shaped like a Kodak slide carousel, of ninety-seven rounds of .303 caliber ammunition. After emptying the magazine, the pilot pulled the gun down toward him on a track to reload. Rounds frequently jammed, and Eddie and his fellows spent considerable time at Cazaux learning how to clear them.

Strange recounted the harrowing tale of how he had been closing on an Aviatik near the Flemish town of Menin when his gun jammed. After exhausting his ammunition under furious fire from the German observer, he tried to release the empty drum, which would not budge. Wedging the stick between his knees, he tugged with both hands, still without effect, and finally stood up to get a better purchase. His Martinsyde, then in a steep climb, stalled just as his knees loosened their grip on the stick, flicking the machine into an upside-down spin that threw him entirely out of the cockpit, the only thing left to connect him with the plane being his precarious hold on the drum. His feet now dangled in space. "Only a few seconds previously I had been cursing because I could not get that drum off, but now I prayed fervently that it would stay on for ever." Then the engine quit.

"The only thing I could see was the propeller (which seemed unpleasantly close to my face), the town of Menin, and the adjacent countryside." He started guessing where he might crash. In desperation, he kicked upward behind him until he could hook first one foot and then the other inside the cockpit, wrestling the stick back again between his legs and jamming the aileron and elevator full on, which turned the aircraft right side up. Dropping heavily back into his errant craft, he drew a lungful of relief and tried to move the stick—but couldn't. That was when he noticed that he had fallen through the seat and lay wedged in the bottom of the cockpit. Now upright, the aircraft engine roared back into action, further hastening Strange's earthward plummet.

He braced his shoulders against the top of the fuselage and his feet against the rudder bar, then wrenched away the broken bits of seat to free the controls, pulled up the nose, and cleared the trees along the Menin road "with very little to spare." He got back to his quarters and slept for twelve hours, but "Lord, how stiff I was the next day!" Such sustained coolness under extreme duress often made the difference between living and dying, when a cascade of mechanical problems or, less commonly at the outset, enemy gunfire might take one within seconds to the edge of destruction. Chambers caught something of that quality of enduring courage when he observed that Eddie "wasn't the best pilot in the world. He couldn't put as many holes in the target that was being towed as I could, but he could put more holes in a target that was shooting at him than I could."

It was the daredevil Roland Garros who forced many of the game-changing innovations in aviation weaponry. Born in 1888 and sent to Paris to study music, the dashing Frenchman met the Brazilian aviation pioneer Alberto Santos-Dumont, who taught him to fly. Abandoning music, he flew in the United States and South America before the war. In September 1913, he became the first to cross the Mediterranean by air. At war's outbreak, he was performing exhibition work in Germany and barely escaped via a daring night flight to Switzerland in his Morane-Saulnier.

Shooting forward above the propeller, as Strange found out, proved cumbersome and ineffective, so early in the war, Garros experimented with a light machine gun set at an oblique angle in his cockpit so the bullets would not smash his propeller. The contraption proved too difficult to aim. In Paris, Garros complained about this to the aircraft manufacturer Raymond Saulnier. In April 1914, Saulnier had wrestled with the problem himself, building a cam-operated mechanism that enabled a machine gun to fire only when the propeller blades were elsewhere on their traverse. This was an effective mechanism, but he still dropped the idea because "hang-fire" rounds made firing the Hotchkiss machine gun dangerously uneven. However, he told Garros that he had gained success building metal deflectors to protect the propeller from misfires. Metal triangles were affixed to the blades, their apexes pointed toward the pilot. The concept immediately intrigued Garros. He and his mechanic fashioned their own deflectors but found in tests that the rounds still turned the propellers into matchsticks. By building more solid braces for the mount, which reduced the gun's vibration, and adapting the deflectors to wedge shapes with gutterlike channels to impart safe directions to the rounds, they devised a system that seemed to work.

On April 1, 1915, Garros took off from the Saint-Pol-sur-Mer aerodrome near Dunkirk on the Channel in his modified Morane-Saulnier. He found a two-seater German Albatros whose observer pulled out a carbine, then froze in horror as the French machine pointed directly at them and opened fire. "An immense flame burst out of the German motor and spread instantly," recalled Garros. On April 15 and 18 he scored more kills. Although imperfect, the deflectors conferred an immense advantage. Less than eight months after it had begun, aerial warfare was moving from the small-arm to the machine-tool age that had taken four centuries to reach on the ground.

Shortly after his third victory, a bullet fired from the ground severed Garros's fuel line, forcing him down in German-occupied territory. He failed to set the plane ablaze in time to hide his innovation, whose discovery threw the Germans into an uproar. Building their own deflectors didn't work: Unlike France's copper or brass-jacketed rounds, the steel-jacketed German bullets were not so easily deflected, quickly destroying the blades instead.

The German high command called upon the brilliant Dutch airplane manufacturer and innovator Anthony Fokker to replicate Garros's deflectors. He went on to do a lot more. Historians still argue whether he knew about an existing German patent for an interrupter mechanism developed by LVG's Franz Schneider: a cam-and-rod attachment to a trigger bar that overrode the firing mechanism when the propeller rotated in front of the barrel. Fokker probably did, because he turned out a similar pushrod control mechanism known as the *Gestängesteuerung* almost overnight. Mounted on his own Eindecker (monoplane), the synchronizer turned this rather mediocre "fighting scout" into so potent a weapon system that the RFC tersely dubbed the bloody period from midsummer 1915 to early spring 1916 the "Fokker Scourge."

One British pilot described encountering this deadly new weaponry: "You feel naked and helpless. The panic seeps through your pores . . . everything seems unreal . . . and then you hear guns hacking. All I can do at the controls is stay to a westerly course [i.e., run for home] and summon every trick I know . . . swerving erratically from side to side so the Boche does not have a steady target. Only as a last shift do I give away altitude, since he can climb like an arrow off a bowstring and enjoys an absolute advantage if I go too low . . . It is a harrowing execrable ordeal."

While Fokker's synchronization gear inaugurated a sea change in aerial warfare, this was only one of eighteen seesawing reversals of air dominance during the war. The "Scourge" ended when the new French Nieuport 11 roared up to the front, its top-wing ailerons affording far more maneuverability than the Eindecker, which still relied on Wright-era wing warping to control roll.

At Verdun that spring the French air service, led by such aces as Jean Navarre, Georges Guynemer, and Charles Nungesser, established air superiority and essentially blinded the Germans. In early August 1916, the German air corps only fielded some 250 aircraft at the Somme, half the Allied total.

Hammered at Verdun and the Somme, the German chief of staff, Erich von Falkenhayn, resigned, passing command to Paul von Hindenburg and his deputy Erich Ludendorff. This hard-charging duo ordered a massive reorganization of the air corps into thirty-three new pursuit squadrons designated *Jagdstaffeln,* or Jastas—hunt formations—each equipped with fourteen new aircraft, which would not only fly defensive patrols behind the lines but also undertake offensive operations. The emphasis would also be on flying in large formations, not the lone-wolf sorties that had characterized the war's exploratory days. In addition, they shifted the bulk of these aircraft from Verdun to help meet the great Allied offensive obviously forthcoming on the Somme.

During the Fokker Scourge and afterward, two German aces towered above all others in killing facility—Max Immelmann and Oswald Boelcke, two men who couldn't have had more different personalities: Immelmann, arrogant, moody, and unpopular; Boelcke, mild mannered and well liked. A notable lothario, Boelcke once was disciplined for taking a nurse aloft in the intimate cockpit of a Fokker—perhaps becoming charter members of the mile-high club. (By contrast, Immelman said he thought of no woman other than his mother.) As Boelcke's wins began to mount, he often visited hospitals, bearing gifts for the aviators he had shot down. The young pilot even earned a French lifesaving medal for jumping into a canal to pull out a drowning French boy. Boelcke appeared to be a natural leader, commenting that "you can win the men's confidence if you associate with them naturally and do not try to play the high and mighty superior," not a particularly common sentiment in the rigid German military.

One of Boelcke's great strengths lay in his open, adaptable approach as combat flying rapidly and steadily transformed itself. He had started flying in September 1914, in a world of unarmed reconnaissance machines that could reach only 55 mph; within two years, these had been brushed aside by sleek, dedicated fighters that reached 109 mph and carried two devastating machine guns. In the week before he flew the Fokker Eindecker with the synchronizing gear, he wrote that "I believe in the saying that 'the strong man is mightiest alone.'" He would change his tune as experience proved that flying in formation kept him and the whole outfit safer—simply more eyes on the lookout for enemy ambushes and more concentrated firepower. He and Immelmann teamed up in late 1915 as a particularly effective twosome to originate what is still a basic fighter formation of wingman and leader. The German press played upon their friendly rivalry in kill scores. Immelmann would give his name to the so-called Immelmann turn—today often understood to be a half loop with a half roll at the top of the loop to restore an upright position. Aviation scholars doubt that Immelmann's Eindecker had either the power or control—it still used wing warping for lateral adjustment—to perform such a maneuver. More probably he used a chandelle, a climbing turn, certainly used before, but never applied systematically in combat.

Tapped to run Jasta 2, Boelcke selected his team, which included Manfred von Richthofen, a former cavalry officer with so far only one kill to his credit. Richthofen and the men of Jasta 2 worshipped Boelcke. As they waited for their new planes, Boelcke would frequently sortie alone. Upon his return, the pilots would press around him, demanding to know whether he had scored a kill.

"Do I have a black chin?" Boelcke would famously reply—as frequently he did, left by smoke from the machine gun that he rarely fired to no avail. Now his country's leading ace, he had succeeded to the spot after Immelmann went down in combat in June. "He shot one or two Englishmen for breakfast every day," boasted Richthofen. What Boelcke imparted to his students would prove as devastating an advantage as the introduction of a far more powerful engine. He required that each pilot memorize the tolerances of his aircraft—not only its maximum and cruising speeds but velocity at different altitudes, turn radius, and other characteristics. Embracing the German culture's fixation on doctrine and theory, he developed and codified the first air-combat tactics, eight rules known as the "Dicta Boelcke." However simple and obvious they might seem, they were brilliant because they distilled lifesaving (and -taking) tenets that leaped readily to mind even in the wild disorientation of combat.

The first recommended, "Try to secure the upper hand before attacking. If possible, keep the sun behind you." A truly professional pilot never attacked without an edge, which often came from using the sun's dazzling glare to blind one's adversary. Or one could strike effectively from a superior altitude because it took so long for even the best World War I aircraft to climb. The next rule—"Always continue with an attack you have begun"—rested on the hard-learned fact that rookies often plunged into a fight only to break off under an overwhelming terror at what they had gotten into. Precipitous flight often presented one's adversary with an opportunity to rake an unguarded back.

Implicit in Boelcke's teachings was a raw, battle-taught insight into what later systemic analysis would prove: The first combat engagement would be the rookie's most dangerous. After a fighter pilot survived five such encounters, his survival rate jumped twentyfold. Boelcke knew that by anticipating how he might unnecessarily lay himself open to destruction in his first hostile engagement, whether breaking away from or losing sight of his foe, he could enhance the odds of getting his students through to the next battle and the following, ever more effective, combats. These clear, concise principles addressed not a pilot's ability to perform a difficult spin or maneuver but how to approach an aerial engagement coherently. Along with the synchronizer gear, the widely studied Dicta revolutionized German air corps performance.

On September 16, 1916, Jasta 2 received their new Albatros D.IIs, powered by the formidable 160 hp, in-line Mercedes engines and armed with twin Spandaus, or Maxim machine guns. Watch the Nieuports, Boelcke warned his men; they are "very fast and agile," but generally lose "height in prolonged turning action. Attack from behind if possible and at close range." On that first sortie, every one of Jasta 2's fliers knocked a British plane out of the sky, and the squadron went on to claim forty Allied aircraft during the next month. During September and October, the reorganized German air corps would destroy 211 Allied aircraft while losing only 39 of its own, ruthlessly grabbing sovereignty over the Somme. Even with Boelcke's death on October 28, after a comrade's undercarriage brushed against his wing, the German air corps looked nearly invincible. The next month, in his ninth victory, Richthofen downed the brilliant British ace Lanoe Hawker, playing the superior performance of his machine at concert pitch. Soon he would far outshine his mentor.

By the end of 1916, when Eddie was visiting the Sunbeam plant in England, the Germans, although bloodied, had left the Allies stumbling and shaken: more than 600,000 British and French casualties at the Somme; a third of a million French casualties at Verdun; a million Russians after an initially promising offensive ran down. In January 1917, the Germans would deploy the Albatros D.III, one of the war's finest fighter aircraft.

During the "Bloody April" of 1917, the Germans shot down 150 British aircraft, one-third of Britain's entire fleet, Richthofen alone claiming 21. The life expectancy of an RFC pilot dwindled to two months. The dread appearance of Richthofen's Albatros, immediately recognizable by its bloodred wings and fuselage, was enough to send Allied pilots into headlong flight.

When he made his first kill, the Red Baron had claimed a piece of it, which he then sent home. Soon his mansion was overflowing with machine guns, insignia, wing fragments, and instruments from his scores of victims. With each kill he commissioned a silver cup from a Berlin jeweler, only stopping at sixty when silver ran out under pressure of the war effort. Curiously, Richthofen expressly forbade his pilots to engage in acrobatics. "The decisive factor does not lie in trick flying but solely in the personal ability and energy of the aviator. A flying man may be able to loop and do all the stunts imaginable and yet he may not succeed in shooting down a single enemy."

By June 1917, he was ordered to put together the first *Jagdgeschwader*, or JG (pursuit squadron), made up initially of the pilots from four Jastas combined into a mobile group of fifty planes. Housed in tents and portable sheds, they were rapidly deployable by truck or rail. The Germans sent bombers against London, in part to force the British into diverting valuable interceptor formations from the front. "My reserve is dangerously low," lamented Hugh Trenchard, commander of the RFC.

Richthofen's JG 1 took on all manner of brightly colored paint jobs; one Allied pilot described them as "machines with green wings and yellow noses, silver wings with golden noses, red bodies with green wings, light blue bodies and red wings." It was this formidable "Flying Circus" that Eddie and the other young and unseasoned American pilots would soon be coming up against.

After gunnery training at Arcachon in early 1918, Eddie spent a week's leave in Paris, then was ordered to the 1st Pursuit Group's advanced training center at Villeneuve-les-Vertus in Champagne on February 19. Some 20 miles south of Reims in the Toul sector, Villeneuve was relatively quiet, a good environment in which to take their first hostile sorties. In addition, the men would join the famous 12th Groupe de Combat and the Cigognes Escadrille (these "Storks" were France's most famous squadron), as well as the recently arrived American fliers of the 95th Aero Pursuit Squadron, who had finished advanced training at Issoudun one step ahead of the 94th. The 95th never let the 94th forget that they would be first to go into combat. Remembering how Issoudun's chief engineer had treated them, most still shunned Eddie, although he remained friends with Chambers, Meissner, and Miller.

A minor wrinkle remained at Villeneuve: The Americans had nothing to fly in. "All the time, of course, we were hearing that America was going to ship over 20,000 of the greatest planes the world had ever seen," recalled Eddie, "and there were cartoons of how the sky would be blackened with American airplanes, all a bunch of hokum." Nearly a year earlier, when the United States had joined the war, the first flush of bravado had set government officials and journalists slaphappy at the prospect of mobilizing American industrial might for aircraft production. "Fifty thousand American aviators in fifty thousand flying machines, each dropping one hundred dynamite bombs on German soil, would do the work," enthused the *New York American*. Surely nothing could stop the nation that had put the assembly line to such powerful use in creating the first automobile industry. On July 24, 1917, Congress appropriated the expenditure of $640 million for military aviation—more than the entire cost of building the Panama Canal—seemed to prove the point.

The Allies got caught up in the hype; ominously, the Germans bought into their enemies' rhetoric, too. While General Ernst von Hoeppner, commander of the German air service, questioned Americans' ability to mobilize so quickly, he could not afford to risk it and so instituted the Amerikaprogramm, which called for increasing the German air corps by forty pursuit and seventeen training units. Aircraft manufacture would increase to 2,000 per month, that of engines to 2,500. Only U-boat construction would claim a higher priority.

Meanwhile, a commission of American industrialists led by Colonel Raynal Bolling visited Europe in the summer of 1917 to learn what kinds of aircraft should be built and discovered to their astonishment and dismay that in the air race Europe had wholly outdistanced the United States, in numbers and technology alike. What's more, added Bolling, "in most of the airplane and engine factories, [the Allies] are entirely without complete drawings, specifications and other tabulated information which we should consider essential in the [mass production] manufacture of airplanes and engines." The commission saw no recourse but to recommend that the United States buy aircraft from the French until it could get up to speed in a year. Converting the nation's industrial assembly lines to aircraft production overnight was a pipe dream. In its eighteen months of war, America would not ship a single fighter plane to France.

Paradoxically, the Amerikaprogramm would itself put the industrial production of French aircraft under stress, hampering France's ability to deliver aircraft to the United States. In late August, the U.S. and French governments agreed that the French would supply the Americans with bombers and reconnaissance planes, along with either the SPAD XIII or a new fighter; the Americans promised to furnish large supplies of machine tools and raw material.

As the war ground on, the French would claim that the United States had not met its contract to supply matériel. It appeared that the Americans would have to settle for the Nieuport 27. Finally the French agreed to provide the Nieuport 28, an aircraft that had performed well in trials but had not passed the acid test of combat. The French knew that the Germans were preparing to launch an all-out offensive to break the Allies before America could fully mobilize. French recalcitrance to supply the Americans with better aircraft may have stemmed from chill anticipation: What was the point of siphoning off the best machines as they braced for this possibly final onslaught? "After much discussion, consultation and almost in desperation we took [the Nieuport 28] over for our own use," reported Captain Gordon Rankin. "The French didn't want any part of them . . . [and] we were too stupid to know they were bad," wrote Chambers.

That the Nieuport was already outclassed was evident just by examining the performance of the French units at Villeneuve, which were flying the SPAD XIII. Compared to the Nieuport's 160 hp engine, the SPAD mounted a 220 hp Hispano-Suiza. Although graceful in form and quite nimble, the Nieuport's frame was willowy compared with the sturdier-framed SPAD, which thus could undertake more violent acrobatics and endure greater beatings when it had to put down hard. What nobody yet knew—and the Americans would only find out in bloody combat—was that the Nieuport also harbored a design flaw, which only emerged in the deep dives and sharp recoveries of dogfighting.

Any doubts about their new machine did not reach pilots itching for action at Villeneuve. In late February, word came that the aircraft were ready for pickup in Paris. Just as Meissner, Eddie, Chambers, and others got there, a massive snowstorm struck. For an excruciating week of blinding weather, they tried to enjoy the city's charms. Eddie visited a plant making Liberty engines, saw *Faust* with Meissner, and went out on a date with a woman who was "dark and rather small but has a very sweet disposition."

Finally, on March 6, the weather cleared enough for the fifteen unarmed Nieuports to take off from Orly airport on the 60-mile trip to Villeneuve. Only six made it that day, including Eddie's and Meissner's. The rest, including Chambers's, had "panned" (from the French word for breakdowns), most because they had been inadequately fueled. Three airplanes smashed, but the pilots were unhurt. "Rather bad results for the first time," wrote Eddie in his journal, but he and Meissner were overjoyed at becoming formal members of the 94th on their return. The mess elected Chambers bar officer, most probably because, having sworn off alcohol at the front, he wouldn't dip into supplies; as a budding entrepreneur, he learned how to keep the squadron awash in champagne, cutting deals for twenty-five-cent bottles in Reims and shipping truckloads back to base. Eddie and the others liked to a get "a jolly little bun on" over the weekends, made especially sweet because the 95th's commander, Jim Miller, had forbidden their brother squadron to drink alcohol at any meal.

On the morning of March 9, Miller visited Eddie in his barracks, spilling over with an almost schoolboy excitement. He was heading off to check out one of the crashed Nieuports. He had secretly decided to team up on his way back with two other officers—Davenport Johnson and Millard Harmon—still flying for a French squadron and cross into enemy territory near Reims. Unfortunately, this venture proved disastrous. Engine problems forced Harmon back before he could cross the front. Johnson and Miller pressed on over to the Argonne Forest, where two Germans jumped them. Johnson later claimed that his guns had jammed and, thus unable to fight, he had sensibly turned home. Outgunned, Miller took direct hits and spun out of control. The pilots at Villeneuve learned later that he had died in a German hospital. Some men blamed Johnson, questioning whether his guns had actually failed. Later evidence corroborated the story circulating that Johnson had seen the Germans approach while Miller had not, and left without alerting him. The German credited with bringing Miller down reported the American's dying words as "He's a yellow son of a bitch! You can tell him that, and I hope he's stuck up against a brick wall and shot." The newly and bitterly nicknamed "Jam" Johnson had a difficult time living down his patrol mate's death. Distraught, Eddie vowed never again to "cherish friendships with my pilot comrades so intimately that their going would upset the work I had to do." That the young, supremely confident, and talented commander of the 95th had died so early fell as the first real blow upon the American flying service. There would be many, many more. Eventually, noted Eddie, the pilots of the 94th "came to look with callous indifference upon the sudden death of their dearest chum," a necessity that he believed was "one of the greatest horrors of war."

This first and far from knightly combat revealed how the game had changed. The bonds that had determined one's standing in training were quickly evolving now that lives were on the line, not from impersonal accidents but from skilled enemies. Each man now asked himself, What constituted cowardice? Just what ethic generated the rules of loyalty and mutual support? Together they would have to forge new understandings of fighting as a team, not as single performers. How could these brave yet naive young men come together to match the Flying Circus blow by blow?

Some of these questions were rather miraculously answered with the arrival at Villeneuve of the short, square-faced Major Raoul "Luf" Lufbery. Five years older than Eddie, he had flown in the famous N. 124, the Lafayette Escadrille, a group of 38 American pilots under the French flag. (Another 172 American volunteers serving in other squadrons in the French air service became known as the Lafayette Flying Corps, 63 of whom would die in combat.) Luf had shot down more than a dozen adversaries. Eddie and the others already knew of Whiskey and Soda, the Escadrille's two pet lions, and the stories of the group's high-spirited shenanigans, which included endless dice and poker games played to gramophones belting out ragtime. Luf's fellows had recently bailed him out of a French jail for knocking out the teeth of a railway employee. He "always smelt of cheap perfume," remembered his comrade LeRoy Prinz, because he corresponded with as many as fifty women who sent him love letters on scented paper.

Luf exuded dash and swagger, a confidence no doubt born and battle-tested over three long years on the front. His presence alone suggested to the unformed American pilots that they, too, might survive: If they followed his example and learned from him, he might reveal the secrets of his successes. Eddie and Luf clicked immediately, each recognizing in the other the born survivor. Like Eddie, the French-born Luf had experienced loss early, his mother dying when he was a year old. His father had remarried and emigrated to the States, leaving the boy behind to work in a chocolate factory, much of his wages going to finance his father's adjustment to the new country. As a young man, he had traveled the world, returning to America in 1906, where he eventually joined the U.S. military and served two years in the Philippines. In Calcutta in 1912, he met the renowned aviator Marc Pourpe, who took him on as his mechanic, notably on a pioneering 1,250-mile airmail flight from Cairo to Khartoum in January 1914, and also taught him to fly his Blériot monoplane. While Pourpe was buying a new aircraft in France, war broke out, and he immediately signed up with the French air service, Lufbery soon following as his mechanic. The war claimed Pourpe in December 1917, a death that hit Luf hard. Committed to revenging his mentor's death, he went on to become the most celebrated American ace in French service.

Luf and Eddie bonded as self-made mechanics in a sea of entitled young men. In Luf, Eddie found not only a friend but also a font of critical knowledge, on which he would draw repeatedly. Spurred on by Luf's example, Eddie feverishly set about getting his own Nieuport ready for war, working with his three mechanics to install a compass, clock, and altimeter and to mount the single Vickers machine gun. Rain kept him from the air until March 21, when Luf sent him up to check out the Nieuport's rate of climb and "ceiling," its maximum attainable height. In nine minutes, Eddie had reached 3,000 feet; in twenty-three minutes, 5,000. Another seventeen minutes took him only 800 feet higher. He concentrated so hard on pushing his machine that he got lost, just making it home before dark. "All the boys were sure that I had been out over the Front," he later recalled, "which I let them believe."

On March 25, American headquarters realized that very few of the 95th Aero Squadron had taken the gunnery course, and those deficients were unhappily crowded into trucks for the long trip to Cazaux. Eddie and the others of the 94th could not have been happier that the "foolish virgins of Squadron 95" had been sent away. Now the 94th was the first squadron in line for combat.

BOOK III

FIGHTING

And each man stands with his face in the light
Of his own drawn sword,
Ready to do what a hero can.
—Elizabeth Barrett Browning, *Napoleon III in Italy* (1860), VIII

10.

FIRST BLOOD

By 1917, the combatants in World War I looked like bloodied prizefighters taking punch after punch while somehow just keeping their feet. Their effectiveness had eroded, all energies engaged in just staying alive: Russia disintegrating, France battered senseless, Britain exhausted, Italy barely propped up. Germany, too, swayed under near-fatal weakness but was still perhaps capable of smashing through to Paris in spring 1918.

The strain of all-out war had sown fear and weariness, not only among the French but on the much hungrier German home front. Only ruthless action had broken a strike by 400,000 Berlin workers late that January. The British blockade forced its citizenry into eating their bony dogs and cats, the latter now referred to as "roof rabbits." Bread, if one could get it at all, consisted of potato peelings leavened with sawdust. The cruelest hardships came from the deaths and maimings that seemed to reach into every family, starkly manifest in the thousands of broken men returning home, limbs lost to shells or eyes to gas attack.

By March, with 100,000 to 150,000 Americans steaming into Europe each month, the kaiser, or at least his staff, understood that time no longer favored them in this war of attrition. Yet most of these newcomers remained green, not having received advanced training. They would be ready by year's end, and in full force certainly by 1919, a reality that would tip the scales heavily on the Allied side. The Germans thus sought to knock France out of the war once and for all. Four sledgehammer blows, beginning on

March 21 and finishing in the summer, would offer the last opportunity for victory, and they came within inches of succeeding. They would press close to Paris, take 250,000 Allied prisoners, and inflict nearly a million casualties. At any moment over the coming months, any one of a number of salients—the bulges in the front at which the Germans pressed their advantage—might rupture like a cardiac aneurysm to open a hole that storm troopers could exploit and turn the course. For the first time in the history of warfare, control of the skies would prove critical. While millions of infantrymen ground together in mud and desolation, all too few airmen would fight in tiny numbers for untold strategic knowledge.

In early March, the forbidding Erich Ludendorff invited Richthofen, three squadron commanders of the Flying Circus, and several other officers to field headquarters to brief them on the important role assigned them in the upcoming offensive. On March 3, Ludendorff had watched Lenin's envoys sign the Peace of Brest-Litovsk, taking Germany's great rival to the east out of the war. The imperial railroad system immediately had begun efficiently shuttling troops and armaments from east to west. Ludendorff impressed upon the airmen how critical their support would be to the ground forces. Strafing and bombing would demoralize the enemy, while observers would keep the general staff apprised of hostile movements and dispositions. Radio-equipped observers would also direct artillery fire upon hardened positions. General Hoeppner toasted his "eagles" and promised Ludendorff that "our planes will guarantee your success." The steely general responded with a bit of humor, "Don't you think, Herr General, that our six million foot soldiers will be useful also?" He exaggerated—he directed some 2 million—but there was no question that this new dimension of combat would be essential from now on.

On March 21, 1918, after a massive bombardment, including tens of thousands of canisters of poison gas, the Germans struck the British 5th Army hard along a 45-mile line from La Bassée to La Fère along the Somme. Foul weather prevented either side from getting aloft until March 24. By then, a

German assault had driven them back 14 miles in full retreat, which astounded the British with its force and speed. For years the front had changed yards at a time; now the storm troopers—a rather new but rapidly famous category of soldier—promised to blow open the salient they had created and altogether divide the French and British, threatening the critical railway hub of Amiens. The French, realizing how close the Germans were to strategic victory, shook up their leadership by appointing the strong-nerved, older General (later Marshal) Ferdinand Foch to command.

Into the first clear skies, the Germans and British put waves of aircraft over the Somme on a scale of aerial war never before seen. In one day, the British claimed forty-five German aircraft while losing eleven of their own, fifty-one more being damaged beyond repair. Stiff British ground resistance to the German thrust, backed by fierce air support, kept Amiens just barely in Allied hands. Two days later, the Germans adopted a defensive air strategy, taking down thirteen British planes without losing any.

At the Villeneuve aerodrome Eddie and the others listened anxiously to reports of the offensive, worrying that their base, although well behind the front, might soon be overrun. Eddie calibrated his gunsights, writing on March 23 that German bombers had struck the nearby town of Châlons, "killing many also wrecking the depot." Bombers even passed over Villeneuve, "naturally we thot [sic] they would bomb us however they did not." Lufbery decided his tyros needed combat vetting, even though machine guns remained at a premium—instead of the stipulated two, the squadron could mount only one per Nieuport. He ran his young charges through one last vigorous acrobatic session, then tapped the two most promising, Eddie and Douglas Campbell, just out of Harvard, to join him over enemy lines the following morning. "Got the opportunity I have worked so hard for during the past 9 months," scribbled Eddie in his diary before trying to get some sleep.

Rickenbacker and Campbell couldn't have been cut from more contrasting bolts of cloth. The short, dapper, athletic Campbell had quit school his senior year when the United States entered the war. Eddie described him as "quiet and thoughtful in manner and gentle in speech." Like many sons of privilege—his father, a noted astronomer, was director of the Lick Observatory near San Jose—he keenly felt the pull of martial patriotism; he and his friend Quentin Roosevelt had quit college to join the air service, Campbell graduating from ground school at MIT. He, Roosevelt, and classmate Ham Coolidge had become good friends, sailing to France together that breathless summer. During those early halcyon days before the relentlessness of daily combat came to weigh upon them, they had been united by many things at Issoudun, one most certainly a disdain for the likes of Eddie, his rough-edged ways, and the rumors of his German connections. Polished gentlemen did not work so hard, nor forever pick at problems with crude mechanical empiricism as Eddie did.

War would soon bring these men together in ways few other conditions could. Eddie's competence, growing leadership skills, and sheer toughness made it impossible for them to dismiss him as one more monkey-wrench-adept rube. Nor could they get a bead on the man who somehow defied any classic expression of the American hero: neither the unassuming, self-deprecating type made for the professional classes, like Charles Lindbergh in decades to come, nor the bang-the-beer-on-the-bar alpha male, like Barney Oldfield. Eddie was neither modest nor self-assertive, nor looking to be the nation's next fair-haired boy. He was altogether too businesslike, and his unemphatic but deep-rooted confidence grew out of reason, practice, and ceaseless toil. His toughness combined with his startling creativity made him appear alien, formidable, and difficult to come to terms with. When the Ivy League boys gathered over port or champagne around an off-key piano to hear Campbell bang out the latest ragtime, Eddie was rarely invited. Another pilot—LeRoy Prinz, a high school dropout—felt the same exclusion. "If it would [be] a nice [social] event I would be left out . . . I didn't realize [it] until suddenly I found these guys were all college men. They were all fraternity men. They were all clubmen. They had grip handshakes."

Campbell had been assigned a staff position at Issoudun, becoming the first assistant officer in charge of training. As with Eddie, his responsibilities kept him from taking advanced instruction, so he snuck in as much stolen flying time as possible. "Campbell learned to fly alone on a fast scout machine," remembered Eddie, "a feat I do not remember any other American pilot having duplicated." Campbell was a natural-born pilot.

Photographs of both Eddie and Campbell show the bright, knowing alpha smile—expressing, however, a confidence springing from very different sources. Eddie's reflected the cheerful pessimism of a fighter permanently on the edge of being brushed off or rolled over, always aware that his greatest asset was his undismayed mistrust of the world. Campbell's shone from a bright star that seemed to guide his life, an effortless directing spirit manifest in his father and such institutions as Harvard, which bestowed a sense of entitlement and the certitude of success. Eddie's rock-hard determination and ambition were fueled by still-potent memories of childhood poverty and misfortune, and his father's angry fists. He had survived those challenges by drawing strength from within his bruised, ill-fed body. For Eddie, standing out and above others was no birthright but a necessity. Merely to be ordinary to him implied a dark, harsh obscurity, a life essentially not worth living. He had seen the sad, listless men coming home from twelve-hour shifts, exhausted and prematurely aged, their wives worn out by repeated pregnancies and unceasing motherhood. Every cell in Eddie's body bore out George Orwell's bitter observation that "any life viewed from the inside is simply a series of defeats."

So, while both came to the job with their veins boiling with similar combustible mixtures of patriotism and testosterone, their motivations were indeed heated by different fuels. Lufbery's experienced eye cared little about what spring had nourished his protégés' talents and determination, only that they could deploy the necessary raw materials. The U.S. Signal Corps knew so little about what it took to make a good pilot that they devised bizarre tests to determine the fitness of the Lafayette veterans for the new service. One, likely dreamed up by a deskbound flunky, placed Lufbery on a piano stool set briskly spinning. When they put his allegedly superior qualities to the test by ordering him to walk backward, he fell over and nearly broke his neck. America's highest-regarded combat pilot fully understood how a robotic ability to withstand disorientation counted, but he also knew that it still paled against other capacities. In Eddie and Campbell he detected a near-fanatical determination to be the best. Flying and shooting skills improved with practice, but nothing could create from scratch the composure necessary to thrive in the most stressful combat environment that humans had yet conceived. "Many fighter aces have been described as fearless; this is simply not true," writes one modern expert. "What they have to do is to control their fear, which demands a high degree of determination."

Dawn broke bright and clear over the Villeneuve aerodrome on Thursday, March 28, 1918, perfect flying weather for the 94th's first hostile sortie. The other fliers enviously ribbed the pair, "wondering what they would do with our equipment and personal effects, should we fail to come back," noted Eddie without resentment. Such gallows humor would proliferate over the coming weeks, as one comrade after another failed to return. Eddie and Reed Chambers took to saluting one another before a mission with "Well, I'll be slapping you in the face with a spade, you old so and so. I'll be burying you." Dragging on a cigarette, Eddie pulled on his bulky teddy-bear suit, his nerves on edge, then climbed aboard his Nieuport. Lufbery strolled over to speak with Campbell, then Eddie. As Eddie watched the supremely self-confident ace come over, his apprehension swelled to fever pitch. Lufbery reminded him to stay close and not to break formation.

In the quiet morning, their engines generated a blasting sound, akin to a modern jet engine's. Lufbery took off, closely followed by his novices, who banked with him north toward Reims. The Villeneuve aerodrome lay at the southern end of the small eminence known as the Mountain of Reims, a few miles south of the city, and Lufbery cleverly used its shadow to hide their approach from the vigilant German observers only 20 miles away. Vines were still climbing in neat rows up the mountain's flanks, bearing grapes for the Taittinger, Veuve Clicquot, and Mumm champagne companies. Pockets of snow lingered from a spring storm of some days earlier.

Campbell assumed position behind and to the left of his leader, Eddie to the right. Almost immediately, Eddie found his plane lagging well behind as they approached Reims.

Ninety miles northeast of Paris, Reims had seen fierce fighting during the first German push into France in 1914. Terribly stung by the fall of Paris during the Franco-Prussian War of 1870–71, the French had fortified the border, particularly at such critical points as Reims, adding forts to those already commanding the rises circling the plain on which the town sat.

Nothing prepared Eddie for the immense cruciform of Notre-Dame de Reims, thrown into crisp relief by the sharp early-morning sunlight. The world's largest and most imposing symbol of the Middle Ages, the great Gothic church had witnessed the coronations of twenty-five French kings from that of Louis VIII in 1223 to Charles X in 1825. Joan of Arc herself had traveled here in 1429; her visitation was commemorated by an equestrian statue with sword raised, which Eddie spotted near the cathedral in the Place Cardinal-Luçon. Her posture seemed to defy all those who should menace such a nobly historic town, but the Germans had, with a vengeance. Their swift August 1914 offensive had swept into Reims like a tide, which then rolled back before heroic resistance. The invaders had dug into its northward hills, close enough to shell it. The cathedral, which the Germans considered an appropriate target because of the observers sweeping the landscape from its 260-foot towers, felt war's inhuman blows. Wooden scaffolding caught fire, burning and melting the lead-and-wooden roof. As Eddie flew over it, he peered into the debris-strewn nave. The French denounced such havoc as an example of German barbarism, and the American poet Florence Earle Coates was moved to write that

The generations yet unborn shall feel
This wrong to Beauty, and lament her loss;
Here royal kings, unhappy ghosts, shall steal
Through ruins where no carillon shall peal,
Nor altar gleam, nor Christ bend from the cross.

Most of the other stone buildings in Reims had suffered damage as well, the townsfolk taking refuge in the vast network of champagne cellars.

Lufbery circled back around and settled in front of his slower charge, Campbell following suit. The flight turned toward Suippes, 25 miles southeast, Lufbery now beginning a gentle corkscrew motion, a technique of continuous "banking and turning from one side to the other, in order to see at all angles," as Campbell later explained. Lufbery was teaching them to overcome the multiple blind spots imposed by wings, tail, and fuselage (not to mention the absence of a rearview mirror) by rotating their vision so as to avoid surprise. Should some "Boche" jump them, such corkscrewing would make them the more difficult targets—hard-earned knowledge that the Royal Air Force ace Geoffrey Wellum was going to echo a generation later when he summed up his wisdom about combat flying. "Never, never fly straight and narrow for more than twenty seconds. If you do, you'll die."

As Eddie began weaving himself, the cold chilled him to the bone, and the stiff wind pitched and rolled his Nieuport like a small boat riding heavy swells. As he wondered how his leader could corkscrew so effortlessly, bile began to rise in his stomach. He had been concentrating so hard since leaving Reims that he hadn't looked over the side; now what he saw astounded him, "nothing below but these old battered ditches, earthworks, and billions of shell holes . . . nothing but the chaos of ruin and desolation." He clenched his teeth against his nausea. It didn't help that the thin air left him gasping for breath, forcing him to inhale even more castor oil than usual.

Just then an explosion directly behind him pitched his machine up, then dropped it. He fought to regain control as the aircraft pitched and rolled wildly in the concussive wake of antiaircraft fire. In the next moments, more shells exploded, hammering his ears; he jerked around in his seat to see five puffs of black smoke just below and behind. Typically fired from German Krupp 77mm guns, the 15-pound shells with a 1,600-foot-per-second muzzle velocity could deliver jagged shrapnel anywhere up to 14,000 feet. Pilots called them "Archies" after a popular British song whose refrain of "Archibald! Certainly not!" was a wife's response to her husband's desperate entreaties to consummate their marriage. For vulnerable airmen, the comic reference seemed somehow to soften the deadly indifference of the shells.

With each concussion, Eddie learned a little better how to meet the blunt upward force with a gentle counterpressure on the joystick. Excitement swept away his nausea, replacing terror with the elation of meeting and surviving his first test of combat.

By the time they touched down, both Campbell and Eddie felt deep satisfaction, their countenances reflecting the casual indifference that was Lufbery's own trademark. As the other pilots peppered them with questions, their mentor broke through to ask what aircraft they had noticed. Both shook their heads. "Just what I expected," he grumbled. "They're all the same!" He then counted off a formation of SPADs that had passed 500 yards below them before they reached the front, and another group that had flown by them fifteen minutes later. Four Albatroses had later come into his view 2 miles ahead, and another enemy two-seater much closer. These revelations showed just how far these two cocky greenhorns were from gaining what Eddie would later call "the vision of the air." Lufbery was "the owner and manipulator of the best pair of eyes in existence," gushed Campbell in a letter home. The ability to register potential threats at great distance, while scanning three-dimensionally above, below, and behind oneself, marked a critical power of "situational awareness," the pilot's ability "to keep track of events and foresee occurrences in the fast-moving, dynamic scenario of air warfare," as one modern-day student of the subject has summarized it. No pilot on his first time out, regardless of how good he promised to be, could have developed such a skill overnight, much less on his first combat mission. It would take practice. As Lufbery spoke, a wave of almost debilitating doubt swept over Eddie as he contemplated whether his damaged right eye might prevent him from ever attaining such abilities.

Lufbery walked over to Eddie's machine, almost everyone at Villeneuve who could fly crowding around. "How much of that shrapnel did you get?" he asked. Eddie couldn't help but laugh nervously, wondering what he could possibly mean, until Lufbery poked his finger into one ragged hole in the

Nieuport's tail, then into another in the wing, and pointed out "part of the shell [that] had gone thru the wings one piece just a short way from my head," Eddie told his journal. The other pilots said that Eddie turned pale and stayed that way for half an hour.

Mechanics placed frayed inch squares of Irish linen over the bullet holes and painted them with aircraft dope, a plasticized lacquer. The planes themselves were ready to fly again within the hour. Although the physical scars had disappeared, the effect of that encounter on Eddie and Campbell remained vivid and permanent memories, searing, frequent reminders of the enemy's deadly intent. How these new pilots handled this recognition would affect their ability to survive and thrive in this new arena of war.

That afternoon, the 94th learned that they must evacuate Villeneuve to make room for French bombers who would be carpeting the advancing German front. Heavy rains over the next few days, however, grounded everyone. On Easter Day, a hangar fire destroyed four Nieuports and damaged Eddie's plane. Finally, on April 2, twenty-two pilots from the 94th flew to a new field near Épiez-sur-Meuse. Later that day, they heard the whine of a rotary engine and rushed out of their barracks to watch the last of the Nieuports come in, expecting it to be a green new pilot at the controls. As the plane touched down on the muddy field, its nose suddenly pitched forward. It flipped onto its back and slid tail forward toward the onlookers. The pilots hurried to the wreck, some of them making "rather caustic comments about the authorities sending us such unsophisticated aviators"—only to be astonished, then delighted, to find the upside-down grinning countenance of James Norman Hall. They dragged him laughing out of the ruined fuselage, his unflappable calm and wry humor already magnetizing the young pilots.

While indeed new to the 94th, Hall was certainly no rookie. The Iowan had begun his journey to that wet field four years earlier, when he presented himself as a Canadian in order to join the British Army. Serving as a machine gunner in the Royal Fusiliers, he fought bravely as a lance corporal at

Loos on the Western Front in the fall of 1915, one of the few of his company to walk away from a bloody engagement that took the life of Rudyard Kipling's only son (a loss memorialized in Kipling's famous poem "My Boy Jack").

Eventually learning of his nationality, the British honorably discharged him; the irrepressible Hall went home, wrote his first book, *Kitchener's Mob: The Adventures of an American in the British Army,* and promptly found his way into the Lafayette Escadrille. Of those experiences, he would write, "To tell of aerial adventure one needs a new language, or, at least, a parcel of new adjectives, sparkling with bright and vivid meaning, as crisp and fresh as just-minted bank-notes." Before the United States joined the war, the Chaucer-loving pilot crashed with a bullet through his lungs but returned to the front. (After the war, Hall would move to Tahiti and most famously coauthor the three *Mutiny on the Bounty* novels. His somewhat melodramatic prose could indeed claim to be rooted in a life of genuinely high drama.)

That March afternoon in 1918, Hall seemed to be just what the 94th needed as they pondered their highly uncertain future. Lufbery told Campbell that Hall was "a comer" who "has developed an unerring judgment in picking and timing his attack." Joining Hall as new flight commanders were two other Lafayette veterans, the taciturn David M. Peterson and the gregarious Kenneth Marr, the latter an Alaskan recruited into the war by a French agent seeking malamute sled dogs to help evacuate casualties in the snowy Vosges. Its leadership now filled with seasoned combat fliers, America's preeminent air squadron drew ready for battle. Even more auspiciously for Eddie, the three new additions had not flown at Issoudun and so harbored no resentment toward him. His star now had more space to rise. A new sense of unit consciousness swept over the 94th Squadron, confidence and anticipation spreading infectiously. They were players on the world's largest stage.

On April 7, the 94th moved to active duty at Gengault Aerodrome near the front at Toul. They were delighted by the cement buildings with rooms for two, and a separate building containing showers with quick-heating apparatus. "No mud, good roads, fascinating country, and beaucoup Boches.

Can't beat it," Campbell wrote home with unconcealed excitement. Now that the 94th was no longer a training unit, tradition required that it display a logo, as earlier chevaliers had flaunted coats of arms. The men liked the gesture of a boxer pitching his hat in the ring to show his readiness to fight. Each pilot painted a top hat emblazoned with stars and stripes sailing through a circle on his fuselage. It wasn't elegant, but it did the trick.

Eddie spent April 12 painting the insignia on his Nieuport. Lufbery had returned at noon "with another Hun to his credit," he recorded in his journal. The next day Eddie wrote that "we were a happy lot," the Operations Board listing "the first war-flight order ever given by an All-American Squadron Commander to All-American pilots." Hall would lead the two-hour sortie with Eddie and Chambers behind him. Starting at 6:00 A.M., they would patrol the lines from Pont-à-Mousson to Saint-Mihiel at 16,000 feet.

Now Eddie had the chance to make his first official kill, an honor that he almost desperately craved. Others perhaps yearned for the accolades such a feat might bestow, the adulation due a hero. To Eddie, who resisted being defined by others, winning came as an extension of authority. Like the Duke of Wellington, who hated applause from his men because one day it might turn to jeering, Eddie knew that such glory can die and fade, while hard achievements—the track wins and speeds he had steadily run—would endure. For a boy who grew up one slipup away from the next hard beating, he wanted only what he could command: to be a master, not a hero. Every solid achievement marked a step back from the abyss of those childhood terrors that could never be forgotten but might at least be distanced.

That night he cataloged everything he knew about aerial combat. When he finally nodded off, he passed into a nightmare in which enemy airplanes crowded the sky. Just as he knocked one down, an orderly tugged at his elbow, reassuring his mumbling, disoriented superior that things were okay but that he'd better get up for breakfast.

Peterson took over as flight commander for the sick James Hall. Douglas Campbell, Alan Winslow, and Jimmy Meissner joined them for breakfast, all three on call during Eddie's sortie in case bombers or other intruders should threaten the aerodrome. A heavy mist hung over the field, but the trio still took off promptly at 6:00 A.M. Peterson immediately turned back because of the weather, which should have cued Eddie and Chambers to do the same, as they had been instructed. Instead they continued to climb. Eddie wrote later that he believed Peterson was having mechanical troubles and the less experienced Chambers was following Eddie's lead. The truth was that Eddie was too excited to let a little weather stop their appointed patrol.

To imagine the geography that the pilots needed to memorize, visualize an inverted pyramid, Toul airfield at its bottommost point. The front ran along its inverted base from Pont-à-Mousson to the northeast of Toul, on the banks of the Moselle, to Saint-Mihiel to the northwest, on the Meuse. From Saint-Mihiel, the front snaked north another 18 miles to Verdun. Twenty miles to the north of Pont-à-Mousson lay Metz, the hub of several German aerodromes.

The pair followed the Moselle and climbed high, only realizing that they had passed over enemy lines in the fog when antiaircraft fire lit up beneath them. Never having encountered Archies before, Chambers skittered so dangerously close that Eddie feared they would collide. Chambers finally regained control, and they made four round trips up and down the line without seeing any enemy aircraft. As they turned home, low on gas, dread suddenly clenched Eddie's stomach when he realized that thick cloud cover now obscured the ground and all identifying features that could help them navigate home. Pushing down blind into the fog was extremely dangerous, the area being rife with hills and trees, but he had no alternative but to trust the notoriously fickle altimeter. Chambers peeled away, concerned that they might collide. He would have to make his own way home.

Eddie pushed his nose down and kept going until he broke clear only a few hundred feet above the ground. "Believe me," wrote Lansing Holden, "when the ground suddenly disappears in favor of a bank of mist your instinct shoots the machine down so fast your heart and breakfast start racing for your throat. In fog there is no way of keeping your machine level except by balance." At that altitude Eddie couldn't discern the major landmarks, but he did remember the telltale Y where a railway divided between Épiez and Toul. To his relief and by a stroke of providence, he found this intersection and flew low toward Toul and then on to Gengault. When he landed, the normally quiet Peterson justifiably called him a bloody fool for flying into such conditions. The real blow came when he added that Chambers had not yet arrived. Had Eddie led his best friend to his death?

After shaking off his teddy-bear suit, Eddie walked over to the Operation Room to begin his report. He thought it peculiar that Campbell, Alan Winslow, and Meissner were gone, the remains of a Russian Bank card game scattered on the table. Then Eddie heard the roar of two Nieuports taking off. Walking outside, he headed back to the field, then sprinted over to a private who was yelling and pointing to a fire and smoke. While he stared, he heard more shouts and twisted around to see a plane crash into the ground. As he sprinted over to one of the burning wrecks, he heard the *br-rppp, br-rp* of two Nieuports coming in to land. Crazy as it seemed, in the few short minutes that it took Eddie to get to the field, Campbell and Winslow had just scored America's first aerial kills.

The sound of Eddie's and Chambers's engines over the line had alerted the Germans. A Pfalz and an Albatros set off in hot pursuit, only to find themselves equally lost. An Allied antiaircraft battery crew heard them pass over Toul at 6,000 feet and alerted Gengault at 8:44 A.M. Winslow, a popular former Yale rower and editor of the college's *Sheffield Monthly* science journal, fielded the call, then raced out with Campbell and Meissner to their waiting planes. He yelled for them to meet him at 1,500 feet over the northeast corner of the field. Meissner's plane was being worked on. Campbell took off, followed by Winslow forty-five seconds later.

Winslow had barely cleared the trees at the edge of the field when he spotted a German biplane bearing down on him from only a few hundred feet ahead. Filled with sudden rage, he swore and veered toward it, ripping off some rounds "until I could see my line of tracer bullets entering its fuselage." The Albatros D.V turned on one wing to avoid his fire, which it returned dangerously close to him. "I pulled my Nieuport sharply in a vertical climb, kicked over my right rudder, and went plunging down on his tail, spraying his wings and fuselage with a long rattling burst of fire. In another instant he dashed toward earth in an uncontrollable dive." Winslow watched his adversary crash and somersault some 300 feet from the airfield.

The airborne Campbell heard the machine guns and looked over to see the tracers "going toward an airplane which had black crosses on it." The moment when something so long dreamed of takes animated form often realizes itself rather calmly, indeed oddly. "I had never seen a German airplane before but that obviously was one." Campbell was turning to support Winslow when a stream of tracers zipped terrifyingly near from above and behind; he jerked the stick up to fire at the interloper, only for his machine to stall, dropping to within 100 feet of the ground before he recovered. Now behind and below his foe, he again pulled up his nose—this time more judiciously—and fired again. In moments he gained altitude on the diving Pfalz D. IIIa and maneuvered behind it. As Winslow roared up to help, Campbell set his enemy's fuselage ablaze. The Pfalz crashed behind the 94th's hangars.

Winslow gave a cigarette to the pilot he shot down, who had suffered only bruises, and noted that Campbell's foe had not fared as well, resembling "the charred sacrifice of some huge animal." From takeoff to landing, the entire engagement had lasted only four and a half minutes. Campbell and Winslow did not even have time to think, only react.

Within moments, French civilians started flocking to the aerodrome "on foot, bicycles, sidecars, automobiles," wrote Winslow. "Soldiers, women, children, majors, colonels, French and American—all poured out of the city; in ten minutes several thousand people must have gathered." One of his bullets had pierced the ear of a peasant out plowing a nearby field; he proudly showed Winslow the wound, blood drying on his neck. *"Un grand souvenir!"* he exclaimed.

Eventually the crowds dispersed and headed back to Toul. Only then did Eddie hear the welcome sound of Chambers's machine coming in. After they separated, Chambers had flown until he landed in a pasture just inside Allied lines, concerned that he would soon run out of fuel. French soldiers, who had never seen either a Nieuport or its American markings, immediately surrounded the downed craft with pointed rifles and marched him off to find an interpreter. By the time he scrounged up enough fuel and returned, he had missed all the excitement.

Morale skyrocketed, but not everybody was ecstatic. "The 94th squadron continues to receive congratulations from all parts of the world for their Sunday results," wrote Eddie the following day. "No flying today weather is rotten," which directly reflected his mood. He had not only missed the first kill, but his impetuosity had nearly killed him and Chambers. It was little consolation that their sortie had laid the groundwork for the dual victories. It had been the sound of their engines overhead that had sent the Germans planes aloft in the first place. Campbell's detailed letter home made no mention of Eddie's sortie. Somehow they both already knew that the other was the one to beat. For the next two days, Eddie's diary, usually crammed full of his spidery cursive, is nearly blank. In the silence of those pages, one can hear Eddie girding for the next round, doubling his focus. If he couldn't be first to down a German, then he could become the first to shoot down five and earn the title of America's first ace.

Still not even brevetted as a pilot, Campbell went into Toul and bought himself a shiny pair of pilot's wings.

Over the next two weeks, Eddie's frustrations mounted as the drenching spring rained out most flying. When he did get aloft, he was lucky not to face any German veterans, as his rookie mistakes piled up thick and fast. "We had a bunch of guys across the lines from us just as stupid, if not stupider than we were," remembered Chambers. "Fortunately for us, they had no 'hotshots.' The hotshots were over at Château Thierry . . . fighting the British." Opposite them was Jasta 64, who were as green as the 94th, having reached the front at the same time they had. When Eddie and Chambers responded to one alert, they got so lost in the clouds that they had to turn back, Eddie admitting to a "definitely bad" sense of direction. On one solo venture, he only saw a machine diving on him at the last second—fortunately a French SPAD, which broke off its mistaken attack.

Out on his own again that April, he spied what he thought was a German closing with him and waited until he could confirm. Something was odd, though: Either the pilot didn't see him, which didn't seem possible, or something else was amiss. It was too easy. Remembering Lufbery's firm admonition about avoiding traps, he violently craned his neck to scan the skies and saw an Albatros jumping out from behind a cloud. He jerked back his stick into a steep climb, managing to loop behind the Albatros, which had a black-and-white roundel on its wings. That struck him as strange because he had never "heard of the Boche using anything for insignias other than the Maltese Cross." Just as he decided to fire, he noticed two more airplanes heading toward him. Perhaps just uncertain enough about the Albatros and feeling vulnerable, he aborted his attack and bolted back to Gengault. One of the planes gained steadily on him, his fears increasing because it was common knowledge that the Albatros could not match the Nieuports' flat-out airspeed. Taking no chances, he corkscrewed and feinted until he could find refuge in a cloud, within which he zigzagged for half an hour, finally emerging to find the skies clear. On landing he discovered that two members of his squadron, Campbell and Charles Chapman, another Lafayette pilot, had seen him evade the German trap, then followed and watched him maneuver right behind the enemy only to break off what appeared a certain victory. When they tried to escort him home, he had acted bizarrely, eventually disappearing into a cloud, and they had come home without him. The ribbing he received only magnified his frustration.

Particularly mortifying was the thought that others might say that he had passed up a sure kill for lack of nerve. On more than a few occasions, pilots froze during their first combat, fear and the full import of their power to destroy immobilizing their trigger fingers. Ernst Udet, the German pilot second in kills only to the Red Baron, candidly described his first interaction with an enemy:

He is now so close, I can make out the head of the observer. With his square goggles he looks like a giant, malevolent insect coming toward me to kill. The moment has come when I must fire. But I can't. It is as though horror has frozen the blood in my veins, paralyzed my arms, and torn all thought from my brain with a swipe of the paw. I sit there, flying on, and continue to stare, as though mesmerized, at the Caudron now to my left. Then the machine gun barks across to me. The impacts on my Fokker sound like metallic clicks. A tremor runs through my machine, a solid whack on my cheek, and my goggles are torn off. I reach up instinctively. Fragments, glass splinters from my goggles. My hand is wet with blood.

Udet's wounds proved only superficial, but that evening he tormented himself "Is it cowardice when one fails in the first moment of combat?" He finally came to understand over the course of that sleepless night that real soldiering can only come from thinking of the enemy as an object, not an individual. "Is it possible," he asked himself, "that the line of demarcation between the man and the coward is narrow as the edge of a sword?" The true warrior "must, at the moment of decisions, have the strength to choke off the animal fear within himself, because the animal within ourselves wants to live at any price."

Certainly these were questions that most pilots wrestled with, Eddie himself acknowledging that "there is no courage unless you're scared." Later he would boil his combat philosophy down to its very essence: "If I was master of myself I was master of my opponent, also." This was an extension of the determination to control his environment, found and polished so early in childhood, which liberated him from the stresses that broke so many others.

On Saturday afternoon, April 27, 1918, Eddie and Hall were sitting in the ready room when word came in of an enemy two-seater flying south near Beaumont. They raced to their planes, the waiting mechanics swinging the propellers. A speck in the sky to the north had to be their quarry, but, maddeningly, they couldn't take off before the squadron's commanding officer gave the specific orders. He was nowhere to be found. Frantic that they'd lose their chance, Eddie flailed at Hall, who finally "gave the signal to the boys to pull the blocks from under the wheels, leaving the camp with me in close pursuit." Both were risking reprimand, but greater things awaited.

They headed toward Pont-à-Mousson, seeing an immense observation balloon like a dirty low-hanging cloud over the American lines. Catching sight of an aircraft heading toward them, Eddie assumed it to be their enemy. Despite waggling his wings and waving madly, he failed to catch Hall's attention and so peeled off anyway, easily overtaking the intruder, maneuvering underneath its tail. Finally, heart racing, he had his chance, only to recognize, just as he started to pull the trigger, the French tricolor cockade— blue bull's-eye set in concentric circles of white, then red—and pulled away cursing. He had come far too close to shooting down a friendly.

He broke back west toward Saint-Mihiel to rejoin Hall, whom he found taunting an antiaircraft battery with a string of acrobatics. Concussive bursts rocked his dancing plane. Hall broke off his aerial nose-thumbing to take up with Eddie, now heading back toward Pont-à-Mousson. Shortly thereafter, they saw a real German; Hall signaled to Eddie to climb steeply westward so that they could position themselves between the enemy machine and the setting sun. Eddie followed. The Pfalz D.III, no blinder than they, climbed flat-out but was unable to match the Nieuports' rate of ascent.

As Hall initiated the attack, Eddie took in the whole three-dimensional scene with a quiet clarity, maneuvering against the German's other flank to head off his escape. Their prey hurriedly banked right and then dove "like a scared rabbit" for home, Eddie and Hall now on his tail. In the excitement, Eddie completely forgot to use his gunsight, aiming entirely by the flash of his tracers. They pressed the Pfalz to 2,000 feet, at which point they finally saw it lose control and crash at the edge of some woods a mile inside enemy lines. Back at Gengault, "we jumped out quite happy with glad hands for each other and we were amazed to see the personnel of our Squadron, with their hats and coats off dashing from the barracks across the field to us." American observers had seen the Pfalz crash and telephoned it in to the aerodrome. Eddie was ecstatic but drained. "Indeed, an aviator, and a fledgling aviator in particular, often runs the whole gamut of human feelings during a single flight," wrote Hall.

Eddie's published account of his first victory, which he split with Hall, would soar with dash and confidence. "Raising the nose of my airplane slightly the fiery streak lifted itself like a stream of water pouring from a garden hose," runs the passage in *Fighting the Flying Circus*. "The swerving of the Pfalz course indicated that its rudder no longer was controlled by a directing foot." Embellished by his ghostwriter, these words reflect a bravado—even arrogance—that did not characterize Eddie in the flesh, and also suggest that he had brought down the Hun almost entirely by himself. His original report, which he submitted to the writer soon after the war, paints a different and more modest picture. "To me, it was a great deal like taking something which did not belong to me rightfully, as I shall always be convinced that it was Captain Hall's victory and not mine, due to his superior marksmanship." Eddie understood that Hall had given him the greatest of gifts, a role in a first kill that engendered within him a "wonderful feeling of self-confidence." For a man who always felt at the edge of falling off into the deepest obscurity, his first victory would come as an enormous relief, helping move him beyond the mishaps and bad judgment calls that had plagued him over the last several weeks as he fought to master the dauntingly steep learning curve of aerial combat. In recognition of the kill, Eddie would receive the Croix de Guerre avec Palme. Despite this award, he knew how far he still had to go.

James Hall often took up the question of whether a flier had "plenty of sand": the grit, guts, and skill essential to making oneself a true combat flier, not just an adept flying-school pupil. Hall and Lufbery certainly had sand enough. Did Eddie?

11.

WHEN GIANTS FALL

Three years of war had taken their toll on Manfred von Richthofen, who now wore the hollow-eyed stare of the overstressed. Little stood in his way in the air; his advance toward an unparalleled kill count thrilled a country starved of heroes. For the Red Baron, however, food had lost its taste; he avoided parties, slept terribly, and spent long hours by himself staring at the ceiling. The hunter had lost much of his joy in taking prey, but love of a desperately beset nation still whetted his cunning to a razor's edge. He became increasingly preoccupied with his young charges, now often setting up an encounter so that one of his own might make the kill, thus gaining valuable confidence and experience. He worried particularly about his headstrong and often reckless younger brother, Lothar, who was becoming a star in his own right and on his way to forty kills. A few weeks after his interview with Ludendorff, as the offensive grew imminent, Richthofen learned that Lothar had crashed, gravely injuring his head. His eyes welled up. "It was touching to see his tears, for they showed him to be human after all," wrote one his men. "Those of us who knew him in the early days at the front had kept our doubts."

Early in April 1918, JG 1 moved to an advanced base at Harbonières and within four days shot down twenty-two enemy machines while losing none of their own. Whatever happened in the skies, though, the first phase of the German spring offensive stalled on April 5, the Second Battle of the Somme ending with the great salient still unbreached. Ludendorff only paused for a moment before launching the second phase against the French to the north, seeking to capture Ypres and close the crucial channel ports of Dunkirk, Boulogne, and Calais. Ludendorff believed that the French would divert valuable men and armament to Ypres, thus weakening their position farther south, but stiff resistance slowed and then halted the German advance.

On April 20, the Red Baron landed from a patrol, saying only the number "Eighty" to the delight of the mechanics and riggers who crowded his trademark scarlet plane. It marked an achievement of fourscore kills that stands as the ultimate ace record in any service during the First World War. That night they toasted "our leader, our teacher, and our comrade, the ace of aces." Even the exhausted wunderkind believed that he had brought off something of significance. No one imagined what the next day would bring.

The following morning, for the first time in nearly a month, he joked and laughed over breakfast. He even partook of a little roughhousing, overturning a sleeping pilot's cot. A few minutes later, his hound dog, Moritz, came up to him whining, a wheel chock tied to his tail. Trying to put on a stern face, Richthofen confronted the pilot he had so unceremoniously dumped on the floor. "But why make poor Moritz suffer for my crimes?" "Because it would be improper to hang a weight from the tail of a superior officer," replied his dutiful subordinate. Richthofen couldn't keep up the serious face and laughed out loud.

Later that morning he and nine other Fokkers rendezvoused with Jasta 5's Albatroses in a twenty-five-plane formation. Over Morlancourt Ridge, near the Somme, the colorful outfit jumped fifteen Sopwith Camels in a frenetic fifteen- to twenty-minute dogfight. No longer were most combat engagements lone-wolf duels, wrote Alan Winslow, instead, they were "violent mob riots in the air." "Most of the very high scoring aces tried to keep out of the confused, whirling fight, and contented themselves with trying to pick off the stragglers," observes a contemporary expert. Well versed in their limitations, aces had come to learn that a brawl among multiple machines became more than any one person could keep track of. The Red Baron bided his time.

A young, inexperienced Canadian, Lieutenant Wilfrid "Wop" May of

No. 209 Squadron, Royal Air Force, had been instructed to stay above and away from any fighting unless necessary. When the formations drifted together and all hell broke loose, engines screaming and machines pirouetting, tracers going every which way, May saw a German pass directly beneath him. When a second did so, he simply could not hold back and threw his Camel into a dive. In his eagerness he overshot his quarry—and found himself in the midst of the melee. Before he blinked, a completely red-painted plane appeared on his tail. No matter how hard he banked or what maneuver he tried, the Fokker not only matched him effortlessly but grimly and patiently moved in for the kill. By now the frightened May, having cashed out all his altitude in a last bid for escape speed, was reduced to terrain jumping, the terrifying low-level flight of pulling up just to barely clear trees and hillocks. The shadow loomed ever larger behind him. From above, Captain Roy Brown swooped down to rescue his charge, pulling hard on his machine gun. About the same time, a fusillade burst from Australian infantry below. A .303 bullet pierced Richthofen's chest. The scarlet Fokker came down precipitously but under control on a hill near the Bray-Corbie road, just north of the village of Vaux-sur-Somme. Reports differ, but the scourge of the Allied air services was already dead or died very soon after coming down.

Debate rages to this day as to whether Australian ground fire or Brown's machine gun killed the baron, although the former appears the most likely. Of far greater interest remains why this supremely experienced flier ignored the very advice he hammered daily into his apprentices about the dangers of becoming so fixated on the quarry that one becomes vulnerable oneself. Perhaps he had let up just a little bit after hitting the extraordinary mark of eighty kills. Some have suggested that an earlier bullet graze to his head had somewhat clouded his ace-caliber judgment. Or maybe the day's odd weather of a 25 mph easterly wind, directly the reverse of the prevailing westerlies, may have thrown him off by pushing him farther and faster over enemy lines than he had reckoned. Most likely, sheer cumulative stress, which had already torqued this young man into appearing nearly twice his age and sucked the life from his eyes, took its final toll. The British called it "staleness," some attributing it to oxygen deprivation, while others saw plain nervous exhaustion in his shaking hands and numb stares. What a later century well characterized as post-traumatic stress disorder could not but have contributed to his final failure of judgment that spring day. Even the finest combat pilot of the war finally bowed under the almost unimaginable strain of year-round aerial combat. The baron himself compared the "hunter," who carefully weighed the odds, eschewing outrageous risks, with the mercurial and impulsive "shooter," who triumphed by sheer audacity. He knew his JG needed both types, but he—and the other finest fighters—fell unequivocally into the hunter category. For some reason that day, the wholly uncharacteristic tug of the shooter drew him to his death.

As befit his standing as the ultimate hero of the newest mode of warfare, the Allies buried him with full honors.

Tucked away in the quiet Toul sector, away from the real intensities of combat, the 94th could hardly restrain their desire to find "Huns" and knock them out of the sky. Like many other young men new to their uniforms, they fretted that the war might be concluded before they got a chance to fight. More often than not, fog and rain socked the 94th in for long days at a time, leaving them to rowdy games of cards; Campbell and Lufbery buried themselves in epic rounds of evening bridge. They banged on a piano, with Yalies like Alan Winslow teaching the mildly sexual songs of their school years, such as "The Whizz-Fish," about a hungry fish biting a monkey's tail "in far off Uruguay." They would trade books; detective stories were popular, but they also read *The Wind in the Willows,* Shakespeare, and poetry. They spent hours staring at maps, it being impractical to take these aloft "because the minute you start to look at it some wily Boche is 'on your tail,'" noted Coolidge. In the evenings, they would drink as only young men can. "Quent . . . the only person I've ever seen who had a sword-swallower's throat," remembered Chambers, would "stretch his neck—and he'd let the champagne, a whole quart of champagne, run right down him without ever swallowing." He'd do it twice in an evening if someone bought the champagne.

High spirits spilled over as they added decorative touches to their aircraft. John Winslow painted his girlfriend Priscilla's name underneath his cockpit, Wentworth a dragon, while Eddie and Jimmy Meissner adorned their wings with war-bond posters of a young woman unfolding the flag over the slogan "Fight or Buy Bonds." Everyone joked that they'd have to buy bonds themselves if the weather didn't improve soon. Like all young men, they bridled and pushed, hungry for a chance to prove themselves.

All too soon their wishes were granted, May 2 offering fairly good conditions all day: The 94th mounted eight separate sorties. For the first time in three weeks of active duty, Jimmy Meissner saw German planes, and he returned with the squadron's fourth kill but also a horrifying tale of how a midair collision had stripped the top edge of his uppermost wing. At 15,000 feet he had reflected, "What beastly luck to die just as my first victory had been won." After long frightening moments in a spin, he realized that his bottom wing would not in fact collapse, thus leaving his ailerons intact and affording just enough lift to limp home. The blush of that early victory faded fast the next day when enemy rounds set Lieutenant Charles W. Chapman Jr.'s Nieuport ablaze, cremating him long before he struck the earth. The first of the 94th to die in combat, Chapman posthumously received the Distinguished Service Cross for "extraordinary heroism in action," having attacked five enemy aircraft and shot one down before he himself fell. "All the Boys feel very blue," Eddie wrote in his diary, "but same must be expected."

It's hard to imagine a more combustible creation than the World War I–era airplane, a virtual flying pyre made of cotton fabric or linen stretched over wooden frames and doped with highly flammable finish to stiffen the whole assembly. Not enemy tracers alone but a spark from one's own engine might instantly turn a smooth, routine flight into mortal agony. Fanned by the stiff breeze of flight, flames could consume a machine in moments, leaving the pilot himself wrapped in fire far above the ground. Few if any combat experiences gave a warrior such a Faustian choice as between a martyr's immolation or a leap to the earth thousands of feet below. After Chapman died, the pilots wrestled with this decision, no longer able to ignore the possibility that they might be forced to make it in a few crazed seconds. Some opted for a third option and took their service revolvers aloft with them.

Rudimentary but workable parachutes existed—the Germans would use them for balloon observers, and during the last six weeks of war for combat pilots—but the U.S. military bureaucracy never cleared them. The reason given appears ludicrous, even callous, clearly the thinking of swivel-chair commanders who never had to contemplate burning to death 2 miles up. Headquarters believed that a pilot would be far more inclined to leave his airplane at the first hint of trouble if he could bail out, thus unacceptably wasting equipment. A moment shared with the young men who took such desperate risks just to go aloft, much less to challenge a skillful, well-armed adversary, would have given the lie to this assumption.

"We knew [parachutes] were being worked on," noted Campbell, "and we didn't know why we didn't have them . . . We would have been glad to have them." The understanding that pilots were difficult to train and far more valuable than aircraft didn't sink in until a year after the war ended, when parachutes finally were issued. For the men of the 94th, this callous valuation of their safety amounted to yet another conflicting factor that each man carried with him each time he climbed into these highly dangerous machines.

On May 7, Eddie, Hall, and the darkly handsome, round-faced Lieutenant M. Edwin Green, very recently a student at Carnegie Institute of Technology, responded to an alert at 7:27 A.M. Enemy had been spotted over Pont-à-Mousson on the Moselle. Unbeknown to the Americans, King Friedrich August III of Saxony was visiting his troops; Jasta 64 mounted a patrol to protect the royalty. Unable to find targets by Pont-à-Mousson, the intercepting Americans turned westward toward Saint-Mihiel, where Eddie gazed down upon the Moselle as it wrapped around the mountains surrounding the town and disappeared north toward Verdun, the site two years earlier of perhaps the most savage protracted battle in history.

Looking to the horizon, Eddie focused a little closer in, a technique he had learned to better help his "vision of the air." (As Campbell described it, "If you focused on some point in the sky, looking for aircraft, you probably wouldn't see them if they were over here, so you had to sort of gaze around with a sort of vacant stare, and if anything was moving you'd see it right away.") The slight shadow of a German machine flickered a few miles within Allied lines. Eddie waggled his wings, and the patrol turned toward it. Just as Eddie identified it as an Albatros two-seater, a German battery fired a warning shot. Eddie cursed as the Albatros dove for home. The Germans had perfected a simple but effective signaling system to warn a friendly craft by directing a shot at the converging foe's altitude. In another moment, the battery discharged three more shells ahead of the retreating Albatros, "three hostiles approaching from the East"—displays that poked the hornet's nest, alerting nearby aerodromes of the intruders' number, direction, and height. Eddie kept sweeping the horizon, now fully aware that they could expect company and wondering why the Allies themselves did not systematically imitate "this admirable liaison between German artillery and their aviators."

Another gift that the German ace and tactical mastermind Oswald Boelcke had delivered before he crashed eighteen months earlier centered upon creating forward combat airstrips, an idea that his student Richthofen had enthusiastically embraced. Just a mile or so behind the lines—well within artillery range—the Germans established temporary airfields replete with reclining chairs, their airplanes gassed up and ready to go at a moment's notice. When enemy aircraft were sighted through binoculars, the pilots raced to intercept. "Standing patrols are not flown," wrote Ernst Udet, believing it a waste to fly out in search of quarry. Indeed, noted Richthofen, the "business of standing sentry duty in the air weakens the pilots' will to fight." Or, as the Red Baron put it more prosaically on another occasion, he liked to "let the customer come to the shop."

Eddie fixed his gaze toward Pont-à-Mousson; sure enough, four Pfalzes were coming up but at a lower altitude, angling to cut off their retreat. Eddie pulled in front of Hall, again waggling his wings. Yet again Hall seemed slow to register the enemy. Without radios, each pilot had to interpret the actions not only of the enemy but of his comrades, adding even more complexities to real-time aerial decision making. Hall again took the lead, but curiously pushed northward and deeper into enemy territory. Did he see something else, wondered Eddie? Had he even seen the approaching Pfalzes? Taking charge, Eddie again dove ahead to bank eastward and toward the oncoming enemy.

During his time with the Lafayette Escadrille, Hall had described the almost dreamlike first blush of combat. At first "we seemed, all of us, to be hanging motionless, then rising and falling like small boats riding a heavy swell. Another glance would show one of them suspended bottom up, falling sidewise, tipped vertically on a wing, standing on its tail, as though being blown about by the wind, out of all control." In a moment, the peacefully undulating sortie jumped into screaming action, as Eddie threw his Nieuport in a steep attack dive, his guy-wires singing under the stress, Hall and Green close behind.

Eddie pounced, pouring a burst into his foe's wings at 200 yards; as he closed to 50 yards, the Pfalz tumbled into a death spin. Eddie pulled up sharply until he was vertical and standing on his tail, rolling his head around frantically to see if anyone was on his back. No one was, but he did see a death fight not 100 yards away to his right, as a pursuing Pfalz poured its magazine into a Nieuport. Suddenly the Nieuport's pilot executed an exquisite, beautifully timed pirouette, pulling up steeply until he stalled and twisted upside down as the startled enemy swept beneath him. Then, with another twist, the American fell back into the dive, right on his assailant's tail, predator now prey—exactly the cool, composed handiwork in extremity that Eddie had expected of Hall. The Pfalz caught fire and hurtled into the ground.

Eddie searched the skies for Green without success, and so was taken aback when coming up on the other Nieuport, he saw Green beaming in the cockpit. Hall was nowhere to be found. Now vulnerably low over enemy guns, the pair reluctantly pushed homeward. After landing, Green described how Hall had spun down in a vrille, leveling out low over a forest before going down. He was probably dead. When Lufbery heard this, he jumped into a Nieuport in immediate search of revenge, found three enemy planes, and ferociously attacked.

"America's greatest loss today," Eddie noted in his diary, simple words that belied the devastation that Hall's crash wrought upon the 94th. If that self-assured, highly experienced flight leader could go down so quickly and easily after joining the squadron, what chance did that offer the greenhorns? Some consolation came when the Germans sent word, as was customary, that Hall had survived a bad crash with a broken leg and nose, but the brave, dynamic leader was lost nonetheless for the rest of the war.

With Hall gone, Eddie took over command of 1st Flight, one of three groups within the 94th, an indication of just how stretched the air service was for experienced pilots. Even flying every moment he could, Eddie could count no more than 150 hours of air time and only a handful of actual engagements—no substantial experience by any reckoning. Only a month and a half after his first shaky flight across enemy lines with Lufbery, it was now his job to lead others into danger. The sudden, unexpected course changes and urgencies of war press deeply upon the skills and inner resources of those who fight in the air. Rarely is there time for full preparation. Eddie was no stranger to embracing new challenges, but these would prove of a new order of magnitude compared to anything he'd ever put his shoulder against.

The friendship between Eddie and Reed Chambers now flowered into a strong working combination. They often stayed up late "trying to hit on some extra little trick that would assure more victories over the Germans." During one such session they decided to take off before dawn and gain high altitude just as the sun rose to win the double advantage of height and

surprise. They agreed that dabs of axle grease on their faces would protect against the cold. (The grease worked but caused their skin to peel when
they had to remove it by scrubbing with gasoline.)

So on May 17, they took off in the predawn darkness, spiraling higher
and higher yet. Chambers would later say with poetic exhilaration that a
high-altitude dawn patrol enabled one to "see the sun coming up the day after tomorrow." Such heights held their own dangers. They climbed through
8,000 feet (the pressure at which modern passenger jets keep their cabins in
flight) to beyond 14,000 feet (the pressure at which supplemental oxygen
masks automatically drop) and on to 20,000 feet, where significant physiological changes occur swiftly. Lower pressure denies oxygen to the blood,
starving the brain and muscles and impairing judgment.

At this attenuated pressure, the heart beats faster, and breathing grows
labored to offset the scanty intake of oxygen, which, compounded by the
searing cold of the open cockpit, visits a euphoric confusion upon the best-
prepared mind, often bringing headache and dizziness, possibly even tin-
gling in the fingers and toes. Above 12,000 feet, wrote Ham Coolidge, one felt
dizzy, but that usually passed. During one combat at high altitude, amid the
frantic tracers of a Rumpler, Chambers remembered that "you were so doped
up with lack of oxygen, you didn't mind it at all." While the pilots' sheer
youthfulness minimized the discomfort, they were also often hungover or
dehydrated. Walter Avery wrote that at 16,000 feet on one flight, he threw up
the half pound of candy he had gobbled the night before. "It froze instantly
into a solid sheet on my shoulders and back of the seat, also before I could jerk
out my handkerchief it had frozen solid on my mustache, cheek and goggles
so that during the next hour I had to fly without goggles. Nice trick!"

Flying the 15 miles east to Nancy, Chambers left Eddie's side—probably,
surmised Eddie, because of engine problems, or perhaps due to the subzero
temperature's sludging effect on oil and gas lines. Eddie had already turned
back to base when he spotted three Albatroses far below. His thinking
probably clouded by the altitude, he pushed his joystick hard forward into a
steep dive, the so-called zoom, while Archies burst to alert his prey. Too
late. Coming right onto his first target's tail, he squeezed off fifty rounds

into the belly of its fuselage and saw it death-spiral away. Any feelings of exultation evaporated as he saw the team leader swing into place above and behind him.

Once initial surprise passes and dogfighting begins, the laws of physics wield overriding influence on the encounter. Rapid maneuvering—turns, banking, loops, the deathly circus of a new way of fighting—increased drag upon the airframes of the day, considerably slowing them. The under-powered engines, unlike today's, could not quickly make up speed. So a pilot who resorted to one maneuver too many would eventually find himself slowed to the minimum speed necessary just to keep aloft. As with the first few wobbly pedal strokes on a bicycle, such slowness gives virtually no ability to maneuver. Eddie could transform altitude into speed—that's what he had earned from climbing so otherwise dangerously high—but he obviously couldn't keep this up indefinitely: The ground would intervene once and for all. The worst and usually rather brief outcome would be to find himself flying at sitting-duck slow speed only a few hundred feet up.

At this point, Eddie had conceded major altitude in his first pass, the lead Albatros now cashing in his newly bestowed height advantage for speed and a chance to rake the intruder. Devoid of any other fighting chance but that of regaining altitude as quickly as possible, Eddie jerked his stick back hard into his stomach to reverse that precipitous dive. This threw him back into his seat, the engine shrieking in protest. With a loud crack, the leading edge of his upper right wing ripped back from the wooden ribs and started snapping like a flag in a stiff wind. Eddie craned his neck violently—he must have hit his adversary, he thought. The engine coughed, then stopped.

Deprived of starboard lift, the Nieuport slid into an uncontrolled tail-spin, the two Germans blazing long ropes of bullets at him. With the uncanny detachment of the mortally stricken, he thought it strange that they would waste ammunition on a goner. Next to go would surely be his lower wings—but somehow they held. With every revolution he felt "a regular jar as the shock of the air cushion came against the left wing after passing through the skeleton of the right one." Suddenly galvanized, he kicked into activity, fighting to break the death spiral, wrenching the stick from side to side, stomping on the rudder, even throwing his body with all his force in one direction, then another. Still he could not "modify, even in the slightest, the gyrations of the Nieuport."

As the plane plummeted 10,000 feet, "My whole life seemed to go through my mind like a moving picture. I wondered whether the airplane would disintegrate around me and let me fall free, whistling through the wind. Would I strike the ground and splatter all over? Maybe I would be lucky and land in the trees with only a few broken bones."

Some German soldiers stood mesmerized at his Icarus-like fall; he imagined how they would pick over his body and carry off pieces of his shattered machine as souvenirs. He could see his mother opening the door of their little house in Columbus to receive the cablegram announcing his death in action. A "spasm of longing" rose up within him.

He had at most a few seconds to live. Virtually all those so doomed would have bowed to the sovereignty of fate. No emergency procedures came to mind—no such manuals had yet been written; no body of experience had been marshaled from which lifesaving lessons could be culled. For Eddie there were "no formulas" for escape, only the crippling reality of a wildly disorienting, stomach-screwing spin into the earth.

Yet something within him cooled into steely resolve. Just a couple of hundred feet off the ground, he threw his "weight to the left hand side over the cockpit and jammed the controls, crossed them and jammed the engine wide open." An explosion lit the cowling with blue flame, but "the whole thing suddenly sputtered and vibrated violently, and finally went off on one wing headed for France." Intuition suggests that engaging the engine should only have launched him more forcefully into the ground, but instead the speed so gained imparted just enough lift to tear him out of the spin. Flying almost horizontally, he jerked on his stick with all he had and reversed the rudder to counter the gyroscopic momentum of the rotary engine. The Nieuport crept along just above stall speed. He pitched around in search of his two enemies, expecting at any moment to feel bullets smash into his back. Fortunately, the Albatroses had left him for dead.

Experienced pilots speak of the almost intimate relationship they forge with their craft. The Canadian ace Billy Bishop described how the thrum of his engine was as important as his own heartbeat. "No matter how many cylinders you have whirring in front of you, the instant one misses your heart hears it even before your ears do." Eddie maneuvered his broken machine, integrating and then responding to hundreds of real-time details, many only just consciously registerable: the sound of the engine, the tension on stick and rudder, the pitch of the wind in his guy-wires, the uneven pressures on his seat. He corrected, gently pressed upon, almost caressed the controls to keep it aloft.

To his relief, the deeply incised front trenches came into view only 2 miles ahead. He talked to his Nieuport all the rest of the way, so grateful "to her for not letting me down that I actually cooed words of endearment." He got across, but only 1,000 feet up and sinking fast. Had the providential aerodrome sat even a half mile farther away, he wouldn't have made it. As it was, he barely cleared his own barracks, bringing down his machine like a bird with a broken wing. Enraged French pilots charged out to discover who had dared to attempt such a "hot" landing, his engine at full roar.

He stumbled ashen-faced behind the barracks and vomited. The pilot's code, which he was helping to write by hard experience, brooked no whimpering over such brushes with death, and so he summarized the episode to the French commander with feigned nonchalance. In contrast, a picture taken not long after he landed shows a man stunned beyond all measure by the shadow of the angel of death. His color has drained; the eyes reflect an exhaustion that conveys just how far he had to reach into himself simply to survive. "As for me," he wrote later, "the pride and gratitude I felt for the little ship overshadowed all other emotions."

A few weeks after he took command of 1st Flight, several new pilots joined the 94th, including one Walter Smythe. Eddie liked the New Yorker right away—a no-nonsense fellow who handled his Nieuport with confidence— and, after watching his acrobatics, took him up for his first sortie over the lines on May 19. Eddie had not forgotten the vulnerability of that first time out. "A moment's forgetfulness, a trifling foolhardiness, a slight miscalculation, and even a man who has been carefully and expensively trained and who possesses all the characteristics of a successful pilot, may fall before the skill of a more experienced flier."

Eddie led Smythe as Lufbery had led him and Campbell to Saint-Mihiel and then across the trench line to Pont-à-Mousson. Seeing no enemy activity, he pointed northwest toward Verdun, recrossing the lines near the enemy aerodrome at Mars-la-Tour. Lufbery had been satisfied with that for Eddie's first sortie, feeling no need to press deep into occupied territory. Hungering for action—Campbell had bagged his second Hun the previous day, evening their score—Eddie pushed harder and finally spotted an Albatros observation plane below them some 2 miles ahead. Waggling his wings to alert Smythe, he then maneuvered to place the blinding sun at his back and dove. His tracers missed, probably from opening up at too great a distance. All surprise blown, Eddie and the other pilot, who maneuvered with the confidence of experience, pulled out their bag of tricks. However, Eddie had not reckoned with his Nieuport's usual nimbleness being compromised by the thin air at this height. Steering into a steep bank, it slowed, then stalled and fell into a tailspin. By the time he recovered control, the Albatros was gone—not the lesson that Eddie wanted to teach Smythe, who was watching from above.

On the way home, Eddie spotted telltale white puffs of artillery-shell explosions over Saint-Mihiel—American gunners firing at an enemy ship. The Albatros had simply continued its mission after shaking him off. His blood rising at this perceived challenge, he again maneuvered to attack, but the Albatros called it quits and dove for its friendly field. Eddie tried to cut it off but was again deftly evaded. To cap it all, when he turned to look for Smythe he couldn't find him. They were 10 miles behind enemy lines. Which way had Smythe headed? Stomach clenching, he circled higher but, still unable to see his pupil, finally turned back to Gengault with a heart buffeted by doubt. What would Lufbery say of his leadership now?

Approaching the aerodrome, Eddie felt his heart sink as he saw pilots and mechanics milling about, all too likely around a crashed Smythe. As he put down he remembered joking with Smythe, who had been so delighted to go up. How could he maintain his leadership as flight commander if he'd lost his first charge? He rolled to a stop and jumped out, but the men gazed blankly when he asked for Smythe. Then someone broke the news that Lufbery had crashed and was probably dead, leaving Eddie "dumb with dismay and horror." The impossible had happened—just how remains a source of contention to the present day.

It is indisputable that Lufbery had been piping mad and hot for revenge ever since Jim Hall went down on May 7. When an alert sounded at about 10:00 A.M.—Eddie and Smythe were already long clear of the base—indicating a German reconnaissance plane crossing the lines, the squadron commander, Major Jean Huffer, immediately took off in pursuit. Accompanying him was Lieutenant Oscar Gude, a pianist of some talent and the son of a wealthy advertising executive, who had never flown in combat. Huffer turned back right away after experiencing engine trouble. From the field, the pilots and mechanics watched Gude approach the enemy and loose two hundred rounds from hopelessly far away. His effort appeared so weak and halfhearted that they knew he had fired solely to discharge his minimal duty and get back to the field. There had already been murmurs that, for all his excellent piloting abilities, the New Yorker might lack nerve. Now it was out there for all to see. It was one thing that some young fliers could not bring themselves to take life, yet another when they could not even draw close to their adversary. Any willingness to accommodate such hesitation was in limited supply among men who feared that any sign of weakness would infect the group and validate the terror that lurked just behind every noisily cheerful face in the mess. As if attacking an infection, they dealt with Gude without mercy. He soon transferred out of the 94th.

At the sight of this debacle, Lufbery leaped onto a motorcycle and roared down to the hangar, where in a white heat he commandeered a warmed-up Nieuport—his was being repaired—which he took up immediately. From the field, they watched him chase the enemy, pushing his craft all out. Just at the edge of their vision, he went into an attack, swooping with his customary hyperaggressiveness so close to the enemy's tail that it seemed the two planes might collide, in breathtaking and perhaps purposeful contrast to Gude's tepid efforts. He fired a burst before breaking off to avoid collision. On his next pass, the German gunner got off a few shots, one punching into Luf's fuel reservoir, which set it on fire, and severing the ace's right thumb on the joystick, which caused the plane to snap-roll and flip over. Two shapes fell from the cockpit: Lufbery himself, then the cushion he had been sitting on. He was impaled on the picket fence of a shoemaker's house close to the Moselle; his machine crashed not far off.

Word reached the aerodrome only a few minutes later, just as Eddie landed. He, Chambers, and Major Huffer jumped in the squadron Cadillac and raced east across the Moselle to the tiny village of Maron, some 8 miles southeast of Toul. There they quickly found the house, but the body already had been taken to the Toul *hôtel de ville*, where it lay covered in spring flowers. The shoemaker's old wife told them that he had fallen while she had been gardening. The picket fence had pierced his left leg; he had struggled up, then fallen over dead. They found the imprint of his body in the soft spring soil.

Debate immediately broke out over whether he had jumped to avoid a terrible death in flames or had simply fallen when his plane inverted. The nearness of the river supported the notion that he might have been trying to jump in the water. However, his headlong takeoff also suggested that he might have neglected to buckle into his harness, by any measure cumbersome and virtually impossible to connect while taxiing or flying. Straps across both shoulders meet at a lap belt, all of which had to be fastened into one central joining mechanism. In addition, the belt was adjusted for another pilot who was much shorter than him. If unbuckled, nothing would have kept him aboard after his machine flipped.

As the pilots wrestled with the harrowing loss of their confident and seemingly invulnerable comrade, the squadron united to a man on the explanation that Lufbery had jumped. Nothing ever swayed Eddie from that position, even the recollection of a conversation only days earlier during which Lufbery had told him that he had never considered jumping because "there is always a good chance of side-slipping your airplane down in such a way that you fan the flames away from yourself and the wings." For Eddie and the others, the awful pointlessness of dying a tyro's death from failing to secure his seat belt was simply too painful to even entertain. Jumping at least suggested that he had chosen his own death, an ending that befitted the outstanding pilot and honored the needs of those who had idolized and drawn their confidence from him. Lufbery's jump, wrote Eddie, was a "hopeless but a heroic attempt to preserve his life for his country." The squadron's collective belief about their most horrific catastrophe would make them a tougher, tighter unit and evoke from them a greater will and capacity to survive. As Eddie's leadership flowered, he would put such un-brookable commitments to use in building morale and unit cohesion for tackling difficult odds.

That evening Smythe flew back in, much to Eddie's relief. Mechanical difficulties had forced him down in a French field. The next day he and hundreds of others, including Colonel Mitchell and several generals, marched in somber procession up a hill at Gengault to the cemetery near the hospital. Banks of flowers surrounded Lufbery's grave. Overhead, Eddie led five Nieuports to shower the cortege with blossoms. Luf's passing blew the cold winds of death into the deepest recesses of every heart, but it also raised a signpost in the growing maturity of the 94th. For one thing, their bewitchment faded, the pilots now looked more critically at the performance of the Nieuport 28. A small fuel reserve tank, called the *nourrice* (nurse), was located to the pilot's front and right in a position especially vulnerable to enemy fire. A single near-miss could spray the cockpit with raging, ignited gasoline, consuming plane and pilot within seconds. Meissner's diary records "flying with side tank empty now to lessen fire danger." It is likely and entirely comprehensible that others did as well.

Two days later after the funeral, Eddie took up Chambers and another novice, Lieutenant Paul B. Kurtz, whom he was glad to see because Kurtz had learned to fly with him at Tours before being sent to Britain to study teaching techniques of aerial gunnery. He had arrived at Gengault with orders to acquire combat flying experience. Eddie took no chances, telling Kurtz not to engage but to observe any action from up and behind. Should they become separated he was to keep the sun behind him, so he would be heading west and into friendly territory. Kurtz did as he was told, remaining high above as Eddie and Chambers engaged an enemy formation 6 miles inside their own lines. Eddie brought down his third Hun, again evening the score with Campbell, but on the way back lost track of Kurtz, only catching sight of him as he circled in preparation to land at base. One eyewitness saw Kurtz put on power to avoid a machine taking off. Then, to Eddie's "unspeakable horror," Kurtz's craft hurtled into the ground and exploded in a ball of fire. Throwing his plane into a dive, Eddie landed flat-out and tore over to the smoldering wreck on the squadron motorcycle. Kurtz's charred body gave him nightmares for the rest of his life.

Eddie would later learn that although aerobatic activity gave Kurtz fainting spells, he had been so eager to get into the mix that he concealed this problem from his squadron leader. Eddie, who hid his own infirmities from others, certainly could not blame him and chalked the accident up to an inopportune blackout. "I had got my Boche," he wrote, "but I had lost a friend, and he had perished in the manner most dreaded by all aviators, for he had gone down in flames." Another officer speculated that Kurtz had cut off his engine to glide in for a landing but blipped it back on to avoid the other aircraft and in doing so ignited the unburned fuel in his cowling. Eddie kept to the idea that Kurtz had fainted from some lurking physiological weakness. Later he would institute a rule that pilots must circle the field twice before landing, not swoop down from thousands of feet. "Could I live for a million years," wrote Eddie, "I should not forget that awful sight of the charred remains of the man who had been my companion in the schools, and who only one brief hour before had set out with me full of life and hope."

Eddie and the others carried the small box of remains uphill to the cemetery three days after they had borne Lufbery there. Stepping into Lufbery's shoes would not be easy, even for Eddie.

How does one assess the toll exacted by the destruction of such a re-vered figure as Raoul Lufbery upon the young men of the 94th? His pres-ence had been their one constant. He could always be found leaning against a fuselage or in a game of cards, a wry grin on his lips and an ever-burning cigarette casually gripped between index and middle finger, dispensing homegrown wisdom. When arguments broke out about air tactics, it seemed that conversation soon died away as all eyes turned upon him, waiting for an opinion in that heavy French accent. He didn't show much emotion or deliver many words, but those he did speak counted. He wasn't so much a father figure as an older brother, or perhaps a younger uncle. They watched him working with the mechanics to keep his plane pristine, never knew him to miss a chance to go up, registered the unquenchable fire in his eyes.

Leaders such as Lufbery supplied the hard-to-define cohesion that holds a combat group together, the critical source of sustenance that keeps them going back and back yet again into adversity and danger. He had nothing of the commanding presence of Pershing, but he provided important intan-gibles on mastering "one of the most challenging and difficult professions, air to air combat," as one historian has characterized it. The air combat en-vironment was changing so fast—and no ready-made role models, nor standards of behavior, had had the chance to evolve before the Archduke Franz Ferdinand had been killed, so few years before. In that crazy, uncer-tain turmoil, Lufbery had supplied solid, crucial leadership.

His death, on the heels of Jim Hall's crash and capture, along with the news that Peterson was off to run the 95th, tore a gaping leadership void in the 94th. In times of such duress, groups can turn inward, like a football team recharging flagging spirits with a call to remember the injured and rekindling memories of ancient rivalries. Teams can also splinter or founder destructively off course. Fatalism can infect morale. Out there on the fields of Gengault, the stakes were high. How could they stem the tide of the attri-tion that threatened to wash them away before they even got a fair shake at combat?

12.

RACE TO ACE

It's easy to think that Lufbery's death must have seemed like a great oak crashing down in the forest, ripping a hole in the canopy through which light could spill to afford wispy saplings a chance to reach for full growth. In fact, northeastern France in that bloody spring of 1918 was no stable forest, but rather a hothouse in which the cream of America's finest fought to survive the debilitating toll of fatal or crippling accidents, technical malfunctions, and a skilled enemy eager to exploit them. As the world order swayed in the balance, these young men were on the cutting edge of a struggle that would remake the contours of the political world.

Their journals, if anything electrified by daily extreme risk, began to change in timbre and tone from the almost carefree early days at Issoudun and Cazaux—not really that fatalism takes over their pencils, but rather that a certain hardening becomes manifest in those being pressed into adulthood at deadly speed. To most, these insistent calls to maturity were new, but not for Eddie, who had felt such demands since his bruised childhood. Most were still boys at heart, drinking anything alcoholic that passed in front of them, prone to horsing around and gibing at one another, painting the world in passionate simplicities. While their voices might already ring deep, their curses still crackled boyishly when they opened yet one more parcel from home to find soap and toothbrushes. Moments of pure joy still peeked through. "Have you ever looked up at a fleecy cloud with the sun glistening on its top and wished you were there?" wrote one breathlessly.

"I saw one and in five minutes had reached it." Overall, however, a growing sobriety begins to creep into their writings.

If young men often know no bounds and must press forward until they meet them—and themselves—in the process, then this environment gave them the room literally to soar. "Flying that people are called fools for doing in the States is simply everyday life here," wrote Lansing Holden of the 95th, "and the man that isn't perfectly at home in his machine at any position is gone." Among this cadre, all culled through manifold trial and test, all potential leaders, two within their midst pulled far ahead of all others. Lufbery had been right all along in anointing Campbell and Rickenbacker.

The first and second kills for both could have been chalked up to good fortune more than seasoned skill; from then on each raced ahead of the others in victories, awakening a heated competition for bragging rights as the first ace in American service. Their fellow pilots—themselves all strong fliers—began to understand they were witnessing something extraordinary, even in extraordinary times. Like two elite tennis competitors who keep pushing one another to reach beyond what either thought possible in himself, these two born competitors used courteous competition to hone their already sharp competitive edges.

Campbell had scored his first kill that day with Alan Winslow in early April, then took more than a month for his second. Eddie scored his first on April 27 with Hall, then a second just before that near-fatal moment when the leading edge split off his Nieuport's upper wing. A day later, Campbell drew even, going on to a third on May 19, which he celebrated by drawing a tiny Iron Cross on the hatband of his machine's insignia. On the May 22 sortie in which Kurtz died, Eddie again tied the score. Campbell nailed his fourth on May 27; Eddie the following day. None of the others exactly took sides in this unacknowledged competition; that would have struck everyone as somehow petty, not in keeping with their responsibilities as patriotic Americans on the front line against a tidal menace to democracy. Neither would Eddie let it get to that. They were bent in competitive common purpose, not zero-sum opposition. Nor would Campbell, ever the gentleman. There was simply no tolerance for self-aggrandizement.

Where the term "ace" originated, or why the number five became its universal benchmark, has aroused much speculation but unearthed few answers. The first aces had appeared in 1915, the realization dawning in Europe as both sides settled into their foul, muddy trenches that this conflict would drag on long after the joyful anticipation of quick decisive victory had receded. In contrast to the legions wiped out in the hellish mud of no-man's-land, the contests of will and cunning in the sky lent themselves to celebration, victories marked by a clean, hard-edged number. Across cultures the number of aircraft downed by this warrior elite carved a rock-hard and ratable hierarchy of excellence—if not measurable by scalps on a belt or notches on a pistol grip, then something equally tangible.

Between World War I and Vietnam, hundreds of thousands trained to become fighter pilots, but fewer than 1 percent went on to see combat; of those, only one in twenty became aces, superstars amid an already exalted few. These workhorses also bore more on their broad shoulders, accounting for 40 percent of all aircraft destroyed; their presence alone could change a battle's dynamics. Back home, these young men found themselves lit gaudily by the klieg lights of national idolization, as civilians of all stripes hungered for heroes who personified courage, craft, and the mastery that brought triumph. Men such as Richthofen, Boelcke, and Max Immelmann, along with René Fonck of France and the Canadian Billy Bishop, received trunkfuls of adoring letters with marriage proposals and offers of unattached sex. Of the 1,500 aces to emerge from World War I, more than half would come from Britain; the Americans would count 110, the French 160, the Germans 363.

The American race to ace played out in the waning days of May. At 8:00 A.M. on the thirtieth, a formation of six Nieuports under Jimmy Meissner and another six from the 95th took to the skies to escort British bombers home from striking a German railhead east of Verdun. Not tasked to go, Eddie decided to join them anyway—a flight leader's prerogative—and took off a few minutes later, planning to rendezvous near Verdun. As he climbed well above the others to 15,000 feet, the clear light of a bright morning revealed a riveting scene more chessboard than classic battlefield, the

Elizabeth Rickenbacher, William Rickenbacher, and Eddie Rickenbacher, c. 1903, Columbus, Ohio. (*Courtesy of Auburn University, Special Collections and Archives*)

Columbus Buggy Company's quality control team, which Rickenbacher (wearing tie) supervised, October 1908. (*Courtesy of Auburn University, Special Collections and Archives*)

Mason Team Racing Team, August 1913: (from left) Rickenbacher, Eddie O'Donnell, Billy Chandler, Fritz Walker. Both O'Donnell, who served for a while as Eddie's mechanician, and Walker, would die in crashes. (*Courtesy of Auburn University, Special Collections and Archives*)

Rickenbacker and Lee Frayer driving politician William Jennings Bryan in a Firestone-Columbus in Abilene, Texas, 1909. (*Courtesy of Auburn University, Special Collections and Archives*)

Daredevil Lincoln Beachey. *(Courtesy of the National Archives)*

Lincoln Beachey's *Little Looper* racing Rickenbacker's Duesenberg. Iowa State Fair, August 1914. *(Courtesy of the San Diego Air & Space Museum)*

Johnny Aitken, Rickenbacker, and Dario Resta at the Indianapolis Motor Speedway, c. 1916. *(Courtesy of Auburn University, Special Collections and Archives)*

A Locomobile takes the Westbury Bend at the 1908 Vanderbilt Cup race. *(Author's collection)*

Rickenbacker takes a pit stop at an unidentified track. *(Courtesy of Auburn University, Special Collections and Archives)*

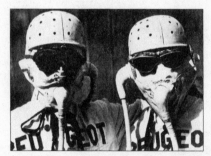

Rickenbacker designed a mask-and-tube assembly to ease communication between racing car driver and his mechanician Fred McCarty. Corona Road Race, November 1914. *(Courtesy of Auburn University, Special Collections and Archives)*

Rickenbacker in Blitzen Benz, c. 1915. *(Courtesy of the National Archives)*

The nose-heavy Nieuport 28 often flipped on landing. *(Courtesy of the National Archives)*

A pilot's first landing, probably in Issoudun. *(Courtesy of the National Archives)*

Manfred von Richthofen, the Red Baron, and feared creator of the German Flying Circus. *(Courtesy of the National Archives)*

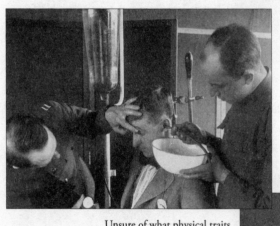

Unsure of what physical traits made a good pilot, the Signal Corps put its aviators through a battery of tests (top), which many already confirmed aces, such as Raoul Lufbery (left), failed. *(Courtesy of the National Archives)*

A 1930s artist's rendition (above) of the April 18, 1918, dogfight, in which Douglas Campbell and Alan Winslow (below) claimed the first official U.S. air victories, gets aircraft details wrong but captures the close immediacy of a dogfight. Gengoult Aerodrome near Toul, France. *(Author's collection)*

Douglas Campbell and Alan Winslow shortly after their surprising first victories, April 18, 1918. *(Courtesy of the National Archives)*

Eddie Rickenbacker in a Nieuport 28, the aircraft in which he earned his first kill. *(Courtesy of the National Archives)*

The body of twenty-year-old Quentin Roosevelt, son of the former president, lies beside his broken Nieuport, July 14, 1918. *(Courtesy of the National Archives)*

Nieuports of the 147th Pursuit Squadron are readied for flight after an alert. *(Courtesy of Ted Hamady)*

Officers of the 94th Pursuit Squadron at Gengoult Aerodrome: (kneeling from left) Douglas Campbell, James Meissner, Edwin Green, unidentified, Oscar Gude, unidentified, unidentified; (standing) unidentified, Raoul Lufbery, unidentified, Jean Huffer, Ken Marr, unidentified, Rickenbacker, Reed Chambers, John Wentworth, Harvey Weir Cook, Bill Loomis, Alan Winslow, Walter Smythe. *(Courtesy of Ted Hamady)*

An artist imagines Rickenbacker's wing-stripping episode. *(Drawing by Michael T. O'Neal, ASAA)*

Rickenbacker with the damaged top right wing. *(Courtesy of Ted Hamady)*

A distraught Rickenbacker just after landing his damaged Nieuport. *(Courtesy of Ted Hamady)*

Arizona Balloon Buster Frank Luke of the 27th with his SPAD ten days before his death. *(Courtesy of the National Archives)*

A hydrogen-filled observation balloon. *(Courtesy of the National Archives)*

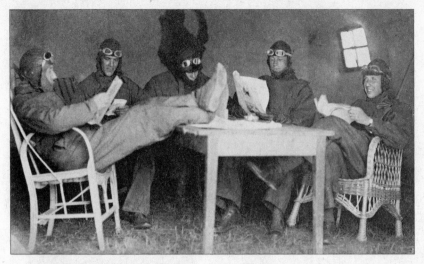

On-call pilots await an alert in a ready room.
(Courtesy of the National Archives)

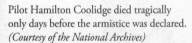

Pilot Hamilton Coolidge died tragically
only days before the armistice was declared.
(Courtesy of the National Archives)

Rickenbacker and other 94th pilots examine what appears to be an aerial map on a roller device,
which could be attached to a pilot's thigh. *(Courtesy of the National Archives)*

Rickenbacker Six

A · CAR · WORTHY · OF · ITS · NAME

A brochure promotes the Rickenbacker Car Company's six-cylinder offering, branded with the logo of its namesake's Hat in the Ring Squadron. *(Courtesy of Auburn University, Special Collections and Archives)*

Adelaide Rickenbacker. *(Courtesy of Auburn University, Special Collections and Archives)*

Returning American hero aces arrive in New York City: (from left) Douglas Campbell, Rickenbacker, James Meissner, Paul Baer. *(Courtesy of the National Archives)*

Rickenbacker at a New York Mobilization Rally of the Commerce and Industry Committee, February 24, 1943. *(Courtesy of the National Archives)*

Rickenbacker inspects troops. Long Beach, California, March 27, 1942. *(Courtesy of the National Archives)*

Emaciated by his three-week raft ordeal in the Pacific, Rickenbacker is helped off a plane. *(Courtesy of the National Archives)*

Pacific rafters dig into a meal: (from left) James Whittaker, William Cherry, Rickenbacker, unidentified, John De Angelis. *(Courtesy of the National Archives)*

Sailors examine two of three rafts on which the eight castaways were stranded. *(Courtesy of the National Archives)*

colors and types of aircraft standing out as in a hyperrealistic painting. He could see the almost stately procession of their cumbersome British charges returning from the East, black Archie bursts marking their path. Above and behind, readying to attack, gathered a German formation. The two American flights raced up from the south, each aircraft bobbing in the buffeting wind, a swarm of angry bees. From his Olympian vantage, Eddie espied more Germans angling out of the west to intercept the Americans before they could cover the bombers. The only analogy to such wide-open battlefields in the past would have been two mighty sailing fleets tacking majestically for advantage over a smooth sea, but that ocean scenario lacked the extraordinary speed of these new machines and their all-complicating third dimension. Eddie watched in fascination as the two sides closed with deadly intent.

As the cloudlike formations mingled, the clear order of only seconds before dissolved into a frightening anarchy of swooping and twisting, turning and banking. Eddie watched one Nieuport spin out of control, two Albatroses hot on its tail, then, pulling out of its brilliant ruse, bank toward one of its pursuers to renew the dogfight on different terms. "With a savage sort of elation," Eddie saw his chance. Unseen by the others, he zoomed onto the tail of one Albatros, firing until it went down in flames: his fifth kill. (When Hall returned from Germany after the war, he confirmed that Eddie had shot down a German in the action in which he crashed on May 7, so this latest score would actually be his sixth, while Campbell only had four.)

Meanwhile, the Nieuport he had just saved maneuvered violently to avoid the path of the stricken enemy; suddenly the leading edge peeled away from its upper right wing—exactly what he himself had experienced earlier. Had the two aircraft touched? Watching the Nieuport's pilot deftly coaxing his machine—just as had Eddie, with full throttle and precision—he escorted his comrade back to Gengault.

On the field, he walked over to the ruined machine to be greeted ebulliently by Jimmy Meissner. "Thanks, old boy, for shooting down those Boches on my tail," he said. "I'm beginning to like coming home without any wings on my machine." Campbell and Thorne Taylor raced up to ask

Eddie which pilot had lost a wing, swearing that they had seen the other injured Nieuport go down. Eddie pointed to Meissner.

"Was that really you, Jimmy?" asked Campbell, then gave him a hug. "And this is the second time you've gotten away with it!" Both Meissner and Eddie recorded in their journals that the wing fabric had been detached in midair collisions. It struck them as peculiar that this should be Meissner's second such experience. They couldn't quite be sure that he had brushed the other aircraft, but if a collision hadn't done this, then what had?

When the Nieuport's ill-placed reservoir tank so terribly caught fire on Lufbery's plane, it had raised the specter that design flaws could account for some of these accidents. Meissner and the others huddled, and it soon became apparent that their wing-shredding experiences came not from glancing collisions but from leading edges ripping under the stress of violent climbs out of steep dives. Only when the Armistice freed Hall would they learn that a similar misfortune had forced him so low that the Archies got him. The day before Meissner's second unpleasant experience, a similar problem had compelled the 95th's Bill Casgrain to land and be captured in no-man's-land. A structural weakness lay where the hollow poplar ribs attached to the spar that formed the wing's leading edge. When these broke under stress, the leading edge peeled back. Had they known about the wing's limitations, they could have avoided situations in which wing-stripping occurred.

The 95th's Harold Buckley claimed that this defect "had been immediately hushed up by the authorities as much as possible. No doubt they were afraid we would all get the 'wind up.' All inquires were met by mysterious smiles." Brigadier General Benjamin Foulois, chief of the 1st Army Air Service, wrote on June 12 to Major General Mason M. Patrick, chief of the American Expeditionary Forces air service, that "the defects in this type of aeroplane are of such a serious nature that in my opinion they cannot be corrected sufficiently to authorize the use of this type of aeroplane on an active sector of the front, except at the risk of considerable unnecessary loss of life." He recommended that "immediate steps" be taken to replace Nieuport 28s with SPADs.

This sour knowledge settled uncomfortably among the fliers. Who could guess what evasive maneuvers might be necessary were a Fokker to bear down on one's tail in the heat of combat? Did they have to rule out completely one of the best evasive tactics available? "We were all afraid of the Nieuports," remembered Chambers. Yet they had no choice but to continue flying and fighting—only now they had to integrate this new wrinkle into their way of war until new planes arrived, heaping one more layer of strain onto men already overloaded.

As was customary, Eddie filed a report, ending with a request for independent confirmation of the kill, required by the French system under which they flew. Such proof often proved difficult or even impossible to obtain when the action took place well behind enemy lines; this time, as so often, it didn't come that day or the next.

The day following, Campbell took off on a lone sortie, knowing full well that confirmation could crown Eddie at any moment. After fruitlessly patrolling the front, he finally discovered a Rumpler two-seater returning from a photography mission near its aerodrome at Mars-la-Tour. Closing with the classic advantage of the sun at his back, he zoomed onto its tail and let loose with his single Vickers machine gun—which, however, jammed after the first few shots. The German pilot did not attempt to flee in the long moments while Campbell struggled to clear the jam. The Boche could not hope to match the Nieuport's speed or maneuverability, but he clearly liked his plane's edge in firepower—not only the Parabellum machine gun firing through his propeller but the one his observer wielded to cover their tail.

Having cleared the jam, Campbell began maneuvering for a safe approach, diving, twisting, and banking like a sparrow harassing a much larger crow. Such air combat, he later noted, is the "most fascinating and absorbing game I have ever tackled; it is a real problem which involves eyes, ears, nerves, delicate touch, a lot of brain, and a sixth sense which is called 'air sense,' which consists in knowing, by feeling the machine, whether it is in the right position or not."

His capable foe danced with him for fifteen minutes, an eternity in dogfighting. Biding his time with the uncanny composure of the hunter,

Campbell conserved ammunition by firing only the shortest possible bursts to limit his enemy's options. Suddenly he realized that his adversary had changed tactics, maneuvering to keep his tail away and out of sight, a clear indication that the rear gunner had exhausted his ammunition; whereupon, coming in at a new angle, he saw the observer tear up his map and rise with his arms crossed, awaiting death with a grimly mocking smile. Campbell hesitated, doubt compromising his deadly determination. Was it decent to shoot an unarmed man? If he let them go, his racing brain countered, the film they took back might bring countless Allied deaths. He pressed the trigger and watched the observer slump over, then the ship itself stumble off course and spin out of control. "He was a real man and a loveable character," Campbell acknowledged in a letter home. The air war was the last place, however, where death could be treated with a gentleman's elegant contempt. Campbell's encounter was the kind of story Americans thrilled to hear, vaguely aware that their nation was stepping into world ascendency—and that its Ivy League aristocrats could match those of the Old World.

Over the course of the engagement, the duelists had drifted westward within sight of Gengault. Dozens of fascinated onlookers witnessed the Rumpler's demise. With confirmation of his yesterday's kill still outstanding, Eddie joined the others to swarm the first ace produced in the American air service. Once more he had lost to the fair-haired Harvard boy, but his journal entry of that day shows no disappointment: Campbell was "certainly going some," he noted. Elsewhere he described how "for a month the congratulations of the world came pouring in upon [Campbell]." Years later, Campbell confessed that "I think Rickenbacker may have beaten me to it"; indeed, Eddie's earlier fifth would soon enough be confirmed.

As Campbell and Rickenbacker stepped into the exalted ranks of acehood, they began to confront the queer doings of those strange bedfellows, fate and fortune. Certainly they knew that their talents had carried them forward, blending a brew of will, hand-eye coordination, nerve, and scores of other intangibles. Still, none but the most arrogant—and neither was—could dismiss the blunt fact that each had made amateur, ill-advised decisions and somehow escaped the consequences. How much, they asked themselves, had simple luck played a part, or how far had the critical factor been the good fortune that so often comes from careful preparation?

In late May the aviation section was at last detached from the Signal Corps to become the U.S. Air Service. The 27th and 147th squadrons, who had trained with the British, joined the 94th and 95th at Gengault to become the 1st Pursuit Group. A couple of days later, a German aircraft dropped a canister on the airfield containing a photograph of the aerodrome with a note on the back reading WELCOME 27TH AND 147TH, PREPARE TO MEET THY DOOM. "Clever people, those Chinese!" quipped Major Harold Hartney, now commanding the 27th.

On May 27, nineteen German divisions surged across a 25-mile front for the third blow of the spring offensive, quickly took the Chemin des Dames ridge that the French had sacrificed so much to recover, then crossed the River Aisne. In eight days they reached the Marne, as they had at Château-Thierry in 1914, driving a 35-mile-deep salient to within 55 miles of Paris. General Foch simply had no one left to counter them—no more reserves, no reinforcements to pull from other sectors. The French had run out of options. The only soldiers not committed were those of the American Expeditionary Forces—more than half a million men, though only one-third of these had undergone advanced combat training. Throughout the spring offensive, the Allies had begged Pershing to allow American troops to fight under French or British command, but he had refused, set on keeping them until they were ready to fight under the American flag. The situation now had grown dire. Pershing finally relented, knowing that his army wasn't quite ready; he raced the 2nd and 3rd U.S. Infantry divisions to the front in cars and trucks. No one knew how these unseasoned troops would fare against the German storm troopers.

Their fresh infusion made an indelible impression on the tired French and British, including the bright young Voluntary Aid Detachment nurse Vera Brittain, who paused in the street to let through a column of soldiers and noticed that an "unusual quality of bold vigour in their stride caused me to stare at them with puzzled interest. They looked larger than ordinary men; their tall, straight figures were in vivid contrast to the under-sized armies of pale recruits to which we were grown accustomed . . . I wondered, watching them move with such rhythm, such dignity, such serene consciousness of self-respect."

In June and early July, American doughboys and leathernecks struck back against the western flank of the salient's furthest reach, recovering Vaux, Bouresches, and, most famously Belleau Wood, where the marines fought with such ferocious determination ("Come on, you sons of bitches—do you want to live forever?") as to earn the sobriquet "devil dogs" from their adversaries. When asked if they should consider retreating, Captain Lloyd Williams of the 2nd Battalion, 5th Marine Regiment, famously said, "Retreat, hell. We just got here." The stand came at a huge price; 40 percent of the marines committed went down in nineteen brutal days. Nonetheless the Americans had shown a mettle that shook their enemies as much as it heartened their allies.

In the air above, the German JG 1, bereft of its formidable leader but flying the new Fokker D-7, perhaps the war's best fighter, was truly out for blood, shooting down fifty-four enemy aircraft in less than nine weeks after the Red Baron's death, a positive ratio of 6:1. Overall in June, the Germans destroyed 505 Allied aircraft, losing only 153 of their own.

On June 4, as Eddie and his now solid friend Walter Smythe were flying back home from a sortie, Archie alerted them to a low-flying Rumpler photographing positions at Toul. The pair snuck up and swooped down on it. Eddie got so close that the enemy's tail filled his vision for his easiest shot yet, but his Vickers jammed after a couple of rounds—and in an instant he had to switch from offense to defense, dodging a stream of bullets from the now-alerted observer. The Rumpler, bearing a rising-sun insignia and an orange-outlined number 16, beelined for home. Boiling with anger at the missed opportunity, Eddie jerked the wayward round free from its chamber and continued the chase, regaining altitude in the knowledge that his greater speed would grant him another chance. Miles behind the lines, as the Rumpler descended into the approach path to Mars-la-Tour, he again zoomed in for the kill, so eager for one more victim that he had forgotten all about Smythe and the endless painstaking lessons he had learned and sternly passed on to his charges. Going in so vulnerably low that close to an enemy aerodrome ranked near the height of folly, almost as bad as attacking an enemy formation alone. Sure enough, tracers "crackled and sparkled around me like a dozen popcorn kernels, except, that they had a far more consistent and regular rhythm." He'd been jumped by a pair of enemy machines, whose pilots no doubt couldn't believe their luck that so careless a fly had flown into their web.

Scared almost out of his wits, Eddie reflexively kicked his right rudder and shoved his joystick over "with a single spasmodic jerk," turning the Nieuport onto its wing and sliding several hundred feet, the speed of his response disconcerting his attackers. They continued their dive, ceding enough valuable altitude to give their target a reprieve.

Straightening out, he saw a patch of clear air and beat it for home. Risking a quick slideslip and crane of the neck to see with relief that his pursuers were gone, he cursed himself for being a "blessed idiot," lucky to emerge with only a few holes through his wings. "Most of one's troubles in this world come from something wrong inside one's self," he would later write revealingly. Letting anger get the better of him had blinded him. From these formative experiences, he drew deep lessons that would soon distill into clear-eyed self-knowledge. A primary element of the strong fighter pilot, he wrote in more tranquil times, was a "quick-thinking, unburdened mind."

That didn't mean he could have easily let that Rumpler go, and he still hadn't received confirmation of his fifth kill. So on the following morning, June 5, when he walked into the hangar to find his mechanics dismantling his Vickers machine gun, he commandeered Smythe's Nieuport, even though his buddy immediately warned him of its gun alignment problems. By 9:30 A.M., he was flying high along the line when he spotted two enemy fighters escorting an observation plane. Waiting for the escorts to peel off, Eddie then moved in close enough to see that it was yesterday's number 16. Approaching diagonally from above on its tail, he poured a stream of bullets into its path, using the "deflection" technique that he had learned at Cazaux. Incredibly, both guns jammed. Again the Rumpler ran for safety; again Eddie freed a jam, then sparred a bit more with the Rumpler until his remaining gun locked irretrievably. As he finally broke away, the observer fired a few rounds after him as a final insult. After he had pointed home in exasperation, he realized that he had not checked the time: two hours and thirty-five minutes had elapsed, twenty more minutes than the usual complement of gas would allow. The engine spluttered, then died. At 17,000 feet he had plenty of glide room, but it still proved close—and he negotiated a very tight landing just across the line in a small space between shell craters. Doughboys ran up to see if he was hurt. The very stubbornness that had brought so much success had this time nearly killed him.

He got a ride back to Gengault, learning as he arrived that Campbell had just got in, terribly wounded. Eddie met Meissner on the field to watch Campbell climb out unaided, a "long jagged tear" in his teddy-bear suit amid "frightful blood stains." With flyboy macho, Campbell called for a motorcycle to ride to the hospital, but Eddie commandeered a car.

Campbell's troubles had begun when he and Meissner set out Boche hunting and found one more Rumpler flying low, perhaps on its way home. Campbell dove on it; as they circled and twisted down to 500 feet, he noticed that the observer wasn't firing, so assumed a jam. Figuring he could now close from behind however he wanted, he dove at a dangerously exposed angle into the observer's range of fire; it was a cocky, dangerous gamble that he assumed would pay off handsomely. "Nerve is necessary," he had written in April, "but the head picks out the time to use it."

The gunner had in fact quickly cleared his jam and promptly opened up. Campbell heard a loud crash, then felt a blow like "a swift kick in the back." An explosive bullet had struck a wire behind him, sending a piece of shrapnel up his spine to lodge in his lower shoulder. Fighting off searing pain, he somehow stabilized his craft, then, shock and concentration binding in this supremely urgent moment, focused his bleeding body homeward as Meissner shot the Rumpler down.

The wound proved clean; Campbell waved off ether, and doctors removed the fragment using cocaine as a local anesthetic while Meissner and Eddie watched. Only once Campbell was "safely tucked away in bed" did they return to barracks. In the hospital for a week, then on to Paris and Biarritz to recuperate, he was eager to get back to the squadron, but headquarters sent him stateside to train new pilots. He would get back to the 94th just a few days before the Armistice.

Eddie would always express courteous respect but never warmth for his dissimilar comrade, saying years later that Campbell "would undoubtedly have one of the highest scores claimed by an air fighter, for he was just entering upon his full stride." Yet the loss of so personal a competitor, who had shown himself a more natural pilot and better shot than Eddie, would prove unsettling, although not debilitating to a former race-car driver who had seen competitors die in front of him. Eddie understood that he had not been flying as smartly as he should have—and could have easily suffered Campbell's fate, or worse. In the air, stressed beyond all measure, compelled to make instant decisions, personal characteristics become wildly magnified. Eddie's stubbornness and competitiveness had led him to take almost terminal risks. One split-second of injudiciousness had ended Campbell's passionately overeager career. Perhaps more difficult than outstaring fear was wrestling down the always potentially mortal flaws in one's own character.

Fatigued by overexertion, Eddie came down with a bad cold, and his discerning CO packed him off on leave to Paris.

The City of Light had changed indeed since he had last been there in March. Much lay deserted, the bleakest acknowledgment of recent German successes. Train after train pulled into Paris, overflowing with refugees from Château-Thierry, 55 miles northeast, upon which the Germans were rapidly pressing. If fear took a tangible form, it stared from the faces of the old and young women, children tugging at their skirts, and the old men carrying the few belongings that they had hurriedly packed, "the grim horrors of war as I had never seen them before." One could now only enter Notre-Dame through a narrow opening between sandbag ramparts, laboriously raised to protect the carvings against bombs and shells. Four days after the spring offensive opened, strange, seemingly random, explosions had ripped the streets. "Mysterious air torpedoes or long range shells are dropping in Paris," the Paris-based pilot Walter Avery wrote in his journal. "No one knows where they come from or what they are." Parisians would soon learn that these shells came from a newly developed supergun that could wreak havoc from more than 55 miles away. At night, they would hear Gothas droning overhead and wonder what their cargo would destroy. Such random destruction by unseen hands recalled nightmare memories of the starving siege of 1871. Many bought the tiny rag dolls Nénette and Rintintin, which they hung about their necks or kept in pockets, believing them to bring good luck.

Back at Gengault in mid-June, Eddie found the 1st Pursuit Group raring for transfer to a hot sector of the front. Headquarters kept it back, waiting for the new squadrons to integrate and sending it out on countless escort assignments for British bombers. The pilots also learned new strafing techniques—diving low to fire their machine guns or simply to demoralize batteries and marching columns. After initiating one such mission from 300 feet, wrote Eddie, "undoubtedly my appearance was quite a surprise for upon diving and shooting at the battery, I was quite amused to see the battery crew scatter in all directions and leap for their dug-outs." On that same sortie, he saw a "dense white fog" blanketing the German lines for at least 3 miles—the result, he thought, of a German gas attack gone wrong when the wind blew it back. In fact, he had witnessed the secret first American use of poison gas.

A few new men joined the 94th, including Ham Coolidge, finally released from duties at Issoudun. Eddie took them up to train in formation flying on protection detail. On one of Coolidge's first times out, he somehow got turned around and, instead of landing, headed east toward enemy lines. Eddie went fast after him, managed to catch up, and by waggling his wings got the novice to reverse direction and follow him home. If Coolidge harbored any residual irritation with Eddie, it soon evaporated as he recognized that the dynamics of leadership and command had changed considerably from his training days.

On June 26, the 1st Pursuit Group got the word they were waiting for, orders relocating them to the Touquin airfield in the Château-Thierry sector, right smack in the midst of the hottest action. "Every body seems real happy to have an opportunity at the Big Show," wrote Eddie in his diary. The next day, he woke up with a fever worse than that he had before. No matter how desperate to go on with the men, he physically couldn't; he was sent instead to the American Evacuation Hospital No. 7 in the elegant Château de Montanglaust in Coulommiers, a dozen miles from the new airfield. Frequent exposure to high altitude and the precipitous changes inflicted by diving and climbing had badly damaged his ears.

For now, the 1st Pursuit Group would have to take on the finest German pilots, including the masters of the Flying Circus's bloodred Fokkers, without what they had come to acknowledge was their main man.

13.

THE GERMANS STRIKE BACK

When young men first match their powers against those of experience-hardened veterans, failure often comes hard, fast, and strongly laced with humiliation—a central rite of passage. So it was when 1st Pursuit met the best German pilots above Château-Thierry that summer of 1918. "There was trouble ahead," noted the 95th's Harold Buckley of their arrival in late June at the new base at Touquin, only 25 miles from the nose of the Château-Thierry salient. "Gone were the days when we could dive into the fray with only a careless glance at our rear."

"Clouds of ash and dust often blotted out the sun to an altitude of 12,000 feet," recalled Reed Chambers, "and above the swirling dust and debris huge concentrations of Fokkers hunted their American prey." Prepping for the last-throw offensive due in two weeks, the Germans concentrated forty-six of their seventy-eight fighter squadrons in this sector to destroy reconnaissance planes and their fighter escorts, and thus blind the western powers to their designs on the ground. Along this sector the massing German air service outnumbered the Allied by at least four to one, which included the three gaudily painted squadrons of the Flying Circus. From Richthofen, command had passed first to Ernst Udet, himself a formidable killer on the way to sixty-two victories, then to Hermann Göring, later Hitler's confidant and architect of the Third Reich's formidable Luftwaffe. That bloody summer, the American rookies would come up against individual German pilots who boasted more kills than all of 1st Pursuit.

The rules had changed, too: The patrol tactics instilled at Toul, shaped around three- to five-machine formations, often had to be discarded before the overwhelming power of new hunting packs of fifteen to twenty Fokkers. Deploying such numbers manifestly complicated combat, multiplying the chances of collision and confusion when cohesion fell apart. No longer were the Allies fighting outclassed early Fokkers or Albatroses; they faced instead the new, fast, and effective Fokker D.VII. The transition to SPADs was slow in coming; until then, the now-obsolescent Nieuport would have to do, the pilots playing on its maneuverability with the full knowledge of its fragile wings.

Desperation also drove their adversaries, who knew that the initially slow-to-mobilize Americans were by now reanimating the moribund Allied war machine. The need to win before the full weight of the New World bore down upon the exhausted Old invested the German forces with all-or-nothing intensity. Their wives and children were starving, so many of their comrades buried. Now or never.

The skies over Château-Thierry became a high-vaulted slaughterhouse for Allied airmen: In three months, the 1st Pursuit Group, usually mustering twenty pilots for each of its four squadrons, would lose forty-one men killed or captured. "None of us will last a month," fretted Walter Avery. The 94th, which by late May had scored sixteen kills—mostly at the hands of two aces—registered only three and a half victories but lost eight of their own. "Protection patrols became the synonym for sudden death," wrote Buckley, "and when dawn broke on a really perfect day, the only doubt in our minds was which of us would be the one to get it."

Despite the press of death all around them—"I never expected to live" was a common refrain, delivered without any hint of self-pity or dramatization—the American pilots strained every fiber to get into the fight, no matter how rigged or deadly it seemed. Youthful naiveté or testosterone comes nowhere close to explaining this rock-hard will to push so resolutely into the face of death. These unyielding young men also shared a sense of destiny, the overwhelming feeling that they stood at the very hinge of world history.

A generation later it would be easy for Americans to look back at World

War I as little more than a warm-up for the big showdown with totalitari-
anism. That summer, nothing was certain except that Germany stood on
the brink of a victory that would confer on it a territorial control far outreaching Alexander the Great's or Julius Caesar's. World power still seemed
firmly rooted in Europe. All African nations except Liberia and Ethiopia
flew European flags; Russia claimed control over much of East Asia; Britain
ran India and South Asia. The United States certainly was a rising star, but
as yet it was internationally unproven and unsophisticated. America's 100
million people did not far outnumber Germany's 70 million. Its industrial
engines might outweigh but could not overwhelm it. Germany had exhausted
Russia, nearly overrun Italy, pushed France to the edge of despair, and sorely
tested Britain. The German Reich wielded formidable new technologies
and was using them with imaginative aggressiveness.

   In only a matter of months, events would decide the way the human
world would turn—and the United States would play a decisive role in them
and forever change the balance of world power. At the cutting edge of America's broadsword were the young men of the 1st Pursuit. These suddenly
exalted young men—Quentin Roosevelt, Ham Coolidge, Eddie Rickenbacker,
Reed Chambers, and Jimmy Meissner—largely unknown barely a year ago,
represented the new American nobility, the best of a young nation sent out to
match wits with the best of the Old World. These young Americans—bright,
mechanically adept, businesslike, and brave—reflexively melded courage
with efficiency in ways the world had not quite seen before.

Leading six Nieuports on one of the first sorties out of Touquin, Jimmy
Meissner encountered an equal number of the enemy. The American formation collapsed; the German didn't. When Harold Tittmann Jr. peeled off
to chase a Fokker, he discovered several others on his tail. Bullets pierced
his lung and extremities; crash-landing on the south bank of the Marne, his
wheels caught on barbed wire, flipping the plane and catapulting him, still
belted into his seat, 30 feet away. The bloodied yet still conscious Tittmann
was rushed to the 103rd Field Hospital in La Ferté-sous-Jouarre on the

Marne River; his awed rescuers counted nine bullet holes in the back of his seat, two hundred in the aircraft wreckage.

His debilitating fever finally gone, Eddie joined with Chambers, Ken Marr, commander of the 94th, and several other pilots in Paris for the celebration of Independence Day. When Chambers developed severe abdominal cramps and nausea, Eddie booked him into the Hôtel Meurice and summoned an American doctor, who called for an appendectomy. Chambers brushed him off, erroneously believing an operation to be more dangerous than the condition. The 94th's surgeon, Paul H. Walters, delivered orders from his commanding officer either to go into the hospital or get back to the front. The pain having subsided, Chambers traveled to Touquin with Walters. Over the next month, he felt periodic discomfort, but little more.

Meantime, Eddie visited the American Experimental Aerodrome at Orly, where pilots inspected new aircraft going to the front, "hoping to find a plane assigned to our Group, which I could return with." The new SPAD XIIIs that had been promised to the 1st Pursuit a month earlier had not yet materialized, but here he was excited to find three fit for service. The depot commander let the persuasive ace fly one back to Touquin. Without a lick of training on it, nor any instruction beyond a few hurried whispers from French mechanics, and carrying no authorizing paperwork, Eddie took his new craft up in high excitement, allowing no thought of the ramifications of stealing off in a new plane with no orders.

The SPAD indeed proved itself a new beast altogether, with entirely different handling characteristics from the Nieuport's. If the Nieuport had been light, maneuverable, and fragile—a barn swallow—then Eddie's new mount proved itself a sturdy red-tailed hawk. Heavier than the Nieuport, with a thinner wing cross-section, it enjoyed higher "wing loading," the aerodynamic term for the ratio of an aircraft's total weight to the surface area of its wings. Weight is everything in flying; given identical engine power, a heavier craft requires more wing area to generate compensating lift. An elephant could fly if it could grow wings that covered a quarter of a football field. Weighing only an ounce, a bat can soar on wings that lift only ounces per square inch. As engines rapidly developed greater horsepower, early aircraft designers discovered that as planes pushed faster, the wings engaged more air and could therefore exert more lift, enabling wing area to be contracted without diminishing lift. Today's stubby-winged, heavy-airframed fighter jets travel so fast that the extraordinarily high loading of their tiny wings more than compensates for diminished area. Compare that to the Wright glider or the (original, lowercase) albatross, whose immense ratio of wing surface to weight can still impart only very slight loading.

Higher loading generally entails lower maneuverability and climb rate, while delivering more potential for speed—not least because smaller wings offer less wind resistance and drag. The SPADs soon enough earned the telling sobriquet "flying bricks," because their weight and smaller wing area sank them fast and precipitously when engine power fell away. Unlike the Nieuport and its rotary engine, which demanded the judicious use of the blip switch to reduce airspeed for landing and could be brought down with the engine off in order to come in more safely, the SPAD had to run full out.

That day, Eddie managed to figure the SPAD's handling characteristics in the course of one brief flight. Despite its sometimes frightening tendency to drop like its nicknamesake, he felt reassured, knowing that he could put the sturdy machine into a headlong dive and pull out without fear of peeling away the leading edge of his wing. He also learned, however, that should his engine cut out at low altitude, he could not just slide down into some inviting meadow.

His arrival in the shiny new number 1 caused a stir. The boys crowded around, eager to see the shape of their future. Nor did Eddie disappoint them, waxing eloquent about the new design's handling characteristics and top speed of 138 mph. They admired the roominess of the cockpit and contoured fuel tank beneath the fuselage, much less vulnerable than the Nieuport's to ignition by enemy fire. The water-cooled engine would also throw off welcome heat at altitude. In the SPAD, the Americans would be getting an instrument that would help level the aerial playing field. Predictably, Eddie's commanding officer, Major Bert Atkinson, bristled at the breach of his authority. "I found that I had acted unwisely in bringing this

SPAD out without going thru military channels," wrote a chastened Eddie, "and that I had upset the Major's plans in doing so." Atkinson let slide what could have been a court-martial offense, partly because of Eddie's skill and reputation. As always, Eddie had a knack for appearing entirely task-oriented, exhibiting no apparent self-promotion. The rest of the 94th were relieved that he was back as they braced for their toughest challenges yet. Eddie immediately set about mounting his Nieuport's machine guns aboard the new aircraft.

Shortly after his return, 1st Pursuit learned of its transfer to the nearby, much smaller field at Saints to make room for a large complement of British Sopwith Camels and Handley Page bombers. A recently harvested wheat field served as the landing strip, across from which white cows looked on. The squadron was billeted in private homes, some in the famous Hôtel de Marie, "which was once used as an Arabian Hospital," reported the official history of the 27th, for French Algerian and Moroccan units in the French forces. "The Arabs left their friends the justly celebrated 'cooties.'" Eddie found Saints "terrible."

A leaking fuel line cut short his first official SPAD flight on July 10—perhaps just as well; he developed so painful an ache in his right ear that Walters sent him to a Paris hospital. The following day, the doctors operated on an abscess and lanced his eardrum. He experienced a "terrible night," although attended by a pretty nurse whom he imagined taking out for dinner. Three days later and still bedbound, he listened to the Bastille Day celebrations outside his window, only later learning that the 95th's Quentin Roosevelt had crashed that same day, brought down by a high-scoring ace in the Flying Circus after he broke formation. A photograph of his body next to the wood-and-wire ruins of his machine circulated shortly thereafter as a postcard. The horrified Kaiser Wilhelm, who had known and admired Quentin's father, forbade its sale.

The beaming second-year Harvard man with the broad forehead and shy smile had been a favorite with the men for being "gay, hearty, and absolutely square," recalled Eddie. His lack of airs equally endeared him to his brother officers. In college he had studied math and mechanics but had stolen away every chance he got to tinker with motorcycles and cars. In his war memoir Eddie described how Roosevelt, elevated to flight commander upon reaching the front, handled his first combat sortie with three seasoned pilots, well aware that his inexperience could endanger the others. Before they took off, he queried each of them, established who had the most experience, and instructed him to take the lead in the air. Soon the men of 1st Pursuit began to notice that Roosevelt's growing confidence also created a new, dangerous dividend—a brashness that uncomfortably blurred the line between courage and recklessness, bringing repeated warnings from his commanding officers. He would simply "laugh away all serious advice," but everyone understood how large were the boots he must fill.

On a July 10 patrol, Roosevelt had detached from his formation and fell in with a second, taking the last position and proceeding north well into enemy territory, only then noticing that his comrades sported Maltese crosses; he hastily shot down the machine in front of him and then beat it home, the Germans too startled to follow. It made a rousing good story in the mess hall.

Roosevelt's "bravery was so notorious," reflected Eddie, "that we all knew he would either achieve some great spectacular success or be killed in the attempt." Chambers perhaps came closer to a harder truth when he recalled him as "a wonderful guy" but "a little slow, a little clumsy" for fighter combat and perhaps better to have been deployed as a bomber pilot. The loss of so popular a man, apparently destined for such great things, left a ragged void. One officer's letter of condolence to the stricken ex-president said that his son had given his life "with a high heart in the performance of duty of prime importance,—for the photographs which were obtained played no small part in enabling one French army to know with some precision the nature of the attack which sixteen hours later was launched against it." The heartbroken Teddy Roosevelt died less than six months after his favorite son. Roosevelt Field on Long Island, whence Lindbergh would depart on his famous transatlantic flight, was named in Quentin's honor.

The cream of American youth were falling, although at nothing of the rate of their European counterparts over the past four years. Still, they were falling fast. When Lieutenant Norman "Jim" Archibald of the 95th returned late from a patrol, he discovered to his irritation that his messmates had assumed the worst and already distributed his cot, blankets, and wardrobe among themselves.

The working conditions at Saints began to get even uglier. The 94th drew its complement of SPADs, the first squadron to undertake the transition. "Some of the other guys had a lot of trouble with them," noted Chambers. "We lost two men there—coming in too slow, hitting, bouncing over, and taking the tops of their heads off." Unlike the Nieuports with their air-cooled rotary engines, the SPADs were powered by water-cooled, high-compression V8 Hispano-Suizas, more complicated setups that bedeviled the mechanics. Gears connecting crankshaft to propeller proved particularly troublesome. "Our 'machines available' for each day's work dropped from about 90 per cent to 50 per cent, despite long hours of night work and extra men on each job," reported the commander of 1st Pursuit.

On top of the technical issues, the 94th suffered from a leadership vacuum, and morale had tanked. Once the stellar squadron in American service, it had lost its top guns Lufbery, Miller, and Campbell; Peterson had been promoted to head up the 95th, Jimmy Meissner the 147th. Eddie's hospitalizations had taken him away for long stretches. The squadron's commander, Kenneth Marr, who had distinguished himself in the Lafayette Escadrille, had suffered a bad crash that seemed to have spooked him—he drank heavily, avoided flying, and rarely showed up at the aerodrome. He "was not the type to lead men," remembered Eddie, "nor morally consistent with the type of life a fighter had to learn." Leadership fell to the assistant squadron commander, Reed Chambers.

Two days after Tittmann had crashed earlier that month, Chambers had used a rainy day to search for his missing friend, finally locating him in the 103rd Field Hospital; its staff, overwhelmed with so many wounded and dying, had no time to report admittances, as their corridors were lined with "dead Americans stacked up just like cordwood," wrote Chambers. The stench and the moaning of the gravely wounded overwhelmed him. An orderly led him to Tittmann, who was so badly torn up that Chambers marveled how "he ever lived" and worse yet was "out of his head," badly torqued by pain, disorientation, and morphine. It undermined the spirit to see so warm and resilient a figure thus reduced. Chambers left convinced that he would never see his friend again. Remarkably, Tittmann pulled through minus a leg, albeit beset by horrible infections, bedsores, and bouts of dysentery, his wounds attacked by enormous horseflies. After almost two years in the hospital, he ranked as the worst-wounded-in-action American soldier to have survived, going on to a distinguished foreign service career, serving as the envoy to the Vatican during the Second World War.

Tittmann's horribly battered and broken body haunted Chambers, who tried to remain upbeat but bowed steadily under a descending gloom that showed through to the men. He dutifully joked with them, trying to buck himself up as well. "Look, we're going to live to be killed by an automobile when we get back to the States, so let's go out and go after them." Together, beneath his alert vigilance, he seemed to be saying, they would come through. Yet these increasingly stressed young men saw almost every sortie return without someone who had lifted off. A steady stream of new faces only reminded them regularly of just how often many had "gone west." They needed a leader who could outstare the daily toll, not sugarcoat it. Only then could they go about figuring how best to do their job of killing while also staying alive. For the men of the 94th, the iron will of the German air corps had simply raised the bar too high. No one yet—certainly not Chambers—could persuade them otherwise. Only later, under Eddie's instruction, would Chambers come to temper his carefulness with courage—and begin to score.

Ten minutes after midnight on July 15, the pilots at Saints streamed out of their tents to watch an immense light and sound show brightening the eastward sky—a barrage seeking to smash the way open for the last great German offensive. Alerted by air observation and German prisoners, the French had been ready, their own guns opening up minutes before the Germans'. "Rockets and signals were appearing everywhere," wrote Billy Mitchell. "Searchlight beams were sweeping the sky; the buzz of airplanes going and coming, and the noise of their bombs dropping covered the whole line." Five miles north of Château-Thierry, the Kaiser Wilhelm Ge-schütz, a massive 8-inch gun, launched a 228-pound artillery shell toward Paris, which covered some 65 miles in three minutes and demolished a building not many blocks from Eddie's hospital. "From the unusually seri-ous expression on the nurses' faces, I noticed it must be something more or less serious," he would write. Thirteen more rounds landed on Paris over the next several days.

At 3:00 A.M. that morning, Mitchell met with his French counterpart and learned that a mixup in orders would delay French air response for hours. Furthermore, the French had no idea where the Germans intended to force passage over the Marne. They agreed that American and British air support should move in at once. Mitchell raced over to Saints, where, un-willing to risk a subordinate's life, he took off by himself, following the dirty ribbon of the Marne first downstream then up. "Suddenly as I rounded a turn of the river east of Dormans, I saw a great mass of artillery fire hitting the south bank, and, spanning the river, five bridges filled with German troops marching over. I looked everywhere for German airplanes but there were none in the sky at the time."

Returning to Saints, he ordered a dawn attack and informed army head-quarters. Indeed, fourteen divisions of the 7th Army had crossed the Marne on pontoon bridges, rafts, and canvas boats—a thrust that Ludendorff be-lieved would pull French reserves away from the Somme, where he planned another blow. With yet another strike aimed against the British to the north, the Germans would press on toward Paris from three directions and throw the British back against the English Channel in the Fatherland's last chance for complete victory.

For the next three days, French and British fliers, plus 1st Pursuit—minus the 94th, still refitting to SPADs—threw themselves against this last surge of German might, dueling with Fokkers in the sky, strafing columns on the ground and bridges, and covering badly needed artillery observation planes. "Boche didn't have a look in," wrote the 95th's Waldo Heinrichs, so full was the air with Allied formations. On the ground, the French had raced in the American 3rd Division, which stubbornly attacked the Dormans bridgehead and held the line, earning it the title of "Rock of the Marne." With Allied airpower pounding the crossings, the Germans on the rough side of the river could not expect resupply or reinforcement. Chambers led a squadron to strafe the resolute German infantry as it crossed the river. "These fellows, Germans, were marching just as close together as they could across this pontoon bridge and we just clobbered them. I mean, we must have killed two or three hundred of them."

Ludendorff bitterly ordered a retreat. In three days, the final offensive had ground to a halt, an Allied triumph to which 1st Pursuit had substantially contributed. Airpower had indisputably become essential in war. During a brief lull in the fighting, the 95th transferred rapidly to the SPAD, its well-led and motivated pilots taking only a fraction of the time that the lethargic 94th had required.

The Allies mounted a nineteen-day counterattack, the French relying mainly on Moroccan colonial units and the U.S. 1st Division, which used tanks to break through the German lines. During late July, the RAF's 9th Air Brigade left the area. "They were the best scout squadrons the British had," noted Holden. "They say in all their experience they never struck so active or deadly a sector as this." The British departure left only three American squadrons to patrol the area, the 94th playing only an anemic role.

The 95th, 27th, and 147th squadrons stepped up to the task, some pilots flying as many as three or four two-hour missions daily. After more than a week of inaction, the 94th's first patrol ended with three SPADs out of eleven making forced landings. The diaries of the 1st Pursuit Squadron grew grim. "The 27th lost seven men in two days," wrote Lieutenant Joseph Eastman, a veteran pilot of the 94th.

On July 20, his ear still draining, Eddie transferred to a new hospital with beautiful gardens, but he grew stir-crazy and started taking trips against doctors' orders. Visiting a Hispano-Suiza plant, he saw a 300 hp aero engine with a cannon that fired through the propeller hub. He hit it off with the chief engineer; a few days later they enjoyed dinner at a château on the banks of the Seine, Eddie writing afterward that "the ear is not much better but am going back to the front regardless as there is much work to be done."

Somehow he managed to dodge orders sending him stateside; the doctors who told him he would never fly again he simply ignored.

Getting back to Saints on Sunday, July 28, his ear no better (he was still unable to fly), he found 1st Pursuit under deadly attack. "They are shooting down a few of our fellows every day," recorded Walter Avery. "Gee but it's tough to see one's friends going out, have them come back and hear their stories of fights I should have been in," Eddie lamented to his diary. Unable to wait any longer, he took a short hop on Wednesday for the first time in three weeks but became dizzy. "I'm crazy to get back but don't dare," he confessed. The good feelings that attended his return shattered that afternoon when Alan Winslow, who had scored the squadron's first kill, did not return from a sortie. Jumped near Oulchy-le-Château, he maneuvered away but "had not given sufficient credit to the remarkable climbing ability of the new Fokkers," as he would later admit. Sprayed with bullets from behind, he nearly passed out from the pain but struggled to right his spinning SPAD when he saw red. "Thinking I was in flames, I put my remaining hand on the release button of my safety strap, intending to jump. Just in time, however, I realized that with a stunned brain what I had first thought to be flames was in reality blood." Winslow managed to bring his gore-spattered machine to a rough landing in enemy territory. He would languish in a prisoner camp, where his wounded arm grew so infected from indifferent care that it was amputated.

The following day, a large formation of the 27th, sent out to protect an observation plane, lost cohesion when attacked by at least four different German squadrons, including two from the Flying Circus. In the resulting free-for-all, six Americans were either killed or taken prisoner, 30 percent of the entire squadron gone on one flight. The ground offensive might have stopped, but the German air service had kept its teeth sharp. The next few days the weather socked in, affording 1st Pursuit a brief respite.

Desperate to get aloft again, Eddie prayed his malady would "get better soon for if it don't I realize the war is over for me this year." Pushing pain aside—even though he could hardly move his neck—he joined a formation flying near Reims. During a close encounter with a Fokker from the Flying

Circus his gun jammed. On the way home he got "madder than six wet hens" at the malfunction that had cost him a possible victory. After landing and taxiing up to the hangar, his gunnery sergeant, Abraham "Abie" Karp, met him and asked, "How did the guns work, Captain?" Eddie started to tell him that they were no damn good; the feisty sergeant, no more than 5'2" with great, winglike ears, began to object. Eddie stopped him cold, "the only time I ever . . . used the prerogative of an officer in my lifetime over an enlisted man."

"Dammit, Abe, you're talking to an officer, so shut up and let me talk."

"Well, Captain," retorted the quick-talking Brooklyn mechanic, "sometimes good comes out of an argument." This struck Eddie as terribly funny; he slapped Karp on the back. "Abe, you win." Conversation swung profitably back toward preventing jams, Karp coming up with the idea of passing a live round through a template to check for the irregular surfaces that caused the problem. If it didn't go through, the round could then be filed down until it did. They also considered the possibility of attaching a 1-pound copper hammer to the pilot's wrist with a leather thong so he could rap the recoil mechanism and break the jam loose. Eddie's practice of filing rough gun parts at night reduced both jamming and the gun's tendency to freeze at altitude. Others soon adopted the practice. That night he wrote, "I'm praying to God same will get well soon. I shan't go to a hospital."

Pain crippled him so badly the next morning that he couldn't get up. Lieutenant Edward Green took Rickenbacker's SPAD to lead a formation that included Smythe and a recent addition to the 94th, Alexander Bruce of Harvard. In a semistupor with bags of hot water on his ear to relieve the pain, Eddie had a waking dream that Smythe and he had been engaged in severe combat when Smythe's plane went down. Shortly thereafter an orderly knocked on his door. "Sir, I have bad news," he had started to say when Eddie interrupted him with "I know, Smythe is dead." The man hurried off a bit startled, Eddie remembered. Green came in minutes later with the grim details: Smythe and Bruce had collided. The 95th's Lansing Holden wrote about a similar midair collision at Issoudun, which left "not wrecked machines, but just flat patches of torn linen—no shape—no volume." The 1st Pursuit fliers knew that German pilots had begun to wear parachutes—one had recently saved Ernst Udet's life—and it put Eddie into "a very bad state of mind" to think that this relatively cheap technology would "without question" have saved the two men's lives. "Cannot help but feel," Eddie confided to his journal, "that it was criminal negligence on the part of those higher up for not having exercised sufficient forethought and seeing that we were equipped with parachutes for just such emergencies."

A quarter century later, at the height of a vastly different war, T. L. Maloney, late of the 94th, would vividly recall that hot midsummer's evening in 1918 after Smythe's and Bruce's deaths. Complete silence reigned in the mess hall as the pilots of the 94th and 147th ate dinner. In the flickering candlelight, Maloney sneaked a glimpse at Eddie, who sat at the head of the table, big tears quietly furrowing his cheeks, his two friends' empty chairs on his right.

This moment undoubtedly etched itself in Maloney's mind's eye, not because Eddie conceded a rare vulnerability or because his tears simply revealed a caring soul beneath a gruff exterior, but for a far more profound reason. Early, hard, and unrelenting life experience had taught Eddie that no amount of bluff could beat away all the adversity that would confront him and everyone else. In stark contrast, the far more experienced Lufbery had responded to Miller's loss with volcanic anger. The day he died, he intended to show the boys that one can discharge grief and feelings of impotence by smashing back—but, alas, all too often anger becomes all-consuming, crowding out the capacity to think clearly, as it did for Lufbery that fateful day. Eddie's quiet weeping before his squadron mates was a far healthier response to the sheer ugliness of war than Lufbery's or Chambers's faux bravado. To Maloney and the others, Eddie showed that one must look with unclouded—if sometimes tear-stained—eyes at life's unforgiving realities. Only then could one move away from being a slave to the rage, a thirst for revenge, and undermining grief that must surely unravel confidence and judgment. The philosophically minded Scottish historian Thomas Carlyle once described genius as "the transcendent capacity of taking trouble."

Indeed, while trouble seemed to be Eddie's constant companion, it never seemed to master him, in large part because he never pretended that it wasn't there.

His awful earache steadily worsened. He had willed himself over his fear of heights, compensated for his injured eye, and choked back the airsickness that routinely washed his cockpit with vomit, but this new agony grew so excruciating that no amount of focus could overcome it. Back again he went to the hospital for the third time in as many months. The next day, doctors operated on an infected mastoid bone in the middle ear, whose honeycombed structure had filled with infected fluid. Before antibiotics the condition could prove fatal and was a leading cause of childhood death.

The mastoid had been the source of Eddie's pain from the beginning. "It was a success and am feeling quite some better," he reported a few hours later. Over his long recuperation, Eddie systematically pored over every one of his combat missions, seeking to identify his vulnerabilities and opportunities to learn. (In a similar period of creative focus, the French philosopher Blaise Pascal had coped with a painful toothache by retreating into his mind for eight days, coming up with a mathematical description of a geometric form called the cycloid, the gateway to calculus.) During those long twilight times, Eddie picked and poked, queried and examined every one of his hostile encounters. His wife would later joke with him that the hairless peaks that ran up the sides of his head came about from his rubbing them when deep in thought. It is rare for men of action to have the time or inclination for such arm's-length review, but Eddie drew not only insight but deep sustenance and strength from this time away.

He came to see danger as something to be interrogated, not defied, which helped him hew the fine line between timidity and arrogance. Before military scientists broke down human reactions to danger into probabilities, the early combat flier needed to settle his own uneasy relationship with risk, glory, death, and killing. The combat pilot in World War I simply had to learn on the razor's edge; Campbell recalled that "we did a lot of talking to people that had been at the front . . . They gave us a lot of pointers about what you should do and what you shouldn't do, but you got no lectures . . .

You had to get that by hearsay and figure it out for yourself." That experience-squeezing ability came in real time, under incredible duress. These were men who survived not just by exercising hyperanimal instincts but by putting their expansive imaginations to work at the fullest speed; in terrible danger, they came up with altogether new ways to emerge victorious.

Nerve did play a role. Across the twentieth century, one study shows, only 35 percent of the pilots given an opportunity to engage the enemy did so—nearly twice as many avoided combat altogether. For the aces, however, nerve was rarely the problem. The hardest was to master arrogance. The top fliers of every nationality came up with idiosyncratic responses to help them survive. Some were recluses, given to plain odd behavior. The British boy ace Albert Ball liked to build bonfires and walk around them playing the violin. Richthofen sharpened his innate talents as a hunter, carefully stalking his prey and relishing in the raw alpha-maleness of bagging one more trophy. For Eddie, the killing part was simply the business of war. The closest analog for his philosophy on war may have been the famous words of Confederate general Nathan Bedford Forrest, "War means fighting and fighting means killing"—rather proletarian phrasing, but a sentiment that Eddie would have endorsed as the plainest good sense. Such frankness did not mesh well with the romantic vision of the flyboy ace, but it offered the compensatory benefit of being businesslike—and extremely effective. Today, such an approach to just about everything helps to define the American experience. In his day, this emerging paradigm was just beginning to distinguish American attitudes from those of the Old World.

Eddie's enforced time in the hospital gave him a valuable, lifesaving chance to adjust his behavior, not unlike a brilliant football coach making the halftime adjustments that change momentum and win games. His musings and wonderings distilled into clear-eyed resolve. When his ear finally healed, he would become a new kind of leader, the latest kind of flying killer.

14.

A SECRET COUNTEROFFENSIVE

On August 28, 1918, Major Harold Hartney, the tidy, bantam-sized thirty-year-old ace recently elevated from command of the 27th to head the 1st Pursuit Group, made his way to Ligny-en-Barrois, a small medieval town now the headquarters of Pershing's 1st Army. Forty miles west of Nancy, its red-tiled, somber gray buildings bestrode the 180-mile east-west canal connecting the Marne to the once French city of Strassburg (Strasbourg), a German possession since 1871. Five hundred years before, Ligny had been torn by charges of witchcraft, but these would prove nothing compared to the secret grand designs now unfolding, as Pershing huddled with his subordinates and his French counterparts to formulate a plan to drive the Germans back to the Fatherland once and for all. He had combined sixteen U.S. divisions into the 1st Army, augmented by French troops, including artillery and tanks, which the Americans would heavily rely on to bolster their growing numbers. Among the talents at Pershing's disposal: Colonel George C. Marshall, who worked on the planning for the so-called Saint-Mihiel offensive; Brigadier General Douglas MacArthur, who would lead a brigade in the 42nd Division; and Lieutenant Colonel George Patton Jr., who commanded the 304th Tank Brigade.

Another rising star in the American Expeditionary Forces, Billy Mitchell, had ordered Hartney to headquarters. Mitchell's command performance on the recent Château-Thierry battlefront had won him high praise and promotion to chief of the 1st Army's Air Service, the highest post in

American combat aviation. Gripped by his big-plan mentality, he had immediately put into place a grand design for what would prove the war's largest single air operation—all with his usual frenetic energy. One of his first orders of business was to replace Atkinson with Hartney, who had hands-on combat and leadership experience, to command 1st Pursuit. No longer under the wing of the French 6th Army, 1st Pursuit was now an element of the U.S. 1st Army, supporting the U.S. 5th and French 2nd Colonial Corps.

At Ligny, Mitchell ushered Hartney into a room on whose table rested an astoundingly detailed 12-foot-square topographical representation of the region, embodying not just towns and key rail lines but also ravines and hilltops, even large buildings and quite small copses—the fruit of three years' obsessive French balloon observation. Such tridimensional verisimilitude brought home a level of urgency beyond that of more typical battlefield maps, making it immediately apparent why these odd salients—bulges in the battle line—had stubbornly endured for more than three years of history's greatest deployment of armed force. In this sector the Saint-Mihiel salient made particular sense as the object of the upcoming offensive. The Germans had targeted Verdun, a city on the Meuse set within a crescent of hills crowned by a nearly continuous ring of fortifications. It had been the last French stronghold to surrender to the Prussian invaders of 1870, and further and greater works had been constructed since then. In 1916, the Germans had failed to take it with terrible cost on both sides, but their offensive had driven forward a southwestward-pointing bulge some 15 miles deep and 25 miles wide just south of the city and touching Saint-Mihiel, a position the Germans could retain because it held easily defensible high ground; not enough for staging a large offensive, but sufficient to prevent direct Allied communication between Verdun and Nancy to the south. Pershing determined that a mostly American pincer attack on both flanks could clip it off.

Hartney had a penchant for cocking his head and saying, "Precisely, precisely." His almost effeminate manner belied the toughness of an ace who had engaged the Red Baron in single combat and emerged—however narrowly—unscathed. Mitchell, who found in Hartney the kind of leader he most valued, reached across the display to point out the tiny medieval town of Rembercourt, immediately west of Saint-Mihiel and south of Verdun. Just visible to the east of town, the ground opened into a few acres of open farmland.

"Hartney, I want you to go over to that map and look at that tiny field, then go back and prepare to slip in there overnight when I give the word, without fuss of any kind. The enemy mustn't know we're coming. Can you do it?"

Hartney must have swallowed before responding, "Certainly." He then asked the size of the field.

"Thirty acres," said Mitchell. "The only thirty acres left in France, so don't squawk."

The designated strip's size, along with the hills behind it, would require each pilot to "do expert work with stick and rudder to avoid smashing himself and his plane to bits," Hartney later recalled. Getting eighty planes in and out of there on a regular basis would be a nightmare.

If the Germans got wind that America's top pursuit group was moving to the Saint-Mihiel area, the entire offensive could be compromised. Hartney must move 1st Pursuit piecemeal so as to escape notice. On the ground, planes not prepped for takeoff would be kept in camouflaged Bessonneau hangars pushed right up to the tree line. One aircraft would be kept circling above at all times to engage any approaching enemy observation planes. Pilots would be strictly forbidden to cross enemy lines, thus denying critical intelligence should a machine go down. Hartney was stunned—yet at the same time inspired—by the boldness of the plan.

He was somewhat relieved when he and his driver had difficulty finding Rembercourt; this surely meant that the Germans would have similar problems. However, ground conditions were even worse than he had imagined, the area "unbelievably small and incredibly rough." General headquarters would have to crowd into a dilapidated shack, the officers sleeping on cots in tents beneath a birch and fir copse, into which all the enlisted men's barracks, oil and gas reserves, and truck support must also fit; its understory was so damp as to boast a carpet of moss. Hartney could already foresee how the mechanics would grumble at working in such cramped hangars.

He registered the shell holes and uncountable large stones cumbering the irregular, muddy fields. Rembercourt would offer little in the way of supplies or relaxation for the men. The fifteenth-century church on which it centered, along with many of its other buildings, had long since been pulverized. The town's newest feature lay on its west side: a cemetery for the hundreds of French soldiers who had died to hold this byway. Nearby ran the twisty Voie Sacrée, the Sacred Way, along which had struggled the men and matériel desperately needed to hold Verdun in the face of intense bombardment and assault.

Hartney set about his task with a certain grim relish, coordinating the move from Saints between August 29 and September 3, establishing a well-lit dummy field 4 miles distant, which the Germans would eagerly bomb but which would also serve as a beacon for pilots homeward bound in the dark. He built what he would later claim was the first control tower for night flying, "a rough two-by-four scantling affair on top of the Group headquarters shack." Incoming pilots, given their bearings by the fake base, would blink flashlights at the tower, whereupon Rembercourt's own lights would snap on for a minute. Pilots who missed were to circle for ten minutes and try again.

Chambers briefed Eddie at bedside. The closeness of the airfield to the heart of the upcoming offensive was a clear sign that this was it, the real thing. He was "crazy to get back," Eddie told his doctors, who kept him for several more days, but there was no more talk of going home or never flying again. On September 6, he called the aerodrome; a driver delivered him at midnight among the pitch-dark trees. It took him some time to discover his billet, but he was then delighted to find his bedroll laid out in welcome. His squadron buddies clapped him on the back and teased him about his ear condition. "We were frothing to get to the Front," wrote Archibald. "Not because of war . . . not because it meant the gruesome thing of killing . . . not because of any heroism but because the Front meant a culmination of our flying lives and progression to our goal. It was the ideal, the purpose, the thing for which we had worked and lived." Eddie was right where he was determined to be.

Foul weather and strong winds socked in the squadron for the next three days. The trees provided little protection from the pounding rain, which left tents sodden and turned the earth inside to mud. Relentless artillery fire made sleep difficult. Finally, on September 9, the weather broke enough for Eddie to fly his SPAD for about an hour, only to return frustrated once more by jammed guns. That same day, Lieutenant Archibald broke the rules and flew a mile into enemy territory, paralleling the front; but his rpms dropped, and he descended. Shrapnel from Archies had wrecked his engine. The Germans discovered one of his guns loaded with incendiary rounds. One soldier waved two of them in his face, raging, "*Sprengstoff!*" (explosives). An informal understanding existed that fliers on both sides could carry incendiary rounds only along with express written orders to destroy observation balloons; Archibald lacked any such document. Desperate for information about the obviously upcoming offensive, the interrogator threatened to have him shot. Archibald held his tongue until asked who should be notified of his death, when he blurted out the name of his squadron commander and unit, establishing the presence of America's primary aerial strike force.

It was exactly what Mitchell and Hartney had sought to avoid. Forty-eight hours later—the day before the offensive—a communiqué to the German Supreme Headquarters read, "The conversation of several American aviators captured the past few days, reveals that the American 1st Army with about 10 divisions is to attack between Saint-Mihiel and Pont-à-Mousson in the very near future."

As the clock ticked down to H hour—dawn on September 12—rain still lashed the runways. The pilots crowded into the operations office, a bleak room containing a few desks with phones, a large sector map on the wall, an equally big mission board identifying pilots, squadrons, and flights, and the day's schedule. The one board commanding the attention of every single young man was a simple listing of each 1st Pursuit pilot's name—followed, if deserved, by a small black cross. Each flier yearned for that symbol next to his name, mark of an unmistakably personal contribution to the struggle. This offensive might give them the chance: Waves of Allied planes would be swarming in vital support of the mighty ground assault. Mitchell didn't like to do anything small. He would commit 1,481 airplanes from the American, French, and Italian services against the Germans—701 pursuit machines, 366 observation planes, and 323 day and 91 night bombers.

Eddie was shaken awake at 5:00 A.M. by thousands of guns opening the preparatory barrage. He sprang out of bed, stuck his head out of the tent— "I suppose every American in the world wanted to be in that great attack"— and ran through the sodden darkness to the operations office, already filling with highly strung men awaiting assignment. The morning brought "a howling gale," remembered Eastman, that rattled the canvas hangars. Nobody would be going up today, he thought, but headquarters ordered them "to get off double quick," weather or not.

Whistles sounded along the front, and doughboys fighting under the American flag for the first time in Europe jumped from their trenches to struggle forward through a mist and chill wind, which at least masked the advance. The front that day was "at once picturesque and terrible," wrote Pershing, "aflame with exploding shells, star signals, burning supply dumps and villages." The infantry carried Bangalore torpedoes, wire cutters, and axes to sever the barbed wire. Others carried rolls of chicken wire, which afforded passage when thrown over entanglements.

Despite the downpour and low-hanging clouds, 1st Pursuit undertook sixty-two sorties that day. The extremely limited visibility kept most patrols down to two planes to minimize collisions; many of these could only fly just above tree level.

In the basket swinging below the 5th Balloon Company's Goodyear No. 169, Lieutenant Maurice Brown Smith of Oklahoma and a companion were just completing their four-hour stint—duty that would fray even the steadiest nerves, especially on that first seismic day. Swaying quietly at the end of his metal-cable tether about 3,000 feet up just behind the front, the observer could see some 20 miles in good weather. Often the observers needed only a few minutes aloft to identify key enemy positions and coordinate an artillery barrage. Telephone wires strung up along the cable enabled observers to relay real-time observations directly to a central command station, a hub in a complex communication web that, when working well, coordinated divisional headquarters, artillery battalions, divisional artillery, and antiaircraft batteries.

That day, however, the weather hampered their ability not only to monitor artillery positions but also to spot enemy planes. When such attackers flew into view, the ground team engaged a motorized winch that pulled the vulnerable gasbag down in minutes, but often the "busters" gave much less warning than that.

Although the huge sausage-shaped balloons appeared to be sitting ducks, they had proved such dangerous targets that veteran airmen tended to avoid them. The balloons' height compelled pursuit aircraft to come in hazardously low. The artillery set their shells to explode at the balloons' set altitude, making them far more deadly than random shots at formations passing at only guessed-at higher altitudes. Even so, floating beneath huge cloth sacks that contained clouds of hydrogen remained extremely dangerous. The vital, immediate intelligence gathered made such odds well worth it—certainly for everyone but the observers.

That day, Smith had worried whether the old winch with its broken brake arm could bring him down quickly. He wore a rudimentary harness to which was connected a large oblong canvas parachute container, which hung low on the outside of the basket. Should he jump, the harness ought to pull the parachute clear of the container, but Smith did not relish the prospect, given the considerable chances of its becoming entangled, especially while the ground crew was hauling the balloon frantically earthward. Jumping from a basket proved so stressful that German observers were automatically relieved of that duty after four such experiences.

Smith couldn't believe his eyes when he saw a SPAD coming at him in attack mode. The dawning realization that he would die from friendly fire gave him a sickening feeling. It was too late to jump. At the last extreme moment, Lieutenant Frank Luke of the 27th recognized the balloon's insignia as American and narrowly swooped up over it, then banked to bring his SPAD down on the field with the balloon's ground crew. They promptly put him on the phone with Smith in the basket, who had sufficiently regained his composure to remind Luke that he should heretofore limit his balloon hunting to Boches, and then told him about the four German *Drachen* he had seen rising behind enemy lines, adding that he would be happy to confirm a kill should Luke bring one down. Needing no more encouragement, that eager pilot took off within minutes to follow Smith's instructions. Through his binoculars, Smith watched him cross the front and close in.

No simple patriotism or youthful resolve sped Luke toward his target, but rather a near-desperate, almost adolescent desire to win the respect that he felt his fellow pilots had denied him. A blond, steel-blue-eyed athlete from Arizona, he brought a southwestern swagger to 1st Pursuit from his summers in the copper mines. It was rumored that he had stepped into the ring with a pro welterweight and knocked him out in the first round. Perhaps it was the cut and upward sweep of the popular civilian—certainly not "soldierly"—haircut known as a pompadour that radiated his ego; or his self-conscious talk, "twelve things at a time, changes from past to future and to present in one sentence," recalled one pilot. Certainly his boasting clinched his fellow pilots' angry impatience. Seeing a German overhead one day, he told an enlisted man, "Gee, that plane would be a cinch for me."

A month earlier he had wandered away from his formation and claimed to have shot down a Fokker deep behind enemy lines. This could never be confirmed, but he would still tell anyone who listened about it, breaking the unspoken rule "that you never mention your victories unless they are official, even though there is no doubt," as Lansing Holden put it. Archibald wrote that Luke's "self-heroism sickened us. His cocky assurance made us fume . . . We would not tolerate such talk. We would not listen. Luke . . . was an outcast." Still, the "four-flusher," as the men called him, had real if latent talent, perhaps the most of any pilot in the American service; still smarting from his colleagues' visibly chill assessment, he yearned to establish himself by killing memorable numbers of Germans.

When Lieutenant Willi Klemm, newly arrived at Ballonzug 55, spotted Luke's SPAD, he considered jumping. This was his first trip up as an observer, though, and he anticipated his commanding officer's anger should he bail prematurely. After all, part of the business of being an observer was gutting it out. What if the SPAD pulled away? He had already seen many Allied planes that morning and registered with satisfaction that artillery fire was pitching the SPAD about violently. Yet the SPAD kept on coming, and seeing that the time had come, Klemm straddled the basket's side.

Too late. Luke was on him, riddling the *Drachen*, then pitching his nose forward to rake the basket. One round struck Klemm in the chest and threw him back to dangle over the other side, grievously wounded and tangled in his harness. Down below his support crew toiled frantically at the screaming winch, but to their horror they saw the SPAD turn for a second pass. Archies pocked the surrounding air, syncopated by machine-gun rattle. Luke felt the sustained tapping of shrapnel and bullets' impact on his wings and fuselage but kept on undeterred, again within yards of the great undulating form, his balloon gun going until it jammed. Again he turned, pounding to free his gun, the balloon by now closing to earth, and got off another burst. He clearly saw Klemm's figure hanging from the basket. As he prepared for a fourth go-round, hydrogen flashed into a ball of flame, and the wreck crashed atop Klemm, who struggled to breathe in the conflagration. It took them six minutes to pull him out, miraculously still alive but terribly burned. He died three days later.

Luke got his battered machine back to the friendly balloon field that he had left only minutes earlier, where he was at last surrounded by the congratulations of Smith and the rest of the 5th Balloon Company. He spent the night there, his plane too damaged to fly home, pumping the crew for information about their work. He gleaned new tips about how best to down these ungainly aircraft, learning, for instance, that morning dew dampened balloon fabric and made it harder to ignite.

A few hours later, Eddie and Reed Chambers sortied toward Saint-Mihiel, turned northwest to Verdun, then finally flew southeast across the line to Vigneulles, the salient's main road hub and a prime objective. Eddie found the main highway north toward Metz "black with hurrying men and vehicles. Guns, stores, and ammunition were being hauled away to safety with all possible speed."

On their way back, they strafed a half-mile-long column of horse-drawn 3-inch guns into "the wildest confusion." On landing, Eddie's phoned-in report to headquarters clearly came as "splendid news and exactly what G.H.Q. had been anxious to know." Orders came back to bomb the road.

This apparent retreat was in fact a carefully orchestrated retrenchment, ordered by Ludendorff once he had determined that their position was no longer defensible. Behind the front line of trenches, barbed wire, and pill-boxes, the Germans had prepared yet another line, and behind that lay the Hindenburg Line proper, the main glacis of Fortress Germany. If that formidable redoubt was not enough, there lay within it the heavily fortified towns of Metz and Thionville. Though the Germans had started to pull back before the Americans moved, however, they had underestimated the speed of the offensive. When the pincers closed upon Vigneulles on September 13, the Allies captured some 16,000 prisoners and 250 heavy guns, at a cost of 7,000 casualties, and liberated some 200 square miles of occupied territory. While the push continued for several more days, the real work had been accomplished in the first two. The critical railway between Paris and Nancy reopened, and the Meuse could now be used to float matériel and troops—to the Americans a success smelling more of rout than retrenchment. It built a false confidence that would be quickly deflated by stiff resistance in the upcoming Meuse-Argonne offensive.

Nonetheless, the victory was definitive—and clearly the Americans now drove the chariot. The first coordinated air and land offensive had worked, if not seamlessly, then effectively. Mitchell's strategy of gaining ownership of the skies through sheer numbers had been vindicated. Massed strafing had disrupted the retreat, adding substantially to the number of prisoners. On the first day, for all the foul weather, the Americans had flown 390 sorties and dropped 14,300 pounds of bombs. Eleven pilots and four observers were missing, one of those being the American ace of aces, David Endicott Putnam of the 134th, operating out of Toul. As square-jawed as he was square-shouldered, Putnam personified the popular ideal of the air hero: taciturn but friendly, president of his class at Harvard, and a lettered athlete. Unlike Eddie, he didn't need to invent a middle name; his illustrious heritage traced back to General Israel Putnam of the Revolutionary War. "There is no question about the hereafter of men who give themselves in such a cause," he wrote in a letter to his mother. "If I am called upon to make it, I shall go with a grin of satisfaction and a smile." It may well have been such a sense of chivalry that impelled him to join a doomed, lopsided effort to save an Allied observation plane from an entire German formation. He was buried in the graveyard at Evacuation Hospital No. 1 at Issoudun among Lufbery, Kurtz, and ever more of his fellow fliers.

On September 14 the weather cleared, and the 1st launched 123 sorties, issuing twenty-seven aerial engagements, one of which involved Eddie flying solo. The German air service, which had been quiet for the first two days, now bristled with reinforcements and stiff resolve. High above Metz in the early morning, Eddie saw four Fokkers rapidly closing in on a formation of American DH-4 bombers, nicknamed "flaming coffins" for their fuel tank's propensity to catch fire in combat, now returning from a 12,000-foot bombing run on Metz. Eddie climbed unseen 1,000 feet above the Fokkers to shadow them. The diamond-shaped enemy formation pursued the bombers to the line, then peeled off to head farther west, unaware of the lone SPAD above and behind them. Patiently aligning the bright sun exactly at his back, Eddie launched into a half-speed dive and came within 50 yards of the last plane. The lead pilot pulled into a climbing virage—a banked vertical turn to send the pilot heading in the opposite direction—but too late: Eddie's stream of bullets either severely wounded or killed the pilot.

Only then did he see the Fokker's red-splashed wings. Rumors had circulated that Richthofen's widowed squadron had come to the sector (after action against the British to the north), but there had been no sightings—until now. Never had he been up against such veterans. He threw his SPAD into a steep zoom, counting that his superior speed would enable him to escape. The lead Fokker, with a superhuman response, initiated a virage, its pilot kicking his rudder over to reverse direction right onto Eddie's tail. It was a breathtaking maneuver, the bullets tearing past Eddie's head convincing him that he "would be very lucky if I got away with a whole skin." The exact details of this frenetic dogfight are lost to time and the flood of adrenaline, but Eddie recalled how his opponents "whipped their machines about me with incredible cleverness" and had him "twisting my head off to follow their movements." No matter where he turned, "there were always at least two of them there before me!" Only after pulling "several frantic virages and a long pique into our lines" did he finally outspeed his determined enemy. It had been a close thing, but those minutes erased whatever lingering doubts he'd had since his last kill three and a half months ago. Never had he quite felt so elated: He had gotten away with his sixth kill against the ultimate enemy.

The following day he followed with a seventh. He had headed toward Conflans, a favorite target for Allied fighting scouts and bombers not only because of its airfield and railroad station but because of its easily locatable position at the confluence (hence its name) of the Moselle and Madon rivers. Six Fokkers came into sight from the direction of the airfield, at his own altitude of 10,000 feet. He figured they had spotted him, too, because they were climbing steeply as they headed toward the Moselle. A half mile away, Eddie mirrored their action, and they all made three circling round trips. "I decided it was better to wait for a more promising opportunity," he recalled. Patience paid off some twenty minutes later, when both he and the Germans saw four SPADs—probably from the 2nd Pursuit Group, because some were retrofitted to carry light bomb racks—flying very low. Waggling his wings, the lead Fokker led a steep dive on the vulnerable formation. After a hasty glance for other enemies, Eddie plunged onto the tail of the last Fokker and set it ablaze, a stunning blow that scattered the survivors home.

With his seventh victory, and Putnam having gone down five days earlier, Eddie now became the ace of aces, a distinction he had simultaneously craved and feared because its holders seemed beset by an "unavoidable doom." Most of his predecessors had died or were shot down in action, including Lufbery and Frank Baylies. Eddie recalled, "I began to feel that this superstition was the heaviest burden that I carried with me into the air"—a thought that remained with him the following day, when he encountered three Fokkers near the Three-Fingered Lake. The Germans may well have identified the American ace by the markings on his fuselage—they spent time learning about their opponents—and raced back toward Metz. Eddie chased them for 4 or 5 miles, getting in position to intercept them as they dived on their airfield. A few short months ago, he would have gone in for the kill; now, a heightened risk awareness tempered his fierce desire for one more victory. Seeking action so low and deep in enemy territory made for unacceptable odds, and he turned back reluctantly for home.

That same day, a bright new star of the 1st Pursuit did not exercise such comparable caution—and in so doing, shot down two enemy aircraft and surged past Eddie's one-day title to become the next ace of aces. Frank Luke had decided to make that most difficult of targets, the *Drachen*, his specialty. No longer were his words empty boasting.

Early on the afternoon of September 16, three highly agitated officers burst into group headquarters at Rembercourt, Leo Dawson pulling up before Hartney to say, "Listen, Major, we want to take that all back. Boy, if anyone thinks that bird is yellow, he's crazy." Hartney knew this "bird" had to be Frank Luke. "The man's not yellow; he's crazy, stark mad. He went by me on that attack like a wild man. I thought he was diving right into the fabric."

Then Luke's flight commander, Captain K. S. Clapp, broke in. "Gosh, Maj', who spread that dribble around that Luke is a four-flusher? . . . He's gone, the poor kid, but he went in a blaze of glory. He had to go right down to the ground to get that second balloon and they've got the hottest machine gun nest in the world around it. They couldn't miss him."

The phone interrupted Clapp—a near hysterical call from the 27th's operations officer from the opposite side of the field. "Major, you'd better come down here and ground this bird, Luke!" Luke had indeed made it home, but in a machine "so badly shot up it's a wonder he flew her at all." Immediately after landing, he had ordered it gassed up to be taken right back into action and, "crazy as a bedbug," was going up straight again with or without permission.

Hartney sprinted over, with Alfred Grant, commander of the 27th, and Clapp close behind. On the quarter-mile run, Grant barked at Clapp, "You're his flight commander, Clapp, I hold you responsible."

They pounded up out of breath to find Luke standing casually beside a SPAD with its longerons shot up, bullet holes peppering wings and fuselage. One round had entered Luke's seat 6 inches from his body. To frustrate his mad idea to take such a wreck back aloft, his adoring mechanics had already conspired to pull off several feet of fabric, claiming that it needed replacement. While Luke fell for the ruse, he begged for another plane. Before Hartney could open his mouth, Alfred Grant, the stiff, not-well-liked leader of the 27th—Luke's commanding officer but Hartney's subordinate— demanded that Luke follow orders like everybody else. Luke glared at him but slunk off. A few minutes later, Hartney found Luke and congratulated him on that day's victories, then gripped the ace's arm, "Listen, Frank, old boy. Have patience. In flying, patience is the best virtue you can have. I want you to live to be an old man."

Even if Hartney had needed to show outward displeasure, he was inwardly delighted. Only that morning, Mitchell's headquarters had phoned with orders to take the two balloons down. In the wake of the Saint-Mihiel offensive, Mitchell had directed pursuit pilots to limit offensive missions to no more than 3 miles across the lines unless accompanying a bombing or reconnaissance patrol. The Germans figured that Pershing's next move would be to complete the Saint-Mihiel push to strike for the railroad hub of Metz—just as many of his advisers, including Douglas MacArthur, were urging. With pressure from the French, he had decided instead to bring the full force of the hammer down north and northwest of Verdun, upon the hilly confines of the Argonne Forest, which the Germans had spent four years fortifying. If the Allies could take the railroad hub of Sedan, they would cripple the German resupply web. This penultimate offensive of the war, the largest engagement of the conflict for the Americans and the costliest, would require a massive undetected shift of men and matériel from the Saint-Mihiel sector some 60 miles to the north. In one of the war's most remarkable operations, Colonel George C. Marshall, who would play so great a part in organizing victory a generation later, directed the extraordinary feat of moving some 600,000 troops, 90,000 horses, 3,000 field guns, and thousands of supply trucks by night in only ten days, using trains, motor transport, and marching columns. Air command took on the crucial task of blinding the Germans by downing their observation balloons. Failure to do so would have grave consequences for the masses of soldiers and supplies bunched in transit and extremely vulnerable to bombing and strafing.

On September 15, Luke, again accompanied by Joe Wehner, shot down three balloons. A tall, athletic loner, son of a German cobbler, Wehner had undergone the same humiliating suspicions of disloyalty as had Eddie. The rage induced by heavy-handed investigation had morphed into a determination to prove himself as a warrior. Luke and he understood one another perfectly. On the sixteenth, Luke shot down two more balloons, his eight kills now exceeding Eddie's total. These last two victories, noted Eddie in his journal, came in the evening. Luke "returned after dark and landed with flairs [sic] and was shot at all the way home by French." Luke had taken to heart the recommendations of the American balloon crew to attack just as the light was failing.

September 18 brought more blows of war but also extraordinary successes. On a dusk sortie with Wehner providing cover from above, Luke shot down two balloons near Labeauville. During the second action, Wehner suddenly found his hands full with a whole formation of Fokkers. As Luke climbed to join the melee, two Fokkers roared in behind him, guns blazing. His back to the wall, Luke responded the only way he knew how—by turning on a dime to savage his attackers. "We came head-on until within a few yards of each other, when my opponent turned to one side in a nose dive and I saw him crash on the ground. I then turned on the second, shot a short burst, and he turned and went into a dive." Unable to find Wehner, he dashed home, gas tank emptied by a round that miraculously had not set it ablaze, forcing him to pump gas from his small reserve. Even now the drama was not yet over. Falling in with four French SPADs harassing a Halberstadt observation plane over Allied territory, he banked sharply and, not caring that this would stop his engine, quit working his emergency pump to dive between two SPADs and finish off the German. He landed his ruined plane not far from the fresh wreckage.

The twenty-one-year-old executioner walked over to the tangle of wire and fabric, between an old French concrete bunker and a grove of trees, immediately seeing a helmetless German officer, thrown facedown from the plane, one arm twisted behind his torn flight jacket, fingers bloodied, the other arm reaching out as if in some last-second supplication. The other corpse lay beneath the wreckage, face to the sky. Seeing the grotesque trophies of his work close up shocked Luke. A reporter who had watched the fight overhead rushed up to photograph him in front of the wreckage. No smile, nor even the remotest glimmer of satisfaction, plays across the handsome countenance; the mouth is set with hard determination; the eyes no longer glow cockily but seem those of a much older man of grim experience. Although he hadn't seen Wehner go down, somehow he knew his pal was dead, his mangled body probably being examined by German officers just as he looked at the fruit of his own victory.

The reporter pressed for a few words, no doubt expecting the knightly, self-deprecating commentary of a flying cavalier. He got no such reward, but he did carefully take down Luke's exact utterance: "Saw balloon. Saw another . . . Lieutenant Wehner [was] above. Set fire . . . uh . . . set another afire. Fokker—two Fokkers. Wehner, myself. Gasoline pressure. Got . . . uh . . . both. We . . . er . . . they . . . the Archie shells."

Late that afternoon, Luke had downed two balloons and three aircraft in under ten minutes. On May 9, the great French ace René Fonck had brought down six, but over more than three hours of flying in two sorties. Later that same month, the RAF ace Mick Mannock made four kills in one day, but again on two patrols. The Red Baron himself had only achieved four victories in one day in April 1917, on three successive sorties against outclassed observation planes. Any satisfaction Luke derived was chilled when word arrived that Wehner was indeed dead.

The following evening, Eddie helped the 94th and 147th host a banquet for Luke. Tellingly, Luke's own 27th squadron, which messed with the 95th a quarter of a mile across the field, did not celebrate his achievements as a group, many of its fliers still resenting "the Arizona Balloon Buster," as he was coming to be known. Its commanding officer, Grant, a stickler for authority, had grown increasingly furious at Luke's independence and disrespect; this would soon come to a head. Eddie harbored no ill will toward this shooting star, even joking with him about their rivalry. "For Luke's very mischievousness and irresponsibility made every one of us feel that he must be cared for and nursed back into a more disciplined way of fighting—and flying—and living." Luke's desperate bid for acceptance must have keenly reminded Eddie of his own struggles uphill. To Eddie at least, Luke had earned the right to belong. Chambers remembered Eddie asserting that "I think I can control him," if given the chance.

That night the drinking was heavy. When Luke climbed up onto a table, words again failed him, but he was clearly moved by his comrades' thunderous approval. Eddie, Hartney, Wilbert White, and Peterson gave speeches. For Luke, even though still grieving for his friend and wingman, that night would mark the high point of the war. Yet, unlike for Eddie, the respect he earned from his skills would not bring him reflective satisfaction but in fact would erase what little caution he still could muster. "As doctors say to the press, he is not expected to live," observed Eastman in his journal.

The next day, Hartney wisely ordered Luke on a few days' leave to Paris and then returned to the important business of squadron leadership, particularly that of the 94th, which was "badly slipping" even given Eddie's string of victories. The lethargy that had plagued it all summer still lingered. America's first and most formidable attack squadron remained a burned-out husk of its former self, with listless leadership, its ranks ravaged by the enemy, seemingly unable to overcome the switch to SPADs, which continued to bedevil the mechanics.

From the outside, Hartney's solution to these problems could seem highly unorthodox and improbable—and he understood that it would be next to impossible to convince his superiors that Eddie was the man to take over. After all, Eddie's wicked slang and profanity, easy smile, and roughneck ways bore the marks of an effective master sergeant far more obviously than of an officer in the army's most elite branch. Hartney would need to elevate Eddie over the heads of three other excellent senior fliers—Reed Chambers, Ham Coolidge, and Thorne Taylor. All of the 94th's pilots had received formal flight-school training stateside, which Eddie had skipped.

Yet for those three and the others of the 94th, there was no one else they would rather have making decisions on the ground or on sortie with them. In this maelstrom, the intangibles of leadership came clearly into focus—hundreds of fleeting moments evidenced every day as they set out to overcome fear, weather, cunning adversaries, equipment malfunctions, deadly exhausting boredom, and the unending loss of comrades. Short of giving orders, Eddie had already taught and recharged those around him, providing the hard-to-quantify substance that not only held a unit together under extreme duress but enabled it with startling consistency to produce remarkable examples of truly courageous battle flying. Throughout history the best-prepared fighters in all of combat's endlessly changing forms have faltered, stumbled, and failed without strong leadership. The best equipment and knowledge, the most superior battle plan, all the advantages of surprise or topography—these cannot guarantee victory absent effective direction. ("Wars," said George Patton famously, "may be fought with weapons, but are won by men.") However easy it may be to identify this combination of qualities in hindsight, it is far more difficult to discern its exact characteristics through "the fog of war," when every situation's uncertainties are changing by the second, threatening disaster at any moment. Certain times demand a brutal, unbending allegiance to the rulebook, while others must be bent to the deadly flow of combat. By the time there is opportunity to write the playbook, it is already out of date. Effective leadership requires the seeming contradiction of being one of the team and yet simultaneously holding oneself apart. Only then can a leader push his people beyond what they thought possible.

It would take a month of hard lobbying that would reach all the way up to starched regular-army Pershing for Hartney's designs to bear fruit. The American general had told the head of the British air service that "natural airmen have a visionary faith in three-dimensional warfare that owes more to intuition than to the teachings of West Point." The latter philosophy persuaded leadership to deem parachutes inappropriate because these would encourage pilots to bail out prematurely. Still, legitimate questions did raise themselves for Mitchell, and certainly for Pershing. No one argued about Eddie's formidable flying record. Mitchell himself would comment that "in Rickenbacker we had the rare combination of sound judgment and fighting spirit, quick thinking, and great manual dexterity in handling his craft." By no means did such skills automatically translate into the ability to command men or bear up effectively under the operation of a squadron and all its administrative details. Call it snobbery or good sense, but career army types looked askance at men such as Eddie, who had virtually walked into the service. His bona fides as a race-car driver did not impress, as evidenced by General Squier's humiliating rejection of his offer to raise a squadron of drivers. Were that not enough, questions still lingered about the man with the German-sounding name and his loyalty, despite his extraordinary capacity to shoot down the enemy.

Hartney visited Mitchell with three senior pilots to help argue his case and cleverly pressed upon his boss a point that no one could ignore. The SPADs were still spending far more time in the hangar getting repaired than flying, their finicky Hispano-Suiza engines hampering the air effort. Eddie's clear mechanical abilities, which Mitchell knew firsthand, could stand the squadron, and the entire group, in critically good stead. Mitchell, who had tapped Hartney because of his commitment to the "free exchange of new ideas" and hands-on master qualities, listened carefully. "With proper officers an army can, and frequently does, perform miracles," Hartney would later write. "But such officers must have an instinctive fellow feeling with their men plus a superior knowledge of the work at hand and a definite capacity for leadership." At first surprised and dubious, Mitchell came around in the face of Hartney's persuasive case. Pershing, ever eager to press supreme advantage for the critical upcoming Meuse-Argonne offensive, agreed.

"It is no small good fortune that Rick has been given command over the 94th," noted Eastman in his journal. Even that, it would soon prove, was a major understatement.

15.

SQUADRON COMMAND

On September 24, 1918, the day Hartney announced Eddie's promotion, the 94th's new commander scheduled two evening meetings. To his gathered pilots he delivered a ringing speech, part rally booster, part call to action. He got to the point in a flash—after all, life had been preparing him for something like this from the outset. Eddie's focus had always been on clarifying his mission, whether putting food on his family's table or winning one more race to keep the Duesenbergs alive another day. The war offered a clearer—and harder—mission than anything even he had ever faced. Later he would write that "it suddenly dawned on me that I was pitting myself against a gigantic evil."

He reminded those assembled how the 94th had so swiftly and decisively lost its primacy among the twelve active pursuit squadrons. Under Frank Luke, the 27th had soared far ahead of them in kills. That would need to change now. Most listened gravely as he laid down the rules: Everyone was to fly often, and aggressively. He may well have invoked Lufbery's adage that one couldn't shoot down Germans with one's feet propped up in front of a fire. They were in this together, which equally extended to the mechanics, whom, Eddie added, they would respect by babying their new SPADs and temperamental Hispano-Suiza engines. Flying full throttle would be kept to a minimum. (Even decades later, Eddie would get worked up recalling that the average life of an engine for squadron members was twelve hours before their misuse either burned out the engine or caused mechanical troubles. "Think of it!" he exclaimed.) Eddie "always patrolled at just enough rpm's to prevent stalling," noted Chambers. "When he fought, however, he called for maximum performance and drove the plane until it nearly fell apart." The others were to do the same, as well as to closely inspect their ammunition to reduce gun jamming. Nothing but their fullest effort could bring victory over the supremely motivated German veterans.

To his assembled mechanics and support staff, he asserted that their contributions matched those of the pilots, something they had heard often enough before. Luke's CO, Alfred Grant of the 27th, had glibly told his mechanics that half of each medal won by a pilot belonged to them, until an irritated enlisted man had logically inquired what they would have to show their girlfriends and families at home after earning such credit. Eddie did not sugarcoat the differences between the vaunted pilots and their hard-working ground crews, but he did make authentically clear their critical role in the squadron's coming success. They could count on him as he would on them, much as he had on his pit crews at Indy, where every grease monkey could voice an opinion. Eddie threw down the gauntlet: Engine overhaul times must improve so that more machines were in the air longer. He suspended operations to muster the entire squadron outside in front of a hangar. He told them that while he "respected the uniform," he "didn't want anybody wasting time saluting somebody else . . . a waste of good energy and time." It was time to get down to business. "He made [the squadron] back into a team," said Chambers.

Well aware that actions, not speeches, cement leadership, Eddie took off on a lone sortie on his first full day of command. Near Billy-sous-les-Côtes, he found five Fokkers escorting a pair of reconnaissance two-seaters. Pulling out his signature élan, he climbed high between them and the sun, then pitched headlong into an attack dive. "Most of the pilots he killed," said Chambers, "never knew what hit them. Out of the sun, a quick burst and gone. That was Rickenbacker."

One Fokker spun away trailing smoke. Then, exploiting the confusion that comes in the seconds right after such complete surprise, Eddie maneuvered extremely close to one of the slower two-seaters and destroyed that,

too—his eighth and ninth confirmed kills, a sudden and catastrophic assault that sent the smashed formation milling away to regroup. A pattern
was emerging from the operation reports, which singled out the aces from
the others: They drew extremely close to their targets, often needing only
fifty to a hundred rounds for a kill.

By such actions, Eddie communicated to his new command that he
would not ask anything of anybody that he wasn't going to demand of himself. He would, in fact, go beyond this, logging longer time over enemy
territory and engaging in more combats than any other U.S. flier. "He drove
himself to exhaustion," said Chambers. "He'd fly the required patrol. Then
he and I would come back to the field, have a cup of coffee, get into our second ships and go hunting by ourselves." At the same time, his philosophy of
combat had evolved to the point where he was helping shape a new pattern
of air tactics. He had seen too many friends go down in flames to romanti-
cize air war. Styling combat flying "scientific murder," he set out to perfect
supremely businesslike techniques of making it yet more precisely murderous. "The experienced fighting pilot does not take unnecessary risks," he
later wrote. "His business is to shoot down enemy planes, not to get shot
down. His trained eye and hand and judgment are as much part of his armament as his machine gun, and a fifty-fifty chance is the worst he will
take or should take, except where the show is of the kind that either for offense or defense justifies the sacrifice of plane and pilot." Stripped to its core,
this clear, cold-eyed perspective was beginning to elaborate the early, effective use of applied risk management, decades before its universal adoption
in American business.

It was good that the squadron was settling in quickly to the new order. The make-or-break Meuse-Argonne offensive would be launched
the next day.

The swathe of battleground the pilots would come to know so well over the
following days had been forged partly out of its natural topography and
partly by the vicissitudes of history and nation building that stretched back

at least to the ninth-century Frankish emperor Charlemagne. His continental-scope conquests of the Saxons of the German plains, the Lombards of Italy, the Bavarians of southern Germany, and the Moors in northern Spain briefly imparted to Western Europe a unity that it hadn't seen since the Roman Empire of the West had collapsed three centuries earlier. By the Treaty of Verdun of 843, his three grandsons settled a civil war among themselves by dividing the sprawling empire: Charles the Bald receiving the western portion, whose lands would eventually encompass most of modern-day France; Louis the German being given the eastern realm, including the lands of the Germanic tribes; Lothair, the eldest, inheriting the in-between region of middle Francia, a reach of land that stretched from the North Sea to the Mediterranean, including the modern-day Low Countries, Lorraine, Alsace, Burgundy, Provence, and northern Italy.

Long borders and generally flat contours made Lothair's realm difficult to defend; it lacked the mountains of Switzerland, the encircling seas protecting England, or even the Netherlands' maze of waterways. Middle Francia became a land of multiple loyalties and historic presences, a confusion of encroachments, rebuffs, and betrayals. More than a thousand years' worth of French and German nobility would spill much blood, with little to show. In 1815, British and Prussian armies would frustrate Napoleon's grand designs at Waterloo in Lothair's former realm of Flanders. Yet further complications ensued, particularly when the Prussians annexed much of Lorraine in 1871, its German-speaking people loudly voicing their attachment to France, not to a reconstitution of the Germanic nation. The 1918 Armistice, which reestablished the southern half as French, the northern half remaining independent as Belgium, the Netherlands, and Luxembourg, would not silence the bitter quarrels over this ethnically indeterminate middle ground. While the borders looked clean to the Americans staring at a map, a rich and bloody history blurred distinctions and heated deep prejudices between the two great confronting powers.

Through this region the Meuse runs like a backbone. At well over 300 million years, it is one of the world's oldest rivers, rising in France to flow 575 miles through Belgium and the Netherlands into the North Sea. In a quarry on its banks, geologists discovered the remains of gigantic sea lizards, or mosasaurs ("Mosa" for Meuse, "saur" for lizard). The river's sinuous curves cut deep embankments, along which perched historic and strategically significant but not particularly large cities nested within centuries-old fortifications, drawing their sustenance from rich floodplain fields. Verdun, Sedan, Neufchâteau, Saint-Mihiel, Dun-sur-Meuse, and Charleville-Mézières became key theaters of Franco-German struggle. In the 1870–71 Franco-Prussian War, the newly united German army trapped Napoleon III and his army at Sedan, taking 104,000 prisoners after killing or wounding 17,000 more (losing 8,300 themselves), and then rolled into Paris after a long, terrible siege. In the hot ashes of that war, the kings and princes of the various German political entities gathered in the Hall of Mirrors at Versailles to ratify a unified German nation-state under the primacy of King Wilhelm of Prussia, now dubbed Kaiser (Emperor) Wilhelm I. Four months later, in accordance with the uneasy peace settlement, the new German Empire annexed most of Alsace and northern Lorraine, including Strassburg (Strasbourg to the French), the fortress city of Metz, and much of the territory containing France's rich iron resources.

In 1918, the penultimate forty-seven-day offensive of the First World War centered on a 20-mile section of the southern front, defined to the east by the unfordable Meuse and the heights on its right bank, and to the west by the high, rugged outlines of the Argonne Forest. In between ran an east-west hogback, upon which stood several heavily defended eminences, the most evident being 1,100-foot-high Montfaucon. To break the German army and win the war, the U.S. 1st Army would have to take Montfaucon, the Cunel Heights, and other staunchly held prominences in this devil's labyrinth. Pershing had no option but to take Montfaucon by attacking up the defiles that cut toward it on either side of the ridgeline. The German 3rd and 5th armies, which had set up four separate defensive lines, would be waiting with the still-formidable firepower of the world's most powerful land military.

The night before the offensive, Major Hartney plotted 1st Pursuit's coordinated attack on all thirteen enemy observation balloons floating over the Meuse-Argonne sector. Each of his four squadrons would take responsibility for a quadrant and the balloons within it, starting at the first light of 5:45 A.M. Once the balloons were shot down—hit preferably through the front of each ship, which contained the most hydrogen—formations of up to six planes were to fly low patrols and take out enemy aircraft, denying further intelligence about the offensive.

On September 26 at 4:00 A.M., an orderly awakened Eddie. Allied artillery had been hammering the enemy for the past two days, a barrage that would continue after the infantry assault slated for 5:30 A.M. left the trenches. Captain Harry S. Truman's battery fired "3,000 rounds of 75 ammunition from 4 A.M. to 8 A.M." Such was the roar that Truman complained of "trouble hearing what goes on when there is a noise" even decades later.

By the time the 1st Army, flanked on its left by the French 4th, had pushed out toward the German entrenchments, Eddie and four pilots of the 94th had been airborne for ten minutes, on their way against the first two targets. Most of the 1st Pursuit's pilots had never flown at night. "Overhead the stars shone coldly," wrote the 95th's Harold Buckley. "Beneath us the dusty roads were dimly visible, crisscrossing the fearsome blackness with strips of gray. The canals and rivers were ribbons of silver. Here and there the fiery exhaust of some other ship glowed for a minute, then faded away." All of this changed as they approached the front. From above, the early-morning sky glowed with a breathtaking artillery light show, shells bursting so often that they melded into a blinding continuity that came close to resembling artificial day. "From Lunéville in the east to Rheims on the west there was not one spot of darkness along the entire front," wrote Eddie, struggling to convey the overwhelming impact. "The picture made me think of a giant switchboard which emitted thousands of electric flashes as invisible hands manipulated the plugs." Indeed, no one had ever seen the likes of this nocturnal glare, before electricity would transform dark urban skies into brilliant temples of human-made luminosity. Mesmerized, Eddie almost overflew Verdun and the turnoff along the northward-snaking Meuse.

He knew exactly where to swing into occupied territory and find his assigned balloon, every inch of the journey now as familiar as the path "around the corner of my old home."

Just as he closed in, tracers streaked up ahead, turning an enemy balloon into a fiery blossom of light. Before it died out, another flamed nearby. Eddie continued along the river toward a balloon nest near Damvillers as dawn broke. In the early light he watched as that balloon, too, went up, but jubilation evaporated a moment later when a glance to his right revealed a Fokker not 100 yards away. In a moment, they were hurtling directly at one another. "Four streams of tracer bullets cut brilliant lines of fire through the sky. For a moment it looked as though our two machines were tied together with four ropes of fire." Would they collide? Who would blink first? At the last moment, the Fokker tipped beneath him. Immediately Eddie pulled into a renversement—a half roll followed by a half loop—to maneuver onto his foe's tail, delivered a quick burst into the center of its fuselage, and watched his tenth victim fall from the sky. Only a few seconds later, a tremendous jerk shook his entire machine, bouncing him around like a rag doll. His engine began vibrating as though possessed. Eddie quickly banked back toward Verdun, the closest point of Allied territory, racing the terrifying prospect of coming down on enemy ground to face the rest of the war as a prisoner.

Throttling down reduced the pounding but maintained just enough speed to avoid stalling. At 1,000 feet in his heavy SPAD, he surely would not make it if the engine cut out, but he just managed to locate a small advanced aerodrome operated by a flight of the 27th and land his crippled bird. Hopping out to inspect his engine, he discovered that a round had destroyed a third of one propeller blade, miraculously without splitting its top off until he had pulled his renversement and chased the Fokker down. Had he not reduced his throttle, the other blade might well have disintegrated under the increased strain. He also counted twenty-seven bullet holes and scars within a 5- to 6-foot radius around his seat. Even more unnerving, he discovered a hole in the windshield through which a bullet had passed so close to his forehead that it had singed his leather helmet. A cold feeling settled over him. Because of his eye injury, he habitually used his healthy left eye to look through this gunsight; had he used his right, as most pilots did, the round would have taken him squarely in the temple.

The mechanics mounted another propeller, and by 8:30 P.M. he was back at Rembercourt. That day, 1st Pursuit logged 143 sorties, destroying five balloons and five planes. Frank Luke had cut short his Paris leave and downed yet another gasbag. The Pursuit Group was hurting the German artillery's capacity to disrupt the American ground offensive. "When daylight came," wrote Meissner, "we saw the effectiveness of our work, not an enemy sausage was in the air." On the Allied side, the balloons went up so thickly that they resembled a massive picket fence. At Rembercourt, spirits bubbled into excited chatter in the mess hall, as famished but exhilarated fliers gulped their food and swapped stories. The men doubled over as Lieutenant Wilbert White Jr. of the 147th regaled them with the saga of his heroic dive onto a *Drachen*, only to find that he'd been pouring good machine-gun fire into a puff of Archie smoke.

On the ground that day, American troops had pushed 7 miles into the foreboding darkness of the Argonne Forest, a brutal tangle of crisscrossed ravines. Enemy machine guns commanded each trail, whole nests perching atop each height. Infantrymen navigated by guess or dead reckoning, the gloom and chopped topography blinding their sightlines. Although he had intelligence to the contrary, Ludendorff still believed that Pershing would concentrate his attack against Metz. Only five German divisions lay between the Meuse and the Argonne; eighteen were massed at Saint-Mihiel, with twelve more held in reserve. The huge American divisions were twice the size of French ones and four times that of the Germans. Yet while the U.S. 1st Army's three corps outnumbered the Germans by eight to one, the combination of a determined enemy, challenging geography, and well-designed defenses evened the odds. Pershing had counted on surprise and speed to achieve his goals, but scheduling the offensive only ten days after the Saint-Mihiel campaign ended had forced him to compromise and send in largely inexperienced and ill-trained infantry, holding his most experienced troops back to hold those recent gains. Of nine divisions, only four had seen combat; many of the rest had not even completed training. Some divisions even lacked artillery units.

The green troops, facing brutal machine-gun fire and artillery barrages in the dark mazes of the forest, simply could not execute their ambitious orders to advance 10 miles and take Montfaucon that first day. The only two roads feeding the area quickly became jammed and barely passable. Artillery could not reach the front; the "battle of a nightmare" stalled bloodily. The surprise surge, designed to storm objectives before they could be reinforced, had failed. The Germans lost no time in racing up veteran divisions. As the offensive mired, a French general recalled that "I could read clearly in [Pershing's] eyes that, at that moment, he realized his mistake. His soldiers were dying bravely, but they were not advancing, or very little, and their losses were heavy." Once and future French prime minister Georges Clemenceau, who had got caught up in the immense traffic jam, demanded Pershing be immediately relieved. Marshal Foch held Clemenceau off, instead pressing upon the American commander the need to place a number of divisions under the Allied high command. Pershing angrily refused. Foch told Pershing to reengage the enemy even harder.

Bogged down and bloodied, the 1st Army now depended on the air service to keep enemy airpower and air-prompted artillery from taking advantage of the huge jam of men and supplies. A well-placed counterattack, supported by strafing German pursuit planes, could potentially end the offensive outright. Mitchell urgently directed his pursuit groups to fly low and do whatever they could to blind the enemy, flinging bombers behind the lines to draw German attack planes away from the front. "Had we not done so," he wrote later, "I believe that this whole mass of transportation would have been destroyed and burned." Tactical airpower had arrived.

Over the next four days, Luke shot down four balloons and one aircraft but, with the headlong disobedience that continued to drive his commanding officer to distraction, often broke formation in his single-minded quest for balloons. He brought in five of his machines damaged beyond repair, frequently landing at another field without finding the time to inform his base. "Luke mingled with his disdain for bullets," recalled Eddie, "a very similar distaste for the orders of his superior officers." Unlike Hartney, who could work with such individualists, Grant, only two years older than Luke, could not handle the headstrong Arizonan. Taking such behavior as a personal affront to his authority, he grounded him on September 27; Luke promptly flew off to an advanced base near Verdun. The enraged Grant called ahead to order his arrest, simultaneously if paradoxically proposing to recommend him for a Distinguished Service Cross. Grant then called Hartney to demand action. As a group leader, Hartney faced a difficult choice: He certainly didn't want his best balloon buster under arrest, but neither could he countenance such open insubordination. He had already considered Eddie's offer to take Luke under his wing in the 94th, which now appeared his only good option. Before that could happen, though, he had to defuse the present situation.

To buy time, Hartney told Grant that he had given Luke permission to fly to the forward base, an outright lie he would later confess to in his memoirs. Luke understood, too, that he remained only a step ahead of Grant. His only hope lay in continuing to bring down balloons. At dusk that evening, he flew to an American balloon nest about 30 miles north of Rembercourt and dropped a message informing its crew to expect fireworks in the next several minutes. Sure enough, the crew watched wide-eyed as three successive *Drachen* went up in flames near Dun-sur-Meuse. Even as they cheered, a round pierced Luke's lung, forcing him down near a small village behind enemy lines. Accounts vary, but he did manage to crawl out of the plane and make his way to a small creek, where he was certainly clutching his Colt .45 when German soldiers approached. Whether he dropped dead from his wounds or his adversaries' bullets, he kept his vow to never be taken alive. Fittingly, Grant got him the Medal of Honor. He had gone where his equally well-deserved court-martial exercised no jurisdiction. Over eighteen days on the front, he had shot down fourteen balloons and four airplanes, despite being on leave for five of those days and being fogged in for several more—an intensity of performance unmatched by any other ace.

Had that brilliant loner survived just one more day, he would have come under Eddie's wing. Eddie had never doubted that Luke's reckless courtship of death would soon destroy him were he not placed under a truly firm but respectful hand. Eddie could never quite forgive Hartney for not stepping in more sternly. A little part of Eddie died that day; the starburst of Luke's talent had awed him, reminding him of his own brilliantly raw days on the track, charged only with an overabundance of nerve and talent. The loss stung, not only because Eddie judged that Luke's death clearly could have been avoided, but also because it let down the whole group—and weakened the effort against an enemy so much greater than insubordination.

"Did I treat him right?" Hartney mused about Luke in his memoirs, still clearly picking at the wound. "I think so. Did I give him too much leeway? I think not." Hartney clearly tolerated Luke's recklessness because his brilliant kill rate furthered the cause. It's difficult to imagine Eddie brooding over such issues if given the chance to supervise Luke. Eddie might have been unable to tame him—and the white-hot daredevil might likely still have found a way to die—but there would have been no ambiguity about expectations and a failure to meet them. For Eddie, survival had depended on wiping out that fuzzy gray world, and it had to be the same for those for whom he was responsible—an approach that led some to call him brusque but didn't stop them lining up to be led by him. Hartney struck a bargain with the devil over Luke, something that Eddie would have never done. Even so, he could not see—or did not want to see—that he had put Luke at risk during a particularly critical moment in the air war. Hartney ultimately judged the strategic advantages to be worth the risks. This did not square with Eddie, who, judging himself at least the equal of any of his charges, saw his role as their steward, not their iron-ruled superior officer.

Journalists stateside began writing about Rickenbacker's seemingly homespun approach to squadron dynamics. A senior pilot in the 94th was known as a "gimper," a term that Eddie had picked up from a mechanic in his racing days: "A gimper is a bird who will stick by you through anything," explained Eddie. "If you were up in the air and ran into a dozen

Boches and were getting the worst of it, perhaps, and the fellow with you stuck with you and gave it to them until the Heinies went back into Hunland, you'd know he was a gimper." A gimper did everything "just a little better than he has to." In effect, Eddie had rewritten the rules of what defined acceptable behavior within a combat environment. From the days that his schoolmates had laughed at his mismatched shoes, he had been too poor, too profane, too little educated—just plain not acceptable, certainly not officer material. Yet he had become the "head gimper," a role that demanded far more than bitter self-justification. Had he set about developing this system only to avenge past personal wrongs, this new "rulebook" would have failed, but it worked precisely because it rallied the pilots to the deepest common purpose and established critical standards and expectations with knife-edged clarity. Out of whole cloth, Eddie was creating the equivalent of a fraternal organization as coherent as the Shriners or the Masons, as fiercely loyal as a fire brigade or burns unit.

A newcomer started out as an "egg," moving up through proving himself to a "vulture," thence "gopher," and finally to "gimper." Being a good scout or friend wouldn't cut it alone. "This pursuit and fighting part of aviation requires a type of aviator who will stick, especially the way we fly in groups. To do your best work you must have a mutual feeling of confidence in the gimper flying beside you that is unequaled anywhere else." Gimpers didn't lose their nerve. "It may seem strange that a man who had gone through flight training and had flown patrols in wartime would be leery of combat. Fighting, however, requires a different kind of bravery from that involved in flying. The combat pilot must be mentally prepared to shoot to kill and to be shot at in return. Some pilots had sufficient motivation and bravery to learn to fly, but going out to kill or be killed over the lines required a different type of courage. Some did not have it." Eddie thus pinpointed that concern universal to all combat fighters—whether they possess "what it takes," or what a much later generation would term "the right stuff." Richthofen had been brutal but operationally savvy when it came to sending home those who were not up to the task—as was Eddie, but his power to discriminate came cloaked in the midwestern storytelling vernacular of

Abraham Lincoln, whose deceptively simple tales got people grinning at their absurdity, yet at the same time clarified important truths. For Eddie, "a man who is not a gimper can't stay with the squadron."

As new pilots filled in for their fallen countrymen, they understood clearly the expectations defining behavior in the air. "When you're flying around up there over Germany," expounded Eddie, "and being followed by a string of black puffs from the German archies, and hear them exploding around you, and then see some German planes off to one side of you, it is the easiest thing in the world to pretend you don't see them, and keep straight ahead until you pass them. Usually, the Germans are willing to do that too, unless you attack them. But a gimper never lets himself fail to see them." There were other terms, too. "Going to a pink tea," Eddie told a reporter, "is going up in the air after a German. Cuckoo birds are always talking about pink teas, though they never have them. A cuckoo bird is an aviator who does all his fighting while none of the gimpers are around, and then comes back and tells about it."

"The squadron," reported one pilot, "had begun to love him. I don't know how to explain it. At first he was just an uneducated tough bastard who threw his weight around the wrong way . . . But he developed into the most natural leader I ever saw." Said Hartney, "He not only led them always but ruled them with a rather firm hand, and they liked it."

During the last week of September and the first week of October 1918, the enemy considerably beefed up its air pressure against the 1st Army, increasing pursuit squadrons from five to twelve, appearing in large formations, bombing and strafing the American front lines, going for observation balloons. The fight for air supremacy was on.

Eddie bent the 94th's will toward this deadly challenge with unified intensity, bringing everyone from the newest mechanic on up together in common cause. He drafted into service his roommate from basic training at Tours, Lieutenant Cedric E. Fauntleroy, from a staff post at an aircraft acceptance facility near Paris. Eddie would order spare parts, and "Faunt" would find them. The 94th would sneak vehicles at night to Faunt's room, which was so crammed with spare SPAD parts that "there was literally an aisle-way from the door to the bed, with no other available empty space." Eddie also drew on his friendship with the chief engineer at Hispano-Suiza. Soon the 94th's aircraft could fly an average of a hundred hours between overhauls—far longer than any other squadron's, as other intangibles of his leadership rapidly took form. Reed Chambers began to strike an effective balance between courage and caution and started making the kills that had so long eluded him. Within a week of Eddie's taking command, the 94th regained its long-lost ascendency and never looked back as it flew more hours, engaged in more combats, and soared past every other frontline American unit in terms of planes and balloons brought down.

Eddie set up headquarters in a hangar, putting up blackboards and charts on which the pilots could see who had earned kills against what German formation. Mealtimes, one reporter wrote, turned into brainstorming sessions: "conferences on methods, blackboard talks, and ideas for air-battle tactics," which reminded him of "a big-time coach and the football team boning up for the season ahead." While there might be no richer sport, this was no game. The next several weeks in the air would be critical to the offensive. Should this push not prove decisive, the weather would likely push the war into 1919, bringing untold consequences upon the ravaged European nations on both sides, especially as civil war boiled over in Russia. On the second day, 1st Pursuit flew another 143 sorties, making ten kills.

The 1st Army's prime objective was to smash beyond Montfaucon to the deeply fortified Cunel Heights and pierce the Kriemhilde Stellung, the stiffest German line of defense anchoring the Hindenburg Line's eastern end. Should Cunel hold out, the offensive must fail. On October 3, right before the 1st Army set out to resume its stalled advance, Mitchell detailed 1st Pursuit's four squadrons to take down three critical *Drachen*. Thirty aircraft, including thirteen from the 94th, would cover three assigned balloon busters against the inevitable fighting-scout counterstroke. Rickenbacker was the only squadron commander to accompany the raid, which would take off in broad afternoon, when the enemy was not expecting them.

By now, Eddie routinely gathered all the pilots in an upcoming mission to review all possible details with intense care. One pilot acknowledged that the meetings were an excellent practice, although he would have preferred them conducted "in a more off-hand manner." Eddie's elaborate presentations of how things might go wrong could try the spirits of men seeking to keep their game faces. These were no pep talks, but rather a risk manager's careful endeavors to outline the range of scenarios, particularly the worst case, with the aim of giving the pilots options they could use when such all-too-likely contingencies broke upon them. The wide Eddie grin lightened the mood, as did his salty witticisms.

Eddie assigned his most experienced fighter pilot, Ham Coolidge, as one of the balloon strafers, along with a recent addition to the 94th, Charles Crocker. Leading them would be the 95th's Walter Avery, who on his maiden combat flight had shot down the much-respected German ace Carl Menckhoff. The shooters would fly in low formation with the rest of the 94th and 95th above and behind, Eddie flying higher yet to survey the action.

Planning the mission down to the minute, he orchestrated each pilot's part and established the exact time for the strafers to go in. The sortie would rendezvous 3 miles behind the Allied lines above Cuisy, then reach for their objectives at Montfaucon.

As he shepherded the formation toward Cuisy, Eddie's satisfaction suddenly soured when Avery inexplicably darted over the line, followed by Coolidge, several minutes ahead of the appointed time. Perhaps eagerness overrode operational discipline with the targets so alluringly close. Whatever the reason, it left the escort out of position to assist.

Coolidge dove on the first *Drachen,* only to see that it had no basket or observer—likely a decoy; he had heard about such traps. He was still able to veer low and fast toward the second—this one manned—while Archies shook his ship and machine-gun fire whined around him. His explosive incendiaries "poured into the old gas bag"; the observer's parachute blossomed small and white below. A few seconds later the balloon burst into flames. As Coolidge pulled up, he saw Avery flying suicidally into the midst of seven Fokkers breaking from around their dummy bait.

Perhaps Avery had mistaken the dappled Fokkers for his own team. Or perhaps, in one of those snap judgments that constitute aerial combat, he sought to divert the enemy and give Coolidge time to finish the job. Whatever his intentions, all hell broke loose, and Avery's machine plunged earthward streaming smoke, the Fokkers "swarming low over the ground like a bunch of vultures over a dead mule," reported Coolidge.

In a moment, Avery had broken the enemy's formational cohesion, and the eight aircraft spun in a strange descending pirouette. "Look out, Walter!" shouted Coolidge futilely, pitching his SPAD after one Fokker, "so mad I saw red," until he had riddled it and watched it go down. When he swiveled his head, "the most god-awful mess of Huns you ever saw" was spilling out of the sky, two of them pulling onto his tail. "I knew it was 'fini.'" Then, like "galloping cowboys over the hill," a swarm of Allied escorts pounced on the "birds that had me cold-cocked." Without time to think, Coolidge threw his machine into madhouse evasions. For the next frantic fifteen minutes, three dozen airplanes swarmed around him, the air "streaked in every direction with the smoke of the tracer bullets."

When Eddie saw the balloon strafers dart away, he immediately changed direction from the rendezvous to the balloons themselves, signaling the others to follow. Two other Fokkers roared up; one he scared off, the other he shot down. Their task completed, he surveyed the smoke-filled air. SPADs were everywhere, their formation "hopelessly destroyed," taking terribly unwise risks 10 miles behind enemy lines. However difficult it was to coordinate so large a force without radios, he was still determined to "call them together and take them back." Somehow, with cool persistence and the tenacity of a sheepdog, he herded what even the strong-nerved Coolidge called that "awful combat" back over Allied lines—whereupon the Fokkers broke off the biggest "rat-fight" yet, as one participant justly termed it.

That afternoon, the 94th Squadron scored six official victories, including Coolidge's balloon. They had lost Avery and another pilot, both of whom survived to become prisoners of war. Although events had veered dangerously out of control, Eddie's careful preplanning, placement of talented flight commanders in critical positions, and calm presence at the heart of the melee had averted what easily could have become a catastrophe. Far from Lufbery's approach to combat as a drama of all-out individual duels, the development of formation warfare was dictating new and different levels of leadership. Eddie and his team were showing the Germans that Americans could match—and even, indeed, outmatch—them in the air, not just as cowboys but as skilled group practitioners. On the ground, American troops moved with weary confidence to storm Cunel Heights, their movements almost entirely concealed from the sky.

Building on the multisquadron approach to balloon busting that had proven itself on October 3, Hartney and his squadron leaders continued to formulate new approaches in which six units of four planes, flying in parallel and within visual range across a 3-mile front, would provide cover for two strafers. Not rendezvousing at a designated spot but passing over certain landmarks at 3:40 P.M., they would then close with the targeted balloon at Doulcon at 3:46. Instead of the strafers forming their own group, they would fly slightly ahead and below their assigned escort.

Eddie took command of the mission, tapping Chambers to strafe and deploying fourteen of the 94th's pilots. The 147th's William E. Brotherton would serve as the second strafer; ace Wilbert W. White Jr. would cover Brotherton. Eddie flew several thousand feet above the formation, which reminded him of a huge crawling beetle, the two lead SPADs its stingers. Then things began to unravel. The Germans quickly winched the target out of play; then eleven red-nosed Fokkers broke out of the west while eight more raced in from Metz to the east. From his godlike seat above, Eddie watched Brotherton lead his closely following outfit headlong across the Meuse to attack a balloon on the ground at Dun, but the Flying Circus arrived just as he began his dive, a swirling dogfight boiling up over the river. Eddie set the last Fokker ablaze. To his surprise, the pilot jumped out, his earthward fall slowed by a "dainty parachute pulled from the bottom of his seat." Antiaircraft fire brought Brotherton down in flames—and he had no parachute to save him.

White saw that one of the new pilots, Charles Cox, had fallen into desperate trouble as a Fokker swung onto his tail. Grasping that "Cox would be shot down unless he put the Boche out of the fight," as Meissner remembered, White brought off what Eddie characterized as the most heroic feat but "the most horrible sight" he had witnessed during the war: He "zoomed up in a half turn, executed a renversement and came back at the Hun leader." Without firing a shot or swerving from the path, White flew right into the Fokker as it lined up on Cox; "the two machines actually telescoped each other, so violent was the impact." Wings sheared off in a burst of splinters and pieces of fabric, and the irretrievably tangled fuselages plunged earthward in a last fatal embrace, "spinning like tops." In White's pocket were orders sending him home the following day to his wife and two small children. Yet his gimper's end somehow seemed to belittle death by saving the newbie.

In the ensuing dogfight, Eddie saw two Fokkers close on the tail of a SPAD, which he later learned was Jimmy Meissner's. Diving flat-out, he brought one down with a single burst, "the third time together during our association on the front that I had appeared like a guardian angel from heaven in his hour of distress." Reed Chambers and Ham Coolidge also brought down a Fokker each. After being bailed out by Eddie, Meissner and his squadron mates shot down a Rumpler. That day 1st Pursuit scored nine confirmed kills, including ones by Brotherton and White on earlier sorties before they themselves died. Eddie would add numbers seventeen and eighteen to his swelling list, once more becoming the American ace of aces, a title he retained for the rest of the war.

Shaken by White's fate, Eddie took a three-day leave in Paris, where he escorted Lois Meredith, a curly-haired silent-screen actress in town to entertain the troops. That same day, in the face of terrible casualties and the millions-killing influenza pandemic, Pershing passed command of the 1st Army to his able subordinate Hunter Liggett. Two days later, the newspapers reported signs that Germany was seeking a settlement under terms outlined in President Wilson's Fourteen Points, a document delineating a European peace based on democracy, free trade, and self-determination of its constituent peoples. Battered by four years of war, the Allied leaders were rightfully nervous of Wilson's idealism—but equally alarmed that the United States might negotiate a separate peace. *Le bon Dieu n'avait que dix!*" Prime Minister Clemenceau reputedly responded to the Fourteen Points ("The good Lord only had ten!"). Even so, the war was drawing down.

After an initial costly push, Liggett rested the 1st Army in preparation for a renewed offensive later that month. The Germans beefed up their resistance in the Meuse-Argonne to hold out for a better settlement. On October 22, Reed Chambers returned from a sortie in which he had shot down his seventh German, complaining of awful abdominal cramps. This time he could not disregard doctor's orders and was rushed to the hospital for an emergency appendectomy. The following day, Eddie saw an American balloon go down in flames and pursued its destroyer behind enemy lines, only to find himself suddenly under attack by four Fokkers; with a coolness and precision exceptional even for him, he shot down two before "zig-zagging for all I was worth" to get home.

Four days later, Eddie and Ham Coolidge led an eleven-plane afternoon sortie to escort four Allied bombers on their way back from a run on the tiny town of Grandpré. Twenty minutes later, flying above Coolidge to the northwest of the village, Eddie saw three Fokkers dive on the SPADs below. It was short work to take the last one out of the sky with 125 rounds at close range. Five minutes later, antiaircraft fire directed at the bombers "carried away [Coolidge's] wing and set him in flames," as Eastman noted in his diary.

Eddie followed the bombers to Bois de Money, where he dove on yet another Fokker. After delivering 200 rounds at close quarters and noticing that the German's engine had cut out, he stopped firing and began maneuvering so as to force him down intact in Allied territory. Eddie got so close that he saw clearly its blue fuselage with white circles and unusual crosses on the wings, the insignia of Lieutenant Max Kliefoth of Jasta 19. Out of nowhere a SPAD dove on Kliefoth with guns blazing, but Eddie flew between the two and waved it off, giving Kliefoth the grace to bank into a swift, steep crash landing. Circling the wreck, Eddie noted with satisfaction that the pilot climbed out unhurt.

Arriving back at Rembercourt, he learned of his long-promised promotion to captain, all too dampened by Coolidge's "indeed . . . most untimely death, for we well knew the war was soon to be over." Their friendship had seemed the most unlikely of all; Coolidge's loathing of Eddie at Issoudun had gradually transformed at Rembercourt into a profound respect for his "remarkable C.O.," as he wrote home only just before he died. The next day, the disconsolate new captain drove a staff car to the front to recover his comrade's mortal remains. An officer walked Eddie to "a terrible sight," he recorded in his journal later that day. "The motor was four feet in the ground and poor Ham on top all burnt to a crisp." Doughboys dug him a shallow grave. On the way back, artillery shells showered Eddie's car with dirt. At Rembercourt Eddie ordered a cross with Coolidge's name and unit on it, which was placed over the grave.

As his victories mounted, Eddie had become famous. Newspapers at home couldn't get enough of his plainspoken practical humility and huge success. Celebrity of the kind recognized today had not yet developed; it would be during the Roaring Twenties when F. Scott Fitzgerald would glamorize celebrity for celebrity's sake. In 1918, without radio, television, or talking films, few opportunities arose for such sustained fame as Eddie was now coming into.

While he struggled with Ham's death, someone handed him newspaper reports that he was engaged to the film actress Priscilla Dean, with whom he had briefly corresponded. Years before he had taught her to drive in California. After his eighth victory, he had received a letter with photos from her, to which he returned a note that began "Hello, my California Sunshine!" and went on to say, "Gee, I'd give some years of my life for just one week in dear California—but, no—I must stay to the finish for there's lots to be done." The newspapers printed his letter, then went on to publish wholly fabricated statements that they had already married in Paris or were planning to do so when he came home. Irritated and perplexed, Eddie cabled news sources to deny any such intention. He had yet to understand that the image of Eddie Rickenbacker as hero was something he no longer could control. He now belonged to all Americans.

On October 30, he scored his last two victories—numbers twenty-five and twenty-six—a Fokker and a balloon, which left him behind enemy lines with little fuel as night came on. Back over friendly lines but unable to locate the fake aerodrome, he fired off two shots of his Very signal gun. Nothing happened, but then a thin row of lights broke out below, and he was able to put down just as his engine coughed and quit, rolling to within 100 feet of the 94th's hangar. Even he acknowledged that he had pushed his luck.

During the first week of November, events started to close down upon Germany and her allies. Warfare had ended on the Italian front after Austria-Hungary signed an armistice with Italy: Bulgaria and the Ottoman Empire had come to terms with other of the Allies earlier. A giant mutiny, set off when the long-blockaded German High Seas Fleet in Kiel was ordered on a suicidal last attack, kick-started a revolution that would bring soldiers' and workers' councils into being across Germany, eventually toppling the imperial monarchy and more than twenty lesser dynasties.

On November 10, the mess phone rang, and as Eddie answered the room went quiet. Captain Mitchell of the 95th verily shouted into the receiver that the war would officially end the following day at 11:00 A.M. Eddie dropped the phone and paused, the men around him aware of something momentous. Antiaircraft guns went off. Pandemonium broke loose as the pilots tumbled out the door, grabbing pistols, flares, and whatever made light or noise, blazing them away into a sky now crisscrossed with searchlights and filled with the glare of rockets and flares, all punctuated by machine-gun fire. Released suddenly from the immense pressure of daily death, the men yelled, whooped, and laughed riotously.

At the sight of some of his pilots rolling gas containers out onto the field, Eddie, instead of ordering them to stop (which would have been in vain), helped push them himself, then lighted the pyre of war. "A dancing ring of crazy lunatics joined hands and circled around the blazing pyre, similar howling and revolving circuses surrounding several other burning tanks," he later recalled. One ace shrieked, "We won't be shot at anymore!"

A brass band appeared and the dancing grew wilder, until someone tripped in the ankle-deep mud—and soon everybody had jumped in, wrestling and howling with delight. "Upon this foundation human forms in the spotless uniforms of the American Air Service piled themselves until the entire Group lay prostrate in one huge pyramid of joyous abandon," wrote Eddie in *Fighting the Flying Circus*.

"When again," Eddie claimed to have wondered, "will that pyramid of entwined comrades—interlacing together in one mass of boys from every state in our Union—when again will it be formed and bound together in such mutual devotion?" Though the actual words came from his ghost-writer, they reflected what Eddie and all those young men felt that celebratory evening.

The next morning, although thick fog clung tenaciously to the earth and flights near the front line were prohibited, Eddie took off anyway at 10:40 A.M. so that he could be in the air when fighting stopped at 11:00. He flew at treetop level toward Verdun, using a road as guidance. Just minutes before the appointed hour, he turned his SPAD toward German-held territory and fired until emptying his magazines. It seemed that both sides were furiously sending off their last salvos. Then sudden quiet fell, followed in moments by a rising chorus of cheering from both sides of the line. Below him he saw Americans leaping from their no-longer-necessary trenches. Not long after, German soldiers scrambled out to join the Americans.

Eddie was surprised to wake "up to the realization that the war had ended, leaving me hale and hearty and America's ace of aces." Under such relentless attrition, no one had been able to take staying alive for granted. A fatalistic perspective had proven necessary and effective against constant worry for experienced airmen.

What's more, Eddie's leadership had spurred the 94th far ahead of every other squadron in every index of deathly excellence. Their forty-four confirmed kills during the Meuse-Argonne campaign outshone the 95th's twenty-nine, the 27th's twenty-three, and the 147th's seventeen. The 94th had flown more hours and engaged in more combats than any other U.S. outfit. Perhaps most tellingly, its wins came at the least cost: 3.9 aircraft downed for each casualty incurred, the 147th ranking second at 3.4, the 27th with 2.5, and the 95th with 2.1. Five pilots had become aces while serving

with the 94th: Campbell, Chambers, Harvey Weir Cook, Meissner, and Eddie. Of all American aces, Eddie had shot down by far the most, his twenty-
six kills the more remarkable because his active service totaled less than
five months once his hospitalizations, convalescence, and leave have been
factored out.

After wrapping up loose ends, Eddie returned to Liverpool, where he managed to pick up the briefcase of engineering drawings confiscated during
his days with Coatelen. As he boarded the steamer that would take him
home, he wondered if that deeply offensive hook-nosed sergeant was still
around. Sure enough, he was, now a captain.

"Ah," he observed without any noticeable change of tone, "I see you're
back again."

"Yes," responded Eddie, who no doubt had dreamed of this moment.
"I've got my briefcase, and that isn't all I've got"—at which he pushed out
his chest so that his nemesis could get a good look at his decorations. Wonder of wonders, the captain congratulated him, which "made up to some
extent for all the brow beating and insults that were heaped on my shoulders by the Scotland Yard boys."

He stepped aboard, now America's most recognizable and famous hero
of the war. Never again would anyone claim that the poor Columbus boy
was not a full-blooded patriot, the best of the bunch. Nor could they ever
dispute his desperately hard-won standing as America's ace of aces. Along
with the medals thick on his tunic, however, Eddie carried the memories of
friends and good men lost, many of them gimpers. The smashed faces and
bodies of Lufbery, Roosevelt, Smythe, Coolidge, Kurtz, and many others
would never leave him. The Canadian war poet John McCrae, who himself
did not live to see victory, seemed to speak directly to Eddie in his famous
poem "In Flanders Fields":

In Flanders fields the poppies blow
Between the crosses, row on row,

That mark our place; and in the sky
The larks, still bravely singing, fly
Scarce heard amid the guns below.

We are the Dead. Short days ago
We lived, felt dawn, saw sunset glow,
Loved and were loved, and now we lie,
In Flanders fields.

Take up our quarrel with the foe:
To you from failing hands we throw
The torch; be yours to hold it high.
If ye break faith with us who die
We shall not sleep, though poppies grow
In Flanders fields.

BOOK IV

IMMORTALITY

Therefore take no thought, saying, What shall we eat? or, What shall we drink? or, Wherewithal shall we be clothed? —Matthew 6:31

16.

PLANE CRASH

At New York's La Guardia Airport on February 26, 1941, Eddie boarded the Eastern Air Lines "Mexico Flyer" DST (Douglas Sleeper Transport), a modified DC-3 seating twenty-four passengers, with sixteen sleeping compartments. The fabric-stretched wooden spars of World War I had morphed into sleek, metal-skinned creations with reset rivets, retractable landing gear, radios, and adjustable props. The DST featured Pratt & Whitney Twin Wasp radial engines, each generating 1,200 horsepower and capable of taking their aircraft coast to coast in fifteen hours.

Eddie shook hands with his pilot, James A. Perry Jr., who, born just two years before the Great War broke out, was understandably nervous at meeting the great man. Now the airline's hard-charging, formidable president and general manager, Eddie did not suffer fools and often spoke his mind with wicked sarcasm. He thought Perry a little inexperienced to pilot them to Atlanta—he had been flying for only a year, much of his 3,000 hours of air time as copilot—but did not give it too much thought. After all, during the war he had flown life-or-death missions with men much greener.

Dressed in his regular dark blue suit and straw boater, the slightly bent fifty-year-old sat down in the Sky Lounge, a small cabin behind the cockpit, and opened his briefcase. Under his leadership over the past five years, Eastern had become the nation's most profitable airline. It was an accomplishment of which he could feel justifiably proud, though the pressure kept him at fever pitch. This trip would take him to Miami, where he would press his board to approve a $5 million outlay on new equipment—no easy sell. He got straight down to work. In a few short hours, fate would conclusively keep him from making that meeting.

Back home after the war, Eddie had been met by an "onslaught of well-wishers, hero-worshippers and fast-buck operators," which unnerved him far more than any squadron of Fokkers and led him to insist that he "had never sought to become a hero, only to serve my country." Nevertheless, the intense nationwide enthusiasm made it clear that he was a bona fide celebrity, whatever his own self-assessment. One newspaper described his arrival in Columbus as "A Kissing Party for [an] Ace." Just off the train, "a comely Red Cross worker threw her arms about his neck and planted a smacking kiss on his cheek," soon followed by "matrons and misses alike," whose "regular osculatory barrage" left the ace blushing. Congress rose in ovation before him. In Los Angeles, 300,000 turned out for a welcome-home parade, the largest crowd for such an occasion the city had ever seen. Promoters begged him to endorse products; publishers and filmmakers pressed him to sign contracts to tell his story; theatrical agents tempted him with a vaudeville tour. He turned them all down, claiming that all such things might cheapen what would later have been called his image; as the ace of aces, he had an "awesome responsibility." At the root, the battered little boy from turn-of-the-century Columbus knew deeply "that it would be easy to go from hero to zero" unless he trod carefully in his new role. A writer he'd met in France was already assembling Eddie's war experiences for what would soon become a Doubleday bestseller. *Fighting the Flying Circus* was a whopping tale of derring-do in the bluest skies, the ghostwriter frequently stretching the story to spin a tale of epic proportions. The undoubtedly thrilling narrative, still in print, reinforced the public impression that Captain Eddie had earned not just flier's but demigod's wings.

William Randolph Hearst had sent journalist Damon Runyon to cover the end of the war, with special instructions to write about Pershing and

Rickenbacker, the star no one could stop talking about. Perhaps with a prod from Hearst, Runyon, who would later become famous for writing the stories that were the basis for the musical *Guys and Dolls*, decided that his old friend from the racing days belonged in the White House. On his passage home he wrote a speech for Eddie, an ode to America that would launch the ace's political career. Runyon's grand dreams crashed the moment Eddie opened his mouth on the stage. This time nerves got to him; his delivery was so leaden that Runyon knew immediately that he had no political career. They remained friends, Runyon penning a series of glowing pieces about Eddie's life. When the writer died of cancer in 1946, Eddie fulfilled his last wishes by flying a DC-3 over Manhattan and spreading his ashes.

Eddie could not say no, however, to a multicity Liberty Bond drive, although he had to fight through terrible stage fright, even at one point hiring an expert to work on his diction. As Runyon found out, he never wore the mantle of public speaker well. Aside from his poor elocution, he was never easy to like, and that showed; many other stars or heroes wore their notoriety far more gracefully, almost as though the mantle had just happened to fall upon them—Charles Lindbergh, for instance, or Douglas Fairbanks Sr. and Charlie Chaplin. Still, Eddie knew that he needed to keep in front of people because the world would push on just fine without him—so his postwar activity smacked of a frantic, almost manic, quality. "A Hero Who Refuses to Be Forgotten," announced *Industry Illustrated*, showing him seated at a desk cluttered with papers.

A week after the Armistice, Eddie announced to a reporter in Paris that he planned "to buy a club-footed mule and cart and travel across the United States. The speed limit will be five miles an hour." Back stateside there were rumors of lucrative offers should he find his way back behind the wheel of a race car. If there were, he showed no interest—nor does it appear that he ever considered the barnstorming career that many former wartime pilots took up. To the public, such reluctance probably appeared to be rooted in the grinding stress and fatigue of keeping alive at the edge, but for Eddie it was far simpler: To resume driving or begin exhibition flying would be a step backward. He believed that his war record and the acclamation that this earned him had justly gained him a seat at the high-risk poker games of car manufacturing and airline development.

History is littered with the overreaches and burned-out careers of highly successful battle commanders who have shone brilliantly under the insane demands and vagaries of war but have fallen correspondingly hard and fast in the civilian world. As late as 1922, Eddie could still acknowledge to a reporter that he did not "yet feel that I have made the readjustment fully . . . Possibly we came too close to our Maker. The result was a frame of mind that would be all right for an old man, but for a young man—the shock was too great for some of them . . . I myself find it necessary to drive my body with my mind." The question remained: What did America need from him now?

In February 1919, the American Automobile Association threw him a lavish dinner, crowded by all sorts of dignitaries at the Waldorf-Astoria Hotel during the New York Auto Show. They even flew in Eddie's mother, "a little woman in black silk whose beaming eyes shone proudly through gold-rimmed spectacles," noted a journalist. Secretary of War Newton D. Baker presented Eddie with wings made of 156 diamonds and 62 sapphires set in platinum and gold. Pershing and former president William Howard Taft sent accolades that were read to the assembly.

Over dinner, Eddie sounded Baker out about his plan of flying with Reed Chambers from New York to Paris to demonstrate the feasibility of long-distance air transport. General Mitchell had already informally approved the idea but recommended that they do it in a three- or four-engined aircraft, which would make government backing critical. Baker listened for thirty seconds before waving Eddie off, indicating politely "that the government couldn't care less."

The master of ceremonies, a former U.S. minister to the Netherlands, spoke glowingly about the ties between France and the United States. Six weeks later, Raymond Orteig, a wealthy hotelier of French descent in attendance that evening, would announce—perhaps inspired by the rhetoric—that he was endowing a $25,000 prize for the first crossing of the Atlantic by an aviator or aviators of any Allied country. Barnstormer and airmail pilot Charles Lindbergh would bring it off famously in May

1927, undergoing a daring solo flight in bad weather from New York to France aboard the single-engine *Spirit of St. Louis.* "Lucky Lindy" catapulted to a hero status the likes of which Rickenbacker had never approached. The emerging mass media of talkies and radio, coupled with a culture of celebrity nonexistent during Eddie's war-hero days, helped shoot this handsome, reticent young man to supernova brightness overnight. His peacetime flight against such great odds bespoke a bright future for an America full of rugged individualists. Given the requisite skill and courage, few things seemed out of reach.

Still, Eddie's new status yielded unexpected dividends in his private life. On New York's Fifth Avenue, he ran into Adelaide Frost, the beautiful but depressed wife of Cliff Durant, playboy racing ace and son of the founder of General Motors. They had first met at one of Cliff's bacchanalian Californian parties before the war. Eddie was surprised to find her still married to the abusive Durant, although the couple had separated. Sorry for his daughter-in-law, Durant Sr. bought her a house and gave her a separate checking account.

On that busy corner they talked so long that Eddie suggested they get tea. After that, Adelaide remembered, he found more excuses to go to New York on business "than a monkey has fleas." Few more eligible bachelors walked the avenues of New York or any other American street in the early 1920s. That he was a "completely impersonal guy," noted one friend, only seemed to goad young women; "girls fell for him largely because he never gave them a tumble." Without trying, this glamorous woman from Grand Rapids had cracked Eddie's practiced tough veneer in a way no one else had—or ever would. She liked life's finer things, and she liked to ride and dance, little of which interested Eddie, who once famously quipped that he'd rather have a million friends than a million dollars. "He's never had a desire for a great fortune," she observed, "and so would never make the concessions to acquiring one that many men will make." He comfortably settled her atop a pedestal, much like the one on which he had placed his mother.

His honesty, often so frank as to be startling, took her aback. He would tell her that most people hadn't given a whit about him even as a famous racing driver—but after the war everyone wanted "to bother with me because I shot down a few planes." His quiet strength translated into a sureness about himself, but she found him far from conceited. She entertained some concerns about his single-mindedness and fears that he would "never live any way but dangerously." Then again, those kinds of traits were intoxicating, too.

Durant finally agreed to grant Adelaide a divorce; in 1922, Eddie and she married in a small Connecticut church, his bride wearing a sumptuous black dress with cream lace and jade trimmings. It wasn't until their honeymoon in Europe, Adelaide reported, that she first saw Eddie really laugh. "His capacity for laughter was enormous but his fear of indulging it was even greater."

They would remain married until Eddie's death some five decades later. They would adopt two boys. When Eddie was stranded on a raft in the Pacific and pretty much given up for dead, Adelaide's desperate appeal to the authorities would launch the effort that saved him. Each, it seems, would rescue the other.

At the New York Auto Show again three years after the banquet, Eddie was back to showcase a new car that bore his name. By all accounts, this six-cylinder, 58-horsepower racehorse with a startling top speed of 60 mph was a beauty. Low-slung and graceful, it featured an engine with two flywheels flanking the crankcase, a vibration-dampening feature that Eddie had discovered when examining the latest German aero engines at the end of the war. The Rickenbacker also offered a four-wheel braking system, the first of its kind to come with a medium-priced car. "At its highest point [romance] is your own imagination pitted against that of someone else. Possibly there is more romance in making and selling automobiles than there was in the war," Eddie told a reporter. However, he sorely misjudged the difficulty of entering a field already crowded with such well-established marques as Cadillac, Packard, and Lincoln.

Sales started well but took a hit when his competition mounted a largely specious campaign claiming that four-wheel brakes were dangerous. Problems compounded in 1923, when a key company designer was killed in an accident. In 1924, the Vertical 8 Superfine offered a high-quality product with an enhanced engine—but also cost more to produce, which cut into the company's margins. By 1925, in the teeth of a recession, Eddie's major investor, Detroit millionaire Barney Everitt, forced the company to cut prices, which imposed dealers with severely narrowing margins. After producing 3,500 cars, the business went bankrupt in 1927, leaving Eddie $250,000 in debt. Instead of declaring personal insolvency and easily shedding responsibility for these obligations, he swore to pay them off.

The failure of Rickenbacker Motors hit him hard. "Adelaide," he told his wife, "the dream of dreams is washed up." They sold their spacious duplex apartment and moved into modest quarters in a hotel. That same year of 1927, America found itself a new hero in Lindbergh, who even received the Medal of Honor within weeks of his great exploit (he was a U.S. Army Air Corps Reserve officer at the time), an award that continued to elude Eddie until 1930, more than a decade after the achievement for which he ultimately received it. Meanwhile, Florida Airways, a venture he had started with Reed Chambers, went bankrupt. He had spread himself too thin, made some bad decisions, and suffered some plain hard luck.

Perhaps the low point came one evening in 1928, when Eddie was out late drinking heavily with a friend and hit a garbage truck in Adelaide's La-Salle. Somehow he got the car home and into the garage. She pretended to be asleep when he crawled into bed, annoyed at the early hour. She heard him whimper, a sound she'd never heard him "make before under any conditions." She ignored it, suspecting he was making "a bid for sympathy." Then he whimpered again. With irritation, she asked what was wrong. He responded that he wasn't feeling well. Without turning on the lights, she walked down to the kitchen and fixed him "a long drink of peppermint."

Soon the whimpering returned. She flipped on the lights and discovered him covered in blood. After calling a doctor, she walked into the garage, which reeked of garbage, and discovered a broken pencil beneath the steering column. The doctor, a personal friend, determined that the crash had driven it into his chest, "which accounted for the strange sounds he made with every intake of breath." One fraction of an inch further would have killed him. They took him to the hospital, where it took him some time to recuperate.

"You crawl out alone or you stay there," Eddie later remembered about this dark period. Once more adversity awakened the indomitable survivor, and he soon vaulted with renewed energy into new ventures. His friend Carl Fisher, whose Miami properties had been ravaged by a hurricane that year, approached Eddie about buying the Indianapolis Speedway. "You are the only real life looking customer at this time who understands the business and could handle the proposition," he told Eddie, who managed to talk his way into a sizable bank loan, then rebuilt and modernized the track, negotiated radio coverage, and built a golf course nearby. He would see the Speedway through the Depression.

Another opportunity arose with the death of James Allison, one of Indy's founding conglomerate. Borrowing yet more heavily, Eddie purchased the Allison Engine Company, which made bearings, superchargers, and reduction gears for aircraft engines. With no money to run the business, he then sold it to the Fisher Brothers Investment Trust, which in turn sold it to General Motors. Thus began Eddie's professional association with GM, which he would push to enter the field of aviation, first encouraging the company to buy 40 percent of the Fokker Aircraft Company, the largest commercial and military aircraft producer, and then becoming the subsidiary's vice president. He would also press GM to buy the Pioneer Instrument Company, later acquired by Bendix Aviation, his finder's fee enabling him completely to make good on the debt he owed from the Rickenbacker Motors bankruptcy. "[His] promise was his bond," a friend remarked.

He would later convince GM to buy North American Aviation, an umbrella over a slew of bankrupt companies, including Transcontinental & Western Air (TWA), the Curtiss-Wright Corporation, and Eastern Air Transport, not to mention a large block of stock in Douglas Aircraft Company. GM made him general manager of Eastern, which owned a potentially lucrative air route from New York to Miami but flew obsolete aircraft. Few held out serious hope that the company could keep going much longer in the dog-eat-dog world of early civil aviation. Low expectations, of course, created an arena in which Eddie particularly thrived, and he worked feverishly to bring the fleet up to date, adding new routes, hiring more workers with better pay and benefits, and quickly boosting passenger numbers.

He did so despite growing tensions with the federal government, which would pit him against President Franklin D. Roosevelt, for whom he voted in 1932 but whom he came to hate because of what he considered his antibusiness policies. Buffeted by the Great Depression, nascent airline companies had fought uphill. Their aircraft was unreliable and expensive to operate; the infrastructure of airfields remained incomplete; passengers were starting to come aboard, but not yet in numbers to justify the formidable outlays. Competition for mail contracts quickly became cutthroat.

GM's purchase of North American also aroused antitrust concerns within the Justice Department. In the spring of 1934, mounting scandals about improper awarding of mail routes during the Hoover administration moved the president abruptly to cancel all private contracts and direct the army to fly the mail—a move that angered Eddie and many other business leaders. FDR had "kicked askew the underpinnings of a $250 million investment shared by 200,000 stockholders," claimed *Fortune* magazine. As if to underscore their irritation, on the last day before the changeover, Eddie and TWA president Jack Frye flew a new DC-1 loaded with mail across the country in 13 hours and 4 minutes, breaking the transcontinental record by five hours. "We hoped to be able to bring forcibly to the attention of the nation, and of the world, what we had accomplished through years of endeavor and the unbounded confidence of the men in our organization," said Eddie.

On the very first day of the new dispensation, three U.S. Army pilots died. Outraged about federal meddling and concerned for military aviators dangerously ill-trained to fly these routes, Eddie spoke out publicly and impulsively about the inevitability of deaths under the new system, calling it "legalized murder." He did not name FDR, but the press quickly cast it as a direct attack on the president. As army pilots continued to die, Eddie appeared prescient. FDR eventually reversed his decision and reinstated private carrier service with the Air Mail Act of 1934, which also contained a series of measures that Eddie and others believed were punitive, such as the reduction of mail-pay rates and prohibitions against airlines owning companies that built airframes or aviation engines. GM's subsidiary North American sold TWA to avoid antitrust charges, divested itself of Douglas stock, and fired some directors who had negotiated contracts with the Hoover administration.

In November 1934, as Eastern's vice president for public affairs, Eddie scored another coup, flying an improved DC-2 from Newark to Miami and back again in a single day. Such invaluable publicity earned him kudos from higher-ups in GM, who—in a striking parallel with Major Hartney's campaign to promote Eddie to squadron command—persuaded the initially skeptical CEO, Alfred Sloan, to appoint him general manager of Eastern.

As with the aero squadron he raised to concert pitch, Eddie knew what needed doing at Eastern right away. Now in charge of day-to-day operations, he fired nineteen station managers, got rid of older aircraft, and raised the orders for the DC-2, which proved not only to be reliable and economical to fly but attractive to passengers for its roominess. In May 1935, he took the bold step of scheduling fifteen daily round trips between New York City (Newark) and Washington, D.C., an innovation later known simply as "the shuttle." Passengers loved it; profits started to grow. It would be the much larger DC-3, with its more stable design and much longer range, which enabled airlines to achieve profitability without carrying mail. Eastern became known as the "Great Silver Fleet" and now had a magazine filled with celebrity photographs, which also served as a platform for Eddie's opinions.

Despite this glowing success, Eddie's relations with Ernest Breech, who ran the line for GM and had fought successfully to promote him, turned chilly. In early 1938, Eddie learned that Breech was negotiating with John Hertz, founder of the Yellow Cab Company and owner of TWA, to buy Eastern out from under GM, a move Eddie knew would leave him out of a job.

If he harbored any doubts of Hertz's dislike of him, they vanished when Hertz himself mistakenly dialed Eddie's home number and launched into a denunciatory rant about the ace of aces, stopping only when Eddie politely informed him whom he was speaking to. Hertz offered GM $3.25 million, a staggering figure considering that GM had considered $1 million a fair price only four years earlier, and a testament to Eddie's success.

Furious that he stood to lose so much, Eddie spoke with GM's general counsel, then jumped over Breech's head and directly offered Sloan $3.5 million in cash—an attractive proposition indeed for GM, because Eddie had not known that his competitor was offering only $1 million in cash, the rest in notes. Sloan gave him thirty days to finance the deal, whereupon Eddie assembled a syndicate that included Harold S. Vanderbilt and Laurance Rockefeller. In a tense showdown at GM headquarters, Eddie and his lawyer beat out Breech and Hertz. In late April, Eddie handed Sloan a certified check for $3.5 million.

"Congratulations, Eddie, and God bless you," said Sloan. "I wish you every success in the world." Further success would indeed come Eddie's way. F. Scott Fitzgerald once wrote that there are no second acts in American lives, but Eddie had proved an exception, shrewdly fighting and negotiating himself into Eastern's general managership, then buying the whole company outright.

As chief officer, Eddie now seemed to be everywhere, reading letters from passengers and making it his business to know about his employees' personal lives, often seeming dictatorial, abrasive, and inflexible. No question existed about who was dynamically in charge. He treated all who worked for him as the objects of a genuine, if markedly paternalistic, benevolence and his competitors with a win-at-all-costs toughness. He rubbed a lot of people the wrong way yet gained the undying affection of many others. He pushed himself hard, sleeping only four or five hours a night and working sixteen-hour days, which stressed his marriage and made harsh demands on those around him. "You'd think the office would walk away unless you come down to see that it's still there," his longtime secretary, Marguerite Shepherd, told him when he came in nearly every Sunday.

Initiatives flew off his desk. Eastern established the industry's first pension plan and was also the first to mandate a forty-hour workweek for mechanics. He stressed safety as well as efficient fleet utilization, pushing for planes to spend more and more time in the air; by 1941, Eastern's crafts averaged 12 hours and 45 minutes aloft per day, more than those of any other airline.

He never stopped crusading publicly and privately to improve "old" airstrips and build new airports all over the country, working sometimes with and sometimes fractiously against the new bureaucracy of airline regulation brought into being by the Civil Aeronautics Act of 1938. Never for a moment did he forget the relationship between aviation and national security, calling in public for a strong and independent air force as a deterrent long before another European war became a real possibility.

On September 1, 1939, Germany invaded Poland. On September 26, the day before Warsaw fell to the Nazis, Eddie took to the airwaves, arguing on New York's WJZ that "while not a pacifist in any sense of the word," and even though "my heart bleeds with sympathy" for the combatant nations, "this can be no justification to me for our involvement again, with the horrible consequences of the probable loss of millions of our young men, and billions of our wealth." The broken walls of Reims Cathedral under the dawn light, the smiling visage of Raoul Lufbery, and the horror of Paul Kurtz's charred body were all too probably crowding into his mind's eye, as fresh then as they had been two decades earlier. He believed that a strong peacetime aviation industry would prove adequate for defensive purposes. Eddie's noninterventionist stance struck a chord with many listeners, but the speed of the Wehrmacht's advance, the chilling proclamation of the Nazi-Soviet Pact, and the reappearance of U-boats were all quickly turning American minds toward the necessity of getting involved.

Soon he himself began to realize that simple deterrence wouldn't be enough, especially after the Third Reich overran Norway and Denmark in April 1940. The destructive powers of bombing became frighteningly apparent when the Luftwaffe ravaged Rotterdam after destroying the small Dutch air force. No antiaircraft guns protected the city, so heavy bombers circled it at low altitude, methodically laying waste to twenty thousand buildings, starting a great fire, and killing and wounding thousands. Those of the Netherlands armed forces unable to escape surrendered the next day; the Belgian government threw in the towel two weeks later. France wilted with stunning speed beneath the Blitzkrieg. Paris fell in June, France capitulating almost immediately thereafter.

That summer, the British hung on as the Germans sought to establish air superiority in preparation for an amphibious invasion of England. Savvy preparation of an early radar system and integrated air defense system, along with the sheer courage of often little-trained Spitfire and Hurricane pilots, denied the Luftwaffe air supremacy; Hitler canceled Operation Sea Lion.

Although Eddie expressed doubts that the United States could keep out of the war, he lent his name that fall to the America First campaign, which argued that preservation of American democracy required neutrality. However, as his reservations about nonintervention grew, bolstered by reports of the Battle of Britain, his resolve wavered. "Should these gallant British withstand the terrific onslaught of the totalitarian states until the summer of 1941, it is my sincere conviction that by that time this nation will have declared war," he told the New York Economic Club on December 10, 1940. It had become increasingly apparent to him that Britain alone, no matter how brave, could not defeat the German military machine. On New Year's Day 1941, he resigned from America First.

Early that winter, bitter disputes had brewed in Congress over American neutrality. FDR promoted the Lend-Lease Act, which established a program to supply material aid to Allied nations. Arrayed against this measure were such powerful isolationists as Lindbergh and U.S. Senators Gerald Nye and Burton K. Wheeler. Eddie, now fully supporting intervention, would have been a voice in these debates had it not been for a perfectly routine Eastern flight to Atlanta that went terribly wrong.

The evening of February 26, Eastern's Mexico Flyer completed its first leg uneventfully, landing at Washington-Hoover Field in Arlington, Virginia, despite the approach of a storm pushing heavy rain and wind into the Southeast. It dropped off the *Washington Post* political columnist Drew Pearson and picked up several others, including the vacationing Maryland congressman William D. Byron, fresh from defeating the popular Washington Senators pitcher Walter Johnson at the polls. On the leg to Atlanta the Mexico Flyer would carry thirteen passengers and three crew members. At 9:05 P.M., James Perry took off with 650 gallons of fuel and set out to parallel the eastern margin of the Blue Ridge at 4,000 feet for the three-and-a-half-hour flight. By the time they reached Spartanburg, South Carolina, he had grown concerned about the front that had by now socked in Atlanta; he handed over the controls to his copilot and walked back to tell the boss that "we may have some difficulty getting in." Eddie remembered telling him not to worry. "I'm in no hurry. If you have to, let's go back to Charlotte. Do you have enough gas?"

"Yes," said the young captain. "There's a ship due in a little ahead of us and one a little after." Eddie questioned Perry about the conditions—a mile visibility under a ceiling of 500 feet—and then left Perry to make the decision: a confidence-building approach, not a responsibility-dodging one. These were marginal conditions, but neither unusual nor difficult for most professional pilots. Perry went back to the cockpit and continued on course as the weather deteriorated.

Near Stone Mountain, Perry patched through to the tower operator at Atlanta's Candler Field, who told him that the ceiling was down to 300 feet, the minimum height for a safe landing. Rain had turned to sleet. Delta had already rerouted two flights, but another plane had landed successfully. The operator cleared Mexico Flyer to land just before midnight. For an instrument landing, Perry relied on three devices: a loop antenna and two altimeters. The former picked up low-frequency radio signals from the airport's transmitter; the pilot simply rotated it until he registered the strongest intensity and then established a compass bearing on that point. The DST also carried two Kollsman altimeters, one calibrated to the plane's altitude above sea level, the other tuned to the current altimeter reading at the airport.

(These readings are based on barometric pressure, which changes with weather conditions, making it important that the pilot adjust the second one to correspond to the airport's current meteorological state. On landing, the second altimeter should read zero.)

By the time they neared Atlanta, Eddie had wrapped up his work and sat looking out the window, chatting with the steward, Clarence "Dinty" Moore, who was dressed in Eastern's red, white, and blue uniform. He could see lights along a highway, then the looming Atlanta Penitentiary. As the DST banked to port, Eddie felt the tilted left wing brush treetops. Instantly recognizing that the plane was doomed, he hurled himself aft. The pilot quickly compensated—but far too much, raising the left wing but sinking the right, which struck a large pine tree. It hooked the plane so forcefully that it somersaulted, breaking off its nose section, then severing its tail in a second flip. What was left of the plane flew up yet again, crumpling the central section the way "a kid would blow up a bag . . . and twist it to hold the air in." Eddie bounced around inside, smashing his left hip as he landed on top of Moore's already dead body between the next two bunks. When the wreck finally came to rest, his head lay wedged between the bulkhead and a gas tank; he could only move it about an inch. The wreck had smashed his hip, ankle, left elbow, nose, and several ribs. He could only move his right leg a few inches, and that brought pain so excruciating it left him gasping. Had he not instinctively thrown himself forcefully to the plane's rear, he would not have been breathing at all.

Eddie's first thought was of fire, and he prepared to end things quickly by inhaling the flames, which, someone in his outfit in France had once explained, "burns your lungs out." To his surprise, no flames came. Later he would learn that one of the pilots, in a heroic last act, had snapped off the ignition. Without that, Eddie would have burned to death.

The awful tangled pieces of the wreck were strewn over a scrub-pine hillside, not a thousand feet from a long clearing that could have afforded a flat touchdown. Rain fell steadily through the cold darkness. Eddie could hear the voices of several passengers who had been thrown free of their berths in the tail. Someone spoke about lighting a fire—and he bellowed out for them to stop: One strike of a match would have turned the fuel-drenched ruin into an inferno.

Rescuers searched all night, but the site of the crash, some 700 yards off a dirt road and in dense brush dissected by deep ravines, stymied all efforts until first light. As the night dragged on, Eddie prayed that he would pass out just to end the pain, but he never did. Others remember him constantly perking up spirits and apologizing. "I'm sorry that it had to happen," one survivor recalled Eddie saying over and over.

All along, Eddie wasn't just apologizing but mustering himself. "What the hell," he thought. "If you have to die, you might as well die trying to get out as laying there and letting the thing happen." With a violent twist and shove, not realizing that a jagged piece of metal pointed daggerlike at his left eye from above, he pulled free a couple of inches, feeling several more ribs crack. The aluminum cut through his eyelid, severing the ocular muscles. The next morning rescuers would find him blood-bespattered, more dead than alive, his left eye hanging on his cheek, a sight that sent rescuers retching into the bushes. It took them an hour to cut him out. He remembered a camera shoved in front of his face, but someone concerned about his privacy "just pasted" the photographer, sending him end over end and breaking the camera. Even though he claimed to be allergic to "dope of any kind" because it made him "wilder than a March hare," Eddie accepted a shot of morphine, then asked for another, and was transported to the nearby Piedmont Hospital.

Wanting to administer last rites to this apparently moribund man, a Catholic priest asked the nurse Eddie's religious affiliation. "A god-damned Protestant, like most people," thundered the near-corpse, disconcerting padre and nurse alike. When the hospital's head surgeon arrived to hold down his chest and sew the damaged eye back into place without anesthetic, Eddie shouted a blue streak of profanity at the pain until quieted by the surgeon's own violent cursing.

The entire staff burst into the operating room to discuss what to do next with this war hero and famous executive who had dropped from the skies into their hospital. Operate on the hip or set it without an operation? His body was so broken, the agony so intense, they didn't know whether he could withstand either approach. "Well, gentlemen, you know we may let him die on our hands," said the head surgeon, "but we'll never kill him."

"Nuts!" Eddie recalled finding the strength to burst out. "Get me a good osteopath and I'll be out of this joint in three days." Everybody laughed, perhaps more in awe than mirth, and the meeting broke up. They wrapped him in a huge cast and waited for him to stabilize. Adelaide and their two sons rushed to the hospital, on the way hearing on the radio that he had died. Coming out of ether, Eddie opened his eyes to find Adelaide. "I'm sorry I interrupted your work, dear," he mumbled. "I guess you'll have to shoot me to get rid of me."

Eddie clung to life, stuck in an oxygen tent, so high on morphine that he hallucinated wildly and frequently tore down the plastic sheeting. He remembered "when I felt myself pushing my toes into the pearly gates." It came as a feeling of great serenity. "Everything was mellow and sweet and beautiful . . . I had that feeling before . . . and so I recognized it instantly. I said to myself, 'Whoa, back away from there,' and I started fighting with all my strength."

It took ten days before he could sufficiently endure the pain to let them set his hip. He learned that of the sixteen aboard, both pilots, the steward, Representative Byron, and four others had died. Of the rest, Eddie was the worst injured. Investigation revealed that the pilots had failed to adjust the second altimeter to the barometric pressure reading reported by the airport, misleading them into believing that they were coming in at a much higher altitude than they were.

Eddie continued to suffer excruciating pain. In his delirium, he tore off a cast on his wrist with his teeth. He made wild claims that the staff had horribly mistreated him, apologizing each time that his mind cleared. Seeing a paralyzed girl rolling by his room on a cart, he ordered one of those and pounded "the hell out of it going up and down the hallway." Finally—inch by inch—he recovered, although he would find his left leg shorter than the other and clumsy with a severed nerve, compelling him to walk with a modified shoe and cane. Nearly four months later, wan, thin, and shaky but back in his trademark blue suit and straw hat, he struggled off the plane back at La Guardia, telling reporters that he was fine, with "only a few aches and pains." Asked whether the United States should enter the war, he replied, "We are in it and have been in it for a year. A lot of people don't realize that. The sooner every one knows we are in, the better it will be. This is no time to waste time. It is vital that we educate the people to the facts of America's future." As to the importance of American intervention, "the sooner we crush Hitler the better." For him, nonintervention was now long forgotten, and he pressed Eastern Air Lines to help prepare the nation for war, which included ferrying war matériel to Miami for shipment to England.

It would take the shock of Pearl Harbor six months later to shake Charles Lindbergh loose from his outspokenly isolationist posture. He had publicly fought FDR's lend-lease bill, which was passed that March, instead pressing for strict neutrality. While scholarship would later identify his seeming support for Hitler as stemming from an authentic and informed anti-Communism, millions of Americans came to loathe him for his apparent cozying up to the dictator. It didn't help when he refused to return the medal that the Führer had bestowed upon him in 1938 for his transatlantic flight. For many others, certain speeches of his that cast Jews as warmongers seemed anti-Semitic and sealed his unpopularity.

Watching this national icon crash and burn as badly as his comrades on the track and in the air gave Eddie no pleasure, and he wisely held his tongue. As Lindbergh's stock fell, Eddie's rose, the public warming to his extraordinary recuperation and his ability to articulate America's responsibilities in an ever-changing world.

Early in 1942, General Henry H. "Hap" Arnold, soon to join the newly formed Joint Chiefs of Staff as the commanding general of the Army Air Forces, asked Eddie whether he would consider a 15,000-mile goodwill tour of domestic air bases. Morale among fliers had flagged in the general disorientation of the massive military buildup. FDR had not helped by downplaying the damage U.S. forces had sustained at Pearl Harbor, intimating that the war would be over soon, which many understandably questioned. A few words from a tough old war hero might do wonders.

Eddie told Arnold that he needed ten more days to recuperate, but the general replied that many fliers would be overseas by then. It was now or never. Although his hip and ankle gave him considerable pain, Eddie agreed and left the following day, visiting forty-one bases in thirty-two days, a pace grueling even for a healthy man half his age. If his gaunt, emaciated features and cane suggested infirmity, his words rang clear and strong. He had turned down Arnold's suggestion to activate him as a major general, preferring instead to remain a civilian so he might more candidly speak his mind.

Not focusing only on boosting morale, he hammered the airmen on the virtues of self-sacrifice, telling them neither to underestimate the Japanese threat nor to overestimate their own abilities, and cautioning that the war might string on for many years. Newspapermen latched on to the words of this withered hero, who now seemed to bear the solemn weight and power of an Old Testament prophet and spoke wherever he could in public forums, as if single-handedly trying to shake the country awake. A Los Angeles paper printed a letter asserting that he "was doing his part in saving us from destruction as he limps his way with his tortured body throughout the land to arouse us. He is grim, powerful, and determined."

Arnold then turned to him for two other high-profile assignments, the first to combat an increasingly popular but harebrained scheme in Congress to short-circuit the U-boat menace by building a fleet of immense seaplanes that could carry matériel and men to Europe over submarine-haunted waters. As that debate found voice in newspapers nationwide, Eddie became the proposal's most vigorous opponent, articulating legitimate concerns that the program would divert critical resources and energy from producing bombers and fighters, not to mention the impracticality of developing such a plane from scratch in such short order. Better to develop the already vetted class of medium air transports, such as the C-47. In the face of Eddie's reasoned arguments and the flop of the prototype, the program withered away.

Arnold also made him the mouthpiece of a campaign to reassure the nation about the quality of American aircraft. Private citizens and pundits alike applauded him. He had once again demonstrated his powers as a team player.

This public relations work drew the attention of Secretary of War Henry L. Stimson, who dispatched him to England to report on the progress of the Army Air Forces. After a flurry of meetings, one with Winston Churchill, he came back with a detailed report recommending improvements for aircraft, intelligence on British policy, and insight into the raging debate about the degree to which heavy strategic bombing's power might help win the war.

Only a week back and still struggling with his health, Eddie responded to the secretary's invitation to Washington, from which came a secret mission that would impose upon him so horrific an ordeal—perhaps the ultimate American story of survival—as to test even his legendary powers. This brutal challenge under unimaginable circumstances evoked so enduring a display of ultimate heroic determination that it played a part in strengthening an entire nation's will to victory.

17.

TRIUMPH OF WILL

A week back from Europe, Eddie headed to Washington to see the secretary of war. Hoover Field, from which he had taken off on that fateful Eastern flight twenty months before, was unrecognizable. No longer a broad expanse of runways, it was now dominated by an unfinished but still prodigious five-sided edifice—the Pentagon, soon to become the world's largest office building, into which Colonel Stimson and his staff had just moved.

Still weak, tired, and gaunt, Eddie limped into the secretary's office, where the seventy-five-year-old statesman received him warmly, thanking him yet again for his invaluable services. Eddie could see that the pressures of the war were already taking a toll on the elder patrician, called up by FDR in his later years to oversee the mobilization and training of some 13 million soldiers and airmen, not to mention the requisition of equipment and its transportation to Europe—his most visible reward being read out of the Republican Party. Stimson's first stint as secretary stretched back thirty years to the Taft administration, before the shots had been fired at Sarajevo.

Believing that he would be asked to tour U.S. air bases overseas, Eddie was surprised when the secretary inquired whether he could conduct a highly sensitive, top-secret mission. There could be no written orders; Eddie must on the spot memorize a stinging reprimand and deliver it in person to Douglas MacArthur, the supreme commander of the Southwest theater, who was now headquartered in New Guinea. The brilliant but abrasive MacArthur had sorely tested FDR, publicly criticizing his strategy of focusing on victory over Germany first. Earlier, to boost public confidence in the war effort, both the president and Stimson had praised MacArthur's command genius, which in retrospect hadn't appeared so wise. With his trademark corncob pipe clenched between his teeth, his radiant confidence, and his ready warrior eloquence, MacArthur enjoyed much popularity, his eye clearly on running against FDR in 1944. (Years before, FDR had famously called him, along with Louisiana governor Huey Long, one of the two most dangerous men in America.) Even at thousands of miles' distance, MacArthur's bite could still be felt. Eddie must tell him to keep it down, particularly his attacks on George C. Marshall, the overburdened but indispensable chief of staff.

Stimson's choice of Eddie was brilliant. Few men could have stood up to such a war god. Both could claim enormous physical courage, backed up with the Medal of Honor. The ace of aces had a legendary reputation for not getting pushed around and for freely speaking his mind. Stimson told him he was to leave immediately for Papua New Guinea, accompanied by Colonel Hans Adamson, who had traveled with Eddie on his early tour of domestic bases. On his return, Eddie was to report back personally to the secretary.

Eddie liked the soft-spoken Adamson, three months his senior, who had written for New York newspapers before becoming director of public relations for the American Museum of Natural History, and whose pioneering work in popularizing its dinosaur collection had done much to ignite the nation's first dinosaur craze. They made their initial stop in California to visit Eddie's mother, eighty years old, then flew on to Honolulu aboard a Boeing B-314 Clipper. On October 20, Eddie toured military facilities.

That evening Brigadier General William Lynd drove them to Hickam Field, up against the naval station at Pearl Harbor, where the wreck of the Oklahoma still listed from the Japanese surprise attack of nearly a year earlier. As Lynd had promised, their transport to New Guinea idled on the runway, a hulking B-17C, two immense engine nacelles and cowlings jutting out from the leading edge of each wing, its bulbous nose mounting a machine gun that gave the plane its nickname of the Flying Fortress. America's most reliable heavy bomber, it would drop more ordnance than any other U.S. aircraft during the war. Eddie had hoped for the newer, more spacious B-24. This was to be the battered B-17's last flight before it was retired.

When young Private Johnny Bartek first saw Eddie on the tarmac, he didn't recognize the man he long considered his personal hero but instead wondered "why they are bringing this cripple aboard." The ace clutched a cane, and his suit hung limply on his wiry frame; he looked "like he should have been in a hospital rather than climbing aboard an airplane."

At 10:30 P.M., Adamson and Eddie squeezed into the jump seats behind pilot and copilot, buckled in, and exchanged perfunctory greetings. The trip had not started auspiciously for the five-man crew, who had been scheduled for stateside leave that evening before being directed to fly the Rickenbacker mission. "A disappointment," said the copilot, Lieutenant James Whittaker, "but it was a thrill, too, because we knew that when Rickenbacker wanted to see something he usually got close enough to look at it." Sergeant James W. Reynolds, the broadly smiling young Californian radio operator, sat in the tight radio compartment aft of the bomb bay, thinking about his fiancée and their wedding day two weeks hence in Oakland.

With the tower's go-ahead, Whittaker pushed open the throttles, bringing the four engines to throaty life, and pilot William T. Cherry Jr. guided the behemoth, "bumping and thumping its tail over the uneven surface," to the end of the runway, to turn and plunge back for takeoff. Halfway down the field, at 60 mph, a brake expander tube let go, locking the starboard landing gear. The plane began swerving wildly, Cherry fighting the out-of-control aircraft with engines, rudder, and stick. They barely missed a hangar and were still headed out toward the harbor waters at a furious clip. Only then did Cherry execute a last-ditch emergency maneuver, turning off the ignition and throwing the craft into a tight spin known as a ground loop to dissipate forward motion, which "almost tore off a wing and nearly knocked two engines out of their mountings." Emergency vehicles raced up, sirens wailing. Cherry calmly unbuckled his safety harness and, turning to Eddie and Adamson, said in a distinctly Texan drawl, "That's the longest no-hop crash landing I've ever made. I'm Bill Cherry—Captain Cherry. And this is Lieutenant Whittaker."

It was the first time Eddie got a good look at the cocky twenty-seven-year-old with high-heeled cowboy boots and a perfectly trimmed vandyke beard. Before the war, Cherry had flown as a copilot for American Airlines; during it, he had already made seven trips between Hawaii and Australia. Eddie didn't much care for the pilot's getup or the man himself but had to admit that he had handled the plane beautifully.

"Any landing you can walk away from is a good one," added the copilot. Eddie noticed Whittaker's shavetail (second lieutenant's) bars, rather odd, he thought, for a forty-year-old, whom he later found out had served in the navy during the First World War and learned to fly in 1927.

Lynd pulled open the bomber's tail hatch and found everybody shaken but all right. Keen to satisfy his high-priority visitors, he told Eddie that he had another aircraft that could be gassed up and ready to go in a few hours.

As the crew unpacked, Whittaker noticed the slight twenty-three-year-old Pennsylvanian navigator, Lieutenant John J. De Angelis, bent over his octant, an optical navigation device used to fix latitude and longitude by measuring the angles between sun, stars, and horizon. The force of the ground loop had slammed the poorly secured instrument across the plotting table into the Plexiglas. De Angelis would claim that he did not have enough time to recalibrate the delicate instrument, composed of prisms, gears, mirrors, lenses, and various adjusting mechanisms, before they left. Flying such distances over the ocean remained something new; only Pan American had flown transpacific before the war. Until recently, military pilots had not crossed great expanses of water, instead skirting the edges of the land masses. Ocean navigation training remained limited. Working an octant for position, then calculating airspeed with a chronometer, while factoring in wind and weather conditions, was exacting work. Although crew members credited De Angelis with a good sense of direction, his experience in handling an octant remained rudimentary at best.

Hearing that they were to take off in another aircraft that evening without undergoing the standard checkout protocol, Cherry strongly objected. Lynd told him that he'd find someone else to fly if he wouldn't. Knowing that his career would suffer, Cherry agreed to pilot the ship, a B-17D. Had anyone checked the radio direction finder, he would have discovered it jammed and unworkable.

At 1:30 A.M., the aircraft took off, quickly climbing to 10,000 feet for the ten-hour flight. Eddie and Adamson clambered back to the bomb bay, where two cots had been set up. At that altitude, their trench coats and thin blankets did little against the cold, and they didn't get much sleep.

The first stop was about 1,650 nautical miles to the southwest, at Canton Island in the Central Pacific, whose 3 square miles of grass-covered coral now carried an airstrip and refueling station established by Pan American in 1938. Canton and the handful of similar tiny atolls that constitute the Phoenix Archipelago lie about halfway between Hawaii and Fiji in the largest of the world's oceans, an expanse vaster than all the earth's land masses combined. Several hundred miles to the northwest lies Howland Island, where Amelia Earhart was heading when her Lockheed Electra vanished in 1937. Few places are so remote—nearly 2,000 miles from a continent in any direction.

Besides the two pilots, navigator, and radio operator, they carried Johnny Bartek as an engineer, a quiet, small-framed New Jerseyite in his early twenties whose mop of red hair overhung a freckled face. The war had sped up and skewed training regimens, leaving Bartek to log only four months' preparation as a flight engineer on four-engine bombers, and none on a B-17. In recognition of that, an engineer familiar with B-17s, Sergeant Alex Kaczmarczyk, had been sent along, even though he had just been released from a forty-five-day hospital stay with yellow jaundice and was still recovering from an appendectomy.

Eddie tossed in his cot, fretting that the tailwind was far stronger than the crew's estimate of 10 miles per hour. Much later, he would speak with a navigator who had been aboard a flight that left Hickam Field only minutes before they did. That crew member recalled that the tailwind was closer to 30 miles an hour, and he had adjusted their position accordingly.

As the sun rose over the Central Pacific at about 6:30 A.M., Eddie climbed forward to chat with Whittaker in the cockpit. Soon joined by Adamson, they drank coffee and orange juice, smoked cigarettes, and ate sweet rolls. "Forward in the cockpit," remembered Eddie, "everything seemed serene." Two hours later with Cherry back at the controls, the B-17 began a gentle descent for their anticipated landfall at 9:30 A.M. The men stared out the windshield and saw no island, just water and blue sky. Sitting directly behind Cherry, Eddie chilled with a premonition that their stronger-than-anticipated tailwind had carried them beyond their refueling stop. They had four hours of gas left.

Fiddling with the crank that rotated the direction finder, Cherry found it incapable of moving more than an inch or so. They queried the Canton operator about giving them a bearing, but he responded that the necessary equipment to do that still lay packed in crates. "Weather and radio aids that are commonplace in commercial airline operations do not yet exist in the Pacific," Eddie later mused. "If the Army had waited for prissy safeguards there would be no American air power in the Pacific today."

Cherry lowered himself into the nose to talk with navigator De Angelis, who revealed that his octant was probably misaligned. All his nighttime calculations were meaningless. A reading off by even a slim margin could mean their having missed Canton by as much as several hundred miles. They contacted Palmyra Island well to the north for a directional bearing, but the radio operator there, mistaking their aircraft for a B-24 approaching Canton at the same time, gave them an incorrect reading.

Remembering how the Germans had cleverly communicated by using Archies, Eddie suggested that Canton Island discharge antiaircraft fire to burst at 7,000 feet. Canton sent up a half-hour barrage, but crew and passengers saw nothing. Options were dwindling as fast as their fuel. Cherry initiated an age-old emergency procedure dating back to the age of sail: In this case, "boxing the compass" entailed flying a square route, forty-five minutes in each cardinal direction, so that those aboard could scan a wide swathe of ocean both inside and outside the area enclosed. They peered into the bright sun-splashed waves until their eyes ached, quickly developing "island eyes," every flicker of cloud shadow holding out an illusory promise of land. "Never had I seen a world so ominously empty," the copilot later recalled.

After fruitlessly completing the maneuver, Cherry instructed De Angelis in his relaxed southern drawl to start sending out SOS's; these went unacknowledged, the awful truth now sweeping over them that not only were they going down but that no one knew their position or where to look for them. Whittaker and Cherry discussed the logistics of a water landing—both leaving unspoken the painful truth that no aircraft this large had ever pulled off an emergency water landing.

The customary procedure of landing into the wind was not viable; they would meet a wave catastrophically head-on. Should they land with the wind and hit the crest, the nose would plunge into the trough and cave in. Cherry decided to go in under power on a crosswind and put down in the trough of a swell.

Eddie and Kaczmarczyk began pitching out everything possible to reduce the force of impact by lightening the ship. The pilots buckled their safety harnesses over the seat cushions now padding their chests. Eddie moved everyone else aft to lie on the bomb-bay floor. Bartek freed the emergency hatches above the cockpit and in the bomb bay. From a port window, Eddie calmly sang out the distance to impact. "Fifty feet!" "Thirty!"

The wind roared as the B-17D came in at 90 miles per hour, landing gear and flaps up to avoid snagging the water. "Five feet!" Now Eddie was shouting. "One foot!"

"Cut it!" yelled Cherry, pulling back on the wheel to hook the tail in the water, as Whittaker flicked off the plane's main-line electricity switch. Inside a trough of 8-foot swells, the bomber lunged forward, its fuselage smacking the water hard. It remained on the surface, slamming to a stop within 30 feet.

"The shock and pressure of that landing [was] almost indescribable," recalled copilot Whittaker, whose safety belt threatened to slice him in two while a vinegary taste flooded his mouth and his eyes seemed to spin wildly. He thought he was losing consciousness, but "then my eyes began to unwind and the pressure inside my head reduced swiftly."

Cherry had pulled off a near-miraculous landing. No one was seriously hurt, although Adamson had wrenched his back, and blood rolled down Reynolds's face—he had struck his nose on impact. Whittaker and Eddie yanked the ripcords, freeing the three emergency rafts, which automatically inflated from canisters of compressed carbon dioxide and were then expelled from the fuselage. Expecting the 25-ton hulk to sink immediately, they scrambled out through hatches onto the wings. Swells that had appeared benign from above now loomed terrifyingly large as they slid aboard the rafts and pushed off. Eddie cut free the cords holding rafts to plane. With foresight, he had wrapped rope around his waist, which they now used to secure the rafts together. A cold dread washed over Whittaker when he saw a dorsal fin slicing the water, attracted by Reynolds's blood.

In six minutes the airship was gone, leaving eight men on three small bobbing yellow rubber rafts without water in a vast salt sea. Nor, in their haste, had anyone grabbed the food and thermoses of coffee they had prepared, provisions they would deeply regret losing. They had no fresh water. Cherry pulled out four small oranges he had tucked into his flight suit—all the food they had between them.

The men floated quietly upon the Central Pacific, a couple of them vomiting from the shock of the landing and the roll of the waves. No one on land knew where they were. Nor did they.

Adamson later described the two large rafts as each the size of an average bathtub, at 4 feet by 7 ludicrously small for three men, much less for its stated occupancy of five. Cherry, Whittaker, and Reynolds lay uncomfortably in one of these; Eddie, Adamson, and Bartek in the other. The slightest-built members of this forlorn party—De Angelis and Kaczmarczyk—sat in the smallest raft, itself so tiny that they had to face one another with one man's legs straddling the other's shoulders. A quick inventory revealed two pumps to keep the rafts inflated, a Very pistol flare gun with eighteen charges (most of which would prove duds), two jungle knives, two service revolvers, two rubber baling buckets, two collapsible aluminum oars, and a first-aid kit that contained only salve for gasoline burns and a bottle of iodine. De Angelis found two fish hooks and a short piece of line, the only items left in the jungle packs zippered into the parachutes cushion, which were supposed to contain a flashlight, jungle knife, hard biscuit, chocolate, and hooks and fishing line. In their later sufferings, the men would come to curse the mechanic who had casually pilfered these supplies.

Even so, spirits initially remained high, as they expected rescue any minute—especially after Eddie yelled, "I'll give $100 to the first man to sight the ship or plane that rescues us." They shot off a flare. The sun set, and a bright moon rose. Sleep proved difficult, the men either snuggling down to the bottom of the raft and several inches of sloshing seawater or sitting up to face the breakers that rolled over them "like being doused with a bucket of ice water." They set up watches and bailed every two hours.

That evening's discomfort soon paled in contrast to what the sun did to them the following day. In his summer blue suit, tie, and battered fedora, Eddie was comparatively lucky. Adamson wore his uniform and hat. Some of the others, anticipating a swim, had jettisoned shoes and pants. Reynolds's bare legs soon turned into "a sodden red mess of hurt," the soles of his feet burning raw. The swarthy-skinned Whittaker and De Angelis tanned, but the rest suffered burn-induced blisters that broke and turned excruciatingly painful with the regular saltwater dousing.

On the second day, in a tacit nod to his seniority, Cherry handed Eddie the oranges. As seven pairs of greedy eyes watched him, he cut the first one carefully in half, then halved each section again, and finally once more. Eddie decided that they would consume an orange every other day, but that soon became too tantalizingly long to wait, and they finished them off. Eddie would remember that first week as the worst, becalmed in a glassy sea, the lines slack between the boats, the sun beating down hour after hour, as if they were "being turned on a spit." At first they took off their clothes, doused them with seawater, and stuck them on their heads, but this cost them valuable moisture through sweating. So they held the clothing up as sunshades instead. Wringing salt water over their bodies afforded short-term satisfaction but exacted longer-term suffering, as the salt that dried on their skins stung and itched. Eddie handed out some handkerchiefs that Adelaide had given him, and the men wore them like cartoonish stick-up artists. Eddie imagined that he smelled flesh burning, along with "the sweet stink of rubber." Reynolds's nose oozed terribly.

When the wind did pick up, the waves pounded the rafts, pushing body parts together, jangling raw nerve ends, and inflaming tempers. So closely intertwined were these outcasts that even the slightest movement of a man's hand or foot in sleep inflicted agonizing jolts on his neighbor. Sharks continually escorted this small convoy, fortunately proving "good humored beasts in their uncouth way . . . We didn't mind the little ones, but the big fellows who ranged up to 12½ feet had a disturbing habit of scraping off their barnacles on the bottom of the rafts," remembered Whittaker. "After a dash to gain momentum, they would scoot under us, rubbing their backs and giving a flip of the tail as they left each raft. A man sitting on the floor would get a wallop jarring him to the teeth."

Hunger tore at their stomachs. Adamson had an issue of *Reader's Digest* in his pocket, its pages stuck together by salt water except for an article about Brazilian aviator Alberto Santos-Dumont. When he read a description of a lavish dinner for that pioneer in Paris, the others hooted him down. Cherry promised to take everybody to a restaurant atop a hill in San Francisco—probably the Top of the Mark above the Mark Hopkins Hotel—and started taking orders. Everybody agreed that strawberry ice cream topped the list.

A bit of orange pulp stuck on a hook brought no nibbles from the fish that the men could plainly see. "The only bait we've got," said Johnny Bartek, "is our own hides," which set off a gruesome conversation about whether an earlobe or small toe would prove the better bait. Cherry fashioned a spear from one of the oars but couldn't pierce the thick carapace of a passing shark.

The others noticed that Bartek had begun pulling out a pocket-sized New Testament—khaki covered, zipper bound, waterproof—and reading it. Eddie thought it a good idea to move the rafts together and hold a prayer meeting, despite the fact that he wasn't particularly religious, although he had attended Sunday school as a child. At first, Whittaker, an avowed atheist, made fun of the Bible meetings, telling them loudly and frequently that "you can pray your guts out and nobody is going to help you." Even so, he found something unexpectedly impressive in the scripture. He stumbled through the Lord's Prayer, but after twice-daily recitations he knew it by heart and claimed that it brought him calm. Things he saw and felt during this experience awakened in him a deep spirituality he had not known before. They passed the Bible around, choosing passages to read aloud. Adamson, also an atheist, joined in. A favorite was the Twenty-third Psalm. Eddie found that bobbing adrift in the Pacific gave the words "a beauty" that he'd never appreciated.

Captain Cherry would begin morning and afternoon prayers with a twangy conversational request to the "Old Master," often mentioning his three-year-old daughter. All he asked was to kiss her one last time. He liked to read the section of the Gospel according to Matthew that included "Therefore take no thought, saying, What shall we eat? or, What shall we drink? or, Wherewithal shall we be clothed?" This passage, with its later admonition "Take thereof no thought for the morrow: for the morrow shall take thought for the things of itself," seemed to speak directly to them and provided some sustenance. De Angelis remembered that Eddie's prayers often seemed like a discussion. "Here we are. We are doing the best we can . . . We believe in you and are seeking deliverance, and it is entirely up to you, if you want to aid us or not."

A week's repeated immersion in salt water left the men with painful ulcers over their abdomens, hips, legs, and feet, which began as rashes before turning into hard, pus-thickened sores that would break open and never dry or heal. Sometimes the only relief was to crouch in a kneeling position. "Our mouths," said Eddie, "became covered with ugly running sores." The salt water also irritated their eyes, virtually blinding them for long stretches because they had neither fresh water to rinse them nor tears.

Although no birds appeared, Cherry cradled his revolver, breaking it open two or three times a day to lubricate the moving parts with the body oil from his nose and behind his ears. This proved a losing battle; his and Adamson's .45s soon locked from corrosion. The men frequently grabbed at the smallest sharks but could gain no purchase on their slippery skins. They tried to sing hymns but couldn't remember more than a few words or bars of the tunes and sank into long silences as it dawned on them that their chances of rescue were worsening with every passing hour. By the eighth day, the baking heat and constant discomfort and pain had combined with desperation to turn them to thoughts of what lay beyond death. "There was no time that I lost faith in our ultimate rescue," said Eddie, "but the others did not seem to share this state of mind fully with me." With a remarkable lack of inhibition, they spoke about their lives, failures, infidelities, ambitions, and regrets. Bartek called it their "confessions." "We let each man talk out as much as he wanted to without interruption." Eddie wrote that "as far as I am concerned, no hint of those long, man-to-man conversations will ever be revealed." It seemed to do some good. Still, in the unrelenting heat, hunger, and sinking despair, even this talk petered out, as the men half-dozed, hallucinated, groaned, and sometimes cried out in despair.

On the afternoon of the eighth day, about an hour after Cherry had again read Matthew, Eddie lay slumped in a waking doze, his battered gray-green felt hat pulled down over his eyes, when he felt something press down on his hat and knew instinctively that a bird had alighted on it. Thoughts raced through his mind, perhaps the most powerful that he'd never have another chance like this; "the whole Pacific seemed to be shaking from the agitation in my body." He inched his right hand up, "the hungry, famished, almost insane eyes in the other rafts" telling him that the bird still perched there. "Sensing his nearness," Eddie closed his fingers, then, feeling a leg, squeezed harder.

It was a miracle. The men described it as a small seagull, but it probably was a tern or sea swallow, because gulls rarely venture so far from land. Species mattered little to those famished men. Eddie wrung its neck; Adamson stripped its feathers. Eddie cut the little creature into equal portions, reserving only the intestines for bait. It tasted "raw and stringy and fishy," said Eddie, and Whittaker likened its muscles to "iron wires," but no one complained, each carefully crunching the bones. With a bit of intestine and Whittaker's ring as a weight, Cherry pulled in a small mackerel. Eddie managed a sea bass. "Each of us received a fish steak about an inch square and a half an inch thick," remembered Whittaker. These few scraps of fish and bird bolstered spirits and strength but did nothing to slake their raging thirst. The copilot likened it to feeling that all the water had been baked out of him. "You just didn't want to drink fresh water. You want to wallow in it. You feel you could soak it up by gallons through the pores." The delirious Adamson longed over and over again for "ice water pie."

That evening came another miracle as a breeze freshened, then picked up into a real blow by midnight, swinging the rafts "crazily back and forth like a Coney Island amusement device." Out of the blackness came a "blinding flash followed by an ear-bursting crash. More lighting, more thunder, and rain! rain! RAIN! Right on the rafts! It was not a gentle downpour. It came with the extravagant waste of a waterfall."

Shouting hoarsely with excitement, the men first squeezed the salt out of their tattered clothing, then, once wet again, handed the rags to Cherry and Eddie, who wrung them out into baling buckets with stiff clumsy hands. They hit on a way of storing water in the air bladders of their Mae West flotation vests. Eddie was given the job of spitting the water into the bladders, the entire group watching his Adam's apple like hawks to make sure he didn't swallow a single drop.

Once the rain had finally stopped in the gray morning light, they slumped over in exhaustion, not seeing an oncoming rogue wave, which suddenly overturned Cherry's raft. Eddie started yelling, then pulled the raft over to him with the cord and, flipping it upright, helped the three chilled and exhausted men back aboard. They had lost a Mae West filled with clean water, but Cherry had clung ferociously to his own partially filled vest. Over the next days, Cherry parceled out the quart and a half, ounce by precious ounce, into the shell casing of a flare gun.

Bartek took to rubbing the leg that Eddie had shattered in the Atlanta crash while the tough elder dispensed homespun wisdom to his eager pupil. "Anything you want to try, you've got to try a hundred percent," Bartek remembered him saying, "and then if you're licked, it's different . . . You've got to fight in order to get it." Bartek said he learned more from Eddie in those few days on the raft than from anyone else he had ever known.

Eddie kept a worried eye on Adamson, whose back pain, along with terribly sunburned feet, legs, arms, wrists, and face, had left him in a semiconscious stupor. His badly corroded colonel's eagles hung almost unrecognizable from his rotting uniform. His eyes were nightmarishly bloodshot and swollen; his usual lucidity had long since deserted him. That evening, when Eddie felt the raft lurch, he thought that a large shark had bumped them; then, registering that Adamson no longer rested against him, he saw Adamson's shape in the water. Leaping to the other side of the raft, he grabbed the colonel's collar—"I'd never seen a man [move] like that," remembered Bartek—and with help from Cherry and Whittaker pulled him back into the raft. Adamson may have slipped overboard for the noble reason of easing his comrades' suffering, but he had nonetheless chosen death—and that was not okay with Eddie.

The next morning, in a moment of clarity, Adamson weakly extended a hand to Eddie, who refused it, swearing at him in a blue streak with a vehemence that shocked the others, unequivocally telling him that a handshake would only come when the quitter had again proved himself worthy of respect. He was indeed boiling mad, believing that Adamson had let his comrades down, not only by betraying them but by hurting their overall chances of survival, a thing he could not pardon. For Eddie, keeping the team together—family, pit crew, squadron—had repeatedly meant the difference between surviving or not. The individual only survived if the group did—and the group couldn't unless the individuals did.

"It was then that Rick[enbacker] took over," remembered Whittaker.

When the plane ditched, Cherry had been in charge, but the exigencies of survival were beginning to change that. The pilot made good decisions, but he could not match Eddie's deep experience, unflinching belief in their rescue, and sheer willpower. Cherry fought to preserve his authority, but the proven, if civilian, hero displayed it in overwhelming abundance when things started to fall apart. For that, Cherry would never forgive Eddie.

"I will not put down all the things [Eddie] said," commented Whittaker. "They would scorch this paper. But from then on, woe betide the man who appeared about to turn quitter or who did anything to lower the morale of the others." With startling clarity, Eddie understood his central function in the group's survival. He had started out telling them of his own experiences, how he'd been in tough spots before and always made it through. Fear and defeatism are infectious, however—and on the rafts these emaciated, battered men were drifting inexorably toward capitulation, two of them inserting in their prayers a petition for something to take them out of their misery. Now, with Adamson so conspicuously trying to end it, Eddie needed a new way to keep them focused—and alive. Here Eddie's particular genius, creative imagination under extreme duress, again produced an unorthodox answer. He did have a weapon left, "and that was to brutalize and jar those whose chins sagged too far down on their chests." There would be kind words and deeds, but mostly a torrent of abuse. If Eddie heard even an inkling of the negative or self-pitying, he would immediately jump on its utterer without mercy.

"What's that? What's that?" he would yell. "So YOU'RE off again, are you? And you call yourself a man! Why, you blankety-blank-blank quitter, when we get out this you'd better crawl home to the women where you belong"—lines delivered with dripping sarcasm, summoning everything he could to scald them into fighting "their way out of approaching coma just because they were mad at him," recalled Adamson. "Lord, how they learned to hate that man! There were times when they would gladly have thrown him into the sea, granted the strength." Somehow Eddie's stinging rebukes did not further deflate morale but instead stirred up such anger as to keep them focused on him, not on the unrelenting agony and proximity of a foul death. "I raged at them until they found reason, in the midst of their suffering, to live." Eddie remembered someone shouting out across a few feet of water, "Rickenbacker, you are the meanest, most cantankerous so-and-so that ever lived." Chances are that the words were far worse, but little ever dented Eddie's tough hide. He was teaching these men how to fight and stay alive. "They had never suffered . . . This was their first, and they didn't know how to attack it; they just didn't." He added, "I have learned that you only learn to appreciate real things and real people, and you only develop real leadership, through suffering and necessity. These are the two basic fundamentals." Eddie's very presence started to affect the others. Liking to cool off with a dip in the ocean, De Angelis reported sometimes slipping below the surface to drink some salty water. He didn't do it much, though, knowing that Captain Rickenbacker "would raise hell with me." This alone may have saved his life.

Alex Kaczmarczyk was not so lucky. Weak from the start, still not fully recovered from his operation and illness, he started drinking salt water, explaining wearily that he could not help it. He began to froth around the mouth, a sign that his kidneys were beginning to shut down. Eddie got Bartek to exchange places with Kaczmarczyk, putting him on the lee side of the raft; all that evening, his arm around him "as a mother cuddles a child," Eddie warmed and comforted the dying man. The shivering finally stopped and broken sleep came, interrupted by incoherent ramblings about his mother and Snooks, his girlfriend. He stayed with Eddie through the next day, then during the evening prayer asked to go back to the small raft. All during the young man's wretched ordeal, Snooks had been receiving a daily letter from him. Bored in the hospital before the crash, he had written thirty letters; a friend posted one per day.

Later that night, Eddie was startled awake by a long, unnatural sigh, then silence. De Angelis said he thought Kaczmarczyk was gone. Eddie told everybody that they would wait for morning to make certain. At daybreak, he couldn't find a heartbeat. In what may have sprung from his memories of splitting up a dead aviator's possessions among the living, they parceled out

Kaczmarczyk's clothing, Bartek getting his jacket. Then they lowered their comrade into the salt water that had killed him and watched him float away. The former altar boy De Angelis croaked out a hymn in Latin and said, "I consign your body to the sea and your soul to the Lord." Whether they discussed cannibalizing the young engineer—an ancient tradition of the seas—no account mentions. It appears that they never considered that ultimate recourse. Eddie reported that the sharks moved in quickly.

It rained frequently from then on, which kept them alive and periodically washed off the accumulation of brine. Little food came their way, apart from some sardinelike creatures and a flying fish that sailed into a raft. Cherry hooked a 2-foot shark and pulled the thrashing creature among his crowded raft mates, finally stabbing it in the head, which slightly pierced the raft's bottom. They patched this as well as they could, then cut up shark steaks. Even for the starving men, however, the meat tasted so awful and sat so badly in their stomachs that they dumped most over the side.

Eddie felt his gums receding; a "cottony substance" had formed under the plate of his new false teeth. He now wheezed with each breath.

Somewhere between days 15 and 20, someone heard a plane, which appeared to be a U.S. Navy Kingfisher, flying low and fast on the horizon some miles away. They shouted as loudly as their weakened frames could manage, but to no avail. Over the next two days they saw six more planes, but each initial exultation chilled when these flew no closer. Cherry decided that they would stand better chances if they split up. Eddie argued angrily against the idea, but Cherry went anyway, taking the small raft without a paddle. Not long afterward, Whittaker and De Angelis decided to float away as well. Again Eddie raged, but soon the pair drifted off, taking with them the near-comatose Reynolds. Eddie sat there with Adamson and Bartek, both closer to death than life.

Among his dreams of wife and kids, others came to Eddie about those he had left behind at Eastern. At sunrise a "strong icy downpour" brought them back to life. The two others spread out their rags to catch the water, then handed them to Eddie, who wrung them into the baling bucket.

Adamson would never forget the image of Eddie clenching his teeth in pain as he wrung the rags, his hands shaking so badly that he could hardly finish, blood rising out of the cracks in the raw flesh whenever he squeezed.

On Friday, November 13, 1942, Eddie administered the morning ration of water. Adamson and Bartek being barely able to lift their heads, he poured a jiggerful from the flare shell into Bartek's mouth, but some of it dribbled down his chin. He gave him more. Sometime late that hot afternoon, they heard yet another plane, then two single-engined seaplanes, traveling only a few hundred feet off the water a couple of miles away. They couldn't stand up, but Eddie got them waving and hollering; the planes still set off frustratingly into the setting sun. Eddie knew his mates were drawing near the end: If the planes didn't come back soon—and there was only a couple of hours' light left—then he wasn't sure that they could make it through another night. Already storm clouds had gathered in the east. Things were very close to over.

Suddenly Bartek heard the planes again, now flying directly toward them, one circling. Eddie could see the pilot grinning at them, but then they headed back to whence they had come. It was like an agonizing dream for Eddie, who had no way of knowing that his rescuers needed to refuel. Three-quarters of an hour later, the same planes reappeared. One left, but the other circled overhead, continuing to do so as the sun went down. Eddie finally realized that they must be waiting for a boat. A plane splashed to a landing near the raft, then taxied over. Eddie paddled to it, grabbing the pontoon for all he was worth.

With room in the cockpit only for the sick Adamson, the two navy fliers tied Eddie and Bartek to the wings in preparation for the 40-mile taxi on the waves back to Funafuti Island, if the PT boat could not find them. In the darkness they hummed along for about a half hour before being caught in PT Boat 26's spotlights. Eddie learned that a navy patrol had spotted Cherry's raft and that the third had washed ashore on another island. All the raft mates then alive would survive, although Adamson and Reynolds both came close to dying. Eddie had started the mission at 180 pounds and now weighed 126.

The survivors didn't know it yet, but they owed their rescue to Adelaide's stubborn refusal to give up on her husband. When he went missing, Eddie's longtime secretary, Miss Shepherd, came to stay with her. When Adelaide received a condolence letter from Arnold two weeks after the Flying Fortress disappeared, she—rightly inferring that they were calling off the search—trained down to Washington and "practically tore the decorations off his jacket." Arnold agreed to extend the search an additional week. Kingfisher patrols had been increased, and their discovery had come right at the end of that reprieve.

Eddie bounced back quickly from the ordeal and received Arnold's approval to continue the mission. MacArthur welcomed the shaky war ace with "God, Eddie, I'm glad to see you" at Port Moresby Airport. Despite the message from Washington, the two got along famously. Meanwhile, Adamson nearly died from a diabetic attack while convalescing in a Samoan hospital. Unfortunately, the hospital lacked any insulin supplies. Only through the chance appearance of a navy doctor who happened to be diabetic himself and offered his personal supply of insulin did the colonel pull through. A bout of pneumonia shortly after that nearly claimed him again, and then an abscess was found on his lung. Miraculously, he survived.

After visiting other bases and touring battle-ravaged Guadalcanal, Eddie returned stateside to something even more exalted than the warmest hero's welcome. Newspapers had trumpeted his survival a week after the turn of the tide of war in North Africa—"the end of the beginning," as Churchill called it—and his story seemed to underscore American perseverance and guts. RESCUE OF AIRMAN DELIGHTS MILLIONS, a *New York Times* headline stated simply. "The news that Eddie Rickenbacker is back with us is wonderful indeed," wrote the president of his rival United Airlines. "Men of his caliber constitute one of our greatest assets in war as well as in peace." When Eddie saw Adelaide again for the first time, he whispered to her, "Hello, honey . . . looked as if I'd stepped off the reservation for awhile, but I'm still around!"

Copilot Whittaker's riveting account of the marooning turned into a thirteen-part series for the *Chicago Tribune*, picked up all over the nation, and eventually became a book called *We Thought We Heard the Angels Sing*. Eddie's powerfully raw telling became the cover story for a three-part *Life* magazine narrative; he donated his $25,000 serial fee to Hap Arnold's charity, the Army Air Forces Aid Society, which helped the families of fallen airmen. Adamson published his own hagiography of Rickenbacker, admitting that he did hate him for those days on the rafts but insisting that they remained good friends during the other times. The seagull story entered popular lore, prompting countless sermons, cartoons, editorials, and newspaper stories. The entire saga registered with near-biblical resonance, something transcending battle triumphs and boardroom successes. Here was America's destiny written in a drama worthy of a playwright but unmistakably true, a morality story of courage, fortitude, and faith that enthralled a nation shaken by war.

Not everyone emerged singing Eddie's praises, however. Cherry's animosity never waned. He did not express his anger publicly, but it's likely that he never bought into Eddie's version of events, which featured the ace as the single-handed savior of the castaways. It's clear that Cherry had not wished to take off so soon in the second B-17; at some level he held Rickenbacker responsible for the haste in which they left. Certainly Eddie's narrative gave Cherry little credit for what probably saved all their lives, the decision to split up, which enhanced their chances of being found.

Indeed, as he had done all his life, Eddie had shaped the narrative of the events to support his role as gritty hero, just as he would later conjure up fantasies of a sunny childhood and had earlier let a ghostwriter embellish his memories of World War I. For many, such obvious self-aggrandizement smacked of pure egotism, but the truth contains far more subtlety. Eddie Rickenbacker never really moved beyond that small boy who marshaled all his available resources to hold off his father and the harsh circumstances of his childhood. Success for Eddie was not just getting out alive but telling the story; not just standing up but also standing out.

On those fragile rafts, surviving became all about Eddie—it couldn't help but be—and he had indeed kept his mates focused on life, not death.

Only he had the authority and the orneriness to push away the soul-choking despair. Never has there been a greater master of that dangerous game.

When Doubleday published Eddie's raft narrative in 1943 as *Seven Came Through*, the cover trumpeted that the book also included "His Message to America." The seventeen-page postscript reminded the United States that it must remain committed to war against a formidable enemy by steeling itself "for a tremendous investment" in aviation, which could prove the difference. Then, after the war, American statesmen must "hammer out a formula that will give all nations free and unhindered access to the new high routes." Otherwise, there would never be peace. The American public had become his family, just like his pit crew, the 94th, Eastern's employees, and the men on those rafts. He would do everything to make sure they all were prepared.

He would be damned if he was going to let them down.

EPILOGUE

The Pacific ordeal changed Eddie, softening him "a very great deal," observed a close friend, and "gave him a reflective side he never had before." Certainly getting older does this to humans; as experience accumulates, the body fades, death becomes more familiar, and the hardest-edged become more contemplative, even generous. The raft experience, though, altered something even more fundamental.

As a young man on the racing circuit, he had relied on cunning and nerves but also bat hearts and black cats, a deep bow to the vicissitudes of fate. In wartime he had traded in his talismans for a growing confidence in his own abilities, brokering youthful arrogance and innate skill into a wild spin above a football game for a shot at the big show. Coming up against the formidable Flying Circus, he had developed a thoughtful, systematic analysis of risk that morphed into strong leadership skills at the helm of the 94th Aero Squadron. All along the way he had tripped so often to the very edge of death that he knew well its cold grip on his shoulder—and how easy it would have been to yield to its pull. Drifting in the Pacific, he had taught a master's class in extreme survival. His raft mates, who even years later raged at the memory of his merciless tongue-lashings, still acknowledged that they would have died without him—and that he was the only one who never gave up.

In the ocean, survival had come not from physical prowess and mechanical genius, or bringing to bear his preternatural ability to gauge a competitor's weaknesses. He was not up against an angry father, a millionaire's son with a faster car, a bloodred Fokker, or even the Axis powers, but something far more elemental in the sea's indifferent enormity, the sun's burning blaze, and the indecipherable rhythms of the wind and waves. Out there adrift, Eddie's courage was the one thing that never corroded, seared, or started dying under the relentless heat, hunger, thirst, pain, and temptations to despair. That singular, extraordinary quality alone had saved them all.

This uninvited struggle had forced him for the first time to grapple seriously with the supernatural: not so much whether God existed or not, but rather whether some form of divinity had touched those dying men, delivering that rainstorm after the prayer, for instance, or bringing their seemingly providential rescue as the end so inescapably loomed. How to explain the seabird landing on his head when things were at their worst? Were these things explainable as luck or simple randomness? Did their thoughts turn to prayer and God just because "there are no atheists in the foxholes"? Or was something else at play, something beyond Eddie that sustained his certainty, his enduring courage? It was new, uncomfortable territory for a man used to looking backward only when he might glean practical information from it.

He wrestled with it in typical Rickenbacker fashion, head-on with soul-baring honesty. In a magazine essay entitled "When a Man Faces Death," he recounted his many near-misses, then boldly jumped into his revelations about the supernatural. He spoke fondly of the crucifix that he had carried faithfully for years; it even weathered the raft trip, though corroding badly.

"I am not such an egotist as to believe that God has spared me because I am I," he wrote. "I believe there is work for me to do and that I am spared to do it, just as you are. If I die tomorrow—I do not fear the prospect at all—I believe my death will have a meaning. It may be only to make others around me to appreciate their own lives even more and use them to better advantage. But it will have meaning." The article hit a nerve; letters poured in. Almost 400,000 copies of the essay were distributed to military personnel. Eddie had cobbled sense and clarity out of the unknowable, exercising perhaps the most critical attribute of leadership, the ability to articulate vision. The bull-headed ace had defiantly reclaimed the narrative of his life, yet somehow remained humble, never playing the victim or ever asking "Why me?" In the uncertainties of a nation at war, Eddie had again shown a way forward.

In 1968, when the seventy-eight-year-old Eddie celebrated the fiftieth anniversary of the Armistice, some of his war-era friends still lived, including Douglas Campbell, who had become the general manager of Pan American Airways after the Second World War, and also Reed Chambers, a cofounder of the nation's first aviation insurance company. The still-doughty Chambers early that year had broken the sound barrier copiloting a Convair F-106 Delta Dart. It did seem that the end of an era was approaching, though, especially when Eddie's great friend and former raftmate Colonel Hans Adamson died in September.

That same year had also seen the retirement of Juan Trippe of Pan American, the last of the four original airline pioneers to pass the baton, following Eddie in 1963, William Patterson of United in 1966, and C. R. Smith of American in 1968. The last years of Eddie's long tenure at Eastern had not been easy; even this visionary was eventually unable to keep up with the rapid changes around him. The end came in sight when he strenuously objected to bringing jets into Eastern's fleet. Eddie's America had changed, too. Women were serving now as flight attendants, another thing the increasingly strident grand old man could not abide. In 1968, he told a journalist that the United States should forget peace talks with North Vietnam and just "bomb the living hell" out of their ports because it was "kill or be killed." Although he considered the American entry into Vietnam a mistake, he had no truck with draft-card burners, because a citizen's job was "to protect the country."

By then his autobiography, published the year before, was a national bestseller, still selling briskly. To get it on paper entailed Eddie's last truly superhuman effort: He sat down with his ghostwriter, Bootes Herndon, and dictated what would turn into some seven thousand typewritten pages of remembrances from which was hewn the official autobiography. His status required that the ghostwriter sand away the rough edges and tint everything nicely. Eddie insisted that Herndon use material gleaned only from the interviews and what Eddie had published before. The original transcripts were anything but polished—like the man himself, they were full of uneven surfaces and contradictions, deep complexities apparent. At times he was difficult, even surly, at others warm and generous, but never was he boring. Even in the dusk of life, he remained a force of nature.

Eddie made sure that every high school and college library received a free copy of his autobiography, later claiming that he had influenced and inspired three generations of kids, perhaps the legacy of which he was most proud. The cover features an oil painting of Eddie in heroic pose, seated atop a mountain crag in the great cloak he had bought in Paris so many summers ago, his Medal of Honor shining upon it. Behind him, a dogfight takes place in the sky. He is unsmiling, his jaw resolutely clenched. It's hard to find a more explicit visual representation of the term "hero."

Yet to his dying day in late July 1973, he insisted he was no hero, his extraordinary feats simply the result of the American way of life. Whether hero or not, it was his courage in extremity that served as a model for successive generations of explorers, adventurers, and warriors, from Charles Lindbergh and Jimmy Doolittle to Chuck Yeager and John Glenn, and an ever vaster host of risk takers, entrepreneurs, and executives. He was many things—daredevil, tinkerer, cool risk manager, improviser, showman, tactician, and leader—but always it was his enduring courage that shone like a beacon for the better part of a century, showing America what it could be and challenging it to get there.

NOTES

ABBREVIATIONS

ER-BH Interview Taped 1965 interview of Edward Rickenbacker by ghostwriter Bootes Herndon for ER autobiography. Transcript in the Eddie Rickenbacker Papers, Library of Congress, Washington, DC. Listed by tape number/side/page.

ER "Life" "Life Story of Captain Edward V. Rickenbacker," Ohio State University Rare Books and Manuscripts, Columbus, OH. Unpublished two-volume interview conducted for background for the 1945 Twentieth Century–Fox film *Captain Eddie*.

ER, Columbia Interview of Eddie Rickenbacker, Columbia Center for Oral History, 1962.

ER "Death" Eddie Rickenbacker, "When a Man Faces Death," manuscript in the collection of Ohio State University Rare Books and Manuscripts Library, Columbus, OH.

ER "Diary" 1918 war diary kept by Edward V. Rickenbacker. National Museum of the Air Force, Wright Patterson Air Force Base, Dayton, OH.

ERWWI. Rickenbacker's nonpaginated typewritten accounts of World War I experiences, assembled for ghostwriter Laurence La Tourette Driggs to write *Fighting the Flying Circus* and transcribed November and December 1918. Edward V. Rickenbacker Papers, Box 91, Library of Congress, Washington, DC.

Leighton Isabel Leighton's "Rickenbacker Material," interviews she conducted of Edward V. Rickenbacker, Adelaide Rickenbacker, and friends, including

Ethel Wilhelm, Steve Hannigan, Mr. and Mrs. Walter Baker, Miss
Shepherd, Dr. and Mrs. Robb, Mrs. "Barney" Everitt, Leroy Peed, Edward
Pospisil. Transcript in Auburn University Special Collections and
Archives, Auburn, AL.

Rickenbacker Scrapbooks Auburn University Special Collections and
Archives, Auburn, AL.

FFC Eddie V. Rickenbacker, *Fighting the Flying Circus* (Garden City, NY:
Doubleday, 1965).

ER Auto Edward V. Rickenbacker, *Rickenbacker: An Autobiography* (Englewood
Cliffs, NJ: Prentice-Hall 1967).

Introduction: When a Man Faces Death

xvii "modify, even in the slightest, the gyrations of the Nieuport": ER "Death,"
      p. 26.
xvii "I wondered whether the airplane would disintegrate around me": Eddie
      Rickenbacker, "Baling Wire and Fabric Crates," *The Airman*, August 1957,
      p. 10.

BOOK I: DRIVING

Chapter 1: Love at First Sight

3 Early Columbus history from Ed Lentz, *Columbus: The Story of a City*
   (Charleston, SC: Arcadia Publishing, 2003), pp. 83–103; *The History of
   Columbus: Past, Present and Future of the Metropolis of Central Ohio, Practical
   Demonstration of Its Development by the Reproduction of Rare Historical
   Photographs* (1900), as reprinted in OSU's Multimedia Histories Section,
   "Columbus Business and History" and "Downtown Columbus" at www
   .ehistory.osu.edu.
4 "a far step from the innate intelligence of the horse": Robert Bruce, "The
   Place of the Automobile," *Outing*, October 1900, p. 65.
4 Steps in starting a Model C: author interviews with Carlton Pate and
   Robert Casey.

5   "the new noise of the automobile": Finis Farr, *Rickenbacker's Luck: An American Life* (Boston: Houghton Mifflin, 1979), p. 14.

6   *a significant part of a car-crazy nation would own cars*: Rudi Volti, "A Century of Automobility," *Technology and Culture* 37, no. 4 (October 1996), p. 665.

6   "a gigantic tidal wave of human ingenuity": Thomas P. Hughes, *American Genesis: A Century of Invention and Technological Enthusiasm, 1870–1970* (Chicago: University of Chicago Press, 2004), p. 14.

6   *Yankee ingenuity of America's independent inventors*: Ibid., p. 13.

8   "The world loves speed": Ritchie G. Betts, "Faster than the Locomotive: The Flight of the Automobile," *Outing* 39, no. 4 (January 1902), p. 399.

8   Material from Lizzie's life and travels to America: Marian Pflaum Darby, *The Inspiration and Lives of Elizabeth Basler Rickenbacker and William Rickenbacker* (privately published by the author, 1963).

10 Detail on Columbus manufacturing: Lentz, pp. 83–103.

11 Material about early Rickenbacher childhood: ER-BH Interview, 1/1/1.

12 *a horse-racing track only three blocks away*: ER-BH Interview, 1/1/6.

12 Description of rail truck escapade: ER-BH Interview, 21/1/3.

12 Stealing mitt: ER-BH Interview, 12/1/1.

12 ER's early life detail: ER-BH Interview, 1/1/15.

13 "does not cry when he gets hurt": George W. Peck, *Peck's Uncle Ike and the Red Headed Boy* (Chicago: Alexander Belford, 1899).

14 "lick the old nick out of me with switches": ER-BH Interview, 1/2/14.

14 Details about William Rickenbacher's death: "Skull Broken by Murderous Blow," July 19, 1904; "Gaines Claims He Hit in Self-Defense," July 21, 1904; "Rickenbacher Is Dead from Blow," August 27, 1904; all from *Ohio State Journal*.

15 "I'll take care of everything": Frazier Hunt, "The Life Story of Eddie Rickenbacker," *Popular Mechanics*, July 1932, p. 37.

16 Brother without same "push" as Eddie: ER-BH Interview, 39A/1/18.

17 "completely undemonstrative": Walter Baker interview, Leighton, p. 37.

17 "emotional shyness": Adelaide Rickenbacker interview, Leighton, p. 20.

18 Olentangy Park: www.clintonvillehistory.com.

18 Cromwell Dixon in Columbus: University District History, Columbus, OH, "Cromwell Dixon," at www.univdistcol.com.

18   Material on Tom Swift: "Bless My Collar Button, If It Isn't Tom Swift,"
      American Heritage 28, no. 1 (December 1976).

19   "My idea was a series of springs": ER-BH Interview, 3/1/10.

20   "I was a dynamic part of progress": Eddie Rickenbacker, "Eddie
      Rickenbacker Tells Own Philosophy," *Los Angeles Times,* November 11,
      1962, p. F2.

Chapter 2: A Most Dangerous Job

21   Early Columbus history, see chapter 1, p. 3 references.

22   *to upend the sleepy rural rhythms:* Georg Simmel, "The Metropolis and
      Mental Life (1910)," in *The Blackwell Reader,* ed. Gary Bridge and Sophie
      Watson (Malden, MA: Wiley-Blackwell, 2010), pp. 103–4.

22   *clearing the oak-maple forests:* "A Snapshot: The State of the Lower
      Olentangy River Watershed in 2001," Lower Olentangy River Watershed
      Inventory, Friends of the Lower Olentangy Watershed, March 2002,
      www.olentangywatershed.org.

23   *birth of more than forty automobile makers:* Richard E. Barnett, "Made in
      Columbus," in *Automobiles* (Columbus, OH: Columbus Historical Society,
      1994).

24   Discussion about the race between three car technologies: Christopher
      W. Wells, "The Road to the Model T: Culture, Road Conditions, and
      Innovations at the Dawn of the American Motor Age," *Technology and
      Culture* 48, no. 3 (July 2007), pp. 502–4.

24   *A fully charged battery today provides:* Rudi Volti, "Why Internal Combustion?,"
      Invention & Technology 6, no. 2 (Fall 1990), p. 44.

25   *To start a Stanley:* Volti, "Automobility," p. 667.

26   "noxious, noisy, unreliable, and elephantine": Jim Motavalli, *High Voltage:
      The Fast Track to Plug In the Auto Industry* (New York: Rodale Press, 2011),
      p. xii.

26   *so few paved roads outside major cities:* John B. Rae, "The 'Know-How'
      Tradition," *Technology and Culture* 1, no. 2 (Spring 1960), p. 144.

27   "in and out of my pocket": ERAuto, p. 31.

27   *a shabby little three-story building:* W. David Lewis, *Eddie Rickenbacker: An
      American Hero in the Twentieth Century* (Baltimore, MD: Johns Hopkins
      University Press, 2005), p. 25.

28   General information on twenty-four-hour race: Bob Brannon, "History of Racing, Part 4—Grinds: The Dawn of 24 Hour Races," www .lastrunclub.com.

28   "the frame was straightened": *Columbus Evening Dispatch* quoted in A. Michael Knapp, "The World's 1st 24-Hour Automobile Race," *Motorsport. com.*

30   "I wanted to bring foreign drivers and their cars over here": Robert Casey, "The Vanderbilt Cup, 1908," *Technology and Culture* 40, no. 2 (April 1999), p. 359.

30   "you've got a good head on your shoulders": ERAuto, p. 35.

30   *a mechanician managed to hang across the vibrating hood*: E. V. Rickenbacher and J. C. Burton, "The Loyal Legion of Speed: Being the Short and Simple Annals of the Mechanician, an Unsung and Unhonored Hero," *Motor Age* 27, no. 14 (September 30, 1915), p. 6.

30   "The next thing you've got to watch for is the tires": ERAuto, p. 36.

31   "Many's the time my mechanic beside me has to kick me": Oney Fred Sweet, "It Wasn't My Fault That a Valve Broke," *Chicago Daily Tribune*, July 30, 1916, p. 41.

31   "He is the Damon of the gasoline circuit": Rickenbacher, "The Loyal Legion of Speed," p. 5.

31   "he drags himself wearily to his garage": Ibid.

32   "I thought sure my ear drums would be crushed": "First Ride with Auto Racing Pilot," *New York Times*, June 19, 1910, p. 54.

32   "but a series of lunges": ERAuto, p. 37.

32   "It killed him, feathered him": ER-BH Interview, 2/2/28.

33   "You've got to learn how to smile and take it": ER-BH Interview, 39C/2/8.

33   "Many Marvelous Escapes": Beverly Rae Kimes, *Automobiles Quarterly* 6, no. 2 (Fall 1967), p. 191.

33   "Again the scrambling, screaming, swearing!": Julian Street, "The Fools at the Finish," *Collier's*, November 7, 1908.

34   *their creator's innovations would survive*: ERAuto, p. 39.

34   About Frayer's work at the Buggy Co.: ER-BH Interview, 2/2/31.

35   Firestone's car breakdown: ERAuto, pp. 41–42; ER-BH Interview, 2/2/32–3.

35   "I would simply listen": ERAuto, p. 43.

35 "I could understand it and it would respond to my mental desires": ER-BH Interview, 39E/1/13.

36 Blanche Calhoun: ERAuto, p. 51.

37 "seriously bruised": *Red Oak* (IA) *Express* quoted in Lewis, *Rickenbacker,* p. 48.

37 "The rear wheels slid sideways": Michael Kernan, "Wow! A Mile a Minute!" *Smithsonian,* May 1998, www.smithsonianmagazine.com.

38 "Average lungs can't overcome the outward force": Ibid.

38 "I did more fighting in saloons getting old Barney out of scrapes": Richard Snow, "Barney Oldfield," *American Heritage* 28, no. 2 (February 1977), www.americanheritage.com.

39 "you have to practice to feel it": ER-BH Interview, 39C/2/24.

39 "It's a very fine dividing line": ER-BH Interview, 39E/1/23.

39 "That's where the tuning comes in": ER-BH Interview, 39E/1/24.

39 "clean, square racing man": Hans Christian Adamson, *Eddie Rickenbacker* (New York: Macmillan, 1946), pp. 97–98.

40 *a burning cinder flew into his right eye*: ER-BH Interview, 11/1/13.

Chapter 3: Death on the Track

41 "A black spot in the distance grew larger as the roar deepened": George Trevor, "Roaring Road," *The Outlook,* June 4, 1930, p. 186.

42 Background on Carl Fisher: Indiana Historical Staff, "The Hoosier Barnum: Carl G. Fisher," www.indianahistory.org; Joe McCarthy, "The Man Who Invented," *American Heritage* 27, no. 1 (December 1975), www.americanheritage.com; Mark S. Foster, *Castles in the Sand: The Life and Times of Carl Graham Fisher* (Gainesville: University Press of Florida, 2000).

43 "More brutal than bull fighting": *Detroit News* quoted in Ralph Kramer, "Centennial—Ten Crisis Moments in Indy's First 100 Years," *Automobile Quarterly* 51, no. 1 (no date), www.autoquarterly.com.

44 "that secular deity, the internal combustion engine": Tom Wicker, "Homage to America," *New York Times,* May 31, 1983, p. A21.

44 "One second my insides were up against my back teeth": Charles H. Owens, "It May Look Like a Cubist Drawing: But It Isn't. It's Just—Speed," *Los Angeles Times,* February 18, 1923, p. VI-1.

44   "My kidneys would scare me": ER-BH Interview, 39D/2/46.

45   "You've no idea how the breeze forces a fellow's cheeks back": Sweet, p. 41.

45   "Take this track out here": Ibid.

45   "built of magnified corrugated iron," Owens, p. 3.

45   *Drivers talked about how the peripheries of one's vision contracted*: Lyn St. James, *Ride of Your Life: A Race Car Driver's Journey* (New York: Hyperion, 2002), p. 5.

45   "When things are right, you can feel the tires in your nerve ends": Parsons quoted in Annie Gilbert Coleman, "Making Time and Place at the Indy 500," *Environmental History* 16 (April 2011), p. 332.

46   On the 1911 Indy: "Marmon Car Wins: Death Marked Race," *New York Times*, May 31, 1911, p. 13.

46   "This is my last race": "Two Winners Jubilant; Two Finish Depressed," *Indianapolis Sun*, May 31, 1911.

46   *pioneer the use of the steel hard hats*: Tony Swan, "Celebrating the Indy 500's 100th Anniversary," *Car and Driver*, June 2011, www.caranddriver.com.

48   License revoked: Lewis, *Rickenbacker*, p. 60.

48   Duesenberg garage background: W. David Lewis, "Eddie Rickenbacker: Racetrack Entrepreneur," *Essays in Economic Business History* 29 (2000), p. 92.

49   "We used to take a connecting rod": ER-BH Interview, 39E/1/32.

49   "we worked for him like football rookies trying to please a great coach": Griffith Borgeson, *The Golden Age of the American Racing Car* (Warrendale, PA: Society of Automotive Engineers, 1998), p. 58.

49   "when a man has taken something": Enzo Ferrari quoted in Robert Daley, "That Blood-Red Ferrari Mystique," *New York Times*, July 25, 1965, p. SM22.

49   *so nationally famous that an imposter traveled the country*: Charles Leerhsen, *Blood and Smoke: A True Tale of Mystery, Mayhem, and the Birth of the Indy 500* (New York: Simon & Schuster, 2011), p. 205.

50   *he riveted half a buggy-wheel rim to the cowling*: ER-BH Interview, 39E/2/38–39.

50   *The kitten clung to the hub*: ER-BH Interview, 39E/2/41.

50   "The direct effect of the jar upon the driver's hands": Street.

51   "This track is very fast": *Sioux City Journal* quoted in Farr, p. 15–16.

51   Sioux Falls race: Reed L. Parker, "Drivers Set for Sioux City Race," July 4, 1914, p. 14, and "Sioux City's Speedway a Surprise to Motorists," July 12, 1914, p. G6, both *Chicago Daily Tribune;* "22 Entries for Sioux City 300-Mile Race," *The Horseless Age,* July 1, 1914, p. 5.

51   *Fifty rich Chicagoans camped in private railroad cars:* Farr, p. 16.

52   *License plates from New York:* Lewis, *Rickenbacker,* p. 66.

52   *Evangelists set up a tent:* Farr, p. 17.

52   *fashioned a protective mesh screen for his dash:* ER-BH Interview, 39D/1/13.

52   *grisly central European practice:* Gary F. McCracken, "Bats in Magic, Potions, and Medicinal Preparations," *BATS Magazine* 19, no. 3 (Fall 1992), www.batcon.org.

53   Bat incident: ER-BH Interview, 4/1/8–9.

53   Wishart lap record: "Spencer Wishart Sets Lap Record," *Hartford Courant,* August 19, 1914, p. 16.

53   Wishart's "out to prove something": Lowell Thomas, *Good Evening Everybody: From Cripple Creek to Samarkand* (New York: William Morrow, 1976), p. 67.

53   Wishart background: "Spencer Wishart Known in New Haven," *Hartford Courant,* August 24, 1914, p. 15.

54   *favorite headgear, a woman's sock:* ER-BH Interview, 39D/2/45.

55   "It can be very painful if you get caught": Lewis, *Rickenbacker,* p. 80.

55   *drifting:* Michael Cannell, *The Limit: Life and Death on the 1961 Grand Prix Circuit* (New York: Twelve, 2011), p. 22.

57   "Speed Demons Annihilate Space": "Speed Demons Annihilate Space in Struggle for Supremacy on Many Courses," *Los Angeles Times,* July 5, 1914, p. VII-3.

58   "Seeing an endless controversy in sight": "Spencer Wishart Claims He Won Sioux City Race," *Los Angeles Times,* July 6, 1914, p. III-1.

59   Wishart's crash: "Wishart Killed in Elgin Auto Race," *New York Times,* August 23, 1914, p. S2.

59   "nodding acquaintance with death": Ken W. Purdy, "Stirling Moss: A Nodding Acquaintance with Death," *Playboy,* September 1, 1962, p. 67.

60   "I tried to dominate death": ER-BH Interview, 21/2/7.

60   "already thrown himself into the maelstrom of life": Lewis, *Rickenbacker,* p. 69.

Chapter 4: Aeroplane vs. Automobile

61   Beachey and Iowa State Fair: Ann Holtgren Pellegreno, *Iowa Takes to the Air, Vol. 1* (Story City, IA: Aerodrome Press, 1980).

62   Beachey background: Richard Reinhardt, "Day of the Daredevil," *Invention & Technology* 11, no. 2 (Fall 1995), pp. 11–21.

62   *donned a flaxen wig and fluttering skirts:* "Beachey Flies as a Woman," *New York Times*, January 28, 1912, p. 6.

63   "You know when a man's in love?": Beachey quoted in Frank Marrero, "Lincoln Beachey: The Man Who Owned the Sky," at www.amacord .com/fillmore/museum/beachey4.html.

63   "If I did tumble from the air": Reinhardt, p. 15.

63   Beachey's contract with fair: Iowa Department of Agriculture, *Fourteenth Annual Iowa Year Book of Agriculture* (Des Moines, IA: Robert Henderson, State Printer, 1915), p. 58.

63   Pain's: "Pain's Pyrotechnic Display," *Sydney Morning Herald*, February 17, 1887, p. 8.

65   Kipling poem: "For All We Have and Are," in George Herbert Clarke, ed., *A Treasury of War Poetry* (Boston: Houghton Mifflin, 1917).

66   "resplendent art and myth": Robert Wohl, *A Passion for Wings: Aviation and the Western Imagination, 1908–1918* (New Haven, CT: Yale University Press, 1996), p. 29.

66   Beachey's fatal crash: "Lincoln Beachey Plunges 3,000 Feet to Death," *Hartford Courant*, March 15, 1915, p. 1.

67   "Chance-taking is not a business with me": Marrero.

67   *In 1910 alone, 37 prominent fliers died:* Reinhardt, p. 13.

67   "It wasn't always recklessness": ER-BH Interview, 39D/2/49.

68   "carelessness and overconfidence are usually more dangerous": Wilbur Wright letter to his father, September 23, 1900, cited in Wohl, p. 11.

68   "an inclination to bust up his mounts": "Dramatis Personae of the Speed Spectacle: No. 5—Eddie Rickenbacher, Maxwell," *Chicago Daily Tribune*, May 14, 1916, p. F11.

68   *twenty-three road and speedway races:* "Automobile Records for 1915," *Chicago Daily Tribune*, December 26, 1915, p. A3.

68 *average winning pace proving nearly 20 miles faster than only two years before*: "Earl Cooper Best of Racing Drivers," *New York Times*, October 24, 1915, p. S3.

68 *recorded speeds jumped*: "Comparison of Speedway Racing in 1914 and 1915," *Motor Age*, November 25, 1915, p. 12.

68 Two million cars in private hands: Reed L. Parker, "Gossip of the Auto Trade," *Chicago Daily Tribune*, October 24, 1915, p. E6.

68 Details about Packard's growth: Reed L. Parker, "Gossip of the Auto Trade," *Chicago Daily Tribune*, August 29, 1915, p. D8.

68 Speedway Park in Chicago: "Summer of 1915—When 'Mercurian Monarchs' Roared," *Chicago Tribune*, September 28, 1978, p. N2.

69 Speaking tube apparatus: Al G. Waddell, "When Scotland Yard Shadowed an Ace," *Radco Automotive Review*, September 1929, p. 78; ER-BH Interview, 4/2/1.

69 "From the minute you touched the pedal": ER-BH Interview, 39D/2/41.

69 Coatalen announcement that he and Resta will drive: *The Horseless Age* 35, no. 5 (February 3, 1915), p. 158.

69 Resta background: L. Spencer Riggs, "Dario Resta: Champion of the Splintered Bowls," *Automobile Quarterly* 43, no. 1 (2003), p. 68.

70 Resta's longshot odds: Lewis, *Rickenbacker*, p. 71.

70 "I am glad to be back at the wheel of an American car": "Great Drivers to Pilot Maxwells," *Hartford Courant*, March 14, 1915, p. Z7.

70 Carlson's mountain race: Al G. Waddell, "Nervy Driver Smashes Mountain Motor Record," *Los Angeles Times*, December 9, 1914, p. III-1.

70 *first adjustable seat*: Anthony J. Yanik, *Maxwell Motor and the Making of the Chrysler Corporation* (Detroit: Wayne State University Press, 2009), p. 109.

70 Maxwell 25's innovations: Lewis, *Rickenbacker*, p. 71.

71 "It's a shame to pick on the ladies": "Pullen Makes Fastest Lap," *Los Angeles Times*, March 13, 1915, p. III-2.

71 "Everybody was watching": ER-BH Interview, 4/2/6.

72 "terrible beating of the rain in his eyes and face": Lewis, *Rickenbacker*, p. 71.

73 "We had to lift him out": ER-BH Interview, 4/2/12.

Chapter 5: New Order of Terrors

73 Indy 500 of 1915 postponed: "500-Mile Race Postponed," *New York Times*, May 29, 1915, p. 8.

73 *rain-chilled bricks*: "Big Indianapolis Motor Race Today," *Hartford Courant*, May 31, 1915, p. 15.

73 *Harroun's latest brainchild*: Yanik, p. 112.

73 Peugeot innovations: Lewis, *Rickenbacker*, p. 69.

74 "to smell a mouse" and material on oil device incident: ER-BH Interview, 4/2/18.

74 *grinned "sheepishly"*: Lewis, *Rickenbacker*, p. 73.

75 "not only a masterful driver": contemporary quote cited in Ian Wagstaff, *The British at Indianapolis* (Dorchester, UK: Veloce, 2010), p. 23.

75 "Resta appeared to drive with his eyes on the stopwatch": Lewis, *Rickenbacker*, p. 72.

76 "perhaps forty, fifty, or a hundred ways of doing each act in each trade": Frederick Winslow Taylor, *Scientific Management: Early Sociology of Management and Organizations* (New York: Routledge, 2003, initially published in 1911), p. 25.

76 "star drivers are good executives": Sweet, p. 41.

76 "The speedway is a fearsome sight": Reed L. Parker, "Hawkeye Track in Poor Shape for Race Today," *Chicago Daily Tribune*, July 3, 1915, p. 10.

77 "I liked road racing better": ER-BH Interview, 39C/2/14.

77 "King of the Dirt-Track Racers": Lewis, *Rickenbacker*, p. 84.

77 *only driver to win three open speedway events in 1915*: "Maxwell Victory Is Popular One," *Tucson Daily Citizen*, May 24, 1916, p. 10.

77 Sioux City race details: "Maxwell—Mercer—Duesenberg July 4 Winners," "Maxwell Leads at Sioux City," and "Sioux City Track Hard on Cars," *The Automobile*, July 5, 1915, pp. 53–56; "Holiday Racing on the Speedways," *The Horseless Age* 36, no. 1 (July 7, 1915), pp. 1–3; "Cox Dies of Injuries," *Motor Age*, July 8, 1915, p. 12.

78 *sobbing as he crossed the line*: Reed L. Parker, "Maxwell Car Wins First in Omaha Event," *Chicago Daily Tribune*, July 6, 1915, p. 14.

78 "Billy was a most lovable chap": "Barney Oldfield Pays Deep Tribute to Billy Carlson," *Los Angeles Times*, July 6, 1915, p. III-3.

78 Carlson's pre-nuptial agreement: "How Racers' Wives Feel," *Los Angeles Times*, March 17, 1915, p. III-4.

78 "Gasoline has robbed the milestones": "Gradual Conquest of Time and Distance by Gasoline," *Motor Age*, July 1, 1915, p. 21.

78 *five of his eight teammates since the Vanderbilt Cup would perish*: Sweet, p. 41.

78 *demoralized Maxwell team disbanded*: Parker, "Maxwell Car Wins," p. 14.

78 *and the catastrophe sealed the decision*: "Accident at Tacoma Ends Brilliant Career of William Carlson," *Motor Age*, July 5, 1915, p. 16.

78 Van's joke about Ricken and Bacher: Adamson, p. 131.

79 "I'll teach that spaghetti eater": L. Spencer Riggs, "Dario Resta," p. 72.

80 "Famous as a speed mad": "Dramatis Personae . . . Eddie Rickenbacher, Maxwell," p. F11.

80 Switching tires at last minute: Adamson, p. 132–33.

80 "You've got to have an imagination": ER-BH Interview, 39C/2/11.

81 "every move, human, mental, physical, mechanical": ER-BH Interview, 39D/2/53.

81 Instructions to pit crew: ER-BH Interview, 39D/2/59; Sweet, p. 41.

82 "I much prefer to travel with Herr": ER-BH Interview, 5/2/17A.

82 "I was entirely too busy trying to be a successful": ER-BH Interview, 5/2/22.

83 Burman and Schrader death: Al Waddell, "Speeding Monster Rolls Over into Parked Autos," *Los Angeles Sunday Times*, April 9, 1916, p. VI-1.

83 "you could almost cover us with a blanket": ER-BH Interview, 4/2/20.

83 Sheepshead race description: ER-BH Interview, 4/2/20–21; "Rickenbacher Wins the Race," *Los Angeles Times*, May 14, 1916, p. VI 1; "Two Are Killed in Automobile Race," *Hartford Courant*, May 14, 1916, p. 1; "Rickenbacker Wins Metropolitan Race," May 14, 1916, p. S1, and "Two Men Killed in Motor Race at Sheepshead," May 14, 1916, p. 1, both *New York Times*; J. Edward Schipper, "Maxwell Wins Trophy," *The Automobile* 34, no. 20 (May 18, 1916), pp. 879–87; "Pay for Thrillers," reprinted from *New York World* in *Los Angeles Times*, June 19, 1916, p. II-4.

84 "I will never drive again": "Aitken to Quit Racing Game," *Chicago Daily Tribune*, November 4, 1919, p. 11.

84 "To be on the wire is life; the rest is waiting": Purdy, p. 70.

84 Aitken background: "Dramatis Personae of the Speed Spectacle: No. 6—Johnny Aitken, Peugeot," *Chicago Daily Tribune*, May 21, 1916, p. G9.

85 Harvest Classic details: A. S. Blakely, "Aitken Wins Every Race," *Indianapolis Star*, September 10, 1916; "Aitken Makes Clean Sweep," *The Automobile*, September 14, 1916, p. 463.

86 "How Aitken got through [the car parts]": ER-BH Interview, 39D/2/48.

86 Eddie can "control that machine with my mind": Eddie Rickenbacker, "Eddie Rickenbacker Tells Own Philosophy," p. F2.

86 *leaving him with about $40,000*: Lewis, "Racetrack Entrepreneur," p. 96.

87 Flight with Martin: ER-BH Interview, 39F/1/1–3.

88 Dodd encounter: ER-BH Interview, 39F/1/18–19.

88 *Resta and Aitken declined to race*: "Resta Is Champion Driver," *New York Times*, November 21, 1916, p. 12.

89 "lucky elephants and four-leaf clovers": Adamson, p. 146.

BOOK II: FLYING

Chapter 6: Storm Clouds Overhead

93 Black Tom: "How Eyewitnesses Survived Explosion," *New York Times*, July 31, 1916, p. 3; Michael Warner, "The Kaiser Sows Destruction," *Journal of the American Intelligence Professional* 4, no. 1 (2002), pp. 3–9; "Plotted Black Tom, Says Von Rintelen," *New York Times*, January 3, 1940, p. 7; "Black Tom Blasts of 1916 Recalled," *New York Times*, July 31, 1966, p. 63.

95 "Rickenbacher's ancestors hailed from the land of the Alps": "Dramatis Personae . . . Eddie Rickenbacher, Maxwell," p. F11.

95 "Great Kaiser Bill has had his fill": "Lautenschlager und Rickenbacher," *Motor Age*, July 9, 1914.

95 Waddell's story about Eddie's Prussian lineage: Al Wolf, "Sportraits," *Los Angeles Times*, July 26, 1945, p. 11.

95 "I'm no baron": "When They Thought Rickenbacker Was a Spy," *Chicago Daily Tribune*, February 20, 1944, p. F4.

95 *more than ninety ships in American harbors alone*: "91 German Vessels in American Ports," *Atlanta Journal*, February 4, 1917, p. 3.

96 Lusitania details: Thomas Fleming, *The Illusion of Victory* (New York: Basic Books, 2003), p. 55.

97 "a violent, hysterical, concerted movement to eradicate everything German": Carl Wittke, *German-Americans and the World War* (Columbus: Ohio State Archaeological and Historical Society, 1936), p. 163.

97 *Germanic surname might bring him trouble:* "British Detain Rickenbacher," *Motor Age,* January 25, 1917, p. 53.

98 English sergeant encounter: ER Auto, pp. 77–8.

98 "colder than the coldest, damnedest icicles": ER-BH Interview, 5/2/35.

98 "the whole thing was so ludicrous that, instead of getting mad, I treated it as a joke": ER Auto, p. 78.

99 *dark-clad women wearing lettered armbands:* Philippa Levine, "Walking the Streets in a Way No Decent Woman Should: Women Police in World War I," *Journal of Modern History* 66, no. 1 (March 1994), pp. 34–78.

100 "All of England's young men are in khaki": "Rickenbacker in Europe for King Motor Company," *Atlanta Journal,* February 8, 1917, p. 8.

100 *thrilled at the sight:* ER-BH Interview, 39F/1/16.

100 Brooklands details: Howard Johnson, *Wings over Brooklands* (Surrey, UK: Whittet Books, 1981); David Venables, *Brooklands: The Official Centenary History* (Somerset, UK: Haynes Publishing, 2007).

102 *death of Victor Chapman:* "Chapman's Opponent," *New York Times,* June 30, 1916, p. 5.

102 Boelcke's exploits: "Dead Man Flew in Aero," *Washington Post,* December 19, 1916, p. 3.

103 Richthofen's description of Hawker dogfight: Manfred Freiherr von Richthofen, *The Red Air Fighter* (London: "Aeroplane" & General Publishing, 1918).

103 "quiet, self-controlled face": Ernst Udet, *Ace of the Iron Cross* (New York: Arco Publishing, 1981), pp. 48–49.

104 *Richthofen and his men would do so five times a day:* Ibid., pp. 49–50.

104 *a British squadron had been formed just to kill the Baron:* Ezra Bowen, *Knights of the Air* (Alexandria, VA: Time-Life Books, 1980), pp. 124–25.

104 *Eddie had also crossed the Channel to visit Peugeot:* "Rickenbacher Is Back from Europe," *Motor Age,* March 1, 1917, p. 16.

104 *he checked in with the relevant authorities:* ER-BH Interview, 39E/2/60.

105 "Yes, my friend, your mail was opened": "When They Thought Rickenbacker Was a Spy," p. F4.

105 "open American eyes": "Rickenbacher Is Back from Europe," p. 16.

105 "That'd be me": ER-BH Interview, 6/1/10.

105 "As a fitting close to the experiences of an American race driver in Europe": "Rickenbacker Is Back from Europe," p. 16.

106 "I leave for the West tomorrow": "Flying Corps of Daring Racing Drivers Plan if War Comes," *New York Times,* February 18, 1917, p. XX2.

106 "But I do want to thank you": ER Auto, p. 82.

Chapter 7: Flying Lessons

109 AEF's welcome in Paris: Charles H. Grasty, "Americans March in Rain of Flowers," July 6, 1917, p. 3, and Charles H. Grasty, "France Brims Over with Gratitude to US," July 8, 1917, p. 64, both in *New York Times;* John J. Pershing, *My Experiences in the World War* (New York: Frederick A. Stokes, 1931), vol. 1, p. 58.

109 "the most inspiring drive I ever took": Carlo D'Este, *Patton: A Genius for War* (New York: HarperCollins, 1995), p. 193.

109 "there is a limit to what flesh and blood and endurance can stand": Martin Gilbert, *The First World War: A Complete History* (New York: Henry Holt, 1994), p. 340.

110 "This adverse situation after three years of struggle was so depressing": Pershing, *My Experiences,* vol. 1, p. 70.

110 "I hope . . . not too late": Ibid., p. 69.

110 *did little to discourage American press coverage . . . that he was chauffeuring Pershing regularly*: "Through 'Rick's' Eyes: Former Racing Champion Writes 'Tribune' Man of Viewing the Big Fight at Pershing's Side," *Chicago Daily Tribune,* December 30, 1917, p. D6.

110 MacArthur anecdote: Douglas MacArthur, *Reminiscences* (New York: McGraw-Hill, 1964), p. 59.

111 Mitchell as "excitable, high-strung individual": ER-BH Interview, 6/2/24.

111 "we are behind all other major powers in the matter of aviation": Aaron Norman, *The Great Air War* (New York: Macmillan, 1968), p. 494.

111   Trenchard's war aviation philosophy: Ibid., p. 497.

111   "I used to lead him out on the end of a limb": ER-BH Interview, 6/2/22.

111   Description of Nancy outing: William Mitchell, "Rickenbacker: The Ace of Aces of the A.E.F.," *Liberty*, May 17, 1930.

113   *earliest bombs remained rudimentary, artillery shells trimmed with bits of horse blanket*: Norman, p. 331.

113   "enables you to have eyes yourself": Charles H. Grasty, "Build Airplanes and Help Us Win, Painlevé Urges," *New York Times*, June 29, 1917, p. 1.

114   Dodd anecdote: ER-BH Interview, 39F/1/26.

115   "Any job that he was given ... was done in the best possible manner": Mitchell, "Rickenbacker."

115   Fashioning a new bearing: ER-BH Interview, 6/2/25.

115   Miller conversation: ERAuto, p. 89.

116   "big, older, tough as nails": Bowen, *Knights*, p. 153.

117   Tours aerodrome: James J. Hudson, *Hostile Skies: A Combat History of the American Air Service in World War 1* (Syracuse, NY: Syracuse University Press, 1968), p. 31; FFC, pp. 9–10.

117   "like church spires in a desert": Hamilton Coolidge, *Letters of an American Airman: Being the War Record of Capt. Hamilton Coolidge, U.S.A. 1917–1918* (Boston: Privately printed, 1919), p. 36.

117   Training in a Penguin: James Norman Hall, *High Adventure: A Narrative of Air Fighting in France* (Boston: Houghton Mifflin, 1918), pp. 24–41.

119   "Now so to do a left hand spin": Douglas A. Campbell interview, U.S. Air Force Oral History Interview, #531, Albert F. Simpson Historical Research Center, Air University, Maxwell Air Force Base, p. 6.

119   Chambers describes French technique: Matthew C. Stafford, "Reed Chambers: The Rise of an Aviation Entrepreneur" (PhD dissertation, University of Alabama, Tuscaloosa, 2003), p. 59.

119   "It made a splendid solid foundation": Edwin C. Parsons, *I Flew with the Lafayette Escadrille* (Indianapolis: E. C. Seale, 1937), p. 67.

119   *killed eleven students out of every hundred*: Hudson, p. 35.

119   "the old trick of patting your head": ERAuto, p. 90.

120   "quickness and sureness of instinct": Hall, *High Adventure*, p. 30.

120   *thrum of the engine softening*: James R. McConnell, *Flying for France* (New York: Doubleday, Page, 1917), pp. 148–50.

120 Experienced pilot acrobatics: Hall, *High Adventure*, pp. 41–42.

120 "They were daily enlarging their conceptions": Ibid., p. 20.

121 "It was a slow moving crate": ER-BH Interview, 39F/1/37.

122 he "couldn't project [his] vision progressively": ER-BH Interview, 39F/1/37.

Chapter 8: A Steep Learning Curve

123 Descriptions of Issoudun: ER-BH Interview, 6/1/30–1; Quentin Roosevelt, *Quentin Roosevelt: A Sketch with Letters* (New York: Charles Scribner's Sons, 1921), pp. 102–3; Coolidge, pp. 24–26, 38, 43; Bowen, p. 149; Robert B. Gill, ed., "The War Diaries and Letters of Walter L. Avery," *Over the Front* 1, no. 3 (Fall 1986), p. 206; Norman, p. 494; Bert Frandsen, *Hat in the Ring: The Birth of American Air Power in the Great War* (Washington, DC: Smithsonian Books, 2003), p. 29; *Stars and Stripes*, March 28, 1919; Douglas A. Galipeau, "Issodun [sic]: The Making of America's First Eagles" (dissertation, Air Command and Staff College, Montgomery, AL, March 1997), p. 22.

124 "Yesterday Philippauteaux fell": Gill, p. 209.

125 Eddie travels to Paris: ER-BH Interview, 6/1/29; Sugar priceless: Coolidge, p. 12.

125 *his first machine shop*: *Gorrell's History of the American Expeditionary Forces Air Service, 1917–1919*, National Archives, College Park, MD, Microform M990, Records Group 120. *History of the Third Aviation Instruction Center at Issoudun*, Series J. vol. 9, p. 266.

125 "masters of difficulties": Ibid., p. 13.

125 *Sam Brownes*: ER-BH Interview, 6/1/30; Coolidge, p. 21.

125 "These were Yale and Harvard and Princeton boys": ER "Life," p. 180.

126 Issued tin buckets: ER-BH Interview, 39F/1/28.

126 "some of them as big as your head": Reed Chambers, "The Reminiscences of Reed M. Chambers," Columbia Center for Oral History, 1960, p. 19.

126 "The more they hated me": ER-BH Interview, 6/1/31.

126 "Lt. Rickenbacker won't give us more planes": Meissner Diary, December 4, 1917, W. David Lewis Papers, Auburn University, Series V, Folder 4.7.

126 "I couldn't get propellers fast enough": ER, Columbia, p. 4.

126 six propellers a day: *Gorrell's History,* p. 262.

126 *Rickenbacker mudguard: Gorrell's History;* ER, Columbia, p. 4.

126 *recalled a three-day period:* "'Worst Mudhole in France' Becomes World's Greatest Flying Center," *Plane News,* November 23, 1918.

126 *Accidents at Issoudun:* Narayan Sengupta, *American Eagles: The Illustrated History of American Aviation in World War I* (self-published, 2011), pp. 103–4; *Gorrell's History,* p. 323.

127 Roosevelt's plane fire: Roosevelt, pp. 79–80.

127 Chambers meets Eddie: "Reed Chambers," interview by great-nephew Daniel Chambers, June 24, 1967, Huntington, NY, transcribed by Matthew Stafford, manuscript kindly provided by Mr. Stafford, pp. 10–12; Chambers, Columbia, pp. 21–23.

127 *flying through flocks of crows:* Coolidge, p. 65.

127 *cut a new road: Gorrell's History,* p. 266.

127 *stocked about 29,000 different parts:* "'Worst Mudhole," *Plane News.*

128 "If you can't smile when you get up from a knockdown": Evan Thomas, *Ike's Bluff: President Eisenhower's Secret Battle to Save the World* (New York: Little, Brown, Company, 2012), p. 30.

128 "I believe and fight like a wildcat": ER "Death," p. 15.

128 Chambers background: Chambers, Columbia, pp. 3–5; Stafford.

129 "Really, the American of the mechanic class": Roosevelt, p. 82.

129 Description of Nieuport: Coolidge, pp. 8, 68; Chambers, Columbia, p. 20.

130 *fitting a cork into a champagne bottle:* Gene DeMarco, "Nieuport 11 Bebe," *The Vintage Aviator,* www.thevintageaviator.co.nz.

130 "pressed the tit": Cecil Lewis, *Farewell to Wings* (London: Temple Press Books, 1964), p. 16.

130 Background on rotary engine: Bill Gunston, *World Encyclopedia of Aero Engines* (Somerset, UK: Patrick Stephens, 1995), p. 97; Fred Murrin, "Shooting Down the Myths of the Rotary Engine," *Over the Front* 20, no. 2 (Summer 2005), pp. 164–75; Forum discussion, "Rotary Engine Throttle?" *The Aerodrome,* www.aerodrome.com; Kimble D. McCutcheon, "Gnome Monosoupape Type N Rotary," www.enginehistory.org

131 "you flew the engine as much as you flew the airplane": Charles D'Olive, "The Reminiscences of Charles D'Olive," Columbia Center for Oral History, 1969, p. 16.

131 "and you were *immediately* ready to take off!": Lewis, *Farewell,* p. 15.

132 "whirling sprays": *Gorrell's History*, p. 16.

132 "I never came so near crashing before": Coolidge, p. 42.

132 *small drops of oil were clinging to the wing's leading edge*: DeMarco, "Nieuport 11."

133 "trying to fly a gyroscope": Charles D'Olive quoted in Hudson, p. 32.

133 Problems with pilot harness clasp: Coolidge, p. 112.

134 *all there was to acrobatics was getting up high*: Thomas E. Kullgren, ed., "The War Diary and Letters of Lansing C. Holden, Jr.," *Over the Front* 1, no. 3 (Fall 1986), p. 233.

134 *It dropped about a degree for every 300 feet*: Technical Notes Prepared for the United States Army School of Military Aeronautics, University of Illinois, 1918, p. 313.

134 "You cannot imagine how bitter it is": William Muir Russel, *Happy Warrior: Letters of William Muir Russel, an Aviator in the Great War, 1917–1918* (Detroit: Saturday Night Press, 1919), p. 97.

134 "I don't know how angels stand it": Roosevelt, p. 78.

134 "a chance to freeze our ass": Gill, p. 207.

134 "My muscles simply would not obey my command": ERAuto, p. 93.

134 *To imagine a spin*: Joseph Bourque, "The Spin Debate: If Spins Can Kill, Why Aren't Pilots Trained to Handle Them?" *Air & Space/Smithsonian*, November 2003.

135 "If the first time you go into a spin is inadvertent": Ibid.

135 the spin as "graveyard spiral": Fred C. DeLaceroa, *Facts About Spins* (Ames: Iowa State Press, 2002), p. 17.

135 "something mysterious and deadly": Duncan Grinnell-Milne quoted in Evan Hadingham, "Spin Control: How Pioneering Pilots Learned to Escape the Death Spiral," *Aviation History*, September 2012, p. 47.

135 "Nobody quite knew how, nor indeed how or why aircraft spun": Lindemann quoted in Adrian Fort, *Prof: The Life of Frederick Lindemann* (London: Jonathan Cape, 2003), pp. 58–59.

135 "spinning was the one thing the young pilot fought shy of": Cecil Lewis, *Sagittarius Rising* (London: Greenhill Books, 2006), p. 41.

136 "the cockpit all messed up": Chambers, Columbia, p. 52.

136 Spin over football game: ER-BH Interview, 6/2/33, 39F/2/51; ER "Life," pp. 180–82; ERAuto, pp. 93–94.

137 *one pilot perished every week on average*: Roosevelt, p. 123.

137 "Who will be next? Me?" Gill, p. 208.

138 "damn fool thing to do": ER "Life," p. 182.

138 *first graduate of the advanced flight school*: Sengupta, p. 100.

138 "He can feel the defects of a machine" and "an eye for little details": Coolidge, pp. 74, 85.

138 Spatz/hospital incident: ER-BH Interview, 39F/2/52; ERAuto, pp. 94–95; ER, Columbia, p. 6.

Chapter 9: Aircraft Morph into Deadly Weapons

140 Arcachon description: Gill, p. 209; Roosevelt, p. 128; Hudson, p. 37; Sengupta, pp. 110–11; ER-BH Interview, 6/2/36.

141 *The pilot aimed by aligning two rings*: Technical Notes, p. 439.

141 "raised more hell than seven boxes of monkeys": ER-BH Interview, 6/2/37.

141 "It is very difficult to keep your sight steadily": Coolidge, pp. 47–48.

141 "the most awful old crocks" and "You get up in the air": Roosevelt, pp. 125, 126.

142 "large group of pilots developed a tendency to roost": *Gorrell's History*, (Cazaux), p. 10.

143 Strange's experience with early machine gun: L. A. Strange, *Recollections of an Airman* (London: Aviation Book Club, 1933), p. 42.

143 Lewis gun: Bill Gunston, *The Illustrated Encyclopedia of Aircraft Armament* (New York: Orion Books, 1988), pp. 8, 10.

143 Strange's plane-flipping episode: Strange, pp. 112–15.

144 Eddie "wasn't the best pilot": Chambers, Columbia, p. 30.

145 Development of synchronizer: Richard P. Hallion, *Rise of the Fighter Aircraft, 1914–1918* (Baltimore, MD: Nautical & Aviation Publishing Company of America, 1984), pp. 8–14; Jon Guttman, *The Origin of the Fighter Aircraft* (Yardley, PA: Westholme Publishing, 2009), pp. 20, 27–28; Bowen, pp. 52–61.

146 "You feel naked and helpless": Bowen, p. 70.

146 *eighteen see-sawing reversals of air dominance*: Theodore Hamady, *The Nieuport 28: America's First Fighter* (Atglen, PA: Schiffer Military History, 2008), p. 37.

147 *Germany's air corps only fielded some 250 aircraft*: Bowen, p. 117.

147 Immelmann/Boelcke comparison: Guttman, *Origin*, pp. 29–31; Bowen, p. 62.

148   "'the strong man is mightiest alone'": Bowen, p. 62.

148   *to originate what is still a basic fighter formation*: Hallion, p. 22.

148   *Aviation scholars doubt*: Hallion, pp. 18–19.

148   Boelcke and Richthofen quotes, Dicta: Bowen, p. 118.

148   *He required that each pilot memorize*: Kelly P. Poiencot, "The Father of Aerial Flight," *Century of Flight*, November 2003, p. 29.

149   Survival rates of airmen: Mike Spick, *The Ace Factor: Air Combat and the Role of Situational Awareness* (Annapolis, MD: Naval Institute Press, 1988), p. vi.

150   *life expectancy of an RFC pilot dwindled*: John P. H. Rayder, "Armed for Success: External Factors of the World War I Aces" (thesis presented to the Faculty of the U.S. Army Command and General Staff College, Fort Leavenworth, 1995), p. 16.

150   "The decisive factor does not lie in trick flying": Hadingham, p. 46.

150   "My reserve is dangerously low" and "machines with green wings": Bowen, p. 134.

151   "America was going to ship over 20,000 of the greatest planes": ER-BH Interview, 6/2/38.

151   "Fifty thousand American aviators": Hamady, p. 39.

152   *Amerikaprogramm*: Walter J. Boyne, *The Influence of Air Power upon History* (Gretna, LA: Pelican Publishing, 2003), p. 114.

152   "[the Allies] are entirely without complete drawings": Hamady, p. 42.

153   "After much discussion, consultation": Frandsen, p. 57.

153   "The French didn't want any part of them": Stafford, p. 68.

153   *date with a woman*: ER "Diary," March 4, 1918.

154   "Rather bad results for the first time": ER "Diary," March 6, 1918.

154   *The mess elected Chambers bar officer*: Stafford, p. 72.

154   "he's a yellow son of a bitch!": Diary of Joseph Houston Eastman, December 19, 1918, Joseph Houston Eastman Collection, Hoover Institution Archives, Stanford University, Stanford, CA.

154   *vowed never again to "cherish friendships"* and "came to look with callous indifference": FFC, pp. 12, 108.

155   "always smelt of cheap perfume": Sengupta, p. 129.

156   "All the boys were sure that I had been out over the Front": Lewis, *Rickenbacker*, pp. 120–21.

156   "foolish virgins of Squadron 95": FFC, p. 15.

BOOK III: FIGHTING

Chapter 10: First Blood

159 Ludendorff meets with squadron commanders: Norman, p. 435.

161 "killing many also wrecking the depot": ER "Diary," March 23, 1918.

161 "naturally we thot they would bomb us": ER "Diary," March 26, 1918.

161 "Got the opportunity I have worked so hard for": ER "Diary," March 27, 1918.

162 "quiet and thoughtful in manner and gentle in speech": FFC, p. 96.

162 "If it would [be] a nice [social] event I would be left out": Prinz quoted in Frandsen, p. 78.

163 "Campbell learned to fly alone": FFC, p. 96.

163 "any life viewed from the inside is simply a series of defeats": George Orwell, "Benefit of Clergy: Some Notes on Salvador Dali," in George Packer, ed., *All Art Is Propaganda: Critical Essays* (New York: First Mariner Books, 2009), p. 210.

164 "Many fighter aces have been described as fearless": Spick, p. iv.

164 "wondering what they would do with our equipment": ERWWI.

164 "Well, I'll be slapping you in the face with a spade": Chambers, Columbia, p. 38.

165 Reims cathedral during the war: Nicola Lambourne, "Production Versus Destruction: Art, World War I and Art History," *Art History* 22, no. 3 (September 1999), p. 353.

165 "Rheims: At the Ruined Cathedral," in Florence Earle Coates, *Poems, Volume II* (Boston: Houghton Mifflin, 1916), p. 211.

166 "banking and turning from one side to the other": Jack Eder, ed., *Let's Go Where the Action Is! The Wartime Experiences of Douglas Campbell* (Knightstown, IN: JaaRE Publishing, 1984), p. 50.

166 "Never, never fly straight and narrow": Michael Korda, *With Wings like Eagles: A History of the Battle of Britain* (New York: Harper, 2009), p. 93.

166 "nothing but the chaos of ruin and desolation": FFC, p. 5.

166 Krupp gun: Sengupta, p. 127.

166 Archies: OED.

167 "Just what I expected": FFC, pp. 7–8.

167 "the owner and manipulator of the best pair of eyes in existence": Eder, p. 54.

167 "situational awareness": Spick, p. vi.

167 ER concern about eye injury: ER-BH Interview, 15/2/1.

168 "part of the shell [that] had gone thru the wings": ER "Diary," March 28, 1918.

168 "rather caustic comments": FFC, p. 13.

169 "To tell of aerial adventure one needs a new language": Hall, *High Adventure*, p. 80.

169 *Hall was* "a comer": Eder, p. 54.

169 Marr and sled dogs: Frandsen, p. 75.

169 "No mud, good roads": Eder, p. 54.

170 "with another Hun to his credit": ER "Diary," April 14, 1918.

171 "when the ground suddenly disappears in favor of a bank of mist": Gill, p. 33.

172 Winslow background: "Daring Exploit in Air in France by Son Makes W. W. Winslow Proud," *Washington Post*, April 16, 1918, p. 5.

172 Winslow/Campbell engagement: Frandsen, pp. 90–93; Campbell quoted in Coolidge letter, Coolidge, p. 116.

172 "until I could see my line of tracer bullets entering the fuselage": Dennis Gordon, "The Ordeal of Alan Winslow," *Over the Front* 1, no. 1 (Spring 1986), p. 62.

173 *the tracers* "going toward an airplane which had black crosses on it": Edward M. Coffman, *The War to End All Wars: The American Military Experience in World War I* (Lexington: University Press of Kentucky, 1998), p. 201.

173 "the charred sacrifice of some huge animal": Gordon, p. 63.

173 *"Un grand souvenir!"*: Ibid., p. 63.

174 Campbell buys pilot's wings: Michael D. Hull, "America's First Home-grown Ace," *Aviation History*, March 2011, p. 46.

174 "We had a bunch of guys across the lines from us just as stupid": Daniel Chambers, "Reed Chambers Interview."

174 Eddie's "definitely bad" sense of direction: ER-BH Interview, 15/2/1.

175 "He is now so close": Udet, p. 22.

176   "there is no courage unless you're scared": Lewis, *Rickenbacker,* p. 124.

176   "If I was master of myself I was master of my opponent, also": ER "Death," p. 17.

177   "gave the signal to the boys to pull the blocks": ERWWI.

178   "the whole gamut of human feelings": Hall, *High Adventure,* p. 204.

178   "Raising the nose of my airplane": FFC, p. 32.

178   "To me, it was a great deal like taking something": ERWWI.

Chapter 11: When Giants Fall

179   "It was touching to see his tears": Norman, p. 436.

180   "our leader, our teacher, and our comrade, the ace of aces" and "But why make poor Moritz suffer": Norman, pp. 453, 454.

180   Ibid., p. 454.

180   "violent mob riots in the air": Gordon, p. 65.

180   "Most of the very high scoring aces tried to keep out": Spick, p. 14.

180   Richthofen's last battle: Hallion, pp. 138–39; Norman, pp. 456–59; Guttman, *Origin,* p. 250.

181   The British called it "staleness": Stafford, p. 109.

182   "The Whizz-Fish": Thomas G. Shepard, *Yale Melodies: A Collection of the Latest Songs Used by the Yale University Glee Club* (New Haven, CT: Thomas G. Shepard, 1903), pp. 66–68.

182   *Wind in the Willows:* Roosevelt, p. 51.

182   "some wiley Boche is 'on your tail'": Coolidge, p. 151.

182   "a sword-swallower's throat": Chambers, Columbia, p. 44.

183   *decorative touches to their aircraft:* Frandsen, p. 80.

183   "what beastly luck to die just as my first victory had been won": Meissner quoted in Charles Woolley, *The Hat in the Ring Gang: The History of the 94th Aero Squadron in World War I* (Atglen, PA: Schiffer Military History, 2001), p. 72.

183   "All the Boys feel very blue": ER "Diary," May 4, 1918.

184   "We knew [parachutes] were being worked on": Douglas Campbell, transcribed interview with Edward M. Coffman at United States Military Academy, September 21, 1977, p. 13.

184   Green background and sortie: "Ace in Hartford Saw Lufbery Hit," *Hartford Courant,* October 9, 1919, p. 8.

184 *King Friedrich August III of Saxony*: Jon Guttman, *USAS 1st Pursuit Group* (New York: Osprey Publishing, 2008), p. 19.

185 "If you focused on some point in the sky": Campbell, "Coffman Interview," p. 5.

185 "admirable liaison between German artillery and their aviators": FFC, p. 45.

185 "Standing patrols are not flown": Udet, p. 50.

185 "let the customer come to the shop": Boyne, *Aces*, p. 27.

186 "hanging motionless, then rising and falling like small boats": Hall, *High Adventure*, p. 130.

187 "America's greatest loss today": ER "Diary," May 7, 1918.

187 *Eddie could count no more than 150 hours of air time*: Boyne, *Aces*, p. 38.

187 "trying to hit on some extra little trick": Eddie, Rickenbacker, "Baling Wire and Fabric Crates," *The Airman*, August 1957, p. 9.

188 *dabs of axle grease on their faces*: Campbell, "Coffman Interview," p. 23.

188 "see the sun coming up the day after tomorrow" and "you were so doped up with lack of oxygen": Campbell, "Coffman Interview," p. 23.

188 "It froze instantly into a solid sheet": Gill, p. 213.

189 Physics of dogfighting: Spick, introduction.

190 "My whole life seemed to go through my mind like a moving picture": ER "Death," p. 26.

190 "I wondered whether the airplane would disintegrate": Rickenbacker, "Baling," p. 10.

191 "the instant one misses your heart hears it": William A. Bishop, *Winged Warfare* (New York: George H. Doran, 1918), p. 35.

191 *so grateful* "to her for not letting me down" and "the pride and gratitude I felt for the little ship": Rickenbacker, "Baling," p. 10.

192 "A moment's forgetfulness": FFC, p. 65.

193 "dumb with dismay and horror": FFC, p. 74.

194 shoemaker's old wife: Campbell, "Coffman Interview," pp. 25–26.

195 "there is always a good chance of side-slipping your airplane": FFC, p. 77.

195 "hopeless but a heroic attempt to preserve his life": FFC, p. 76.

195 "flying with side tank empty now to lessen fire danger": Meissner diary, June 3, 1918.

196 *Kurtz's charred body gave Eddie nightmares*: Lewis, *Rickenbacker*, p. 150.

196 "I had got my Boche" and "I should not forget that awful sight": FFC, p. 71.

197 "one of the most challenging and difficult professions, air to air combat": Boyne, *Aces*, p. 2.

Chapter 12: Race to Ace

198 "Have you ever looked up at a fleecy cloud": Kullgren, p. 236.

199 "Flying that people are called fools for doing in the States": Ibid., p. 233.

200 *only one in twenty became aces*: Boyne, *Aces*, p. 1.

200 *aces . . . accounting for 40 percent of all aircraft destroyed*: Lewis, *Rickenbacker*, p. 60.

200 number of aces by nationality: John P. H. Rayder, "Armed for Success: External Factors of the World War I Aces" (Master's thesis, U.S. Army Command and General Staff College, Fort Leavenworth, 1995), p. 3.

201 "With a savage sort of elation": FFC, p. 89.

201 Meissner's landing with stripped wing: FFC, pp. 91–92.

202 *this defect* "had been immediately hushed up": Harold Buckley, *Squadron 95: An Intimate History of the 95th Squadron First American Flying Squadron to Go to the Front in the War of 1914–1918* (Paris: Obelisk Press, 1933), p. 71.

202 "the defects in this type of aeroplane": Hamady, p. 70.

202 Hall's wing-stripping: James Norman Hall and Charles Bernard Nordhoff, *The Lafayette Flying Corps, Volume 1* (Boston: Houghton Mifflin Company, 1920), pp. 279–280.

203 "We were all afraid of the Nieuports": Daniel Chambers, "Reed Chambers Interview."

203 "most fascinating and absorbing game": Eder, p. 22.

204 "He was a real man": Ibid., p. 66.

204 "Campbell was "certainly going some": ER "Diary," May 31, 1918.

204 "congratulations of the world came pouring in on him": FFC, p. 99.

204 *Campbell confessed that* "I think Rickenbacker may have beaten me": Hull, p. 49.

205 *"Welcome 27th and 147th"*: Hartney, p. 150.

205 Vera Brittain anecdote: Norman, p. 414.

206 *shooting down fifty-four enemy aircraft in less than nine weeks*: Ibid., p. 466.

206 *Germans destroyed 505 Allied aircraft*: Gilbert, p. 436.

207 "crackled and sparkled around me like a dozen popcorn kernels": FFC, p. 104.

207 "Most of one's troubles in this world come from something wrong inside one's self": FFC, p. 104.

207 "quick-thinking, unburdened mind": FFC, p. 86.

208 "long jagged tear" *in his teddybear suit*: FFC, p. 112.

208 "Nerve is necessary": Eder, p. 61.

208 "a swift kick in the back": Campbell, Columbia, p. 15.

209 *Campbell* "would undoubtedly have one of the highest scores": Hull, p. 48.

209 "the grim horrors of war as I had never seen them before": ERWW1.

210 "Mysterious air torpedoes": Gill, p. 211.

210 *tiny rag dolls Nénette and Rintintin*: Harold H. Tittmann, "Memories of Harold H. Tittmann," Maxwell Air Force Base, Montgomery, AL, p. 11.

210 "undoubtedly my appearance was quite a surprise" and *gas attack*: ERWWI; ER "Diary," June 19, 1918.

211 "Every body seems real happy": ER "Diary," June 26, 1918.

211 *sent instead to the American Evacuation Hospital No. 7*: Sengupta, p. 167.

Chapter 13: The Germans Strike Back

212 "There was trouble ahead": Buckley, p. 81.

212 "ash and dust often obscured the sun": Stafford, p. 97.

212 Allies outnumbered four to one: Hamady, pp. 75–76.

213 new hunting packs: Hudson, p. 96.

213 "None of us will last a month": Gill, p. 223.

213 94th registering only three and a half victories: Boyne, *Aces*, p. 42.

213 "Protection patrols became the synonym for sudden death": Buckley, p. 84.

214 Tittmann crash details: Tittmann, p. 30.

215 "hoping to find a plane": ERWWI.

216 "I found that I had acted unwisely": ERWWI.

217 "the justly celebrated 'cooties'": Hudson, p. 98.

217 Roosevelt as "gay, hearty, and absolutely square": FFC, p. 152.

217 *studied math and mechanics*: Frandsen, p. 31.

218 Roosevelt's first sortie: FFC, pp. 43–44.

218 "laugh away all serious advice": FFC, p. 153.

218 Roosevelt's July 10 sortie: Hudson, p. 97.

218 *Roosevelt's* "bravery was so notorious": FFC, p. 153.

218 "a little slow, a little clumsy": Chambers, Columbia, p. 44.

218 "with a high heart in the performance of duty": Philip Roosevelt to Teddy Roosevelt, July 16, 1918, quoted in Frandsen, pp. 176–77.

219 "We lost two men there": Stafford, p. 105.

219 *Gears connecting crankshaft to propeller*: Boyne, *Aces*, p. 44.

219 "'machines available' for each day's work dropped": Jon Guttman, *SPAD XIII vs Fokker D VII* (Oxford, UK: Osprey Publishing, 2009), p. 28.

219 Marr "not the type to lead men": ER-BH Interview, 7/1/3.

219 "dead Americans stacked up": Chambers, Columbia, p. 44.

219 Tittman injuries: Tittmann, p. 46.

220 "Look, we're going to live to be killed by an automobile": Chambers, Columbia, p. 45–46.

220 "Rockets and signals were appearing everywhere": William Mitchell, *Memoirs of World War I: From Start to Finish of Our Greatest War* (New York: Random House, 1960), pp. 219–20.

221 "From the unusually serious expression on the nurses' faces": ERWWI.

221 Mitchell's solo sortie: Mitchell, *Memoirs*, pp. 220–22.

221 "Boche didn't have a look in": Frandsen, p. 187.

222 "these fellows, Germans, were marching just as close together": Chambers, Columbia, p. 46.

222 *1st Pursuit had substantially contributed*: Hudson, p. 105

222 "They were the best scout squadrons": Kullgren, p. 249.

222 *three or four two-hour missions daily*: Hudson, pp. 110–11.

222 "The 27th lost seven men in two days": Eastman Diary, July 20–24, 1918.

222 "the ear is not much better": ER, "Diary," July 25, 1918.

223 "They are shooting down a few of our fellows every day": Gill, p. 223.

223 "Gee but it's tough to see one's friends going out": ER "Diary," July 29, 1918.

223 "I'm crazy to get back but don't dare": ER "Diary," July 31, 1918.

223 Winslow sortie: Gordon, p. 65.

223 "get better soon for if it don't": ER "Diary," August, 6, 1918.

224 Karp exchange: ER-BH Interview, 7/1/17.

224 Smythe/Bruce collision: ERWWI; FFC, p. 179; Adamson, p. 204.

225 "not wrecked machines, but just flat patches of torn linen": Kullgren, p. 209.

225 "criminal negligence on the part of those higher up": ERWWI.

225 Maloney memory: J. L. Maloney, "Comrade of '18 Finds Rick the Leader of Yore," *Chicago Tribune*, January 24, 1943, p. 3.

225 "the transcendent capacity of taking trouble": Thomas Carlyle, *History of Friedrich II of Prussia, Called Frederick the Great, Volume 1.* (New York: Scribner, Welford, 1872), p. 288.

226 "It was a success and am feeling quite some better": ER, "Diary," August 19, 1918.

226 rubbing his head while thinking: Adelaide Rickenbacker interview, Leighton, p. 2.

226 "we did a lot of talking to people that had been at the front": Campbell, "Coffman Interview," p. 4.

227 *only 35 percent of the pilots given an opportunity to engage the enemy did so*: Boyne, *Aces*, p. viii.

Chapter 14: A Secret Counteroffensive

228 Hartney and Mitchell at Ligny: Harold E. Hartney, *Up and At 'Em* (Harrisburg, PA: Stackpole Sons, 1940), pp. 201–2; Mitchell, *Memoirs*, p. 237; Frandsen, pp. 204–5.

228 *Among the talents at Pershing's disposal*: Walter Boyne, "The St. Mihiel Salient," *Air Force Magazine* 83, no. 2 (February 2000), p. 76.

230 Conditions at Rembercourt: Stephen Skinner, *The Stand: The Final Flight of Lt. Frank Luke, Jr.* (Atglen, PA: Schiffer Military History, 2008), p. 45; Sengupta, p. 227.

231 *first control tower for night flying* and *fake base*: Hartney, pp. 257–58.

231 "We were frothing to get to the Front": Norman Archibald, *Heaven High, Hell Deep* (New York: Albert & Charles Boni, 1935), p. 81.

232 *communiqué to the German Supreme Headquarters*: Frandsen, p. 206; Skinner, p. 202.

233 *He would commit 1,481 airplanes*: Frandsen, p. 204.

233 "I suppose every American in the world": ERWWI.

233 "a howling gale": Eastman Diary, September 12, 1918.

233 "at once picturesque and terrible": Pershing, *My Experiences*, vol. 2, p. 267.

233 Balloon observers Smith and Klemm, Luke sortie: Skinner, pp. 50–51.

234 *a complex communication web*: Sengupta, p. 201.

235 Luke's talking "twelve things at a time": Lt. Edward W. Rucker quoted in Skinner, p. 41.

235 "Gee, that plane would be a cinch for me": Hartney, p. 240.

235 "you never mention your victories unless they are official": Kullgren, p. 254.

235 Luke's "self-heroism sickened us": Archibald, p. 124.

237 "black with hurrying men and vehicles": FFC, p. 184.

238 Putnam background: Hudson, p. 161.

238 "I shall go with a grin of satisfaction and a smile": Quoted in "David Putnam" at www.aerodrome.com.

239 "would be very lucky": FFC, p. 189.

239 "several frantic virages": ERWWI.

239 "I decided it was better to wait for a more promising opportunity": ERWWI.

240 "unavoidable doom": FFC, p. 194.

241 Luke/Hartney interaction: Hartney, pp. 250–52.

242 *Luke* "returned after dark and landed with flairs [sic] and was shot at all the way home by French": ER "Diary," September 16, 1918.

243 "We came head-on until within a few yards of each other": Luke's flight report, September 18, 1918, quoted in Frandsen, p. 221.

243 Luke examines the German plane he shot down: Skinner, pp. 63–67.

244 "For Luke's very mischievousness and irresponsibility": FFC, p. 221.

244 "I can control him": Chambers, Columbia, p. 51.

244 "As doctors say to the press, he is not expected to live": Eastman Diary, May 21, 1918.

246 "natural airmen have a visionary faith in three-dimensional warfare": Norman, p. 497.

246 "in Rickenbacker we had the rare combination": Raymond H. Fredette, "Rickenbacker: Most Natural Leader I Ever Saw," *Air Force Magazine* 57, no. 4 (April 1974), p. 65.

246 "With proper officers an army can, and frequently does, perform miracles": Hartney, pp. 192–93.

247 "It is no small good fortune that Rick has been given command over the 94th": Eastman Diary, September 24, 1918.

Chapter 15: Squadron Command

248 "it suddenly dawned on me that I was pitting myself against a gigantic evil": "Rickenbacker—Ace of Aces," *Chicago Daily Tribune*, March 12, 1939, p. G9.

248 *Even decades later, Eddie would get worked up*: ER-BH Interview, 11/1/5.

249 Chambers's quotes: Bowen, p. 174.

249 Grant speaking to his mechanics: Skinner, p. 42.

249 "respected the uniform": ER-BH Interview, 14/2/22.

250 "He drove himself to exhaustion": Bowen, p. 174.

250 "The experienced fighting pilot does not take unnecessary risks": Louis E. Orcutt, ed., *The Great War: Supplementary Volume from the Armistice to Ratification of the Peace Treaty* (New York: Christian Herald Bible House, 1920), p. 145.

253 Captain Harry S. Truman's battery: Gilbert, p. 465.

253 "Overhead the stars shone coldly": Buckley, p. 139.

253 ER night patrol: FFC, pp. 212–24.

255 *the round would have taken him squarely in the temple*: ER-BH interview, 11/1/15.

255 *1st Pursuit logged 143 sorties*: Frandsen, p. 239.

255 "When daylight came": Meissner quoted in Frandsen, p. 237.

255 *Only five German divisions lay between the Meuse and the Argonne*: S. L. A. Marshall, *World War* (Boston: Houghton Mifflin, 2001), p. 432.

255 *huge American divisions were twice the size of French ones*: Norman, p. 481.

256 "I could read clearly in his eyes that, at that moment, he realized his mistake": David Trask, "Foch's General Counteroffensive, Part 1: 26 September to 23 October 1918," in *The World War 1 Reader* (New York: New York University Press, 2007), p. 166.

256 *Foch told Pershing to reengage the enemy even harder*: Lewis, *Rickenbacker*, p. 204.

256 "this whole mass of transportation would have been destroyed": Mitchell, *Memoirs*, pp. 258–9.

257 "Luke mingled with his disdain for bullets": FFC, p. 221.

259 Gimper discussion: "'Gimpers' Theme of Yankee Ace; 'Gimper' Is O.K.," (San Jose, CA) *Evening News*, August 5, 1918, p. 2.

259 "It may seem strange": ERAuto, p. 112.

260 "Going to a pink tea": "Mounted on Trusty 'Can,' Gimper Seeks Pink Tea with Hun," *Salt Lake Telegram*, August 7, 1918, p. 8.

260 "At first he was just an uneducated tough bastard": Chambers quoted in "Durable Man," *Time*, April 17, 1950.

260 "He not only led them always but ruled them with a rather firm hand": Hartney, p. 281.

260 *increasing pursuit squadrons from five to twelve*: Frandsen, p. 243.

261 "there was literally an aisle-way from the door to the bed": Ibid., p. 228.

261 "conferences on methods, blackboard talks": "Rickenbacker's Ambition," *Cleveland Press*, November 20, 1918.

262 Description of sortie in which Avery died: Coolidge, pp. 208–9; Eastman Diary, October 4, 1918.

264 "dainty parachute pulled from the bottom of his seat": FFC, p. 252.

265 Meissner description of White incident: Meissner letter to his mother, October 17, 1918, cited in Jim Parks, "No Greater Love: The Story of Lt. Wilbert W. White," *Over the Front* 1, no. 1 (Spring 1986), p. 53.

265 ER description of White incident: FFC, p. 252.

266 "carried away [Coolidge's] wing": Eastman Diary, October 27, 1918.

267 ER comments about Coolidge and visit to crash site: ER "Diary," October 28, 1918; ERWWI.

267 "Hello, my California Sunshine!": "Airman Denies Engagement: Captain Rickenbacker Says He Is Not to Wed Movie Actress," *Portland Oregonian*, November 17, 1918.

268 Armistice celebration: FFC, pp. 286–8; ERWWI; ERAuto, pp. 133–35.

269 *3.9 aircraft downed for each casualty*: Frandsen, p. 266.

270 "made up to some extent for all the brow beating": ER-BH Interview, 7/2/36.

270 MacCrae poem: John MacCrae, *"In Flanders Fields" and Other Poems* (New York: G. P. Putnam's Sons, 1919), p. 3.

BOOK IV: IMMORTALITY

Chapter 16: Plane Crash

276 "had never sought to become a hero": ERAuto, p. 136.

276 "a comely Red Cross worker threw her arms about his neck": "A Kissing Party for Ace," *Kansas City Star*, February 26, 1919.

276 "that it would be easy to go from hero to zero": ERAuto, p. 137.

276 Runyon writes speech for Eddie: Jimmy Breslin, *Damon Runyon* (New York: Ticknor & Fields, 1991), pp. 174, 180–82.

277 "A Hero Who Refuses to Be Forgotten": "A Hero Who Refuses to Be Forgotten," *Industry Illustrated*, February 1925, p. 18.

277 "to buy a club-footed mule and cart": "Rickenbacker's Ambition," *Cleveland Press*, November 20, 1918.

278 "yet feel that I have made the readjustment fully": "Rickenbacker Sees Romance in Autos," *Cleveland Plain Dealer*, January 25, 1922.

278 "a little woman in black silk whose beaming eyes shone proudly": Lewis, *Rickenbacker*, p. 226.

278 "that the government couldn't care less": ERAuto, p. 139.

278 Orteig Prize inspiration: Lewis, *Rickenbacker*, p. 227.

279 "than a monkey has fleas": Edward V. Rickenbacker interview, Leighton, p. 52.

279 "completely impersonal guy": Steve Hannigan interview, Leighton, p. 23.

279 "He's never had a desire for a great fortune": Adelaide Rickenbacker interview, Leighton, p. 2.

280 "to bother with me because I shot down a few planes": Ibid., p. 9.

280 "never live any way but dangerously": Ibid., p. 1.

280 Adelaide's wedding dress: Ethel Wilhelm interview, Leighton, p. 16.

280 "His capacity for laughter was enormous": Ibid., p. 18.

280 "Possibly there is more romance in making and selling automobiles": "Rickenbacker Sees Romance in Autos," *Cleveland Plain Dealer*, January 25, 1922.

281 "the dream of dreams is washed up": Edward V. Rickenbacker interview, Leighton, p. 46.

281 *sold their spacious duplex apartment*: Adelaide Rickenbacker interview, Leighton, p. 11.

281 Accident in LaSalle: Ibid., pp. 12–14.

282 "You are the only real life looking customer": Lewis, *Rickenbacker*, p. 289.

282 "promise was his bond": Steve Hannigan interview, Leighton, p. 24.

283 he worked feverishly to bring the fleet up to date: David A. Lewis, "A Man Born Out of Season: Eddie Rickenbacker, Eastern Airlines, and the Civil Aeronautics Board," *Business and Economic History* 25, no. 1 (Fall 1996), p. 157.

283 *FDR had* "kicked askew the underpinnings" and "We hoped to be able to bring forcibly to the attention of the nation": Lewis, *Rickenbacker*, pp. 312, 315.

285 *Hertz himself mistakenly dialed Eddie's home number*: Lewis, *Rickenbacker*, p. 329.

285 "You'd think the office would walk away": Marguerite Shepherd interview, Leighton, pp. 38–39.

286 "while not a pacifist in any sense of the word": Lewis, *Rickenbacker*, p. 359.

286 Destruction of Rotterdam: Michael Korda, *With Wings like Eagles* (New York: Harper Perennial, 2010), p. 108.

287 "Should these gallant British withstand the terrific onslaught": Lewis, *Rickenbacker*, p. 363.

287 Atlanta crash: ERAuto, pp. 235–249; ER "Life," vol. 2, pp. 429–48; "Survivor Tells of Tragic Story of Air Crash," *Washington Post*, February 28, 1941, p. 3; ER "Death"; "Captain Is Blamed in Air Liner Crash," *New York Times*, June 14, 1941, p, 3; Wayne Thomis, "Atlanta Plane Crash Blamed on Pilot Error," *Chicago Daily Tribune*, April 15, 1941, p. 1; "7 Dead, 9 Injured in Crash of Plane Outside Atlanta," *New York Times*, February 28, 1941, p. 1; Adelaide Rickenbacker interview, Leighton, p. 26.

292 "We are in it and have been in it for a year": "Rickenbacker, 4 Months in Hospital, Back; He Will Resume His Airline Post on Monday," *New York Times*, June 26, 1941, p. 24.

293 *Eddie* "was doing his part in saving us from destruction": Lewis, *Rickenbacker*, p. 390.

Chapter 17: Triumph of Will

295 Raft episode pulled from the following sources: ERAuto, pp. 296–339; Eddie Rickenbacker, "Pacific Mission, Parts I, II, III," *Life*, January 25,

February 1, and February 8, 1943; Edward V. Rickenbacker, *Seven Came Through: Rickenbacker's Full Story* (Garden City, NY: Doubleday, Doran, 1943); ER "Death," p. 119; "Rickenbacker's Account of Ordeal of Men Adrift on Pacific and His Appeal to Civilians," *New York Times*, December 20, 1942, p. 36; James C. Whittaker, "Diary of Co-Pilot Reveals Epic Story of Rickenbacker," *Chicago Daily Tribune*, 13 installments running daily, January 12–24, 1943; Howard D. Rodgers interview of Lt. John J. De Angelis, Beverly Hills, CA, July 8, 1945, as background for the filming of Twentieth Century–Fox's *Captain Eddie*; Johnny Bartek, *Life Out There: A Story of Faith and Courage* (New York: Charles Scribner's Sons, 1943); Bartek interview, "John Bartek: Interview with Drs. David Lewis and Dwayne Cox," November 20, 1998, Auburn University, Auburn, AL; Bartek speech, "John Bartek's Speech About the Rickenbacker Rescue," November 19, 1998, Special Collections Department, Ralph Brown Draughon Library, Auburn University, Auburn, AL; "Group Kept Alert by Rickenbacker," *New York Times*, November 23, 1942, p. 3; "Col. Adamson Dodged Death by Miracle," *Washington Post*, December 20, 1942, p. 18; "Rescue of Airman Delights Millions," *New York Times*, November 15, 1942, p. 20; Lewis, *Rickenbacker*, pp. 417–99.

296 Adamson background: "Hans Christian Adamson Dies," *New York Times*, September 12, 1968, p. 47.

313 "Hello, honey": Adelaide Rickenbacker interview, Leighton, p. 26.

Epilogue

316 *softening him* "a very great deal": Mrs. Robb interview, Leighton, p. 59.

318 "bomb the living hell": Barbara Carlson, "Rickenbacker Calls Peace Try 'Hokum,'" *Hartford Courant*, May 15, 1968, p. 12.

A NOTE TO THE READER

As a result of leaving school at thirteen, Eddie Rickenbacker never learned to write well, relying on accomplished ghostwriters to pen his two autobiographies, *Fighting the Flying Circus* and *Rickenbacker: An Autobiography*. In both books—with Rickenbacker's blessing—the ghostwriters took great liberties, inflating and in some cases manufacturing heroic details. For his full-life autobiography that Prentice-Hall published in 1967, Rickenbacker forbade freelance journalist Bootes Herndon from using anything outside their conversations or material he had published earlier. Committed to giving America the hero it craved, Rickenbacker brooked no deviations from his storybook bromides of a happy childhood and charmed life. The veneer of untouchable hero covers nearly every incident as thickly as the fiberglass protecting a boat's hull. He applied his legendary toughness to the shaping of his legacy—and that's what has been the largest obstacle to understanding the man behind the broad grin.

The good news is that largely neglected primary sources exist. The National Museum of the United States Air Force at the Wright-Patterson Air Force Base near Dayton, Ohio, has the daily war journal he kept between March 1 and December 1, 1918 in northeastern France, as well as his more lengthy reports, which were transcribed in November and December 1918 and handed over to ghostwriter Laurence LaTourette Driggs for *Fighting the Flying Circus*. Driggs infused Rickenbacker's voice with a confidence bordering on arrogance, which is not evident in the rather self-effacing reports he wrote in the middle of the action.

The richest primary source material on Rickenbacker lies in the extensive interviews he gave in 1965 to journalist Bootes Herndon, which were recorded and transcribed into more than seven thousand typescript pages, a copy of which lives in the Eddie Rickenbacker Papers at the Library of Congress in Washington, D.C., and another at Wright Patterson. Perhaps because he didn't write well, he developed good dictating skills as Eastern Airlines' top executive. The Herndon tapes—part interview, part dictation—are clear and revelatory, full of contradictions and selective memory, and the willful disregard for facts. Again and again the determined Herndon comes back to a topic, and a new side or perspective unfolds. Rickenbacker is at times irascible, hectoring his interviewer, but others he is bemused and generous. It is in working closely with these documents that Rickenbacker's character slowly emerges and crystallizes.

Other revealing insights come from magazine articles with Rickenbacker's byline, but clearly ghosted by editors, the best of these including "Baling Wire and Fabric Crates," (The Airman, August 1957); with J. C. Burton, "The Loyal Legion of Speed: Being the Short and Simple Annals of the Mechanician, an Unsung and Unhonored Hero" (Motor Age, September 30, 1915); "Eddie Rickenbacker Tells Own Philosophy" (Los Angeles Times, November 11, 1962, p. F2); and "Life in Your Hands" (Dime Sports Magazine, no date, Rickenbacker Papers, Library of Congress).

Three major biographies stand out, the first written by his friend Hans Christian Adamson, who was on the raft with him in the South Pacific. Eddie Rickenbacker (New York: The Macmillan Company, 1946) is what you'd expect from an admirer. Finis Farr's lively Rickenbacker's Luck: An American Life (Boston: Houghton Mifflin, 1979) uncovers new detail but he also seems to take liberties with storytelling. By far the best biography is W. David Lewis's Eddie Rickenbacker: An American Hero in the Twentieth Century (Baltimore, MD: The Johns Hopkins University Press, 2005), which uncovers whole troves of new information, sources, and perspectives. A detailed, academic treatment of his life, Lewis's work proved extraordinarily helpful in the research for his book. As a professor of history at Auburn University, he brought to the school a greater number of critical sources that had been in the collection at the Smithsonian's National Air and Space Museum, as well as material from Rickenbacker's heirs. Auburn's research librarians at the university's Special Collections and Archives, led by Dwayne Cox, proved an invaluable resource not only for the Rickenbacker Papers, but for Lewis's own papers. The Rickenbacker collection includes scrapbooks that contain clippings of his early life and the Isabel Leighton Interviews of Adelaide Rickenbacker and a number of their friends. Useful for background on Rickenbacker's parents is Marian Pflaum Darby's *The Inspiration and Lives of Elizabeth Basler Rickenbacker and William Rickenbacker* (privately published, 1963 by the author, and at the Library of Congress).

Other valuable sources include "Life Story of Captain Edward V. Rickenbacker," an unpublished two-volume manuscript conducted for background for the 1945 Twentieth Century–Fox film *Captain Eddie*, currently at the Ohio State University Rare Books and Manuscripts Library, Columbus, Ohio, which also has a manuscript of Rickenbacker's essay, "When a Man Faces Death." The Columbia Center for Oral History conducted an unpublished interview with Rickenbacker in 1962.

I would be remiss not to single out several excellent books on Rickenbacker's 94th Aero Squadron, the best single overall book on the subject being Bert Frandsen's *Hat in the Ring: The Birth of American Air Power in the Great War* (Washington, D.C.: Smithsonian Books, 2003), while Aaron Norman's *The Great Air War* (New York: The Macmillan Company, 1968) remains the definitive source on the overall air war. Gorrell's *History of the American Expeditionary Forces Air Service, 1917–1919* (National Archives and Records Administration, Record Group 120), remains a critical resource for history of the 1st Pursuit Group. Other solid references include Theodore Hamady's *The Nieuport 28: America's First Fighter* (Atglen, PA: Schiffer Military History, 2008); James J. Hudson's *Hostile Skies: A Combat History of the American Air Service in World War 1* (Syracuse, NY: Syracuse University Press, 1968); Narayan Sengupta's *American Eagles: The Illustrated History of American Aviation in World War I* (self-published, 2011); and Charles Woolley's *The Hat in the*

Ring Gang: The Combat History of the 94th Aero Squadron in World War I (Atglen, PA: Schiffer Military History, 2001).

Also particularly helpful were the following: Walter J. Boyne's *Aces in Command: Fighter Pilots as Combat Leaders* (Washington, D.C.: Brassey's, 2001); Jon Guttman's *The Origin of the Fighter Aircraft* (Yardley, PA: Westholme Publishing, LLC, 2009); and Richard P. Hallion's *Rise of the Fighter Aircraft 1914–1918* (Baltimore, MD: The Nautical and Aviation Publishing Company of America, Inc., 1984).

INDEX